MUSIC & WORSHIP
IN PAGAN & CHRISTIAN
ANTIQUITY

by

JOHANNES QUASTEN

Translated by
Boniface Ramsey, O.P.

National Association of Pastoral Musicians
Washington, D.C.

Music and Worship in Pagan and Christian Antiquity,
originally published as
Musik und Gesang in den Kulten der
heidnischen Antike und christlichen Frühzeit.
©1973 Aschendorff, Munster Westfalen.

ISBN 0-9602378-7-9

National Association of Pastoral Musicians
225 Sheridan Street NW, Washington, DC 20011
(202) 723-5800

The National Association of Pastoral Musicians is a membership organization
of musicians and clergy dedicated to fostering the art of musical liturgy.

PREFACE TO THE
ENGLISH EDITION

The present English translation of *Musik und Gesang in den Kulten der heidnischen Antike und christlichen Frühzeit* is based on the second German edition, which was published in 1973. The additions that appeared in the form of a supplement in that edition have been incorporated, for the sake of the reader's convenience, into the notes of this translation. Likewise the appendices have been somewhat restructured in order to make them a little less formidable than they were in the original German.

A second edition had been suggested by many liturgists and scholars in other fields because the first edition had been out of print for a considerable period of time and, more importantly, because the problems dealt with in this study have come more and more into the focus of attention since the Second Vatican Council. There is no doubt that liturgical music today is in crisis. The question of its character has reappeared. The reform of the liturgy in the Roman Catholic and other churches has caused new problems with regard to congregational and choral singing and instrumental music. Under these circumstances a review of the origins of both pagan and Christian liturgical music by a historian of religions seems at once desirable and necessary. It is hoped that the present work in its English translation, which was done in 1973 and is at last being made available to the public ten years later, will be of service to a wider readership in the continuing discussion on the nature of liturgical music.

Freiburg im Breisgau, January, 1983

J.Q.

PREFACE TO THE
FIRST GERMAN EDITION

The present study, which was accepted in the spring of 1927 as a doctoral dissertation by the Catholic Theological Faculty of the University of Münster, was first suggested to me as an undertaking in a seminar on religious history conducted by Professor Dr. F. J. Dölger. He followed the progress and development of the work with continued and lively interest. I am, then, merely paying a debt of gratitude to my teacher when I mention him here with special respect.

A research grant from the Notgemeinschaft der Deutschen Wissenschaft enabled me in 1928 to spend a longer time in Italy and thus to broaden the work from an archeological point of view by including cultic monuments within the scope of the study. Printing of this book has been made possible by the cordial cooperation of the editors of this series, Dr. P. K. Mohlberg, O.S.B., and Professor Dr. A. Rücker, who were also helpful to me in reviewing the proofs, as well as by the magnanimous support of the Verein zur Pflege der Liturgiewissenschaft (Maria Laach).

I also wish to thank all those who have in any way contributed to the completion of this work, in particular Abbot I. Herwegen, O.S.B. (Maria Laach), Professor Dr. J. P. Kirsch (Rome), Dr. Th. Klauser (Bonn), Dr. Küthmann (Hannover), Professor Dr. H. Lehner (Bonn), Professor Dr. M. Meinertz (Münster), Professor Dr. K. A. Neugebauer (Berlin), Professor Dr. G. Schreiber (Münster), Professor Dr. R. Stapper (Münster), and Professor Dr. A. Struker (Münster).

As I write this foreword I call to mind the Christ-Orpheus portrayed in the Catacomb of Saint Callixtus in Rome, whom Clement of Alexandria celebrated in these words: "Truly he has embellished the universe with melody and drawn the dissonance of the elements into the unity of order, so that the whole world might become harmony in his presence" (*Protrepticos* 1).

Johannes Quasten

Münster, i.W., December 1929

FOR MY PARENTS

With Love and Reverence

ABBREVIATIONS

ARW   Archiv für Religionswissenschaft

BKV   Bibliothek der Kirchenväter

BO   Bibliotheca orientalis

CIG   Corpus inscriptionum graecarum

CIL   Corpus inscriptionum latinarum

CSEL   Corpus scriptorum ecclesiasticorum latinorum

DACL   Dictionaire d'archéologie chrétienne et de liturgie

GCS   Die griechischen christlichen Schriftsteller der ersten drei Jahrhunderte

IG   Inscriptiones graecae

PA   Patres apostolici

PG   Migne, Patrologia graeca

PL   Migne, Patrologia latina

PO   Patrologia orientalis

RAC   Reallexikon für Antike und Christentum

RE   Pauly-Wissowa, Realenzyklopädie

RVV   Religionsgeschichtliche Versuche und Vorarbeiten

TU   Texte und Untersuchungen

TU NF   Texte und Untersuchungen, Neue Folge

Table of Contents

21. 1. Detail of a sarcophagus showing a procession from the cult of Cybele. Rome: S. Lorenzo fuori le mura. 2. Votive table for a safe journey. Rome: Vatican Museum.
22. Relief in clay showing a sacred tree and a sacrifice of fruit. Rome: Museo delle Terme. Alinari 27371.
23. Mural from Herculaneum. Scene from the cult of Isis. Naples: National Museum. Anderson 12035.
24. Mural from Herculaneum. Scene from the cult of Isis. Naples: National Museum. Anderson 23422.
25. Pedestal from the Roman Temple of Isis-Serapis. Florence: Uffizi Gallery. Alinari 29347.
26. Musical instruments from Pompeii. Naples: National Museum. Anderson 25380.
27. Detail of a relief showing a procession from the cult of Isis. Rome: Vatican Museum. Alinari 26981.
28. 1. Cover of a sarcophagus showing a lute and a scroll in the hands of the deceased. Rome: Palazzo dei Conservatori. Alinari 6049. 2. Christian sarcophagus with a female lutenist. Rome: Lateran Museum. Anderson 24187.
29. 1. Sarcophagus from Saint-Maximin. Awakening of Tabitha. Photograph after Wilpert. 2. Terracotta fragment. Singer and organ. Rome: Museum of the Campo Santo Tedesco.
30. Grave relief from the Via Latina. Rome: Museo delle Terme.
31. Relief from Amiternum showing a funeral procession. Museum at Aquila. Alinari 36101.
32. Etruscan gravestone with a banquet of the dead and dancers. Fiesole: Museo Etrusco Romano. Alinari 45780.
33. Painting on a Campanian mixing bowl. A deceased person on a gravestone holding a tambourine. Berlin: Antiquarium. Museum photograph.
34. Oil flask from a Greek cult of the dead. The lyre as a gift for the deceased. Berlin: Antiquarium. Museum photograph.
35. Gravestone of Metrodoros showing music-making sirens. Berlin: Antiquarium. Museum photograph.
36. Lyre-playing siren from a tombstone. Athens: National Museum. Alinari 24351.
37. Ash urn of L. Lucilius Felix with music-making cupids. Rome: Capitoline Museum. Alinari 40920.
38. Tombstone of the soldier Marcinus showing a dancing Maenad. Bonn: Provincial Museum. Museum photograph.

INTRODUCTION

"The fact that David danced in the presence of God is no excuse for believing Christians to sit in the theater....[In those days] harps, cymbals, flutes, tambourines and citharas made music to the honor of God, not to the praise of an idol....But through the devil's wiles holy [instruments] have been changed into forbidden ones."[1] With these words Pseudo-Cyprian provides the best commentary possible for an understanding of the attitude toward music which prevailed in early Christianity.

Despite the rich heritage which the young Church received from Jewish worship, she opposed and held back completely from the elaborate musical embellishment of liturgy which was part of Old Testament tradition. The need for such a stand in early Christianity arose from the fact that the music of the day was very closely associated with pagan worship. Moreover, since the pagan cult of the gods and of the dead influenced and permeated every aspect of private life, the Church forbade even private practice of this art.

It was precisely because of this unconditional rejection of contemporary music that Christianity became the formative, creative force in the production of a musical art which served religion not as an instrument of magic but rather as a means of devotion. Within the framework of religious history, therefore, an assessment of the early Christian understanding of music and singing must necessarily take into account the relationship of music to pagan cult.

---

[1]Ps.-Cyprian, *De spectaculis* 3 (CSEL 3.3, 5 Hartel): Quod David in conspectu Dei choros egit nihil adiuvat in theatro sedentes christianos fideles: nulla enim obscoenis motibus membra distorquens desaltavit Graecae libidinis fabulam. Nabla cynarae tibiae tympana et citharae Deum cecinerunt, non idolum. Non igitur praescribetur ut spectentur illicita. Diabolo artifice ex sanctis in illicitae mutata sunt.... *Ibid.* 4 (CSEL 3.3, 7): Graeca illa certamina vel in cantibus vel in fidibus vel in vocibus vel in viribus praesides suos habent varia daemonia: et quidquid est aliud quod spectantium aut oculos movet aut delinet aures, si cum sua origine et institutione quaeratur, causam praefert aut idolum aut daemonium aut mortuum. Ita diabolus artifex quia idolatriam per se nudam sciebat horreri, spetaculis miscuit, ut per voluptatem posset amari. On the instruments used in David's dance cf. E. B. Thomas, *King David Leaping and Dancing. A Jewish Marble from the Imperial Period* (Budapest 1970).

Chapter One

MUSIC AND SACRIFICE IN PAGAN WORSHIP

1. Music as Cultic Action.

The legends and myths of nearly all pagan peoples have sought to explain the elaborate use of music in their worship by indicating that the art of music was a gift of the gods to men. Already in antiquity the true cultic significance of music was no longer so well understood. According to the view which was most widely held, it was to the gods themselves that music was pleasing. This is how Tibullus, for example, interprets the connection between music and worship.[1] In keeping with this is the explanation Horace gives for sacred music when he calls it a means of appeasement which, like the fragrance of incense and the blood of animals, disposes the gods to act favorably toward men.[2] Censorinus is of the same opinion:

> Music is pleasing to the gods, for if it were not pleasing to the gods, then the public games which are intended to placate the gods would not have been instituted; the flutist would not attend prayers of supplication offered in sacred shrines; the triumph in honor of Mars would not be celebrated to the accompaniment of flute music or the trumpet's blast; the cithara would not be dedicated to Apollo, nor would flutes and other instruments be dedicated to the Muses; flutists would not be permitted to perform in public, to eat on the Capitol or to roam about the city on the Ides of June, drunken and disguised in whatever they choose to wear.[3]

Censorinus thus also seeks to use the pleasure the gods found in music to explain the use of music in public cultic ceremonies.

This concept did not prevail only in the world of Roman religion. A Greek hymn from the temple of Zeus Diktaios in Palkaistro on Crete, dating from about the second or third century after Christ, expresses a parallel notion.

> Come to Dikta [Io is invoked], come to Dikta for the anniversary and rejoice with gladness in the song which we play for you on our harps, as our singing blends with the sound of flutes, while we stand before your fully-surrounded altar.[4]

To bring joy to the god who was already well-disposed and to appease the angered deity — this was the task and the goal of music and song in cult, according to the most widely held opinion. The Christian apologist Arnobius ridicules this notion when he asks: "Are the almighty gods pacified by the piping of flutes, and do they give up their anger when soothed by the rhythm of cymbals, just as little boys are startled out of their unseemly screaming by the noise of rattles?"[5]

This interpretation, however, does not express the original purpose of music in pagan cult. At a more profound level music as cultic action was understood to exercise a magical influence over the gods, so that it became a means by which men controlled the deities. This belief is rejected by, for example, the Greek poet Menander when he points out the incompatibility of such an idea with the concept of the divine:

No god, O woman, saves one man on account of another, for if a man could bring a god to do what a mere mortal willed simply by playing the cymbal, then he would be more powerful than the god.[6]

The disagreement expressed by Menander clearly bears witness to belief in the magical significance of music in the cult of the gods. Here we have the specific reason for the cultic use of music. This belief in the magical power of music is most particularly evident in the use of music at pagan sacrifices.

2. THE USE OF MUSIC IN GREEK SACRIFICIAL CEREMONIES.

We find evidence of the use of flute music at sacrifices as early as in the earliest civilization of Mediterranean history. Stengel, it is true, holds that the use of music during sacrifices, like the use of the crown worn by the one offering sacrifice, became customary only in the post-Homeric age.[7] Nevertheless, the sarcophagus of Hagia Triada demonstrates that flutes were played at sacrifices as early as 1300 B.C.[8] The detailed sculptures on this sarcophagus portray a flutist playing a double flute just behind the bull which is to be immolated and, on the other side of the sarcophagus, a citharist next to the women who are offering the libation.[9]

That flute accompaniment of sacrificial action was common in the post-Homeric age is attested by the exception described in Apollodoros[10] and by the passages in Herodotus[11] which report the absence of flute music as a peculiar custom of the Persians. Apollodoros seeks a mythic explanation for the offering of sacrifice to the Graces on Paros without flute accompaniment. Actually, this can be readily explained, since the ritual on Paros was originally the cult of a chthonic deity, and sacrifices in honor of Zeus Lykaios or the Furies show that music was frequently lacking at sacrifices to chthonic deities.[12] Similarly, Lucian recounts that the inhabitants of Hierapolis sacrificed to Zeus (Hadad), whose cult evokes the ritual of chthonic deities, in silence, without singing and flute-playing:

> They sacrifice to Zeus [Hadad] in silence, without singing and without the playing of flutes; but when they begin [the sacrifice] to Hera [Atargatis], they sing, blow the flutes, and make a racket with their cymbals.[13]

In other respects, however, music occupied an extremely important place in Greek sacrificial ceremonies. On the great antiquity of sacrificial music there is the remark by Plutarch in which he mentions the flute, the syrinx, and the lyre already in the cult of the Hyperboreans.[14] From the most ancient times dancing and flute music were integral parts of the sacrificial cult of Apollo, which held a privileged place in Greek religion.[15] According to the testimony of Lucian of Samosata, no sacrifices were offered in Delos without round dances and the playing of flutes and the lyre.[16] The elaborate musical embellishment of ritual in the cult of Apollo at Delphi and Delos was the reason for the choice of this deity as the patron of singers and poets.[17] The playing of flute, syrinx, and lyre is further attested for a special rite of sacrifice in use in Greek worship since earliest times, the *lectisternium.* In the inscription from Magnesia on the river Maeander, published by O. Kern, instructions are given for preparing a *lectisternium* on the agora: παρεχέτω δὲ καὶ ἀκροάματα αὐλητὴν συριστὴν κεθαριστήν.[18] Since the Delphic *theoxenia* very likely furnished the model for cultic celebrations of this kind, one can plausibly assume an influence of Delphi not only with regard to the selection and grouping of the deities, but also with regard to the ritual music.[19]

The extant Greek cultic monuments corroborate the textual evidence in this matter. In sacrifices to Dionysos, the sacred action is usually accompanied by cymbals and tambourines. And this we see in a picture on a vase in the National Museum in Naples depicting a sacrifice in the cult of this god.[20] In the center stands the altar of sacrifice, on which a fire burns. Behind it is the priestess, who is about to slaughter the sacrificial animal. To the left of the priestess two women can be seen striking a cymbal and a tambourine as they accompany the sacrifice with music and dancing. On the whole the scene agrees with the details given by Diodorus concerning sacrificial action in the Dionysian mysteries: virgins are to brandish the thyrsos and exult before the god while the married women offer the sacrifice.[21] In other portrayals of sacrificial ritual the assistant is usually a flutist, either male or female, although the musician is a woman when the ritual is conducted by a woman.[22] Flute ensembles are also found at sacrifices. If there is dancing in connection with the sacrifice, a tambourine nearly always accompanies the flute, since the tambourine is especially suited to marking rhythm. Representations of sacrificial processions furnish additional valuable information regarding Greek cultic practices. On the north side of the Parthenon frieze, four flutists and four citharists are shown preceding the three sacrificial beasts. In other depictions of such processions the musicians follow the animal.[23] In almost every instance, however, the flutist goes before the citharist. According to S. Eitrem, the reason for this precedence may lie in cultic history, inasmuch as the flute was the earlier instrument used at bloody sacrifices.[24]

3. MUSIC IN ROMAN SACRIFICIAL RITUAL.

The link between music and cult is even more apparent among the Romans than among the Greeks.[24a] The Romans were, of course, originally as opposed to dancing and music in private life as they were to gymnastics. Nevertheless, they had from earliest times their own cultic music, as both monuments and texts demonstrate. Cicero reports that the law of the Twelve Tables required that the veneration of the gods be accompanied by singing and the music of lutes and flutes.[25] Accordingly, in nearly every sacrificial representation a flutist is portrayed. The sacrificial action itself is characterized by such expressions as *foculo posito adhibitoque tibicine, ad praeconium et ad tibicinem* and *ad tibicinem foculo posito.*[26]

For sacrifices from the simplest domestic one honoring the Lares to the most solemn state *suovetaurilia*, the flutist was indispensable.[27] A bas-relief on the south side of the triumphal arch of Constantine offers a good portrayal of the *suovetaurilia.*[28] Surrounded by officers and soldiers, Marcus Aurelius is in the act of performing sacrifice. The three animal victims—a swine, a sheep, and a bull—can be clearly seen. The emperor is about to scatter incense on the sacrificial fire. Between him and the ritual assistant (*camillus*), who holds an open box of incense (*acerra*) in his hands, there stands a flutist, crowned with the laurel wreath. To the right of the assistant are two soldiers who are participating in the sacrifice as *tubicines*. Flags and standards decorate the background.

In contrast to Greek ritual, which made use of lyre, tambourine, and cymbals, Roman practice recognized only the flute as the proper musical instrument for cultic use. An attempt to authorize other instruments in Rome was frustrated by the strict prohibition of music in 639 B.C. This law allowed only the "Latin flutist together with the singer." All other music was forbidden,[29] so that even guests at meals sang only to the flute.[30] Ovid mentions the great antiquity of this cultic music in his *Fasti*:

> *Temporibus veterum tibicinis usus avorum*
> *Magnus et in magno semper honore fuit.*
> *Cantabat fanis, cantabat tibia ludis,*
> *Cantabat maestis tibia funeribus.*[31]

Even the ritual of cursing necessitated the flutist, according to the *leges regiae*, a collection of sacred ordinances containing the ancient law regarding customs. Thus, for example, as Cicero informs us, the sentence of *sacer esto* is imposed on all those who harm a tribune of the people or a plebian aedile: in solemn assembly and with covered head the tribune, accompanied by a flutist, is to pronounce the curse over the transgressor in a holy place, invoking the ancient formula, and then to hurl him down from the Tarpeian Rock.[32]

A change occurred in the restriction of Roman cultic music when Greek ritual, ushered in by the Sibylline Books, introduced other instruments such as the lyre and the tambourine to Rome. The characteristic distinction between Greek and Roman ritual consisted in the more elaborate use of music and dancing which was peculiar to the Greeks. Through the infiltration of Greek cultic forms the *lectisternium* also came to Rome. The name of this ceremony comes from the spreading out of the table cushions which were scattered about in a circle of banqueters and on which were placed images of the gods reclining at table and eating—a religious custom which was practiced especially on major feasts of the gods.[33] With the *lectisternium*, the lyre acquired conclusively legitimate status in Roman religious practices, as Cicero attests.[34] Horace refers to the change which had taken place in this regard when he says of the lyre:

> *Tuque testudo—*
> *Nec loquax olim neque grata, nunc et*
> *Divitum mensis et amica templis.*[35]

The *non grata* has become an *amica templis*. It now appears at the supplications as well. From Plutarch we learn that the lyre was used at the sacrificial feast of the Bona Dea which was celebrated annually by women in the residence of the presiding consul.[36] In addition to the playing of the lyre at the *lectisternia,* a special *collegium fidicinum Romanorum* was even organized.[37] In spite of all this, however, the monuments seldom depict a lyrist in cultic action.

One famous monument which portrays a lyrist at the *suovetaurilia* can be seen in the Louvre in Paris.[38] It comes from the Temple of Neptune which was in the Circus Flaminius in Rome[39] and was probably erected during Cn. Domitius Ahenobarbus' renovation of the temple in 32 B.C.[40] A. Furtwängler surmises with good reason that this relief, in the style of a frieze, constitutes, along with three others presently in the Glyptothek in Munich, the casing of a large altar.[41] In the center of the relief a general about to take up a libation stands near an altar. From the right butchers from the sacrifice are bringing the three sacrificial animals; the bull leads, followed by the sheep and the swine. To the left of the altar stands an officer, and next to him, facing the altar, are a flutist and a lyrist. The numerous soldiers as well as the scene of the scribe at the left end of the relief justify the assumption that the *suovetaurilia* are being offered by the general on the occasion of the disbanding of his army as a customary lustration at which he is having the privileges of his veterans inscribed for them on diptychs.[42] The portrayal may, therefore, refer to the victorious homecoming of Domitius Ahenobarbus, the donor of the monument.

4. THE TUBILUSTRIUM.

The special connection of music and cult in Roman ritual has its clearest expression in the so-called *tubilustrium.* This is a feast which had as its purpose the purification or cleansing of the trumpets used at sacrifices. Varro explains the name of the feast in this way:

The day is called *tubilustrium* because on it the sacred trumpets are culticly purified in the Atrium Sutorium.[43]

In agreement with this is what Lydus calls the feast: καθαρμὸς σάλπιγγος.[44] This ceremonial cleansing took place twice a year, on the twenty-third of March and on the twenty-third of May.[45] Nothing certain is known regarding the antiquity of the practice. The lexicographer Festus reports that this sacred custom was thought to have come to Rome from Pallanteum in Arcadia.[46] According to Calpurnius, it was Numa Pompilius who first ordered the use of trumpets in cult.[47]

While the regular trumpets of war were called *tubae*, the form *tubi*, according to Varro, was employed only for the trumpets used at sacrifices.[48] The *tubicines sacrorum publicorum populi Romani*, to whom the performance of this cultic music as well as the cleansing of the instruments was entrusted, were by no means identical with the *symphoniaci*, the *tibicines* or the *fidicines*, *qui sacris publicis praesto sunt.* Rather, they held a significantly higher office. According to Festus, they were priests and *viri speciosi.*[49] The inscriptions demonstrate this also. For example, the *tubicen* who figures in inscr. Orelli 3876 was an officer who occupied the highest municipal position in his home town.[50] As the scenes of domestic sacrifices in Pompeian frescoes indicate, the *tibicines* were used at every sacrifice, private as well as public. The *tubicines*, on the contrary, seem to have participated only in the solemn state sacrifices. They executed their holy office, for instance, at the annual *armilustrium*, offered on the nineteenth of October.[51] The monuments testify that the *tubicines* were also present at the solemn imperial sacrifices, such as those portrayed in relief on the triumphal arches. *Tubicines* are among the sacrificial attendants at the *suovetaurilia* represented on the bas-relief on the south side of the Arch of Constantine, mentioned above,[52] as also on the relief strip of the triumphal arch in Susa.[53] Again, on the reliefs on Trajan's Column they head the lustration procession, crowned with laurel and leading the three propitiatory animals — swine, goat and bull — around the ramparts and the camp.[54]

According to Lydus, the cleansing of the trumpets of sacrifice took place with the immolation of a lamb which was offered in the Atrium Sutorium. J. Marquardt asserts that the feast of the *tubilustrium* stands in close relationship with the Palatine Salii (priests dedicated to the service of Mars) because the Atrium Sutorium was located on the Palatine.[55] In any event the *tubicines* assisted at the *armilustrium* which was carried out by the Salii. This ceremony consisted essentially in a solemn emplacement of the sacred shields in conjunction with sin offerings and sacrifices of purification on the Campus. Lydus points to the active participation of the Salii in a procession on the twenty-third of March when he speaks of καθαρμὸς σάλπιγγος καὶ κίνησις τῶν ὅπλων. Although Lydus alone reports this fact and we are left to conjecture what part precisely the Salii played, it may still be possible from the evidence to infer a relationship between the *tubilustrium* and the festivals of the Salii.[56] However, Marquardt's topographical argumentation is unsound, for the Atrium Sutorium was in fact not on the Palatine and was certainly not identical with the Atrium Minervae, as he seems to assume.[57] The *tubilustrium* was celebrated in honor of Mars and Nerine, a Sabine goddess who bears a likeness to Athena, as Lydus remarks, for Nerine, both in Greek and in the language of the Sabines, signifies ἡ ἀνδρία.[58] Ovid's observation that the *tubilustrium* is dedicated to the "brave goddess"[59] may also legitimately be used against Marquardt, who wishes to find some opposition between Lydus and Ovid.[60] Only the similarity of Nerine to Athena and to Minerva explains the celebration of this feast on the last day of the Quinquatrus of Minerva.

5. THE COLLEGIUM TIBICINUM ROMANORUM.

The flutists who were commissioned to play at the liturgy in Rome built a strong organization, the *collegium tibicinum Romanorum, qui sacris publicis praesto sunt,* which traced its roots back to antiquity. According to Plutarch, this college was founded by Numa Pompilius.[61] If the testimony of Livy is to be accepted, the Romans took over flute playing from the Etruscans.[62] According to the monuments, flute playing must have been very ancient in Etruscan sacrificial ritual. One need simply refer to the portrayal of the sacrifice of Iphigenia on a crudely worked Etruscan ash coffer which is in the Vatican Museum.[63] In the foreground of the relief the round altar is visible. In the background, somewhat elevated, five persons in long robes can be seen. To the extreme left is a woman playing the lyre; to her right a sacrificial butcher holds his axe. In the center another person holds a pot and a dish; next to him is a figure with mutilated head who perhaps represents a singer and who is holding a type of scroll in his hands. At the end a double flute player looks to the altar. On the bronze ornament from Bomarzo the flutist is marching in procession.[64] Considering the powerful influence of Etruscan culture on Rome, Livy's remark seems quite credible. It is further corroborated by Virgil, who mentions the Etruscan flutists at Roman sacrifices.[65]

The *collegium tibicinum Romanorum* later joined with the much newer college of official lutenists, or *fidicines*, who performed at the *lectisternia*; this became known as the *collegium symphoniacorum, qui sacris publicis praesto sunt*.[66] The corporation of flutists enjoyed special privileges from very early times, as the lines quoted earlier from Censorinus demonstrate.[67] These musicians had the right to be fed at the Temple of Jupiter on the Capitoline, where they performed their service. On the Ides of June they celebrated their feast, the *quin-quatrus minisculae*, a carnival of sorts, when they were permitted to wear masks and women's clothing. The origins of this feast, very like-ly long forgotten, were explained by incredible legends. Livy claims that it arose as a result of a decree of the censors in 309 B.C. which prohibited the serving of meals to flutists on the Capitoline. Thereupon, it would seem, the *tibicines* marched in anger to Tibur, so that no one would be available in the city for the liturgical music re-quired at the sacrificial rites. With this the Senate intervened and, in order to appease the angry musicians, granted them this feast.[68] Whatever the explanation, this account points to the important posi-tion held by the *tibicines*.[69]

On May 8, 1875 a portion of a grave monument belonging to the *collegium tibicinum* was found in Rome on the Via S. Croce near S. Vito.[70] This valuable fragment is presently in one of the extensions of the Capitoline Museum in Rome. The inscription reads:

> (L)EGIEI . TIBICIV(M)
> L . PONTIVS . L . C .
> L . LICINIVS . L . L .
> P . PLAETORIVS .

According to Th. Mommsen the entire inscription may have read:

> *magistri quinquennales collegiei tibicinum (qui sacris publicis praesto sunt) L. Pontius L. C., L. Licinius L. L., P. Plaetorius....*[71]

The shape of the fragment led Mommsen to decide that ten names might have followed. The style of the alphabet places the monument about the time of Sulla.[72] Two sculptured remains on it evoke the im-pression of the crudely worked statues of two flutists, clothed in the long tunic and holding two flutes in their lowered right hands. Along with this, other fragments were unearthed; they were fashioned from the same material and evidence a rough execution similar to that of the statues of the two flutists. One figure in this group which deserves special consideration is that of a nude young man wearing a wreath. He seems to be sitting on the trunk of a tree. His mouth is open and his countenance is tranquil, as if he were singing. W. Helbig suggests that a cithara originally on his left shoulder was subsequently broken off. Several animals are pressing about the youth.[73] Of the three quadrupeds at his feet the animal in the middle can be recognized as a lion, while an owl stands by his left leg. Obviously this is a portrayal of the youth Orpheus, charming the beasts with his playing and singing. The place of discovery, the material and the mode of execution identify this fragment as belonging to the grave monument of the *tibicines*. This identification is even more obvious by reason of the subject of the carving, since Orpheus was considered by the ancient world to be the representative of cultic music. Therefore the *collegium tibicinum Romanorum, qui sacris publicis praesto sunt* would have honored him as its patron.

An inscription restored by A. v. Domaszewski[74] indicates that, as a result of the new state religion of Heliogabalus, the old Roman feast of the *tibicines* which (prior to the age of Severus Alexander) was held on the Ides of June, was no longer celebrated. However, the restoration of the ancient cult at the behest of the Empress Mamaea also provoked a change in this situation, since the inscription refers to the restoration of the feast by imperial decree.

6. MUSIC AT THE OFFERING OF INCENSE.

In an attempt to determine the specific aim of music used in sacrificial worship the opinion is sometimes proferred that, in the view of the ancients, music was employed to drown out the disturbing sounds made by the animals to be immolated, since these noises could have an adverse influence on the sacrifice itself.[75] Aside from certain important arguments which contradict this opinion the fact is that music was also played at the offering of incense. If the opinion is correct it is impossible to understand why cultic music was admitted at bloodless sacrifices. The presumption that the custom of playing music was simply transferred from bloody to unbloody sacrifices is untenable. The monuments which depict flutists at incense offerings are very ancient. Consequently we do not know of a time when bloody sacrifices were celebrated to the accompaniment of music while unbloody sacrifices were not. In the case of the Eleusinian initiation, as pictured on the Mimion plate,[76] incense burning and flute music are seen to be simultaneous. Vase paintings frequently portray the offering of incense in connection with flute playing. In the British Museum a vase from Ruvo represents a female slave playing the double flute while another sprinkles incense from a bowl on the altar of incense before her.[77] Again, the relief on the base of the pillar now located in the Forum Romanorum, to the east of the Rostra Vandalicia, depicts a fore-offering made at the incense sacrifice. There the flutist accompanies the sacred action.[78] The presence of flutists at incense offerings is also confirmed by textual evidence. Thus Suetonius speaks of the flutist employed by the Emperor Tiberius at his incense sacrifice.[79] Dio Cassius expressly refers to an exception to the law made at the death of Augustus: on the day following the arrival of the body the Senators went to the Senate, and upon entering the hall they scattered incense as usual upon the censer, but this time they did so *sine tibicine.*[80]

One cultic scene of interest in this respect occurs three times on Roman monuments. In each instance the monument has the form of a pedestal and carries traces of having been used as such. The simplest of these is a rectangular pedestal in the Gallerie delle statue of the Vatican Museum.[81] Two large holes and one smaller one on the surface area demonstrate its use as a pedestal. The holes must have served as fastening points for a bronze statuette with a supporting right leg and a left leg set somewhat back. A spear or thyrsos served as a prop in the right hand. The bas-relief on the face of the pedestal shows a lighted candelabrum in the center and, turned toward this, on both the right and the left, a heavily-veiled figure playing the double flute.

Another representation of this scene is found on a pedestal in the Capitoline Museum. Today this bears the statuette of Artemis of Ephesus.[82] This portrayal, unlike the Vatican monument, counts four persons. In the center is the lighted candelabrum. Immediately to the right and to the left of it is a veiled girl. Both carry in their hands an object which W. Amelung considers to be a distaff.[83] Again, to the right and left of these girls a woman plays the double flute. The flutist to the right is distinguished from the flutist to the left by a mantle which the former wears over her head. Since the two center figures are much smaller than the flutists they appear as very young girls in contrast. It is possible to date this monument from the Flavian era, when the girls' coiffure, with hair rolled in two rows and a garland on the brow, was fashionable.[84] The plinth of the statuette of the goddess Artemis takes up only one-third of the top of this pedestal. It is about four steps higher than the side surfaces, which were originally covered with a rectangular plate. W. Amelung suggests that the form and style of the plate, determined from pieces which have been preserved, is such that it would have held a bronze stag, as is depicted at times on ancient gems.[85]

The third pedestal of this type is in the Museo delle Terme.[86] On the relief there is a heavily-veiled woman to the right, near the lighted candelabrum. She holds in her left hand an object which cannot be clearly identified. Behind her a second woman plays the flute. To the left of the candelabrum is a man holding a staff in his lowered left hand. He wears a *himation* which leaves his head free. Behind him stands a female flutist. As on each of the reliefs already mentioned, the figures are all turned toward the candelabrum. Over the relief three steps lead to the smaller surface on top of the pedestal. The sides of this surface nearest the viewer show a long horizontal cut in which a hole with some iron remains may be found. On the smooth top surface there are two smaller holes and one larger oblong aperture. R. Paribeni identifies this as a pedestal for a small votive temple.[87] The holes and the long cut would have served to fasten a small shrine with two pillars at its entrance. Since the monument in the Capitoline Museum bears similar traces of a like fastening, that pedestal also would have been used for a similar purpose.

Here a question might be asked regarding the significance of the scene portrayed on these monuments. W. Amelung conjectures that a liturgical action from the cult of Artemis is depicted on the Capitoline pedestal. However, he does not specify the character of this action.[88] Nevertheless, the veiled figures suggest the possibility of a sacrificial rite — most probably the offering of incense. The sacrificial implements portrayed on the near side of the pedestal in the Museo delle Terme would uphold this opinion, since there is an incense box among them.[89]

The most famous monument representing an incense offering is the back-rest of the so-called Ludovisi throne, which is of Greek manufacture and dates from the fifth century before Christ.[90] The original is at present in the Ludovisi section of the National Museum in Rome. According to F. Studniczka, the birth of Aphrodite or her emergence from the sea assisted by two Horae is portrayed on the back of the throne. The relief on the right side of the monument shows a seated woman in a gown reaching to her ankles. Over this gown she wears a mantle which almost entirely covers her head, leaving visible only a little more than her face and her forehead. Before her is a censer; the cover has been removed and hangs below it. In her left hand the woman holds a small open box, while with her right hand, which has been somewhat damaged, she is about to scatter grains on the censer.

If the main relief refers to Aphrodite, then it is safe to assume that this scene portrays an incense offering dedicated to the goddess. This can be concluded inasmuch as the censer was particularly connected with her.[91] The left side of the back-rest portrays a nude woman playing the double flute. Following the several monuments and texts which testify, as has been shown, to the use of flute music at incense offerings, it is easy to see this female flutist as a participant in the sacrifice who is providing musical accompaniment for it. Indeed, H. v. Fritze finds that very significance in the side relief.[92] He perceives a single simultaneous cultic action reproduced without regard to spatial dissociation. With E. Petersen[93] he feels that the veiled female figure on the left portrays a bride who may not, however, stand in opposition to the nude figure on the left, whom Petersen considers to be a hetaera. He further holds that the scene depicts an incense offering to Aphrodite, accompanied by the customary flute music, on the occasion of a bridal outfitting.

V. Fritze's opinion seemed the obvious one as long as the Ludovisi monument stood alone. His failure to explain why one figure was nude and the other veiled did not weaken his argument.[94] Now that the counterpart of this monument in Boston has become known, however, v. Fritze's explanation appears doubtful.[95] The nude flutist of the Ludovisi monument has her counterpart in the nude lyrist of the Boston monument. Thus the hypothesis which posits the relation of the sides of both monuments to one another is valid, even though the interpretation of the side reliefs remains unsatisfactory. F. Studniczka wonders if the representations on the sides of the Ludovisi piece might not be portrayals of goddesses who personify different aspects of Aphrodite's personality — now Νυμφία, now Ἑταίρα and now Πόρνη.[96] Analogously he refers to the music-making youth in the main relief of the Boston monument as Adonis. This youth stands in contrast to the shriveled old woman representing the wet nurse Trophos, who plays an important role in the birth of Adonis. Here she is depicted as intent on the care of the myrrh tree from which Adonis was born.[97] Thus Adonis the lyrist of the Boston monument would match Aphrodite the flutist of the Ludovisi fragment. Aphrodite, offering incense, on the other side, would have a counterpart in Trophos and the myrrh tree. The first comparison is more logical than the second. Finally, the better explanation is that which sets the scenes on the two sides in close relation to each other and also provides a connection with the main relief; this is Studniczka's solution, which had not previously been determined.[98]

7. MUSIC AND THE LIBATIONS.

Nothing demonstrates more clearly than the libations how close a bond there was between sacred and profane music in pagan antiquity. Of all the sacrifices offered by Greeks and Romans alike, in cult as well as in private life, none occurred so frequently as the offering of drink, both as partaken and as poured out. Like the incense sacrifice, which was often celebrated as an introductory offering, the libations had their musical accompaniment. Thus a woman striking a tambourine accompanies the offering poured out in honor of Dionysos, represented in the vase painting in the National Museum in Naples which was mentioned above.[99] A libation scene in the Vatican Library portrays a female lyrist in the famous mural known as the "Aldobrandini Wedding."[100] The most diverse views have been expressed regarding the significance of this painting. J. Winkelmann and E. Gerhard see it as a mythological wedding, but their opinions differ with reference to the part of the wedding ceremony portrayed.[101] In any event, the scene on the right side of the painting reproduces a libation accompanied by a female lyrist;[102] because of similar representations on Greek vases, A. Nawrath believes that the libation may have been intended for Hymen.[103]

In general, however, the role of the flutist at the libations is disputed. Among the Greeks the flute player at a libation was called by the special name of σπονδαυλητής. Flute playing at the libations also prevailed as a rule among the Romans. The poet Propertius looked upon flute music as itself a libation for the gods.[104] Thus flute players appear in almost every portrayal of a libation scene which has come down to us from the Roman world. Examples of this are the libation in honor of the *genius familiaris* and the Lares on the Pompeian mural.[105]

The music at the Greek *symposia* must also be understood in this cultic context. The *symposion* opened with three libations — the first for the Olympic gods, the second for the Heroes and the third for Zeus Soter.[106] Occasionally the sequence was modified. Each of these three offerings followed the preparation of a cup in which the liquid was mixed, since generally at least three such cups of mixing were prepared. The sacrificial act was given a more solemn character by the flute music which accompanied it.[107] Plutarch reports that even in later times this libation was performed in conjunction with a solemn paean sung to the flute.[108] Flute playing, then, had not merely an ornamental character but rather a cultic significance, as the religious song of praise which went with it demonstrates. This is the only explanation for the subsequent Christian prohibition of all instrumental music during meals, since music, particularly flute music, was consecrated to the gods.

8. THE CULTIC PURPOSE OF SACRIFICIAL MUSIC.

Tibicinem canere, ne quid aliud exaudiatur, Pliny writes, describing the rite of sacrifice. This would indicate that flute playing at the sacrifices was aimed at the elimination of disturbances from strange noises.[109] Plutarch states that the music heard at the burnt offering to Saturn in Carthage had the same purpose. The sound of the flute and of the tambourine was supposed to cover the screams of the children sacrificed to Saturn so that they would not be heard.[110] Therefore it was most important that music played during a sacrifice not be interrupted. Cicero affirms this in his discussion of the great Megalesian games, which were, to a great degree, liturgical as well, when he asks if the games would be consecrated were the flutist suddenly to be silenced.[111]

There is no question here, however, of music, as G. Appel holds, being played to prevent those disturbances which could have had an unfavorable effect on the devotion of those offering sacrifice.[112] Rather, Plutarch and Pliny envision that euphony which played so important a role in sacrifice that even commands were given silently during the ceremony.[113] A slip of the tongue in sacrificial prayer, a word spoken by the participants or similar disturbances influenced the sacrifice adversely, and the gods were angered rather than placated.

Despite the explanations proffered by Pliny and Plutarch, the real reason for the use of music during sacrifice may lie still deeper. From a purely practical point of view the bellowing of the sacrificial animal — for instance, a bull[114] — would have been louder than any music. Aside from this, the difficulty remains that music was required at libations and at incense offerings. The real reason for the use of music during sacrifice must instead be sought in the belief of the ancients in the magical power of music — and of noise — to drive away the demons. Thus Plutarch explains that the worshipers of Isis made a din with their bells (σεῖστρα) during the liturgy so as to keep the wicked Set away from the sacred action.[115] At the Saturnalia and the Lupercalia the noise of cymbals and bells was supposed to drive away the harmful demons and evil spirits so that they would not negate the ceremonies which were meant to bring about the blessing of fertility. The demons could not endure noise, the blowing of horns or, above all, the sound of gongs and bells.[116] This superstition was so deeply rooted that Christian mothers also hung little bells as talismans around their children's necks and on their wrists to keep away the harmful influence of the demons. Chrysostom had to point out with great severity that only the protection which came from the Cross could keep the children from harm, not little bells or purple ribbons.[117]

The precautions taken by these Christian mothers is understandable in light of the ancients' view with regard to certain noises. The sound of bells and music in general warded off illnesses because it frightened away the demons responsible for sickness. If a woman in Egypt today believes that she is possessed by one of these sickness-bearing demons she sits in the street with other women crouched about her. Together they beat every sort of instrument, howling and screaming with all their might. Since the demon cannot bear such noise for any length of time the sick woman is soon assured that she is healed.[118]

This act of faith in the magical power of music which characterized all of pagan antiquity facilitates an appreciation of the absolute necessity of music at cultic sacrifice. Music was understood to drive away hostile chthonic demons who loved tranquillity and quiet. This concept of music's magical power is found in the formula of a love spell published by S. Eitrem:

> X. X. is bound with the tendons of the holy phoenix so that you will love N. N. with your whole heart and no barking dog or braying ass, cock or conjurer, the clash of cymbals or the noise of flutes or anything else under the heavens will ever set you free.[119]

Here the noise of cymbals and flutes is mentioned as a means capable of breaking the demonic spell. The interpretations of Pliny and Plutarch cited above can be reconciled with this view. The harmful screaming of those who were to be killed in sacrifice was particularly attractive to the wicked demons, with whom the pagans believed the air was filled. Consequently, music was found to be especially appropriate at the time of sacrifice as a means of driving away the evil spirits who could destroy its efficacy. From this it can also be seen why music had to be uninterrupted during the *actio*. It was not necessary, then, that music drown out cries of pain but rather that it simply drive away the demons who had been attracted by those cries.

But our investigation of the aim of sacrificial music is not yet exhausted. In Greek ritual the sacrifice was accompanied by the invocatory cries (ὀλολυγείς) of women. Their purpose was to call the good gods so that they could enjoy the sacrifice.[120] Music had the same character of epiclesis. It was supposed to "call down" the good gods. The text from Menander, already quoted,[121] attests to the attribution of this significance to music. According to Plutarch, the inhabitants of Argos blew trumpets on the feast of Dionysos so as to call the god up from the depths of the river Lerne for the sacrifice.[122] This manner of thinking appears in Plutarch's observation concerning the inhabitants of Busiris and Lykopolis. These people banned the trumpet from their cult because it sounded like the braying of an ass. Since this animal was sacred to Typhon (Set) it was able to summon that deity, who was Osiris' opponent.[123] Because song and music increased the efficacy of the epiclesis the words of epiclesis were nearly always sung to instrumental accompaniment. Thus the Dionysian fellowship used the so-called ὕμνοι κλητικοί of women in order to obtain the appearance of their god.[124] In the Christian era Arnobius alludes to such epiclesis-like songs of the pagans performed to flute accompaniment, and he mockingly asks whether the sleeping deities will be awakened by them.[125]

Belief in music as epiclesis is very old and not specifically Greek. It existed also in the Orient. The cuneiform literature of the Sumerians had already shown examples of it. In the *Hymn in Praise of Enki's Temple Esira*, which essentially contains the benediction of Enki, the god of the watery deeps, over his temple at Eridu, we read:

When one bends the knee in his holy temple
may the harp, algar, drum, algarsurra,
har-har, sabitum, miritum,
instruments of sweet entreaty and humble imploring
    which fill the temple,
accompany the entreaty in its splendor.
Enki's holy algar has [always] sung to him in splendor.
The seven musical instruments indeed [always] accompanied
    [the temple's] entreaty![126]

Again, these words occur:

> In the reverence commanded in the forecourt the seven musical in-
> struments are played and the ceremonies of exorcism are undertaken.[127]

This hymn was published by M. Witzel, who notes the epiclesis-like
character of the music. In reference to the Sumerian word *balag(ga)*,
he states that it was a generic designation of a musical instrument. It
was also used at times to indicate a particular instrument such as a
harp or a drum, which served occasionally to call the gods to their
meal.[128] L. Dürr rejects this view with good reason in arguing that
balag does not mean a drum but rather a gong or a bell with which the
bell-player was thought to call the gods.[129] It seems impossible to
determine clearly the exact meaning of the word. However, both explanations speak of music in terms of epiclesis, although the words
"instruments of sweet entreaty and humble imploring" need clarifica-
tion.

Inasmuch as all of antiquity was convinced that music had the
power of epiclesis, the step to its use at sacrifice was a short one, for
both apotropaism and epiclesis played a major role in sacrifice. The
explanation for the cultic purpose of sacrificial music is therefore to be
found in the pagans' firm belief that through music's power of epiclesis
the god who was to accept the sacrifice could be called down.

This explanation also supports the absence of sacrificial music in the
ritual of the chthonic gods. Because the chthonic demons shrank from
music they had to be offered sacrifice in stillness. Apparent exceptions
to this rule can be explained by the fact that the god in question
originally had another character or, in the course of time, had added
to his own chthonic character that of another deity. According to O.
Kern,[130] the inscription from Magnesia on the Maeander which was
previously mentioned is related to the cult of Zeus Sosipolis, a chthonic deity. The text describes the festal rite of the twelfth day of Artemi-
sion, which was dedicated to this god. We read in the inscription that
the god received a bull and a goat on this day. The *oikonomoi* were to
divide the flesh among those taking part in the great procession, and
the holy action was to be accompanied by the music of flutes, syrinxes
and lyres. At first glance these ordinances seem unclear, for sacrifice
was made to the chthonic deities such as Zeus Lykaios, the Furies and
others without music — "in quiet."[131] Aeschylus too calls the song of
the Furies ἀφόρμικτος, that is to say, performed "without the lyre."[132]
The fact that sacrificial flesh was eaten is not consonant with the usual

ritual of the chthonic gods. At least this custom did not prevail in regard to chthonic deities of a sinister character.[133] Thus the cult of Zeus Sosipolis seems to have had to do with a god who dispensed blessings more freely — like Persephone who, although a chthonic deity, became the distributor of rural blessings. Aside from such exceptions the rule held that music was to be avoided at ritual sacrifice to the chthonic gods. Furthermore, it seems peculiar that the solemn anathema of the Romans, which was nothing else than a *consecratio capitis* to the chthonic gods, prescribed flute music.[134]

In this respect strong similarities exist between the cult of the chthonic deities and the cult of the dead. As in the sacrifices to those sinister gods, nothing was eaten from the sacrifices for the dead.[135] So too the sacrifices for the dead took place without music. This explains the mythical account of Minos, who offered sacrifice without flute music when his son's death was announced to him, just as the Senators offered incense without music at Caesar's death.[136] The omission of music in both instances indicates that the sacrifices in question were not consecrated to the gods but to the souls of the departed. According to Aeschylus and Euripides, libations for the dead, in contrast to libations in the cult of the gods, were also offered without music.[137] One exception to the customary ritual for sacrifice for the dead is depicted in the portrayal of such a sacrifice on the sarcophagus of Hagia Triada, which clearly shows a flutist.[138]

NOTES

1. Tibullus 2, 1, 51 ff. (44 Levy):

> agricola assiduo primum satiatus aratro
> cantavit certo rustica verba pede
> et satur arenti primum est modulatus avena
> carmen, ut ornatus diceret ante deos.

On the concept of *carmen dicere ante deos* cf. J. Quasten, "Carmen," in RAC 2 (1954), 901-910.

2. Horace, *Carmina* 1, 36, 1 ff. (28 Müller):

> Et ture et fidibus iuvat
> placare et vituli sanguine debito
> custodes Numidae deos.

3. Censorinus, *De die natali* 12, 2 (17 Cholodniak): Nam nisi grata esset immortalibus deis [musica] — profecto ludi scenici placandorum deorum causa instituti non essent, nec tibicen omnibus supplicationibus in sacris aedibus adhiberetur, non cum tibicine aut tubicine triumphus ageretur Marti, non Apolloni cithara, non Musis tibiae ceteraque id genus essent attributa, non tibicinibus, per quos numina placantur — esset permissum aut ludos publice facere ac vesci in Capitolio, aut Quinquatribus minisculis, id est Idibus Juniis, urbem vestitu quo vellent personatis temulentisque pervagari.

4. W. Aly, "Ursprung und Entwicklung der kretischen Zeusreligion," in *Philologus* 71 (1912), 470:

> Ἰὼ μέγιστε Κοῦρε χαῖρέ μοι
> Κρόνιε πανκρατὲς γάνους,
> βέβακες δαιμόνων ἀγώμενος.
> Δίκταν ἐς ἐνιαυτὸν ἔρ-
> πε καὶ γέγαθι μολπᾷ
> τάν τοι κρέχομεν πακτίσιν
> μείξαντες ἄμ' αὐλοῖσιν
> καὶ στάντες ἀείδομεν τεὸν
> ἀμφὶ βωμὸν εὐερκῆ.

On the character of the divinity invoked cf. K. Latte, "De saltationibus Graecorum," in RVV 13, 3 (Giessen 1913), 47.

5. Arnobius, *Adversus nationes* 7, 32 (CSEL 4, 265 Reifferscheid): An numquid ut parvuli pusiones ab ineptis vagitibus crepaculis exterrentur auditis, eadem ratione et omnipotentia numina tibiarum stridore mulcentur et ad numerum cymbalorum mollita indignatione flaccescunt?

6. Menander, *Fragmenta* 245 (87 Meineke):

> οὐδεὶς δι' ἀνθρώπου θεὸς σῴζει, γυναί,
> ἑτέρου τὸν ἕτερον· εἰ γὰρ ἕλκει τὸν θεὸν
> τοῖς κυμβάλοις ἄνθρωπος εἰς ὃ βούλεται
> ὁ τοῦτο ποιῶν ἐστι μείζων τοῦ θεοῦ.

Cf. Clement of Alexandria, *Protrepticos* 7, 75, 4 (GCS Clem. I 57 Stählin) and Ps.-Justin, *De monarchia* 5 (144 Otto).

7. P. Stengel, *Opferbräuche der Griechen* (Leipzig 1910), p. 18 and *idem, Griechische Kultusaltertümer* (Munich ³ 1920), pp. 111 ff, n. 15.

8. Cf. F. v. Duhn, "Der Sarkophag aus Hagia Triada," in ARW 7 (1904), 271. D. min, *Zeit und Dauer der kretisch-mykenischen Kultur* (Leipzig-Berlin ² 1924), p. 145, puts the date of the sarcophagus in the second late Minoan period, i.e., before 1400 B.C. W. Aly, "Delphinios, Beiträge zur Stadtgeschichte von Milet und Athen," in *Klio* 11

(1911), 13, agrees, *pace* v. Duhn, on Fimmeen's dating. There is an illustration of the monument in R. Paribeni, "Il sarcofago dipinto di Haghia Triada," in *Monumenti antichi pubblicati per cura della reale accademia dei Lincei* 19 (1908), 5 ff.

9. S. Eitrem, *Beiträge zur griechischen Religionsgeschichte* III (*Videnskapsselskapets Skrifter II. Hist.-Filos. Klasse* 1919, 2) (Kristiania 1920), p. 74, believes that the difference in the types of sacrificial music here indicates that there were different gods. But this view is very hard to prove.

10. Apollodoros, *Bibliotheca* 3, 15, 7 (124 Hercher): Μινὼς δὲ ἀγγελθέντος αὐτῷ τοῦ θανάτου θύων ἐν Πάρῳ τοῖς Χάρισιν τὸν μὲν στέφανον ἀπὸ τῆς κεφαλῆς ἔρριψε· καὶ τόν αὐλὸν κατέσχε, τήν δὲ θυσίαν οὐδὲν ἧττον ἐπετέλεσεν. ὅθεν ἔτι καὶ δεῦρο χωρὶς αὐλῶν καὶ στεφάνων ἐν Πάρῳ θύουσι ταῖς Χάρισιν.

11. Herodotus 1, 132, 1 (I 89 Stein): οὐ σπονδῇ χρέωνται, οὐχὶ αὐλῶν.

12. Zeus Lykaios was sacrificed to ἐν ἀπορρήτω. Cf. Pausanias 8, 38, 7 (II 352 Spiro). On the Furies cf. Sophocles, *Oidipos* C. 489 (426 Papageorgius): μετὰ γὰρ ἡσουχίας τὰ ἱερὰ δρῶσι.

13. Lucian, *De Dea Syria* 44 (III 359 Jacobitz): Διὶ μὲν ὦν κατ' ἡσυχίην θύουσιν οὔτε ἀείδοντες οὔτε αὐλέοντες. εὖτ' ἂν δὲ τῇ ῎Ηρῃ κατάχρωνται ἀείδουσί τε καὶ αὐλέουσι καὶ κρόταλα ἐπικροτέουσι. Cf. F. J. Dölger, ΙΧΘΥΣ II (Münster 1922), p. 243 and also the report of Varro, *Rerum rusticarum* 3, 7, 4 (154 Goetz) who speaks of sacred fish in Lydia which would come to the shore of the lake and go up on to the altar of sacrifice, summoned by flute music, when the time for making the offering had arrived.

14. Plutarch, *De musica* 14 (VI 500 Bernardakis): καὶ τὰ ἐξ Ὑπερβορέων δ' ἱερὰ μετ' αὐλῶν καὶ συρίγγων καὶ κιθάρας εἰς τὴν Δῆλόν φασι τὸ παλαιὸν στέλλεσθαι.

15. *Ibid.*: δῆλον δ' ἐκ τῶν χορῶν καὶ τῶν θυσιῶν, ἅς προσῆγον μετ' αὐλῶν τῷ θεῷ.

16. Lucian, *De saltatione* 16 (II 1, 133 Sommerbrodt): Ἐν Δήλῳ δέ γε οὐδὲ αἱ θυσίαι ἄνευ ὀρχήσεως ἀλλὰ σὺν ταύτῃ καὶ μετὰ μουσικῆς ἐγίγνοντο. παίδων χοροὶ συνελθόντες ὑπ' αὐλῷ καὶ κιθάρᾳ οἱ μὲν ἐχόρευον, ὑπωχροῦντο δὲ οἱ ἄριστοι προκριθέντες ἐξ αὐτῶν. τὰ γοῦν τοῖς χοροῖς γραφόμενα τούτοις ᾄσματα ὑπορχήματα ἐκαλεῖτο καὶ ἐμέπληστο τῶν τοιούτων ἡ λύρα.

17. Cf. F. Schwenn, *Gebet und Opfer, Studien zum griechischen Kultus* (*Religionswissenschaftliche Bibliothek* 8) (Heidelberg 1927), p. 18 and H. Hommel, "Das Apollonorakel in Didyma. Pflege alter Musik im spätantiken Gottesdienst," in *Festschrift F. Smend* (Berlin 1963), pp. 7–18.

18. O. Kern, *Die Inschriften von Magnesia am Maeander* (Berlin: 1900), p. 83 and W. Dittenberger, *Sylloge inscriptionum graecarum* II (Leipzig ³ 1917), p. 113.

19. L. Preller, *Römische Mythologie* I (Berlin ³ 1881) presupposes the influence of the Delphic *theoxenia* on the Roman *lectisternia*. Cf. G. Wissowa, "Lektisternium," in RE XII 1, 1112.

20. Cf. Plate 1.

21. Diodorus Siculus, *Bibliotheca historica* 4, 3, 3 (I 367 Vogel): καὶ ταῖς παρθένοις νόμιμον εἶναι θυρσοφορεῖν καὶ συνενθουσιάζειν εὐαζούσαις καὶ τιμώσαις τὸν θεόν. τὰς δὲ γυναῖκας κατὰ συστήματα θυσιάζειν τῷ θεῷ καὶ βακχεύειν καὶ καθόλου τὴν παρουσίαν ὑμνεῖν τοῦ Διονύσου.

22. Cf. M.P. Nilsson, "Die Prozessionstypen im griechischen Kult," in *Jahrbuch des kaiserlichen deutschen archäologischen Instituts* 31 (1916), 332.

23. Examples in Eitrem, *Beiträge*..., p. 87.

24. *Ibid.* p. 94.

24a. On the use of music among the Romans cf. J. Mountford, "Music and the Romans," in *Bulletin of the John Rylands Library* 47 (1964), 198–211.

25. Cicero, *De legibus* 2, 9, 22 (IV 2, 413 Müller): Loedis publicis, quod sine curriculo et sine certatione corporum fiat, popularem laetitiam in cantu et fidibus et tibiis moderanto eamque cum divum honore iungunto.

26. Cicero, *De domo sua oratio* 123, 124. *Idem, De lege agraria* 2, 93. Pliny, *Naturalis historia* 22, 11.

27. Cf. Plate 2 for a Pompeian wall painting with a sacrifice in honor of the Lares attended by a flutist. We have a similar scene on the fragment of a relief which is presently in the Museo delle Terme in Rome. Cf. W. Helbig, *Führer durch die öffentlichen Sammlungen klassischer Altertümer in Rom* II (Leipzig:³ 1913), p. 188.

An altar in the Palazzo dei Conservatori bears the inscription LARIBVS AVGVSTI on its front. (Cf. Plate 3.) On the front relief the sacrifice of the Vicomagistri is portrayed; they are standing two on each side of the altar and making the preliminary offering. In the middle is a flutist playing a double flute. In the front the sacrificial butchers are bringing the two sacrifical animals — a pig for the Lares and a bull for the *genius* of Augustus. On the sides of the altar, Lares are portrayed, small yet statuesque because they are standing on four-cornered bases; in their right hands they hold laurel, while their raised left hands, which have been damaged, would have held cornucopias. The inscription on the front, which mentions the *mag(istri) vici anni noni*, makes it possible to date this monument with some accuracy. Inasmuch as the cult of the Lares was reorganized in 7 B.C. at the behest of Augustus, most of the *magistri vicorum*, who had charge of the cult, numbered their years from that time; accordingly the altar may belong to either the second half of the year 2 or the first half of the year 3 A.D. Cf. W. Altmann, *Die römischen Grabaltäre der Kaiserzeit* (Berlin 1905), p. 176 and Helbig, *Führer...* I (Leipzig ³ 1912), p. 511.

On the other hand the altar in the Lateran Museum which, according to the inscription on the front, was dedicated to the censor perpetuus Gaius Manlius, probably has nothing to do with an offering to the Lares. There is an illustration of this altar in Altmann, *Die römischen Grabaltäre...*, p. 179. On each of the two near sides a Lar on a rock base between two laurel twigs is portrayed, a bowl in the right hand and a cornucopia in the left. The relief on the front shows a sacrificial bull. The one offering is in the act of pouring the libation. Behind the altar stands an assistant who is carrying a jug in his right hand and who has a towel with fringes over his left shoulder. A flutist can be seen next to him. The butcher is occupied with slaughtering the sacrificial beast. On the back of the altar Fortuna is depicted enthroned, surrounded by three men and three women, the latter with their hands raised in the gesture of prayer. Helbig, *Führer...* II 17, is of the opinion that the goddess is conceived of here in a narrower sense as the goddess of the city of Caere, the place where the altar stood, and that the bull on the front is intended for her.

A flutist is shown in a sacrificial scene on the sarcophagus of a Roman general in the Palazzo Ducale in Mantua. There is a picture of this in A. Levi, "Relievi di sarcofagi del palazzo ducale di Mantova," in *Dedalo* 7 (1926), 3, 225.

A scene of the same type exists on a sarcophagus in the Uffizi in Florence. Cf. W. Amelung, *Führer durch die Antiken in Florenz* (Münster 1897), pp. 18 f. and our Plate 4. From the composition of the individual scenes on the sarcophagus it is evident that the central scene portrays a thank-offering. In the scene on the left the general is showing clemency to a women prisoner and her small child. In the center he is offering a bull to Jupiter on the Capitol in gratitude for his victory. As he pours the libation out upon the small altar — the facade of a temple clearly visible in the background — a flutist accompanies the holy action on his double flute. To the right the butcher is about to give the death blow to the bull with his axe. The scene on the far right shows the wedding of the general.

A sacrifice to Zeus Serapis with a women flutist participating may be seen on Sarcophagus 173 in the Gallery of the Candelabra in the Vatican Museum.

The bottom of a jug handle which was found in Xanten and is now in the Provincial Museum in Bonn (inventory no. 8576) shows a flutist at the sacrifice of a ram. Cf. H. Lehner, *Führer durch das Provinzialmuseum in Bonn. I. Band: Die antike Abteilung* (Bonn 1915), p. 49. There is a reproduction in Ph. Houben and F. Fiedler, *Denkmäler von Castra Vetera und Colonia Traiana in Ph. Houbens Antiquarium zu Xanten* (Xanten 1839), table XXIV, 1.

In a sacrificial scene on gem no. 27 665 in the National Museum in Naples a woman is offering flowers to the accompaniment of flute music. Cf. A. Ruesch, *Das Nationalmuseum in Neapel* (Naples n.d.), p. 350.

A sardonyx cameo in the Münzkabinett in Munich portrays a rustic sacrifice. To the right an elderly man, clad only in an apron, is slaughtering a small goat, while a woman holds a bowl to catch the blood. Behind her a Silenus-like old man blows a double flute. There is a reproduction in A. Furtwängler, *Die antiken Gemmen* (Leipzig-Berlin 1900), table LXIV, 23.

28. Cf. Plate 5. the relief is derived from a monument (probably a triumphal arch) of Marcus Aurelius which was either on the eastern slope of the Capitol or in the Forum of Trajan. A relief which is presently in the Palazzo dei Conservatori and which shows Marcus Aurelius at a thank-offering in front of the temple of the Capitoline Jupiter belongs to the same monument. In the middle of his officers the emperor is performing the preliminary sacrifice, while a flutist plays. The flamen Dialis, or priest of Jupiter, stands prominently behind the emperor, his conical cap (*apex*) upon his head. There is a reproduction of this in E. Petersen, *Vom alten Rom* (Leipzig [4] 1911), p. 23. Cf. Helbig, *Führer...* I 505.

29. Cf. Th. Mommsen, *Römische Geschichte* I (Berlin [5] 1857), p. 230, note.

30. Cicero, *Tusculanae disputationes* 1, 2, 3 (218 Pohlenz): Quamquam est in Originibus solitos esse in epulis canere convivas ad tibicinem de clarorum hominum virtutibus, honorem tamen huic generi non fuisse declarat oratio Catonis. *Ibid.* 4, 2, 3 (362): Dixit Cato morem apud maiores hunc epularum fuisse, ut deinceps, qui accubarent, canerent ad tibiam clarorum virorum laudes atque virtutes.

31. Ovid, *Fasti* 6, 651. Cf. Livy 9, 30, 5 and Valerius Maximus 9, 5.

32. Cicero, *De domo sua oratio* 47, 123 (105 Klotz): Si tribunus plebis verbis non minus priscis et aeque solemnibus bona cuiuspiam consecravit, non valebit? Atqui C. Atinius patrum memoria bona Q. Metelli qui eum ex senatu censor eiecerat, avi tui Q. Metelle, et tui P. Servili, et proavi P. Scipio, consecravit foculo posito in rostris adhibitoque tibicine. *Ibid.* 47, 124 (106): Tu inquam capite velato, contine advocata, foculo posito bona tui Gabini cui regna omnia Syrorum Arabum Persarumque donaveras consecrasti.

33. Cf. F.J. Dölger, ΙΧΘΥΣ II (Münster 1922), p. 2.

34. Cicero, *Tusculanae disputationes* 4, 2, 4 (363 Pohlenz): et deorum pulvinaribus et epulis magistratum fides praecinunt. Cf. inscr. Orelli 2448: COLLEGIO TIBICINVM / ET FIDICINVM ROMANORVM QVI SPPS / TI. IVLIVS TYRANNVS / .MMVNIS PERPETVVS ET / ...VLIVS TYRANNVS F / HCDD / DEDICATVM K. MART / ...RSO SERVIANO II L. FABIO IVST. COS. According to the year of the consulate which is given, the inscription dates from 111 A.D.

35. Horace, *Carmina* 3, 11, 5 (64 Müller).

36. Plutarch, *Cicero* 28, 2 (I 2, 386 Lindskog-Ziegler): ἦν Κλώδιος ἀνὴρ εὐγενής, τῇ μὲν ἡλικίᾳ νέος τῷ δὲ φρονήματι θρασὺς καὶ αὐθάδης. οὗτος ἐρῶν Πομπηίας τῆς Καίσαρος γυναικὸς εἰς τὴν οἰκίαν αὐτοῦ παρεισῆλθε κρύφα, λαβὼν ἐσθῆτα καὶ σκευὴν ψαλτρίας. ἔθυον γὰρ αἱ γυναῖκες τὴν ἀπόρρητον ἐκείνην καὶ ἀθέατον ἀνδράσι θυσίαν ἐν τῇ τοῦ Καίσαρος οἰκίᾳ, καὶ παρῆν ἀνὴρ οὐδείς.

37. Cf. J. Marquardt, *Römische Staatsverwaltung* III (Leipzig ² 1885), pp. 187 and 226.

A *decurio collegii fidicinum Romanorum*, a boy eight years old, is mentioned in the inscription published in Th. Mommsen, *Inscriptiones regni Neapolitani Latinae* (Leipzig 1852), p. 592, no. 6845:

D M

T AVR T F POMT

CLITO DEC COLL FID

R. VIXIT ANN VIII M

IIII d XXII AVR NICE

PHORIANVS ET FILVME

NE FILIO DVLCISSI

MO B M F

38. Cf. Plate 6.

39. Cf. H. Jordan and Ch. Huelsen, *Topographie der Stadt Rom in Altertum* I 3 (Berlin 1907), p. 523.

40. There is no report as to the actual year of foundation of the temple. Yet it is perhaps the same temple mentioned in Livy 28, 11, 4 and Cassius Dio, *Fragmenta* 56, 62, with reference to an omen in the year 206 B.C., which was later renovated by Cn. Domitius Ahenobarbus. Cf. G. Wissowa, *Religion und Kultus der Römer* (Munich ² 1912), p. 227. Thus there is no question here of a temple having been built by Domitius Ahenobarbus, as Jordan and Huelsen, *Topographie...*, p. 522, seem to think, but rather simply of a renovation by him. A. v. Domaszewski, *Abhandlungen zur römischen Religion* (Leipzig-Berlin 1909), pp. 227 ff, seeks a new solution to the problem; he considers Cn Domitius Ahenobarbus, the censor for the year 15 B.C., to have been the builder of the temple, and the consul for the year 32 B.C., who had the same name, to have been its restorer. Against this view cf. J. Sieveking, *Österreichische Jahreshefte* 13 (1910), 95 ff.

41. A. Furtwängler, *Intermezzi* (Leipzig-Berlin 1896), p. 35.

42. Jordan and Huelsen, *Topographie...*, p. 523. On the *lustratio exercitus* cf. v. Domaszewski, *Abhandlungen...*, pp. 16 ff.

43. Varro, *De lingua latina* 6, 14 (63 Goetz-Schoell): Dies tubilustrium appellatur, quod eo die in atrio sutorio sacrorum tubae lustrantur.

44. Lydus, *De mensibus* 4, 60 (133 Wünsch): Τῇ πρὸ δέκα Καλενδῶν Ἀπριλίων καθαρμὸς σάλπιγγος καὶ κίνησις τῶν ὅπλων, καὶ τιμαὶ Ἄρεος καὶ Νερίνης, θεᾶς οὕτω τῇ Σαβίνων γλώσσῃ προσαγορευομένης, ἣν ἠξίουν εἶναι τὴν Ἀθηνᾶν ἢ καὶ Ἀφροδίτην· νερίνη γὰρ ἡ ἀνδρία ἐστὶ καὶ νέρωνας τοὺς ἀνδρείους οἱ Σαβῖνοι καλοῦσιν.

45. For the 23rd of March cf. Lydus in n. 44 *supra*. For the 23rd of May cf. Ovid, *Fasti* 5, 726 (254 Merkel): Lustrantur purae, quas facit ill [Volcanus] tubae. Cf. likewise the stone calendars, the oldest of which call the 23rd of May the *tubilustrium* or the *Feriae Volcano*. On the extent of Greek influence in substituting Vulcan for Mars cf. Wissowa, *Religion und Kultus...*, p. 231.

46. Festus, *De verborum significatu: Tubilustria* (480 Lindsay): Tubilustria, quibus diebus adscriptum in [Fastis est, in atr]io Sutorio agna tubae [lustrantur quos] tubos apellant; quod genus [lustrationis ex Ar]cadia Pallanteo trans[latum esse dicunt].

47. Calpurnius, *Eclogae* 1, 65 (4 Beck): Altera regna Numae, qui primus—Pacis opus docuit, iussitque silentibus armis Inter sacra tubas, non inter bella sonare.

48. Varro, *De lingua latina* 5, 117 (36 Goetz-Schoell): Tubae a tubis, quos etiam nunc ita appellant tubicines sacrorum.

49. Festus, *De verborum significatu: Tubicines* (482 Lindsay): Tubicines etiam hi appellantur, qui sacerdotes viri speciosi publice sacra faciunt, tubarum lustrandarum gratia.

50. Cf. Wissowa, *Religion und Kultus...*, p. 557.

51. Varro, *De lingua latina* 6, 22 (66 Goetz-Schoell): Armilustrium ab eo, quod in armilustrio armati sacra faciunt——ab ludendo aut lustro, id est, quod circumibant ludentes ancilibus armati. Festus, *De verborum significatu: Armilustrium* (17 Lindsay): Armilustrium festum erat apud Romanos, quo res divinas armati faciebant, ac dum sacrificarent, tubis canebant.

52. Cf. Plate 5.

53. Cf. the reproductions in E. Ferrero, *L'arc d'Auguste à Suse* (Turin 1901), table X/XI and S. Reinach, *Répertoire de reliefs grecs et romains* I (Paris 1909), p. 420.

54. K. Lehmann-Hartleben, *Die Trajanssäule. Ein römisches Kunstwerk zu Beginn der Spätantike* (Berlin-Leipzig 1926), tables 8 VIII, 26 LIII, 48 CIII. In contrast to the Arch of Constantine the *tubicines* here are not clothed in military fashion. Cf. also the four *tubicines* in togas and wearing laurel wreathes on the relief pictured in E. Schulze, *Alte Handzeichnung eines Reliefs mit Darstellung eines Saliersumzuges* (Petersburg 1873). The opinion that this is a procession of Salii has generally been rejected. Cf. W. Helbig, "Sur les attributs des Saliens," in *Mémoires de l'académie des inscriptions* 37, 2 (Paris 1905), 255 ff.

55. J. Marquardt, *Römische Staatsverwaltung* III (Leipzig ² 1885), pp. 435 f.

56. This would also explain why on the days designated by Q(uando) R(ex) C(omitiassit) F(as)—cf. Festus, *De verborum significatu* (346 Z.30 Lindsay)—i.e. the 24th of March and the 24th of May, the days after both *tubilustria*, apart from the Rex the Salii were also active. Cf. Wissowa, *Relgion und Kultus...*, p. 557, n. 3.

57. Cf. H. Jordan, *Topographie der Stadt Rom in Altertum* I 2 (Berlin 1885), p. 255, n. 87 and p. 452. It is more likely that the Atrium Sutorium replaced the new Forum, for after Augustus we hear nothing more of its existence. Th. Mommsen also held that the Atrium Minervae and the Atrium Sutorium were identical (cf. CIL I, 369) but he later abandoned this view. Cf. R. Cirilli, *Les prêtres danseurs de Rome. Étude sur la corporation sacerdotale des Saliens* (Paris 1913). pp. 129 ff.

58. Cf. *supra*, n. 44.

59. Ovid, *Fasti* 3, 849 (146 Merkel): Summa dies e quinque tubas lustrare canoras admonet et forti sacrificare deae.

60. Marquardt, *Römische Staatsverwaltung* III, 435 f.

61. Plutarch, *Numa* 17 (I 140 Sintenis): Ἦν δὲ ἡ διανομὴ κατὰ τὰς τέχνας αὐλητῶν. On the serious misgivings concerning the historical personality of Numa Pompilius cf. F.J. Dölger, ΙΧΘΥΣ II (Münster 1922), p. 40, n. 2. On the *collegium tibicinum Romanorum* cf. J. Spruit, "Historie en legende rond het collegium tibicinum te Rome," in *Mens en Melodie* 20 (1965), 135–139 and G. Fleischhauer, *Die Musikergenossenschaften im hellenistisch-römischen Altertum* (Diss. Halle-Wittenberg 1959).

62. Livy 7, 2, 4 (III 97 Weissenborn): Sine carmine ullo, sine imitandorum carminum actu ludiones ex Etruria acciti ad tibicinis modos saltantes, haud indecoros motus more Tusco dabant. Imitari deinde eos iuventus...coepere.

63. Cf. Plate 7. F. Schlie, *Die Darstellungen des Troischen Sagenkreises auf etruskischen Aschenkisten* (Stuttgart 1868), p. 67, gives a thorough description and adduces parallel portrayals on Perugian ash coffers.

64. The original is in the Etruscan Museum in the Vatican. Cf. W. Helbig, *Führer durch die öffentlichen Sammlungen klassischer Altertümer in Rom* I (Leipzig ³ 1912), p. 401. There is a reproduction in *Antike Denkmäler, herausgegeben vom kaiserlichen deutschen archäologischen Institut* I (Berlin 1891), table 21, 1. A god in a long chiton is depicted sitting upon a campstool. Hermes, recognizable from his winged feet and winged helmet, is near him and carries a lance in his right hand. Five Sileni form the sacrificial procession, and they are bringing with them two animals to be sacrificed – either deer or goats. The first Silenus bears an axe, the second blows a double flute, the third carries a wineskin, the fourth an amphora and the fifth a knife in his right, waiting for the sacrificial animals.

A flutist is also functioning in the painting of the Tomba del letto funebre in Corneto-Tarquinia. The newest research seems to indicate that this is a portrayal of a *lectisternium* and not a wake. Cf. F. Messerschmidt, *Beiträge zur Chronologie der etruskischen Wandmalerei* (Diss. Halle 1928), pp. 52 and 57. There is a reproduction in F. Poulsen, *Etruscan Tomb Paintings* (Oxford 1922), fig. 34.

65. Virgil, *Geor.* 2, 193 (50 Janell): Inflavit cum pinguis ebur Tyrrhenus ad aras.

66. A *collegium fidicinum* is mentioned in the inscription in CIL VI 2192, a *collegium tibicinum et fidicinum, qui sacris publicis praesto sunt* in CIL VI 2191, and the *collegium symphoniacorum, qui sacris publicis praesto sunt* in CIL VI 2193. On the identity of the latter two colleges cf. J. Marquardt, *Römische Staatsverwaltung* III, 226 ff. Wissowa, *Religion und Kultus...*, p. 498, considers them to be two different colleges. Yet the change of name after the amalgamation of the *tibicines* and the *fidicines* was natural, so that they may well be the same college. On a *collegium symphonicacorum* (CIL VI 4416) which had its cemetery between the Via Appia and the Via Latina cf. R. Paribeni, "Cantores Graeci nell' ultimo secolo della repubblica in Roma," in *Raccolta di scritti in onore di Giacomo Lumbroso* (Milan 1925), pp. 291 f.

67. Cf. *supra*, n. 3.

68. Livy 9, 30, 5 (III 334 Wissenborn): Tibicines, quia prohibiti a proximis censoribus erant in aede Jovis vesci, quod traditum antiquitus erat, aegre passi Tibur uno agmine abierunt, adeo ut nemo in urbe esset, qui sacrificiis praecineret. Eius rei religio tenuit senatum; legatosque Tibur miserunt, ut darent operam, ut ii homines Romanis restituerentur. Tiburtini benigne polliciti primum accitos eos in curiam hortati sunt, uti reverterentur Romam; postquam perpelli nequibant, consilio haud abhorrente ab ingeniis hominum eos agrediuntur. Die festo alii alios per speciem celebrandarum cantu epularum [causa] invitant, et vino, cuius avidum ferme genus est, oneratos sopiunt, atque ita in plaustra somno vinctos coniciunt ac Romam deportant. Nec prius sensere, quam plaustris in foro relictis plenos crapulae eos lux oppressit. Tunc concursus populi factus, impetratoque, ut manerent, datum, ut triduum quotannis ornati cum cantu atque hac, quae nunc sollemnis est, licentia per urbem vagarentur, restitutumque in aede vescendi ius iis, qui sacris praecinerent. Cf. Varro, *De lingua latina* 6, 17. Valerius Maximus 2, 5, 4. Plutarch, *Quaestiones Romanae* 55. Censorinus, *supra*, n. 3. Ovid, *Fasti* 6, 651 ff.

69. In the cult of Cybele the flutists were also organized; at least we have an inscription which mentions a *collegium tibicinum* of the mother of the gods:

COLLEGIVM TIBICINVM. M. D
D . MAG . CVRAVERVNT

M . SABIDI . M . L . C . ATLIIVS . C . L
CN . EGNATI . CN . S . SALANNIL . S

The first two lines may probably be read: Collegium tibicinum m(atris) d(eum) (I)d(aeae?) mag(istri) curaverunt. The inscription was found Nov. 6, 1911 near the Station S. Cosmo (Albanese), not far from Sibari. Cf. *Rivista Indo-Greco-Italica* 8 (1924), 149 and *Revue archéologique* 22 (1925), II 369.

70. Cf. Plate 8.

71. Th. Mommsen, CIL VI 1, No. 3877.

72. W. Helbig, *Führer durch dio öffentlichen Sammlungen klassischer Altertümer in Rom* I (Leipzig ³ 1912), p. 590.

73. *Ibid.*, p. 591.

74. A. v. Domaszewski, *Abhandlungen zur römischen Religion* (Leipzig-Berlin 1919), p. 190.

75. Cf. also *infra*, chp. 1, sec. 8

76. Cf. S. Eitrem, *Opferritus und Voropfer der Griechen und Römer* (*Videnskapsselskapets Skrifter II Hist.-Filos. Klasse* 1914, 1) (Kristiania 1915), p. 228.

77. Museum Catalogue F 303. There are further examples in the British Museum Catalogue F 556 (a vase picture from Gela) and in the British Museum, Hall IV, cabinet 36, no. G. 132 (a female flutist standing before a censer).

78. Cf. L. v. Sybel, *Christliche Antike* II (Marburg 1909), p. 180; there is a reproduction in table 20.

79. Suetonius, *Tiberius* 44 (144 Ihm): Fertur etiam in sacrificando quondam captus facie ministri acerram praeferentis nequisse abstinere, quin paene vixdum re divina peracta ibidem statim seductum construpraret simulque fratrem eius tibicinem; atque utrique mox, quod mutuo flagitium exprobrarant, crura fregisse.

80. Dio Cassius 3 (220 Dindorf): καὶ τοῦ μὲν λιβαντοῦ, καὶ αὐτοὶ ἔθυσαν, τῷ δ' αὐλητῇ οὐκ ἐχρήσαντο. Cf. Suetonius, *Tiberius* 70 (158 Ihm): Et quo primum die post excessum Augusti curiam intravit, quasi pietati simul ac religioni satis facturus Minonis exemplo ture quidem ac vino verum sine tibicine supplicavit, ut ille olim in morte filii.

81. The pedestal presently surmounts the tombstone of Vitellius Successus. There is a reproduction in F.J. Dölger, ΙΧΘΥΣ IV (Münster 1927), table 235. A detailed description of all three monuments may be found in W. Amelung, *Die Skulpturen des Vaticanischen Museums* II (Berlin 1908), pp. 626 f.

82. W. Amelung, "Zwei ephesische Fragmente," in *Jahreshefte des österreichischen Instituts* 12 (1909), 174 gives a reproduction.

83. Amelung, *Die Skulpturen*... II 626.

84. Amelung, "Zwei ephesische Fragmente," 175, n. 3.

85. Amelung, in Helbig, *Führer*... I 441.

86. Cf. Plate 9.

87. R. Paribeni, *Le Terme di Diocleziano e il Museo Nazionale Romano* (Rome 1928), p. 266.

88. Amelung, in Helbig, *Führer*... I 441.

89. In my opinion a fragment presently in the Provincial Museum in Trier belongs to the same group as the three Roman monuments. There is a reproduction of this in F. Hettner, *Die römischen Steindenkmäler des Provinzialmuseums zu Trier* (Trier 1893),

p. 242, no. 709. The fragment depicts a man holding a staff in his left hand and behind him a woman; both are turned toward a candelabrum.

90. The monument was found in the former Villa Ludovisi in Rome in 1886, not far from the ancient temple of Aphrodite by the Porta Collina. One can only surmise where it might have come from. E. Petersen, *Vom alten Rom* (Leipzig ⁴ 1911), p. 142, suggests Mount Eryx in Sicily. But taking the Boston monument into account this view appears improbable. F. Studniczka, "Das Gegenstück der Ludovisischen Thronlehne," in *Jahrbuch des kaiserlichen deutschen archäologischen Instituts* 26 (1911), 153, holds for Cyprus. F.J. Dölger, IXΘΥΣ II (Münster 1922), p. 339 points to Eleusis, in whose cult pomegranates and surmullets, which we see on this monument, played an important role. There is a reproduction in Studniczka, *ibid.* table 1.

91. Studniczka, *ibid.* 108.

92. H. v. Fritze, *Die Rauchopfer bei den Griechen* (Berlin 1894), pp. 30 f. Cf. also Studniczka, "Das Gegenstück...," 117, n. 9.

93. v. Fritze, *Die Rauchopfer...*, pp. 30 f.

94. The view that this is a ritual nudity is unacceptable.

95. Cf. also Petersen, *Vom alten Rom*, p. 145, who was obliged to correct his earlier view (*Römische Mitteilungen* VII [1892], 55 ff) after the Boston fragment was made public.

96. Petersen, *ibid.*, p. 117.

97. *Ibid.*, pp. 145 ff.

98. Amelung, in Helbig, *Führer...* II 81, also considers the naked flutist and the naked lyrist to be counterparts. Studniczka believes both monuments belonged to an altar. For the significance of the entire work cf. Dölger, IXΘΥΣ II 339, who sees portrayed "a sacred doctrine of birth and death." Against the authenticity of the Boston fragment cf. W. Klein, "Zur Ludovisischen Thronlehne," in *Jahrbuch des kaiserlichen deutschen archäologischen Instituts* 31 (1916), 231 ff.

99. Cf. Plate 1.

100. Although the picture breathes forth the Greek spirit it was, according to Petersen, *Vom alten Rom*, p. 168, painted only about the time of Augustus. H. Licht, *Sittengeschichte Griechenlands* I (Dresden-Zurich 1927), p. 62, is of the opinion that this is a copy of an original from the time of Alexander.

101. A. Nawrath, *De Graecorum ritibus nuptialibus e vasculis demonstrandis* (Diss. Lignitziae 1914), pp. 26 ff, collates the different views.

102. Cf. Plate 10.

103. Nawrath, *De Graecorum ritibus...*, p. 28. Petersen, *Vom alten Rom*, p. 168, believes (without reason, in my opinion) that the flat bowl, which looks like a *patera*, or libation bowl, is badly drawn and represents a dish for incense.

104. Propertius 4, 6, 8, (276 Rothstein): Spargite me lymphis, carmenque recentibus aris tibia Mygdoniis libet eburnea cadis.

105. Cf. Plate 2. Cf. also the libation scene in A. Baumeister, *Denkmäler des klassischen Altertums* II (Munich-Leipzig 1887), p. 1107 and a libation with a lyre playing Silenus in W. Helbig, *Wandgemälde der vom Vesuv verschütteten Städte Campaniens* (Leipzig 1868), p. 397.

106. K.F. Herman, *Griechische Privataltertümer* (Freiburg 1882), p. 246.

107. Plutarch, *Septem sapientium* 5, 150 (368 Bernardakis): ἐπεὶ δ' ἐπήρθησαν αἱ τράπεζαι καὶ στεφάνων παρὰ τῆς Μελίσσης διαδοθέντων ἡμεῖς μὲν ἐσπείσαμεν ἡ δ' αὐλητρὶς ἐπιφθεγξαμένη μικρὰ ταῖς σπονδαῖς ἐκ μέσου μετέστη.

108. Plutarch, *Quaestionum convivalium* 7, 7, 4, 712 (292 Bernardakis): τὸν δὲ αὐλὸν οὐδὲ βουλομένοις ἀπώσασθαι τῆς τραπέζης ἔστιν· αἱ γὰρ σπονδαὶ ποθοῦσιν, αὐτὸν ἅμα τῷ στεφάνῳ καὶ συνεπιφθέγγεται τῷ παιᾶνι τὸ θεῖον. Cf. Sophocles, *Trach.* 217 and Euripides, *Troad.* 126. On the origin and meaning of the paean cf. F. Schwenn, *Gebet und Opfer. Studien zum griechischen Kultus (Religionswissenschaftliche Bibliothek* 8) (Heidelberg 1927), pp. 18 f. A *symposion* with a flutist, after a fresco from the Casa della Suonatrice in Pompeii, is pictured in F. J. Dölger, ΙΧΘΥΣ IV (Münster 1928), table 240.

109. Pliny, *Naturalis historia* 28, 2, 11 (279 Mayhoff): Videmusque certis precationibus obsecrasse summos magistratus et, ne quod verborum praetereatur aut praeposterium dicatur, de scripto praeire aliquem rursusque alium custodem dari, qui attendat, alium vero praeponi qui favere linguis iubeat, tibicinem canere, ne quid aliud exaudiatur.

110. Plutarch, *De superstitione* 13, 171 (420 Bernardakis): παρειστήκει δ' ἡ μήτηρ ἄτεγκτος καὶ ἀστένακτος. εἰ δὲ στενάξειεν ἢ δακρύσειεν, ἔδει τῆς τιμῆς στέρεσθαι, τὸ δὲ παιδίον οὐδὲν ἧττον ἐθύετο, κρότου τε κατεπίμπλατο πάντα πρὸ τοῦ ἀγάλματος ἐπαυλούντων καὶ τυμπανιζόντων ἕνεκα τοῦ μὴ γίγνεσθαι τὴν βοὴν τῶν θρήνων ἐξάκουστον.

111. Cicero, *De haruspicum responsis* 11, 23 (VII 135 Klotz): An si ludius constitit aut tibicen repente conticuit aut puer ille patrimus aut matrimus si tensam non tenui ...ludi sunt non rite facti, eaque errata expiantur et mentes deorum immortalium ludorum instauratione placantur.

112. Cf. G. Appel, *De Romanorum precationibus* (RVV 3, 2) (Giessen 1909), p. 204.

113. Cf. the text in C. Sittl, *Die Gebärden der Griechen und Römer* (Leipzig 1890), p. 214, n. 6.

114. Cf. e.g., the portrayal of the sacrifice of a bull to the accompaniment of flute music on the altar of the temple of Vespasian in Pompeii in Plate 11.

115. Plutarch, *De Iside et Osiride* 63 (537 Bernardakis): τὸν γὰρ τυφῶνά φασι τοῖς σείστροις ἀποτρέπειν καὶ ἀποκρούεσθαι.

116. *Scholia in Odysseam* λ 48 (II 481 Dindorf): κοινή τις παρὰ ἀνθρώποις ἐστὶν ὑπόληψις ὅτι νεκροὶ καὶ δαίμονες σίδηρον φοβοῦνται.

117. Chrysostom, *Homilia 12 in Epist. I ad Corinthios* 7 (PG 61, 105/106): τί ἄν τις εἴποι τὰ περίαπτα καὶ τοὺς κώδωνας, τοὺς τῆς χειρὸς ἐξηρτημένους, καὶ τὸν κόκκινον στήμονα καὶ τὰ ἄλλα τὰ πολλῆς ἀνοίας γέμοντα, δέον μηδὲν ἕτερον τῷ παιδὶ περιτιθέναι, ἀλλ' ἢ τὴν ἀπὸ τοῦ σταυροῦ φυλακήν. These little bells were hung on earrings, arm bands and rings. Many of the bells which have been found bear inscriptions referring to the power which was attributed to them. One gold bell from the Esquiline has on it:

TOI ˮ ΣΟΜ ˮ ΜΑΣ ˮ ΙΝ
ΥΠΟ ˮ ΤΕΤ ˮ ΑΓΜ ˮ ΜΑΙ

i.e., τοῖς ὄμμασιν ὑποτέταγμαι. Cf. DACL III 2, 1958. This custom existed not only among the pagans but also among the Jews. Knots served to protect the children of ordinary parents against the Ajin, while the children of nobles used bells, as the Talmud reports; the knots were tied around the neck and the bells were put on the clothing. Even on the Sabbath the children were permitted to wear these thing. Cf. Mishna, *Sabbath* 66. Cf. also G. Metzmacher, "De sacris fratrum Arvalium cum ecclesiae christianae caerimoniis comparandis," in *Jahrbuch für Liturgiewissenschaft* 4 (1924), 23. K. Mohlberg is reminded of the present-day Roman custom of making noise with bells on the eve of the feasts of St. John the Baptist and St. Stephen—i.e., on the solstice, when the demons, according to an ancient belief, are especially active.

On the apotropaic significance of bells and flutes in the cult of Mithra cf. F. Cumont, *Textes et Monuments figurés relatifs aux Mystères de Mithra* I (Brussels 1899), p. 68. The apotropaic meaning of the bells in the Catholic liturgy has never been demonstrated. The bells found in the catacombs, *pace* Cumont, have nothing to do with the bells which were traditionally used at Mass, since these were only introduced in the Middle Ages and were intended to call the people's attention to the most sacred parts of the liturgical action.

118. Cf. A. Wiedemann, "Magie und Zauberei in alten Ägypten," in *Der alte Orient* 6 (1905), 4 and 25.

119. *Papyri Osloenses* I (Oslo 1925), 9 col. 5, 156: δέδεται ἡ (δεῖνα) τοῖς νεύροις τοῦ ἱεροῦ φοίνικος [ἵν]α φιλῆς διόλου τὸν (δεῖνα) καὶ οὐ μή σαι λύσῃ οὐ κύων βαυβύ[ζω]ν, οὐκ ὄνος ὀνκώμενος, οὐ γάλλος, οὐ περικαθάρτης, οὐκ ἤχ[ο]ς κυμβάλου, οὐ βόμβος αὐλοῦ, ἀλλουδανε[. .]ρανου.

120. Cf. P. Stengel, "Opferblut und Opfergerste," in *Philologus* 41 (1906), 231 ff. On the apotropaic and epiclesis-like significance of ὀλολυγή cf. S. Eitrem, *Beiträge zur griechischen Religionsgeschichte* III (*Videnskapsselkapets Skrifter II. Hist.-Filos. Klasse* 1919, 2) (Kristiania 1920), pp. 52 ff. The opinion of F. v. Duhn, "Der Sarkophag aus Hagia Triada," in ARW 12 (1909), 171 ff, that this ritual calling was accompanied by the flute, is an improbable one. Cf. Eitrem, *Beiträge . . .*, p. 44, n. 3.

121. Cf. *supra*, n. 6.

122. Plutarch, *De Iside et Osiride* 35 (II 506 Bernardakis): ἀνακαλοῦνται δ' αὐτὸν ὑπὸ σαλπίγγων ἐξ ὕδατος ἐμβάλλοντες εἰς τὴν ἄβυσσον ἄρνα τῷ Πυλαόχῳ.

123. *Ibid.*, 30 (II 501): Βουσιρῖται δὲ καὶ Λυκοπολῖται σάλπιγξιν οὐ χρῶνται τὸ παράπαν ὡς ὄνῳ φθεγγομέναις ἐμφερές· καὶ ὅλως τὸν ὄνον οὐ καθαρὸν ἀλλὰ δαιμονικὸν ἡγοῦνται ζῷον εἶναι διὰ τὴν πρὸς ἐκεῖνον ὁμοιότη τα.

124. L. Weniger, *Das Kollegium der sechzehn Frauen und der Dionysosdienst in Elis* (*Jahresbericht des Gymnasiums zu Weimar*) (1883), p. 7.

125. Arnobius, *Adversus nationes* 7, 32 (CSEL 4, 265 Reifferscheid): Quid sibi volunt extationes istae, quas canitis matutini, collatis ad tibiam vocibus? Obdormiscunt enim superi, remeare ut ad vigilias debeant?

126 M. Witzel, *Perlen sumerischer Poesie in Transkription und Übersetzung mit Kommentar* (*Keilschriftliche Studien* 5) (Fulda 1925), p. 7.

127. *Ibid.*, p. 13. Witzel, *ibid.*, p. 23, considers that rites of purification were held in connection with the ceremonies of exorcism. This would only be further proof of the apotropaic use of the music in question.

128. *Ibid.*, p. 19.

129. L. Dürr in his discussion of the work in *Jahrbuch für Liturgiewissenschaft* 6 (1926), 290.

130. O. Kern, *Archäologischer Anzeiger* (1894), pp 78 ff. and *supra*, n. 18.

131. Cf. *supra*, nn. 12 and 13.

132. Aeschylus, *Eumenides* 329 (38 Blass):

ἐπὶ δὲ τῶι τεθυμένωι τόδε μέλος
παρακοπά, παραφορὰ φρενοδαλής,
ὕμνος ἐξ Ἐρινύων,
δέσμιος φρενῶν, ἀφόρμικτος, αὐονα βροτοῖς.

133. Cf. P. Stengel, "Chthonischer und Totenkult," in *Festschrift für Friedländer* (Leipzig 1895), pp. 415 ff.

134. Thus Dionysos of Halicarnassus 2, 10 (168 Jakobi) calls the cursing θῦμα τοῦ καταχθονίου Διός. Cf. Cicero, *De domo sua oratio* 48, 125 (106 Klotz): Sin ista consecratio legitima est, quid est quod profanum in tuis bonis esse possit? An consecratio nullum habet [ius], dedicatio est religiosa? Quid ergo illa tua tum obtestatio tibicinis, quid foculus, quid preces, quid prisca [verba] voluerunt. Cf. *supra*, n. 32.

135. Stengel, "Chthonischer und Totenkult," p. 422.

136. Cf. *supra*, n. 80. Other examples in P. Stengel, *Die griechischen Kultusaltertümer* (Munich ³ 1920), p. 111, n. 4.

137. Euripides, *Iphigenie* 146 (49 Bruhn): βοὰν ἀλύροις ἐλέγοις.... In Aeschylus, *Coephoren* 151 (32 Blass) the paean at the libation for the dead is mentioned, but without accompaniment: τοιαῖσδ᾽ ἐπ᾽ εὐχαῖς τάσδ᾽ ἐπισπένδω χοάς / ὑμᾶς δε κωκυτοῖσ ἐπανθίζειν νόμος, παιᾶνα τοῦ θανόντος ἐξαυδωμένας.

138. F. v. Duhn, "Der Sarkophag aus Hagia Triada," in ARW 12 (1909), 170.

Chapter Two
MUSIC IN
THE MYSTERY CULTS

1. RELIGIOUS CATHARSIS THROUGH MUSIC. RITES OF INITIATION AND THE CULTIC BATH.

At the beginning of the "new life" which the members of the mystery cult were to lead there stood the rites of initiation. These rites were intended to purify the inner man from sin and guilt and place him in the condition of enlightenment.[1]

Because of antiquity's attitude toward cultic music, as explained in the previous chapter, it is clear that these rites offered a wide range for the use of music. In later antiquity sin was believed to consist in nothing more than being stained by the demons.[2] In the context of this belief a power which the ancients thought capable of driving away evil spirits must naturally have been of great value in ceremonies of absolution and purification. Since music was considered to possess such a power, it was particularly important in the religious cathartic rites.[3]

Inasmuch as the ceremonies of initiation often included cultic dancing, rhythmic music came to be added to them. In his accounts of the initiation rites of the Corybantes, Plato reports that those who were already members would dance about those being initiated.[4] Lucian's remarks on initiation are of special significance here. In his book *On Dancing* he states:

> I will say nothing about the fact that one cannot find a single ancient initiation in which dancing does not take place. Orpheus and Musaeus, the best dancers of their time, considered dancing to be something very beautiful. They introduced them [the initiations] and decreed that everyone would be received into the mysteries with dancing. As is the case with such solemnities, many things are not explained to the uninitiated. But everyone has ears, and this is why it is commonly said of those who divulge the mysteries that they dance them out.[5]

The initiation dance spoken of here was particularly enhanced by music. A terracotta from the Campana collection in the Louvre portrays such an initiation scene.[6] The candidate stands between two Maenads, covered with a cloak which also screens his face. One of the

Maenads, striking a tambourine, is turned toward the initiate. The other, with her head inclined, bends toward the candidate who remains in a bowed position. From the left a Silenus-like figure brings a liknon, or sacred basket, containing fruit and a phallus made entirely of pastry, which is to be emptied over the neophyte.[7] This is a portrayal of an initiation into the Bacchic mysteries. A similar depiction can be found on a Roman stucco relief from the Casa della Farnesina, which is now in the Museo delle Terme in Rome.[8] This relief, like that in the Campana collection, shows a deviation from the rite which Plato had in mind: the initiate is not sitting but standing; he holds a thyrsos in his right hand and is covered with a cloak thrown over his head. Behind the candidate a woman in a long garment is visible. She is turned toward another woman who holds a tambourine in her left hand. To the left a Silenus brings the liknon covered with a cloth, ready to empty its contents over the initiate. A mural from the Villa Item in Pompeii presents an excellent reproduction of this initiation rite.[9] This mural portrays the moment of the uncovering of the female initiate. She is kneeling and the lower part of her body is still covered, while the upper part is bare. She awaits the moment when the liknon, carried by a woman in the background, will be emptied on her. Another woman is circling about her, striking cymbals with uplifted hands. In all these initiation scenes music is marked with a cathartic character, like the fire which is carried around the initiate in other portrayals of such purifications. Plutarch mentions a custom which may be appropriately suggested here in explanation of the cathartic religious music described above. He writes that, if anyone consults the oracle, he is immediately "surrounded by tunes."[10] The soul-purifying aim of music, which was thought to facilitate the influence of the god, may be perceived here. This same opinion applies to the boy drawn to magic:

> He should wear only a white garment reaching from the head to the feet. His face is to be turned toward the sun and a little bell should be sounded before him.[11]

Considering the depictions just mentioned, what is said by the commentator on Theocriticus concerning the sound of brass may be extended to instrumental music:

> Brass is of value because it is pure and able to eradicate blemishes. Therefore use it at every absolution and purification.[12]

The religious cathartic character of music is also evident in another rite of the mysteries, the cultic bath. In the *Martyrdom of Saint Theodotus* we read that each year in Ancyra the wooden statues of Artemis and Athena were taken to a nearby lake and bathed to the sound of drums and flutes.[13] Ovid gives this same information in reference to similar baths of the cultic image of the Magna Mater in Almo near Rome and in the Phrygian river Gallos.[14] The demons were also involved in this, particularly at the time when the bathing and washing took place. The Attic *Plynteria*, for example, when the ancient image of Athena was washed, were reckoned among the days of ill omen and were considered to be unfavorable for useful activity.[15]

Still another mural from the Villa Item in Pompeii is significant.[16] A priestess, adorned with a cap and a wreath of myrtle, sits on a backless throne hung with a cloth. Her back is toward the viewer. With her left hand she lifts the cloth over a basket which a young woman offers her. To her right a younger servant girl, also wearing a myrtle wreath, pours water out of a pitcher over the hand of the priestess and into a bowl which stands on a little table. Meanwhile a bearded Silenus plays the lyre, which rests on a pillar. He provides a transition to the following scene, which portrays two female satyrs sitting on a rock. One of them holds a syrinx in her hand. It is difficult to decide whether the lyre-playing Silenus belongs to this scene or to the previous one. The arrangement of the panels does not take the scenes into consideration. Strictly speaking, this is unimportant since, according to the most probable opinion, they all have an inner cohesion. A. Mau explains the action of the mystery portrayed by saying that the seated priestess is about to lay a freshly-watered sprig in the holy basket, which contains the symbol of the cult.[17] Consequently, this is most likely a lustration scene, but it is not possible to determine the specific nature of the lustration. Perhaps a sprig is actually being watered. However, it could also be a kind of washing of the hands prior to the touching of the cultic symbol.

2. ENTHUSIASTIC RITES. ECSTASY AND ENTHUSIASM. SABAZIOS AND CYBELE.

Aristotle tells us that it is the task of the initiate to suffer and to let himself be brought to a certain frame of mind (παθεῖν). He is not to seek to acquire knowledge and increased understanding (μαθεῖν).[18] The significance of ecstasy in the mysteries is strikingly characterized by

this statement. The precise aim of orgies in the mysteries was to induce
such a heightening of consciousness in a man that he would be recep-
tive to the god who came to be united with him. Such a person was
then an ἔνθεος, an enthusiast. Music was the most important element
used to include this condition. Preference in musical tonality was
given to the Phrygian mode.[18a] Because of this, Lucian calls the
Phrygian mode ἔνθεον,[19] and Apuleius coins the expression *Phrygium
religiosum*.[20] This is the mode of Phrygian flute music. "Indeed,"
Aristotle explains, "among the modes, the Phrygian has the same
power as the flute among instruments, for both are orgiastic and both
heighten consciousness."[21] This peculiar capability, which brought on
religious ecstasy, assured to flute music the highest place in all
orgiastic cults. For that reason its use appears very early in the cult of
the Thracian god Sabazios. On that basis, too, Aristotle explains the
phenomenon that everything written in the Phrygian mode is
dithyrambic.[22] Consequently the flute is never absent in portrayals of
ecstatic moments in the cult of Sabazios-Dionysos. Thus the relief in
the National Museum in Naples shows a satyr in the center with his
flute, while a Maenad goes before, already rapt in ecstatic vision,
striking the tambourine.[23]

Among the Oriental cults, that of Cybele strongly resembles the cult
of Dionysos in this respect. Here, too, are the typically orgiastic instruments—tambourines, cymbals, rattles, horns and flutes. To their
accompaniment the worshipers of Cybele, in a state of enthusiasm approaching madness, would untie, pull and shake their hair and then
lash themselves with whips. This rite is described in numerous texts by
the authors of antiquity.

> Come, follow me to the house of the Phrygian Cybele, to the grove of the
> Phrygian goddess! There sounds the clang of the cymbals, there echo the
> tambourines, there the Phrygian flutist plays upon his deep-sounding,
> twisted reed. There the Maenads, adorned with ivy, toss their head wild-
> ly. There they celebrate the holy rites to the sound of shrill screams.
> There the roving band pursues the goddess. There would we also hurry
> with quickening dance-step!

So calls a young servant of the goddess to his companions.[24] The
cultists also took upon themselves emasculation in honor of the goddess. This rite was carried out in a fit of holy frenzy induced by the
Phrygian manner of singing, as well as by the rapturous music of the
tambourine, the cymbal and the flute. Lucian describes such an occasion:

On certain days the throng assembles in the temple. Many Galloi [priests of Cybele] and designated holy persons celebrate the orgies, while the unfortunate people mutilate themselves and beat each other on the back. A great crowd standing nearby accompanies them with flute music, the clashing of cymbals or the ecstatic singing of holy songs. All this occurs, however, outside the temple. Those who are occupied with such actions do not go inside. In these days the number of the Galloi is increasing. For when the others play the flute and celebrate their orgies the frenzy falls on many who have come only as spectators. A young man seized by this madness rips the clothing from his body and dashes into the middle with a loud cry and, snatching one of the swords that stands ready for just such a purpose, he castrates himself.[25]

In a later age Gregory Nazianzus, referring publicly to these orgies, would reproach the Emperor Julian the Apostate, who refused to admire the Christian martyrs but lauded the abominable self-mutilations of Phrygians made ecstatic by flute music.[26]

The tambourine is to be particularly noted among the musical instruments employed in these orgies. This instrument had already occupied an important position in the cult of the Egyptians, for its sound, which was deep and hollow, expelled the evil demons.[27] The rhythmic musical character of the tambourine was highly suited to induce psychic stimulation. In his book *On the Gods*, Philodemos of Gadara reports about the use of the tambourine by those who strive for religious ecstasy and the state of incubation:

So it happens that every place is filled to overflowing with people who are trying to fall into a divinely-inspired incubation and divinely-infused ecstasy. They wish to consecrate their thank-offerings to mere statues and to hold tambourines high in their hands while visiting every possible god.[28]

The tambourine was used primarily in conjunction with the Phrygian flute, the chief instrument of the cult of Cybele. These two instruments recur most frequently in texts and monuments. The Phrygian flute is distinguished from the ordinary double flute by the upward-turned and curved, horn-like end of the right reed. Music of the tambourine and the Phrygian double flute accompanies a sacrifical scene which has been preserved on a relief from the Villa Albani in Rome.[29] In ceremonial dance a woman is circling the altar on which the sacrificial fire burns. With her right hand she appears to be sprinkling incense on the flames, while in her left she holds a pitcher and a bowl of fruit. The music for the sacrifice is being performed by two girls on the right. One strikes the tambourine and the other plays the Phrygian double flute. This monument may well portray a sacrificial scene from the cult of Cybele.[30]

In the cult of Cybele the horn is mentioned only infrequently and at a later date; Lucian knows it as customary in his time.[31] Archaeological monuments show the horn rarely, although it can be seen on a fragment presently in the cloister of S. Lorenzo fuori le mura in Rome.[32] This fragment portrays a Cybele procession which is, more specifically, a circus parade. The image of the Magna Mater is born in front. She is depicted as seated on a throne covered with lions, a tambourine in her hand. To the left, behind the throne, walks a horn player, who accompanies the sacred progress with his music.

In addition to the tambourine, cymbals, kettledrums and krotala were used as rhythmic instruments at ceremonies of the cult of Cybele. The krotalon, a castanet-like instrument, earned for the Mother of the Gods the nickname Χαλκόκροτος. Along with the Phrygian double flute the syrinx received a place in the cult of Cybele, following the merger of this cult with that of Attis. It frequently appears as an attribute of Attis on medals and other monuments. Thus, for example, the obverse of a coin of the elder Faustina shows Cybele with a tambourine in her left hand. Behind her is Attis, with a syrinx in his right hand and a Phrygian flute in his left.[33]

Monuments which show the "holy tree" decorated with cymbals, a syrinx or a tambourine present a difficulty.[34] Did these musical instruments signify a ceremonial consecration of the tree or were they supposed to be votive offerings? The fact that votive plaques were frequently hung on holy trees leads G. Hock to surmise that the instruments were intended as votive gifts to the god and the goddess. This explanation seems all the more reliable inasmuch as other objects such as clothing and hunting weapons are also found on the trees.[35] Again, in depictions on votive plaques where two hands are shown, there are also tambourines, cymbals, krotala and Phrygian flutes, along with knives and whips.[36] However, it is not easy to determine whether these symbols were intended as votive offerings or were meant to indicate the divinity to whom the votive hands were dedicated.[37]

In the Vatican Museum there is a marble tablet which was found with a group of votive offerings to Liber between 1817 and 1823 in the immediate vicinity of Rome, near the Marancia Gate.[38] On the table the soles of two feet are depicted, encircled by a large snake. On the

right is a tambourine decorated with ribbons. The inscription above
and below the picture reads:

KALANDIO . PRO . SUA . SALUTE . DONUM .
LIBERO . KALLANICIANO .[39]

This monument may represent a votive plaque *pro itu et reditu,* with
which the donor wanted to express either petition or thanks for a safe
journey and return.[40] Inasmuch as the purely Italic god, originally
Liber, was at a later date completely identified with the Greek
Dionysos,[41] the tambourine which is depicted must be a symbol of the
divinity for whom the votive plaque was intended. This divinity
would be Liber, who was worshiped as a god of health in the neigh-
borhood of the site of discovery of the monument.[42]

3. MUSIC AND DIVINATION.

The religious ecstasy induced by music expressed itself either in an
outburst of the emotions, thus giving rise to religious catharsis,[43] or in
a transfer to the state of prophecy. In this way music became an important factor in divination. In the mysteries of the Magna Mater this
relationship between music and divination is particularly clear.
Through the din of tambourines, cymbals and flutes the ecstatic wor-
shiper of the goddess prophesied the future to those present.[44] From
time immemorial music had been especially valued in the service of
prophecy. Pliny the Elder gives us a report of the cult of Apis:

> In Egypt an ox is honored in place of the god. He is called Apis and he
> lives in isolation. If he ever goes among the people he stalks along while
> the lictors make way for him and throngs of boys accompany him, sing-
> ing songs in his honor. He appears to understand what is happening and
> seems to wish to be adored. The throngs [of boys] suddenly become in-
> spired and prophesy the future.[45]

Here singing served as a means of inducing ecstatic prophecy. Thus
the essential relationship between music and prophecy can be clearly
seen. This relationship also explains why the expression for "making
music" and "prophesying" was often identical in ancient tongues. So
too, the Greeks called a prophet Χρησμῳδός,[46] and the Hebrew word
Naba signifies not only "to prophesy" but also "to make music." Lucian
states in his *Alexander* that the false prophet Alexander of Abonouteichos selected the right place for his trickery, namely
Paphlagonia above Abonouteichos, where the inhabitants were agape
and believed that they beheld heavenly beings

if a man who prophesies from a sieve appeared with a flutist and a cymbal player.[47]

In cultic action music was used in preparation for prophecy. Julius Firmicus Maternus refers to this fact in his remarks on an African cult. With the air full of flute music, the priests would put on women's clothing and then call on their goddess so that, filled with a wicked spirit, they might predict the future to foolish men.[48]

In considering this cultic background it is necessary to understand the view of music as dispositive to divination, a view which derived from pagan philosophy. This opinion resided in the old Pythagorean school, as Cicero notes.[49] The Stoa also recognized the employment of music in the service of divination. According to Stoic teaching, ascesis and listening to music were preparations for the ecstasy which, along with purity of heart and a relationship with God, was considered to be the most favorable condition for prophesying.[50] The notion which was basic to this conception was closely connected with belief in the purifying power of music. In both instances there was a question of eliminating tensions and obstacles in man which could stand in the way of the infusion of the divine and its revelations.

Among the Old Testament prophets music had this same purpose. Elisha used the music of the harp to prepare himself for prophecy, as we read in 2 Kings 3:15:

"Bring me a harpist!" And when the harpist played, the hand of the Lord came upon him.[51]

Of course this has reference only to the removal of disturbances from outside which might impinge upon the prophet. The state of religious rapture appeared of itself as a result of inner silent concentration which was removed from any exterior stimulation. This use of music in the service of divination was similar to the Pythagorean doctrine that music had the power to bring about an ἐπανόρθωσις τῶν ἠθῶν — to establish an inner balance in man, as Strabo says.[52] On the contrary, the pagan prophets sought first of all to induce prophetic inspiration through external stimulation, and to this purpose they employed music as well as fasting, dancing, honey and intoxicating potions.[53]

4. DRAMATIC RITES. RELIGIOUS PLAYS IN THE CULT OF ISIS.

Dramatic enactments of the mysteries were very closely related to the ecstatic rites. If ecstasy was supposed to mediate the presence of

the god to men, then the religious mystery-dramas were to be concerned with live presentations from the history of the gods, by which the
presence of the deity could be attained by his devotees. Thus in
Eleusis, according to the report of Clement of Alexandria, the fate of
Demeter and Kore was enacted:

> Deo [Demeter] and Kore have become a mystic drama; Eleusis presents
> their wanderings, their rape and their sorrow by torchlight.[54]

The production did not have merely mimic value. Rather the goddess
was actually present to the initiates in the person of the one who portrayed her, and consequently they could also feel her beneficent
presence. This divine presence was an occasion for great joy among
the worshipers, to which they gave expression chiefly in music and
song.

Among the frescoes of Herculaneum which are presently in the National Museum in Naples there is one which depicts a religious play in
the cult of Isis.[55] In front of the temple portal stands a priest who holds
the sacred urn in his covered hands. At his right is a feminine figure,
probably a priestess. With her right hand she shakes a sistrum, or rat-
tle. In her left she carries a pitcher. To the left of the priest is an Ethiopian who is turned toward him and who is shaking a sistrum. In the
foreground of the mural a sacrificial scene is taking place. The action
is accompanied by a flutist who is seated to the right. To the right and
left of the steplike rise to the temple, worshipers of Isis can be perceived. Some are rattling sistra, while others are raising their right hands,
probably in a gesture of prayer.[56] Just in front of the steps there is a
black man who is turned toward the persons on his right. He appears
to be leading the action with the staff which he holds in his right hand.
H. Gressmann is of the opinion that this scene is related to the plays
which were enacted in the forecourt of the temple of Isis in Pompeii,
which he believes was erected about 75 B.C.[57] W. Helbig, on the contrary, considers it to be a picture of a morning or evening liturgy of
the type described by Arnobius.[58] J. Leipoldt also tends to see it as a
morning liturgy because of the prominence of sacred water.[59]

There is available to us still another fresco from Herculaneum
which also portrays a scene from the cult of Isis. This seems to bear
even more distinctly the character of a religious mystery play.[60] In the
middle of the painting there is a black man in the act of dancing before
the entrance to the temple. Near him, on the left, is a smaller feminine
figure who is striking the cymbals. Next to her, rather in the fore-

ground, is an Ethiopian, probably a priest of Isis. He faces the dancer and shakes a sistrum in his raised right hand. To the right of the dancer a woman playing the tambourine can be recognized, but only with difficulty.[61] In the center, before the ascent to the temple, there stands an altar. Around it, grouped in a circle, are those participating in the sacred action. On the right, behind the altar, a priest stands, holding a sistrum in his right hand and a symbol of life in his left. He is turned toward a trumpeter who stands further to his right. This priest seems to be leading the action. That this is a sacrificial action seems clear from the smoking fire on the altar. The small feminine figure, visible on the left side of the picture, is a more definite indication. She holds a libation vessel in her right hand and bears on her head a box of votive gifts, a frequent portrayal on reliefs with sacrificial scenes. Our attention is especially directed to two of the participants in the sacrificial action—a kneeling woman on the left and a kneeling priest on the right. The former, depicted with extraordinary vivacity, is turned toward the altar and is shaking a sistrum, while the latter evidences a singular gesture of prayer. We do not know what this scene portrays. In any event, it is probably not simply a ceremony accompanying the sacrifice. In the opinion of J. Leipoldt it is perhaps a portrayal of Father Nile, and thus, because of the dancing Ethiopian, it would represent Osiris.[62] Whatever the case may be, this scene concerns an action from the mysteries of Isis, in which music played a most important role.

In the cult of Isis music was held in great esteem from the earliest times. It is said that the great temple of Isis in the Field of Mars in Rome had a special temple choir at its disposal. The singing of this chorus, however, seems to have been more cacophonous than harmonious.[63] The flutists employed in the cult were used in sacrifices and processions as well as in hymns.[64] According to Apuleius of Madaura, they fell into two classes, one of which was set apart from the liturgy by a special consecration.[65] The musical instrument peculiar to the cult, however, was the sistrum.[66] This instrument appears first on Egyptian monuments dating from the time of the Middle Kingdom, that is, the beginning of the second millenium B.C. Women at worship usually shook this rattling instrument in the liturgy of Hathor, the goddess of heaven. In the later syncretic merging of the cult of Hathor with that of Isis, the sistrum was incorporated into the service of the goddess, as were the horns and the solar disc. Because of the wide diffusion that the cult enjoyed, the sistrum came to be used throughout the ancient Mediterranean world. It is still employed in the Ethiopian liturgy.[67] According to Plutarch, the shaking of this instrument was meant to keep the wicked Set (Typhon) away from the cultic action.[68] This explains why the monuments which have come down to us portray the sistrum as shaken in the immediate vicinity of the priest who bore the sacred object.[69] Thus a relief preserved in the Vatican Museum[70] shows an Isis procession in the following sequence: a priestess of Isis leads the procession, wearing on her brow a lotus blossom; in her right hand she carries a pitcher, while the Uraios-snake is wound around her left forearm. She is followed by the reader, who holds a half-opened scroll in both hands. He immediately precedes the priest who carries the sacred urn with veiled hands.[71] Finally a woman comes, shaking a sistrum. Below her there seems to be an assistant for the sacrifice, holding a ladle in her left hand. Close to the priest who carries the sacred vessel, both on the right and on the left, a sistrum is being shaken, just as in the mural from Herculaneum already described. The monuments of this period indicate that during the entire second millenium metal rings and perforated tin were added to the sistrum and suspended on wire to increase the sound.[72]

NOTES

1. Cf. O. Casel, *Die Liturgie als Mysterienfeier* (Freiburg ³ 1923), p. 22.

2. Cf. K. Latte, "Schuld und Sünde in der griechischen Religion," in ARW 20 (1921), 296. On how this notion was carried over into primitive Christianity cf. F.J. Dölger, *Der Exorcismus im altchristlichen Taufritual* (Paderborn 1909), pp. 25 ff.

3. The Pythagorean doctrine of the purification of the soul by means of music can only be understood on cultic – and not merely psychological – grounds; in general the views and doctrines of Pythagoras and his school stand in very close connection with the pagan cults and the popular beliefs of antiquity. Cf. F.J. Dölger, ΙΧΘΥΣ II (Münster 1922), p. 350 and *idem, Sol Salutis* (Münster ² 1925), p. 42, n. 1. H. Abert, *Die Musikanschauung des Mittelalters* (Halle 1905), p. 23, has already drawn attention to this phenomenon. On Pythagoras' view of music cf. H. John, "Das musikerzieherische Wirken Pythagoras' und Damons. Ein Beitrag zur Ethoslehre der Griechen," in *Altertum* 8 (1962), 67–72.

4. Plato, *Euthydemos* 7, 277 (III 97 Hermanni): ποιεῖτον δὲ ταὐτόν, ὅπερ οἱ ἐν τῇ τελετῇ τῶν Κορυβάντων, ὅταν τὴν θρόνωσιν ποιῶσι περὶ τοῦνον, ὅτ' ἂν μέλλωσι τελεῖν. καὶ γὰρ ἐκεῖ χορεία τίς ἐστι καὶ παιδιά, εἰ ἄρα καὶ τετέλεσαι· καὶ νῦν τούτῳ οὐδὲν ἄλλο ἢ χορεύετον περὶ σὲ καὶ οἷον ὀρχεῖσθον παίζοντε, ὡς μετὰ τοῦτο τελοῦντε.

5. Lucian, *De saltatione* 15 (II 1, 133 Sommerbrodt): 'Εῶ λέγειν, ὅτι τελετὴν οὐδὲ μίαν ἀρχαίαν ἔστιν εὑρεῖν ἄνευ ὀρχήσεως, 'Ορφέως δηλαδὴ καὶ Μουσαίου, τῶν τότε ἀρίστων ὀρχηστῶν, καταστησαμένων αὐτάς, ὥς τι κάλλιστον καὶ τοῦτο νομοθετησάντων, σὺν ῥυθμῷ καὶ ὀρχήσει μυεῖσθαι. ὅτι δ' οὕτως ἔχει, τὰ μὲν ὄργια σιωπᾶν ἄξιον τῶν ἀμυήτων ἕνεκα, ἐκεῖνο δὲ πάντες ἀκούουσι, ὅτι τοὺς ἐξαγορεύοντας τὰ μυστήρια ἐξορχεῖσθαι λέγουσιν οἱ πολλοί. On dancing in the mysteries cf. S. Eitrem, *Opferritus und Voropfer der Griechen und Römer* (*Videnskapsselskapets Skrifter II. Hist.-Filos. Klasse* 1914, 1) (Kristiania 1915), p. 54.

6. Reproduction in L. Canina, *Descrizione dell' antico Tusculo* (Rome 1841), table LII 2 and S. Reinach, *Répertoire de reliefs grecs et romains* II (Paris 1912), p. 287, no. 1. Cf. Plate 12 of the present work.

7. Cf. E.C. Lovatelli, "Di un vaso cinerario con rappresentanze relative ai misteri di Eleusi," in *Bolletino della Commissione archeologica communale di Roma* 7 (1879), 9. H.G. Pringsheim, *Archäologische Beiträge zur Geschichte des eleusinischen Kults* (Munich 1905), pp. 32 f. H.v. Rohden and H. Winnefeld, *Architektonische römische Tonreliefs der Kaiserzeit* (*De antiken Terrakotten,* ed. by R. Kekulé v. Stradonitz IV 1) (Berlin-Stuttgart 1911), p. 56.

8. Cf. Plate 13. The relief dates from the period of transition from the republic to the empire. Cf. W. Helbig, *Führer durch die öffentlichen Sammlungen klassischer Altertümer in Rom* II (Leipzig ³ 1913), p. 117. The smallness of the initiate here has symbolic value inasmuch as it signifies the situation of a child of the god – a situation in which the initiate has been placed. Cf. A. Dieterich, *Mutter Erde* (Leipzig-Berlin ² 1912), p. 55. The same relationship in depictions as obtains between the god and the initiate also exists in ancient art between the apotheosized dead and men still living. Cf. F.J. Dölger, *Gnomon* 2 (1926), 225.

9. Cf. Plate 14.

10. Plutarch, *Quaestiones Romanae* 10 (II 257 Bernardikis): ὅτι γὰρ ἰσχυρῶς ἐφυλάττοντο ταῦτα, δῆλόν ἐστι τῷ προσιόντας ἐπὶ μαντείαν χαλκωμάτων πατάγῳ περιφοφεῖσθαι. On driving out demons by surrounding a person with the ringing of bells cf. an example from folklore in D.F. Knuchel, *Die Umwandlung in Kult, Magie and Rechtsbrauch* (*Schriften der Schweizerischen Gesellschaft für Volkskunde* 15 [1919]), p. 14: "In the

community of Buchberg near Kufstein, when a woman in childbed is giving birth, the young boys go around her house three times and ring bells."

11. A. Abt, *Die Apologie des Apuleius und die antike Zauberei* (RVV 4, 2) (Giessen 1908), p. 10: Σινδονίσας κατὰ κεφαλῆς μέχρι ποδῶν γυμνηκότα καὶ προκωδωνίσας, παῖδα στῆσον καταντικρὺ τοῦ ἡλίου.

12. Apollodoros, *Schol. Theocrit.* 2, 36 (279 Wendel): ὁ χαλκὸς ἐνομίζετο καθαρὸς εἶναι καὶ ἀπελαστικὸς τῶν μιασμάτων, διόπερ πρὸς πᾶσαν ἀφοσίωσιν καὶ ἀποκάθαρσιν αὐτῷ ἐχρῶντο.

13. *Martyrium S. Theodoti* 14, in Pio Franchi de Cavalieri, *I martirii di S. Theodoto e di S. Ariadne* (*Studi e Testi* 6) (Rome 1901), p. 70: οὔσης δὲ συνηθείας αὐτοῖς ἐν τῇ πλησίον λίμνῃ κατὰ ἔτος λούειν τὰ ξόανα... ἐρχῆν οὖν ἕκαστον αὐτῶν ἐπὶ ὀρχήματι ἐπιτίθεσθαι... συνεξῆλθεν δὲ καὶ τὸ πλῆθος τῆς πόλεως πάσης ἐπὶ τῇ θεωρίᾳ τῶν γινομένων, αὐλῶν γὰρ καὶ κυμβάλων ἦχος ἐθεωρεῖτο καὶ γυναικῶν ὀρχισμοὶ λελυμένους ἐχουσῶν τοὺς πλοκάμους ὥσπερ μαινάδες, καὶ κτύπος ἀπὸ τῶν ποδῶν ἐγίνετο πολὺς κατακρουόντων τὸ ἔδαφος καὶ πολλὰ δὲ μουσικὰ μεθ' ἑαυτῶν εἶχον καὶ οὕτως ἀπῆγον τὰ ξόανα.

14. Ovid, *Fasti* 4, 339 (110 Ewald-Levy): Sacerdos Almonis dominam sacraque lavit aquis. Exululant comites, furiosaque tibia flatur et feriunt molles taurea terga manus.

15. Plutarch, *Alcibiades* 34, 210 (I 2, 301 Lindskog-Ziegler): ὅθεν ἐν ταῖς μάλιστα τῶν ἀποφράδων τὴν ἡμέραν ταύτην [ἄπρακτον] Ἀθηναῖοι νομίζουσιν, which was Alcibiades' undoing. Cf. Eitrem, *Opferritus und Voropfer...*, p. 123.

16. Cf. Plate 15.

17. A. Mau, *Führer durch Pompeji* (Leipzig ⁶ 1928), p. 209. The explanation of T. Warscher, *Pompeji. Ein Führer durch die Ruinen* (Berlin-Leipzig 1925), p. 231, that "another priestess, likewise young, is pouring a libation out of a vessel," I do not consider to be correct. The gesture of the sitting priestess is not appropriate for such an action.

18. Synesius, *Dion* 7 (PG 66, 1133): Ἀριστοτέλης ἀξιοῖ τοὺς τελουμένους, οὐ μαθεῖν τί δεῖ, ἀλλὰ παθεῖν καὶ διατεθῆναι, γινομένους δηλονότι ἐπιτηδείους.

18a. Homer (*Odyssea* 12, 40 ff) labels the effect of music "bewitching" and uses the same word (θέλγειν) to describe the effect of the magic wand. The songs of a singer are called θελκτήζια (*ibid.* 1, 337). According to Plato (*Symposium* 215 c), flute music causes frenzy. Aristotle (*Politeia* 8, 5, 5, 1340 a) remarks that the songs of Olympos accompanied by flute music make τὰς ψυχὰς ἐνθουσιαστικάς; the ethos, i.e., the normal condition of the soul, is changed upon hearing such music. Cf. also Philodemos, *De musica* (Kemke), pp. 25 and 49. Strabo 10, 467. Lucian, *Nigrinus* 37. Diodorus Siculus (*Bibliotheca historica* 3, 57) reports that a woman became ἐνθεάζουσα when she heard the sound of drums and cymbals. Cf. also Polybius 4, 20. Athenagoras 14, 626 ff. Firmicus Maternus, *De errore profanarum religionum* 4, 2. For contemporary works treating of this cf. E. Rhode, *Psyche* (Tübingen¹⁰ 1925), 2, 16 and 48, 1. A. Délatte, *Les conceptions de l'enthusiasme chez les philosophes présocratiques* (Paris 1934). F. Pfister, "Ekstasis," in *Pisciculi F.J. Dölger* (Münster 1939), pp. 178–191. E.R. Dodds, *The Greeks and the Irrational* (Berkeley 1951). "Ekstase," in RAC 4 (1959), 944–987.

19. Lucian, *Harmonides* 1 (I 2, 174 Sommerbrodt): σύμφωνα εἶναι τὰ μέλη πρὸς τὸν χορὸν καὶ τῆς ἁρμονίας ἑκάστης διαφυλάττειν τὸ ἴδιον, τῆς Φρυγίου τὸ ἔνθεον, τῆς Λυδίου τὸ Βακχικόν, τῆς Δωρίου τὸ σεμνόν, τῆς Ἰωνικῆς τὸ γλαφυρόν.

20. Apuleius, *Florida* 1, 4 (20 Hildebrand): seu tu velles Aeolion simplex seu Jastium varium, seu Lydium querulum seu Phrygium religiosum.

21. Aristotle, Politeia 8, 7, 1342 b (290 Immisch): ἔχει γὰρ τὴν αὐτὴν δύναμιν ἡ φρυγιστὶ τῶν ἁρμονιῶν ἥνπερ αὐλὸς ἐν τοῖς ὀργάνοις. ἄμφω γὰρ ὀργιαστικὰ καὶ παθητικά. Consequently

he opposed Plato (who had permitted the Phrygian mode but not flute music) because he felt that neither could be separated from the other. *Ibid.*: δηλοῖ δ' ἡ ποίησις. πᾶσα γὰρ βακχεία καὶ πᾶσα ἡ τοιαύτη κίνησις μάλιστα τῶν ὀργάνων ἐστὶν ἐν τοῖς αὐλοῖς, τῶν δ' ἁρμονιῶν ἐν τοῖς φρυγιστὶ μέλεσι λαμβάνει ταῦτα τὸ πρέπον, οἷον ὁ διθύραμβος ὁμολογουμένως εἶναι δοκεῖ Φρύγιον. On Plato and Aristotle cf. L. Richter, *Zur Wissenschaftslehre von der Musik bei Platon und Aristoteles* (*Deutsche Akademie der Wissenschaften, Schriften der Sektion für Altertumswissenschaften* 23) (Berlin 1961).

22. Aristotle, *ibid.*: ὁ διθύραμβος ὁμολογουμένως εἶναι δοκεῖ Φρύγιον. καὶ τούτου πολλὰ παραδείγματα λέγουσιν οἱ περὶ τὴν σύνεσιν ταύτην ἄλλα τε, καὶ διότι Φιλόξενος ἐγχειρήσας ἐν τῇ δωριστὶ ποιῆσαι [διθύραμβον] τοὺς μύθους οὐχ οἷός τ' ἦν, ἀλλ' ὑπὸ τῆς φύσεως αὐτῆς ἐξέπεσεν εἰς τὴν φρυγιστὶ τὴν προσήκουσαν ἁρμονίαν πάλιν. Cf. H. Abert, *Die Lehre vom Ethos in der griechischen Musik* (Leipzig 1899), p. 15.

23. Cf. Plate 16 and F. Hauser, *Die neu-attischen Reliefs* (Stuttgart 1889), pp. 154 f. Cf. Plate 17 for a relief painting of a sacrificial scene from the cult of Dionysos from the Casa della Farnesina in the Museo delle Terme. A Maenad is lighting the sacrificial fire on the altar with two torches, while a satyr standing behind her accompanies the action on a double flute. To the left Silenus is portrayed, the thyrsos in his left hand, and his right arm resting upon a four-sided pedestal. Behind the pedestal one can see a heavily-veiled woman. Cf. W. Helbig, *Führer durch die öffentlichen Sammlungen klassischer Altertümer in Rom* II (Leipzig ³ 1913), p. 118.

24. Catullus 63, 19 ff. (133 Kroll):

> simul ite, sequimini
> Phrygiam ad domum Cybeles, Phrygia ad nemora Deae
> Ubi cymbalum sonat vox, ubi typana reboant,
> Tibicen ubi canit Phryx curvo grave calamo,
> Ubi capita Maenades vi iaciunt hederigerae,
> Ubi sacra sancta acutis ululatibus agitant
> Ubi suevit illa divae volitare vaga cohors:
> Quo nos decet citatis celerare tripudiis.
> Simul haec comitibus Attis cecinit notha mulier,
> Thiasus repente linguis trepidantibus ululat.
> Leve tympanum remugit, cava cymbala recrepant.

25. Lucian, *De Dea Syria* 50 (III 361 Jakobitz): ἐν ῥητῇσι δὲ ἡμέρῃσι τὸ μὲν πλῆθος ἐς τὸ ἱρὸν ἀγείρονται... πολλοὶ δὲ σφίσι παρεστεῶτες ἐπαυλέουσι, πολλοὶ δὲ τύμπανα παταγέουσι, ἄλλοι δὲ ἀείδουσι ἔνθεα καὶ ἱρὰ ᾄσματα. τὸ δὲ ἔργον ἐκτὸς τοῦ νηοῦ τόδε γίνεται, οὐδὲ ἐσέρχονται ἐς τὸν νηὸν ὁκόσοι τάδε ποιέουσι. ἐν ταύτῃσι τῇσι ἡμέρῃσι καὶ Γάλλοι γίνονται. ἐπεὰν γὰρ οἱ Γάλλοι αὐλέωσί τε καὶ ὄργια ποιέωνται, ἐς πολλοὺς ἤδη ἡ μανία ἀπικνέεται—καὶ γὰρ πολλοὶ οἱ ἐς δέην ἀπικόμενοι—μετὰ δὲ τοιάδε ἔπρηξαν. καταλέξω δὲ καὶ τὰ ποιοῦσι· ὁ νεηνίης, ὅτῳ τάδε ἀποκέαται, ῥίψας τὰ εἵματα μεγάλῃ βοῇ ἐς μέσην ἔρχεται καὶ ξίφος ἀναιρέεται. τὰ δὲ πολλὰ ἑτοῖμα, ἐμοὶ δοκέειν, διὰ τοῦτο ἕστηκε. λαβὼν δὲ αὐτίκα τάμνει ἑαυτόν.

26. Gregory Nazianzus, *Oratio* 4 (*Contra Julianum* 1) 70 (PG 35, 592): καὶ τὰς Φρυγῶν ἐκτομὰς τῶν ὑπ' αὐλοῦ κηλουμένων, καὶ μετὰ τόν αὐλὸν ὑβριζομένων. The musical instruments of the cult of Cybele consequently became, next to the whip, the pine cone and the pomegranate, the most customary symbols of the priesthood of the goddess. Thus a relief in the Palazzo dei Conservatori portrays the tambourine, cymbals and Phrygian flutes of an arch-Gallos. Cf. Plate 18. Cf. also H. Hepding, *Attis, seine Mythen und sein Kult* (RVV 1) (Giessen 1903), 128 and Helbig, *Führer...* I (Leipzig ³ 1912), p. 566, no. 987. The monument of Modius Maximus of Ostia, a high priest of Cybele, portrays a tambourine, a Phrygian flute and a syrinx. There is a reproduction of it in F.J. Dölger, IXΘΥΣ IV (Münster 1927), table 168. On the arch-Galloi cf. F. Cu-

mont, *Die orientalischen Religionen im römischen Heidentum* (Leipzig-Berlin 1910), p. 66.

27. G. Maspéro, *Archéologie Égyptienne* (Leipzig 1889), p. 89.

28. Philodemos, *On the Gods* I 18, 17 ff. (31 Diels): ὥστε πάντα κεκόπηται τῶν ἐφ' εἱερῶν πειρωμένων ἐκ θεῶν κατέχεσθαι κάρωι καὶ τῷ ἐγκαθειμένωι θείωι δαιμονιᾶν καὶ τοῖς ἀγάλμασιν αὐτοῖς προσφέρειν ἐπίχειρα καπίοντας θεοὺς πάντας ὀρθὰ τύπανα διὰ χερῶν ἔχειν.

29. Plate 19.

30. Cf. Helbig, *Führer*. . . II 441. One may see the Phrygian double flute frequently in the stucco decorations in the underground basilica before the Porta Maggiore in Rome. Cf. H. Lietzmann, "Der unterirdische Kultraum vor Porta Maggiore in Rom," in *Vorträge der Bibliothek Warburg*, ed. by F. Saxl, I (1922–1923), 68. Plate 20 gives a reproduction of a sacrificial scene from the left aisle of this basilica. A sacrificial fire burns on the altar in the middle. A woman approaches it on the right; she is dancing and playing the Phrygian double flute, and she wears a himation. Two women in the same clothing are on the left side of the altar. One of them is bending toward the altar in order a lay a bunch of flowers decorated with ribbons upon it. Behind her the second carries a long thyrsos on her right shoulder. Cf. J. Carcopino, *La basilique pythagoricienne de la Porte Majeure* (Paris 1926), p. 88. The predominance of the Phrygian symbols in conjunction with the portrayal of Attis as well as the complete lack of symbols of the cults of Isis and Mithra gives an important indication of the dating of the cultic room.

31. Lucian, *Dialogi deorum* 12, 233 (I 80 Sommerbrodt): ὁ μὲν αὐτῶν τέμνεται ξίφει τὸν πῆχυν, ὁ δὲ ἀνεὶς τὴν κόμην ἴεται μεμηνὼς διὰ τῶν ὀρῶν, ὁ δὲ αὐλεῖ τῷ κέρατι, ὁ δὲ ἐπιβομβεῖ τῷ τυμπάνῳ ἢ ἐπικτυπεῖ τῷ κυμβάλῳ.

32. Cf. Plate 21, 1.

33. Cf. W.H. Roscher, *Lexikon der Mythologie* II 1, 1647.

34. Cf. the portrayal on the clay relief in the Museo delle Terme, reproduced in Plate 22. Cf. R. Paribeni, *Le Terme di Diocleziano e il Museo nazionale Romano* (Rome 1928), p. 293, no. 972. A fruit offering, which a woman is setting ablaze, is depicted. The participants in the sacrifice are a Maenad carrying a thyrsos over her shoulder and a tambourine in her lowered left hand and a youthful Pan who is blowing the double flute. The altar is located under the holy tree, whose branches are decorated with syrinx and cymbals. There is a similar relief, presently in the Louvre, in H. v. Rohden and H. Winnefeld, *Architektonische römische Tonreliefs der Kaiserzeit* (*Die antiken Terrakotten*, ed. by R. Kekulé v. Stradonitz IV 2) (Berlin-Stuttgart 1911), table CXXII 1.

The holy pine of Attis likewise carries the musical instruments of the cult of Cybele. Cf., e.g., the side reliefs of the altar which was found in the summer of 1919 under the Palazzo dei Convertendi near St. Peter's Square and which is presently in the Lateran Museum (Hall 5, no. 342). The relief on the right side of the monument, which according to the place where it was found probably came from the Vatican Phrygianum, shows a pine decorated with a tambourine and a five-reeded syrinx. A pair of double flutes is leaning against the trunk. The pine on the left side is adorned with cymbals, a Phrygian medal and a four-reeded flute. There is a reproduction in O. Marucchi, *Di alcuni monumenti recensemente acquistati dai Musei Pontifici* (*Dissertazioni della Pontificia Accademia Romana di archeologia* 2, 15 (1921), table III 2–3. Cf. also P. Fabre, "Un autel du culte phrygien au musée du Latran," in *Mélanges d'archéologie et d'histoire* 40 (1923), 3 ff. On the pine of Attis cf. Cumont, *Die orientalischen Religionen* . . . , p. 58.

35. Cf. G. Hock, *Griechische Weihegebräuche* (Würzburg 1905), pp. 22 f. On musical instruments as votive gifts cf. Daremberg-Saglio II, 377.

36. Cf. G. Zoëga, *Bassirilievi antichi di Roma* (Rome 1908), tables 13–14.

37. O. Jahn, "Über den Aberglauben des bösen Blicks bei den Alten," in *Berichte*

über die Verhandlungen der sächsischen Gesellschaft der Wissenschaften VII (1855), 105.

38. Cf. L. Biondi, *Monumenti Amaranziani* (Rome 1843), p. 133, table XLI. Cf. also Plate 21, 2 of the present work.

39. CIL VI 463.

40. Cf. W. Amelung, "Ex-voto an Asklepios," in ARW 8 (1905), 159.

41. Cf. Schur, "Liber Pater," in RE 13, 68 f.

42. Cf. Biondi, *Monumenti...*, p. 128.

43. Aristotle, *Politeia* 8, 7, 1342 a (249 Immisch): καὶ γὰρ ὑπὸ ταύτης τῆς κινήσεως [ecstasy is meant] κατακώχιμοί τινές εἰσιν· ἐκ τῶν δ' ἱερῶν μελῶν ὁρῶμεν τούτους, ὅταν χρήσωνται τοῖς ἐξοργιάζουσι τὴν ψυχὴν μέλεσι, καθισταμένους ὥσπερ ἰατρείας τυχόντας καὶ καθάρσεως.

44. Cf. Cumont, *Die orientalischen Religionen...*, p. 66.

45. Pliny, *Naturalis historia* 8, 46, 185 (II 101 Mayhoff). Cf. F.J. Dölger, *Sol Salutis* (Münster ² 1925), p. 105.

46. Consequently Apollo was god of prophets and musicians and Pan was god of medicine, music and divination. On the latter cf. O. Kern, *Die Religion der Griechen* (Berlin 1926), p. 112.

47. Lucian, *Alexander* 9, 217 (II 1, 106 Sommerbrodt): ὁ δὲ 'Αλέξανδρος ἔμπαλιν τὰ οἴκοι προὔκρινε λέγων ὅπερ ἦν, πρὸς τὴν τῶν τοιούτων ἀρχὴν καὶ ἐπιχείρησιν ἀνθρώπων δεῖν παχέων καὶ ἠλιθίων τῶν ὑποδεξομένων, οἵους τοὺς Παφλαγόνας εἶναι ἔφασκεν ὑπεροικοῦντας τὸ τοῦ 'Αβώνου τεῖχος, δεισιδαίμονας τοὺς πολλοὺς καὶ πλουσίους, καὶ μόνον εἰ φανείη τις αὐλητὴν ἢ τυμπανιστὴν ἢ κυμβάλοις κροτοῦντα ἐπαγόμενος, κοσκίνῳ τὸ τοῦ λόγου μαντευόμενος, αὐτίκα μάλα πάντας κεχηνότας πρὸς αὐτὸν καὶ ὥσπερ τινὰ τῶν ἐπουρανίων προσβλέποντας.

48. Firmicus Maternus, *De errore profanarum religionum* 4, 2 (11 Ziegler): Deinde cum sic se alienos a viris fecerint, adimpleti tibiarum cantu vocant deam suam, ut nefario repleti spiritu vanis hominibus quasi futura praedicant. On Firmicus Maternus cf. C.A. Forbes, *Firmicus Maternus. The Error of the Pagan Religions* (*Ancient Christian Writers* 37) (New York 1970), pp. 50, 56, 152.

49. Cicero, *De divinatione* 1, 50 114 (IV 2, 187 Müller): Ergo et ii quorum animi spretis corporibus evolant atque excurrunt foras ardore aliquo infammati atque incitati cernunt illa profecto quae vaticinantes pronuntiant, multisque rebus inflammata tales animi qui corporibus non inhaerent, ut ii qui sono quodam vocum et Phrygiis cantibus excitantur.

50. *Ibid.* Cf. A.J. Neubecker, *Die Bewertung der Musik bei Stoikern und Epikureern* (Berlin 1956) and A. Plebe, *La Sacralità della musica in Platone, negli Stoici, nello Pseudo-Plutarcho* (Padua 1957).

51. Cf. also 1 Sam. 10:5: "...and there, as you come to the city, you will meet a band a prophets coming down from the high place with harp, tambourine, flute and lyre before them, prophesying." Music appears here as a natural means of exciting prophesy. Since the prophets mentioned here were probably chiefly cultic singers, the music could have been intended primarily to accompany religious songs and hymns, especially since these instruments are frequently spoken of in the Old Testament as accompanying religious singing. Cf. H. Junker, *Prophet und Seher in Israel* (Trier 1927), p. 15.

52. Strabo I 2, 3, 16 (38 Meineke): παιδευτικοί φασιν [οἱ μουσικοί] εἶναι καὶ ἐπανορθωτικοὶ τῶν ἠθῶν.

53. The example adduced by H. Gressmann, *Musik und Musikinstrumente im Alten*

Testament (RVV 2, 1) (Giessen 1903), p. 16 must be sharply restricted. The female Hebrew flutist from the *Acts of Thomas* is not a participant in prophecy because she experiences ecstasy, as Gressmann asserts, but merely because she understands the Hebrew which the Apostle spoke. Cf. *Acta Thomae* 8 (II 2, 108 Lipsius-Bonnet): τὰ δὲ ὑπὸ αὐτοῦ λεχθέντα οὐκ ἐνόουν, ἐπειδὴ αὐτὸς Ἑβραῖος ἦν καὶ τὰ λεχθέντα ὑπ' αὐτοῦ ἑβραϊστὶ ἐλέχθη, ἡ δὲ αὐλήτρια πάντα ἤκουσεν μόνη, Ἑβραία γὰρ ἦν τὸ γένος.

54. Clement of Alexandria, *Protrepticos* 2, 12, 2 (GCS Clem. I 11 Stählin): Δηὼ δὲ καὶ Κόρη δρᾶμα ἤδη ἐγενέσθην μυστικόν, καὶ τὴν πλάνην καὶ τὴν ἁρπαγὴν καὶ τὸ πένθος αὐταῖν Ἐλευσὶς δᾳδουχεῖ.

55. Cf. Plate 23.

56. On raising the hand while singing cf. H. Hickmann, "Ägyptische Musik," in *Musik in Geschichte und Gegenwart* 1 (1949), 93. *Idem,* "La musique polyphonique dans l'Égypte ancienne," in *Bulletin Inst. d'Égypte* 34 (1951/1952), 239–244. *Idem,* "Observations sur les survivances de la chironomie égyptienne dans le chant liturgique copte," in *Annales du Service des Antiquités d'Égypte* 49 (1949), 417–427. A. Hermann, "Mit der Hand singen," in *Jahrbuch für Antike und Christentum* 1 (1958), 105–118.

57. H. Gressmann, "Tod und Auferstehung des Osiris nach Festbräuchen und Umzügen," in *Der alte Orient* 23, 3 (Leipzig 1923), 28.

58. W. Helbig, *Wandgemälde der vom Vesuv verschütteten Städte Campaniens* (Leipzig 1868), p. 221. Cf. Arnobius, *supra*, Chpt. 1, n. 125.

59. J. Leipoldt, "Archäologisches zur Isisreligion," in ΑΓΓΕΛΟΣ, *Archiv für neutestamentliche Zeitgeschichte und Kulturkunde* I (1925), 127. On the painting from another aspect cf. F.J. Dölger, "Nilwasser and Taufwasser. Das heilige Nilwasser bei der liturgischen Feier im Tempelvorhof nach seinem Gemälde von Herculaneum," in *Antike und Christentum* 5 (1936), 153–165.

60. Cf. Table 24.

61. Helbig, *Wandgemälde der vom Vesuv...*, no. 1112, 'sees another woman with a sistrum. This would be the person very lightly delineated to the right of the portal. Cf. the etching of the picture in Leipoldt, "Archäologisches zur Isisreligion," 127, table 3.

62. Leipoldt, *ibid.*, 128.

63. Cf. CIL VI 3770. The ἱερὰ τάξις τῶν Παιανιστῶν of Zeus Helios Serapis in Rome is known from the inscription in IG XIV 1084 (146 A.D.). Cf. E. Aust, *Die Religion der Römer* (Münster 1899), p. 158. The relief on a pedestal presently in the Uffizi Gallery in Florence, which comes from the Roman Iseum-Serapeum, portrays an Isis-procession that is particularly instructive. Behind the priest, who is carrying the idol of a god (Anubis?), there is a harpist with his Egyptian instrument – which we see otherwise only in Egypt. A tambourine player follows him. Cf. Plate 25 of the present work. Thus the cult of Isis brought both the sistrum and the Egyptian harp to Rome. Cf. J. Colin, "Une procession Isiaque. Bas-relief de Florence," in *Mélanges d'archéologie et d'histoire* 38 (1920), 282.

64. Cf. F. Cumont, *Die orientalischen Religionen im römischen Heidentum* (Leipzig-Berlin 1910), p. 114.

65. Apuleius, *Metamorphoseon* 11, 9 (272 Helm): Symphoniae dehinc suaves, fistulae tibiaeque modulis dulcissimis personabant. Eas amoenus lectissimae iuventutis veste nivea et cat(h)aclista praenitens sequebatur chorus, carmen venustum iterantes, quod Camenarum favore sollers poeta modulatus edixerat, quod argumentum referebat interim maiorum antecantamenta votorum. Ibant et dicati magno Sarapi tibicines, qui

per obliquum calamum ad aurem porrectum dexteram, familiarem templi deique modum frequentabant, et plerique, qui facilem sacris viam dari praedicarent.

66. Cf. Plate 26 for sistra found in Pompeii and presently in the National Museum in Naples.

67. C. Sachs, "Altägyptische Musikinstrumente," in *Der alte Orient* 21, 3/4 (Leipzig 1920), 3.

68. Cf. *supra*, Chapt. 1, n. 115.

69. Cf. Plate 23. In fact in most other cultic processions there is music near the holy object or the priest. In the vase pictures of Dionysian processions in Athens in A. Frickenhaus, "Der Schriftskarren des Dionysos in Athen," in *Jahrbuch des kaiserlichen deutchen archäologischen Instituts* 27 (1912), 69, the order of procession is such that a trumpeter always leads; following him are a maiden carrying a basket, a youth with a censer, the sacrificial beast decorated with ribbons and the priest, a flutist, and finally others who are taking part in the procession. From the *lex sacra* from Andania the order of procession of a mystery cult has been preserved for us. At the head is Mnasistratos, then the priest of the god, the judge of the games, the sacrificial priests, the flutists, and finally the virgins, who draw the wagon with the box of the sacred utensils (*cista mystica*). Cf. W. Dittenberger, *Sylloge inscriptionum Graecarum* (Leipzig ³ 1917), II, 401, no. 735/736 and J. v. Prott and L. Ziehen, *Leges Graecorum sacrae* I 2 (Leipzig 1906), p. 166, no. 58. Cf. also M.P. Nilsson, "Die Prozessionstypen im griechischen Kult," in *Jahrbuch des kaiserlichen . . .* 31 (1916), 326.

70. Cf. Plate 27. Cf. also W. Weber, *Drei Untersuchungen zur ägyptisch-griechischen Religion* (Heidelberg 1911), p. 44. W. Helbig, *Führer durch die öffentlichen Sammlungen klassischer Altertümer in Rom* I (Leipzig ³ 1912), p. 90. F.J. Dölger, "Das heilige Nilwasser in *der* Isisprozession nach Texten und Bildern," in *Antike und Christentum* 5 (1936), 156–157.

71. On the rite of veiled hands cf. A. Dieterich, *Kleine Schriften* (Leipzig-Berlin 1911), p. 440.

72. Sachs, "Altägyptische Musikinstrumente," 4.

Chapter Three
MUSIC AND MYSTICISM IN ANTIQUITY

THE DOCTRINE OF THE Λογικὴ Θυσία IN ITS EFFECT ON LITURGICAL MUSIC.

The doctrine of the "spiritual sacrifice" was a development of Greek philosophy which rejected the bloody sacrifices of ancient religious worship. It repudiated all empty externals of liturgy and demanded in their place an inner worship of God by the human spirit.[1] This new view could not prevail without consequences for cultic music, which was more closely linked to liturgy than any other art form. This was so because the philosophers who saw the λογικὴ θυσία as the only worthy service of the gods also had a more or less restrictive attitude toward liturgical music.

Premonitions of the elimination of instrumental music from cultic worship appear as early as Plato, who had himself come out against the popular concept of sacrifice and worship. The philosopher spoke with admiration of the thousand year old songs of Isis which he had heard in Egypt. He came to the conclusion that all purely instrumental music should be removed from the liturgy and forbidden because music "without words" contained no more of the spirit in it than the sounds which an animal makes.[2] This severe judgment can be understood only in the context of statements previously expressed regarding the inferior position accorded music in pagan cult. Even more severe than Plato was Philodemos of Gadara (c. 100–28 B.C.). He wrote against the cultic use of music in his work *On Music*. In opposition to Cleanthes of Assos (331–223) and Diogenes of Babylon (c. 240–152), whose writings he cites, he dismisses the notion that music is an indispensable component in the cult of the gods, necessarily bound up with piety, as Diogenes had asserted:[3]

> As far as the worship of God through music is concerned, enough has been said about it in the past and more will be said in the future. What must be said now is this: the divinity needs no worship, but the need to adore divinity is in our blood. This is particularly so because of our pious ideas and especially because of our inherited traditions.[4]

Philodemos considered it paradoxical that music should be regarded as veneration of the gods while musicians were paid for performing this so-called veneration.[5] Again, Philodemos held as self-deceptive the view that music mediated religious ecstasy. He saw the entire condition induced by the noise of cymbals and tambourines as a disturbance of the spirit. He found it significant that, on the whole, only women and effeminate men fell into this folly.[6] Accordingly, nothing of value could be attributed to music; it was no more than a slave of ἡδονή, the sensation of pleasure, which it satisfied much in the same way that food and drink did.[7]

Similar opinions may be found in the writings of the Hellenistically educated Jew, Philo. On one occasion he speaks of the Jewish "Feast of Fasting," a designation used by the Greeks for the Day of Atonement:

> Now, many a man from the false religions, which are not ashamed of criticizing what is noble, will ask: how can there be a feast without carousing and overeating, without the pleasant company of hosts and guests, without quantities of unmixed wine, without richly set tables and highly stacked provisions of everything that pertains to a banquet, without pageantry and jokes, bantering and merry-making to the accompaniment of flutes and citharas, the sound of drums and cymbals and other effeminate and frivolous music of every kind, enkindling unbridled lusts with the help of the sense of hearing? For in and through the same [pleasures] those persons openly seek their joy, for what true joy is they do not know.[8]

Here, too, is a rejection of pagan instrumental music at religious feasts which is made on grounds similar to those of Philodemos — that men look only for their own pleasure in music. According to Philo, the gods of the pagans exploit this weakness of men. For the sake of a better effect, and with the intention of more easily cheating their devotees, they have set their lies to melodies, rhythms and meters.[9]

Philodemos takes offense, as noted above, at the fact that, in cultic music, the inner sentiment is lacking while this so-called worship is offered to the gods only for payment. Philo, too, emphasizes the necessity of religious interiority in preference to the cult of sacrifice:

> God has no joy in sacrifices, my dear sir, even if one should offer him hecatombs, for everything belongs to him. Since he possesses everything, he has need of nothing. He takes pleasure only in a pious disposition and in men who lead pious lives. He accepts the sacrificial cakes, the barley and the most modest gifts from them as if they were the most valuable offerings. He prefers them to costlier things. If they bring nothing other than themselves in the fullness of moral goodness, then they present the

most acceptable offering, as they worship God their benefactor and savior in songs and thankful homage. Sometimes they do so with their tongue, but sometimes without it, when they speak only in their souls and in their thoughts the confessions and invocations which the ear of God alone hears; for men cannot perceive such things with their ears.[10]

In these words of Philo there is a new rigor. He not only abolishes instrumental music in liturgy but also considers singing as merely imperfect worship. The ideal he presents is a worship of silence and of pure intentions, which consequently leaves no room for liturgical song.

However, the transition from bloody sacrifice to divine worship by way of the singing of hymns already marked a strong spiritualization of cult. Thus Philo could describe the "spiritual sacrifice" as one which consisted in ὕμνοι καὶ εὐδαιμονισμοί.[11] At a later date Jerome, too, asserted that Asaph, Iduthun and Eman had been entrusted with the direction of a significantly expanded temple singing, by which the Jews might gradually be drawn from sacrifices to the praise of God.[12]

Philosophy continued to sharpen the notion of the "spiritual sacrifice." The hymn which constituted this divine service was expounded ever more allegorically: the life of each individual person had to become a hymn to the glory of God. This exaggerated spiritualistic tendency would ultimately have eliminated every official cult. It was bolstered by the division of the gods into particular classes as, for example, in Apuleius of Madaura and Celsus. Apuleius distinguished visible gods, the heavenly bodies, and invisible gods. Among these latter he ranked the twelve Olympians, descendants of the highest god and themselves eternal, blessed spirits. Most men worship these gods, but in a completely perverse way. The demons are similar to the gods, for they are immortal like them. They are also like men in that they possess passions, are susceptible to anger and various other experiences and permit themselves to be won over by gifts. The demons are the true objects of the cults of the gods. The customs and rites of the religions of the nations differ completely according to the nature of these demons: the Egyptian gods take pleasure in lamentation, the Greek gods in dancing, and those of the barbarians in the din of tambourines, drums and flutes.[13] Thus Apuleius considered music unworthy of the highest god. Celsus shared this opinion. As he is quoted by Origen, he wished to persuade the Christians to worship the demons, although he warned against too high a veneration of them:

One must beware, however, not to let oneself become too deeply involved in these matters if one becomes occupied with them. One must
not neglect and forget the higher and better things because of love for the
body and earthly things. For we would be foolish if we were to disregard
the opinion of those wise men who tell us that most of the demons of
earth take too great a delight in fleshly pleasures; they have too great a
desire for blood, the smell of fat, sweet sounds and other such things.[14]

The notion expressed in these words of Celsus was not new. It had
long been thought that music pertained only to the lowest gods, the
demons, and that the highest divine being had no need of melodies
and sounds. Theophrastus of Eresos (c. 373-287 B.C.), as Porphyry
tells us, had already hinted at something similar: he had allotted the
sacrificial victims to the spirits of the third rank, the demons, the
sonorous offering of hymns to the spiritual powers of the second rank,
but only the silent offerings of the intentions to the highest god.[15]

These ideas were pursued to their logical conclusions in the philosophy of the time. Cleanthes believed that by word alone the philosopher was unable to express the sublimity of divine things; meter,
melody and rhythm were also needed.[16] Philo was persuaded that

one cannot truly offer thanks to God as the vast majority of men do,
with external effects, consecrated gifts and sacrifices . . . , but rather with
songs of praise and hymns — not such as the audible voice sings, but such
as are raised and re-echoed by the invisible mind.[17]

According to him, too, singing is not sufficiently worthy of the highest
divinity.

Lord [he cries out], how could anyone praise you? With what mouth,
with what tongue, with what organ of speech, with what power of the
soul? Could the heavenly bodies, united in one choir, sing a song worthy
of you?[18]

Philo saw that the high priest had to lay aside his long flowing robe,
set with little bells and colorfully adorned, when he went into the holy
of holies. This was an indication that one must not worship God with
music and colorful array; one should rather pour out to him one's
soul's blood and offer him one's whole spirit as incense.[19] For

if the soul has opened itself totally in word and deed and is filled with
God then the voices of the senses and all other burdensome and hateful
noises cease.[20]

At a later time Neoplatonism held the same view, since in its system
liturgical song and music of any other kind had no place either. For
Porphyry, true worship is that dedication of oneself to God in which

one makes use only of the more noble Logos, which does not pass through the mouth, to ask for something good from the Most Beautiful by means of the Most Beautiful: this is the spirit which needs no instruments.[21]

According to what has been said, it can be seen that the doctrine of the "spiritual sacrifice" not only repudiated bloody sacrifices but also rejected music, particularly instrumental music, as a means of worshiping God. Although the "spiritual sacrifice" was originally explained in terms of hymns of praise to God's goodness and majesty, its logical development eventually considered singing unsuitable for divine worship.

NOTES

1. Cf. O. Casel, *Die Liturgie als Mysterienfeier* (Freiburg ³ 1923), pp. 105 ff. *Idem,* "Die λογικὴ θυσία der antiken Mystik in christlich-liturgischer Umdeutung," in *Jahrbuch für Liturgiewissenschaft* 4 (1924), 37 ff. *Idem,* "Ein orientalisches Kultwort in abendländischer Umschmelzung," in *Jahrbuch für Liturgiewissenschaft* 11 (1939), 1-19.

2. Plato, *Leges* 669 e (56 Schanz): ταῦτα τε γὰρ ὁρῶσι πάντα κυκώμενα, καὶ εἴ τι διασπῶσιν οἱ ποιηταὶ ῥυθμὸν μὲν καὶ σχήματα μέλους χωρίς, λόγους ψιλοὺς εἰς μέτρα τιθέντες, μέλος δ' αὖ καὶ ῥυθμὸν ἄνευ ῥημάτων, ψιλῇ κιθαρίσει τε καὶ αὐλήσει προσχρώμενοι, ἐν οἷς δὴ παγχάλεπον ἄνευ λόγου γιγνόμενον ῥυθμόν τε καὶ ἁρμονίαν γιγνώσκειν, ὅ τί τε βούλεται καὶ ὅτῳ ἔοικε τῶν ἀξιολόγων μιμημάτων· ἀλλὰ ὑπολαβεῖν ἀναγκαῖον, ὅτι τὸ τοιοῦτόν γε πολλῆς ἀγροικίας μεστὸν πᾶν, ὁπόσον τάχους τε καὶ ἀπνευστίας καὶ φωνῆς θηριώδους σφόδρα φίλον, ὥστ' αὐλήσει γε καὶ χρῆσθαι καὶ κιθαρίσει πλὴν ὅσον ὑπὸ ὄρχησίν τε καὶ ᾠδήν, ψιλῷ δ' ἑκατέρῳ πᾶσά τις ἀμουσία καὶ θαυματουργία γίγνοιτ' ἂν τῆς χρήσεως.

3. Philodemos, *De musica* 20, 28 ff. (88 Kemke): ὥστ' ἐφ' ἃ γράφει περὶ τῆς εὐσεβείας μεταβάντες λέγωμεν, ὡς εἰ χάριν τοῦ τιμᾶσθαι τὸ θεῖον διὰ μουσικῆς ὑπὸ τῶν πολλῶν οἰκείαν εἶναι τὴν μουσικὴν τῆς εὐσεβείας οἰηδόμεθα, καὶ μαγειρικὴν οἰησόμεθα καὶ στεφανοποϊκὴν καὶ μὴ Διογένης εἰ ἄρα συνεπείθετο καὶ τῷ τῶν θεῶν ἑτέρους ἕτερα μέλη προσίεσθαι καὶ πρέπειν ἑκάστοις ἴδια.

4. *Ibid.* 4, 1 (66): περὶ τοίνυν τῆς διὰ τῶν μουσικῶν τοῦ θείου τειμῆς εἴρηται μὲν αὐτάρκως καὶ πρότερον καὶ πάλιν τινὰ ῥηθήσεται, τὰ δὲ τοσαῦτα λεγέσθω καὶ νῦν· ὅτι τὸ δαιμόνιον μὲν οὐ προσδεῖταί τινος τιμῆς, ἡμῖν δὲ φυσικόν ἐστιν αὐτὸ τιμᾶν, μάλιστα μὲν ὁσίαις ὑπολήψεσιν, ἔπειτα δὲ καὶ τοῖς κατὰ τὸ πάτριον παραδεδομένοις.

5. *Ibid.* 4, 24 (66): καὶ οὐχ ὑπὸ πάντων ἀλλ' ὑπὸ τινῶν Ἑλλήνων καὶ κατὰ ἐνίους καιροὺς καὶ... νῦν διὰ μισθωτῶν ἀνθρώπων.

6. *Ibid.* 7, 1 (49): ταράττουσιν δὲ καὶ μετὰ συμπλοκῆς δοξῶν. αἱ δὲ τῶν τυμπάνων καὶ ῥόμβων καὶ κυμβάλων καὶ μελῶν τινων καὶ ῥυθμῶν ἰδιότητες καὶ διὰ ποιῶν ὀργάνων τὸ πᾶν συμπλοκῇ μοχθηρῶν ὑπολήψεων ἐξοργιάζουσι καὶ πρὸς βακχείαν ἄγουσι, καὶ ταῦτα γυναῖκας ὡς ἐπὶ τὸ πολὺ καὶ γυναικώδεις ἄνδρας... Cf. H. Abert, *Die Lehre vom Ethos in der griechischen Musik* (Leipzig 1899), p. 31.

7. Philodemos, *ibid.* 18, 24 (85): οὐ μὴν ἀλλὰ κἂν ἀνιῇ καὶ ἱλαροὺς ποιῇ καθάπερ ἀπόλαυσις ποτῶν τε καὶ βρωτῶν καὶ πᾶσ'-ἡδονή. On Philodemos' judgment of cultic music

cf. J. Quasten, "Greek Philosophy and Sacred Music," in *The New Scholasticism* 15 (1941), 255–260 and G. Wille, "Zur Bedeutung und Anordnung von Philodem, Fragment I 24 Kemke über das ästhetische Massenurteil," in *Silvae. Festschrift E. Zinn* (Tübingen 1970), pp. 253–269.

8. Philo, *De specialibus legibus* II 193 (V 114 Cohn-Wendland): Μετὰ δὲ τὴν τῶν σαλπίγγων ἄγεται νηστεία ἑορτή τάχα ἄν τις εἴποι των ἑτεροδόξων καὶ ψέγειν τὰ καλὰ μὴ αἰδουμένων.

ἑορτὴ δ' ἐστὶ τίς, ἐν ᾗ μὴ συμπόσια καὶ συσσίτια καὶ ἑστιατόρων καὶ ἑστιωμένων θίασος καὶ πολὺς ἄκρατος καὶ τράπεζαι πολυτελεῖς καὶ χορηγίαι καὶ παρασκευαὶ τῶν ἐν δημοθοινία πάντων εὐφροσύναι τε καὶ κῶμοι σὺν ἀθύρμασι καὶ τωθασμοῖς καὶ παιδιὰ μετ' αὐλοῦ καὶ κιθάρας καὶ τυμπάνων τε καὶ κυμβάλων καί τῶν ἄλλων ὅσα [κατὰ] τὸ παραλελυμένον καὶ ἐκτεθηλυμμένον εἶδος μουσικῆς δι' ὤτων ἐγείρει τὰς ἀκαθέκτους ἐπιθυμίαις; ἐν γὰρ τούτοις καὶ διὰ τούτων, ὡς ἔοικε τὸ εὐφραίνεσθαι τίθενται ἀγνοίᾳ τῆς πρὸς ἀλήθειαν εὐφροσύνης.

9. *Ibid.* I 28 (V 6): πρὸς δὲ τὸ εὐπαράγωγον μέλεσι καὶ ῥυθμοῖς καὶ μέτροις ἐνηρμόσαντο τὸ ψεῦδος, νομίζοντες ῥᾳδίως καταγοητεύσειν τοὺς ἐντυγχάνοντας.

10. *Ibid.* I 271 (V 56): εἴποιμ'ἄν· ὦ γενναῖε, ὁ θεὸς οὐ χαίρει, κἂν ἑκατόμβας ἀνάγῃ τις· κτήματα γὰρ αὐτοῦ τὰ πάντα, κεκτημένος ὅμως οὐδενὸς δεῖται. χαίρει δὲ φιλοθέοις γνώμαις καὶ ἀνδράσιν ἀσκηταῖς ὁσιότητος, παρ' ὧν ψαιστὰ καὶ κριθὰ καὶ τὰ εὐτελέστατα ὡς πολυτελέστατα πρὸ τῶν πολυτελεστάτων ἄσμενος δέχεται. κἂν μέντοι μηδὲν ἕτερον κομίζωσιν, αὐτοὺς φέροντες πλήρωμα καλοκ'αγαθίας τελειότατον τὴν ἀρίστην ἀνάγουσι θυσίαν, ὕμνοις καὶ εὐχαριστίαις τὸν εὐεργέτην καὶ σωτῆρα θεὸν γεραίροντες, τῇ μὲν διὰ τῶν φωνητηρίων ὀργάνων, τῇ δὲ ἄνευ γλώττης καὶ στόματος μόνῃ ψυχῇ τὰς νοητὰς ποιούμενοι διεξόδους καὶ ἐκβοήσεις, ὧν ἓν μόνον οὓς ἀντιλαμβάνεται τὸ θεῖον. αἱ γὰρ τῶν ἀνθρώπων οὐ φθάνουσιν ἀκοαὶ συναισθέσθαι.

11. *Ibid.*, I 224 (55): Τῆς δὲ τοῦ σωτηρίου θυσίας ἐν εἴδει περιλαμβάνεται ἡ λεγομένη τῆς αἰνέσεως, ἥτις λόγον τοιόνδε.... ἀναγκαίως ὀφείλει τὸν κυβερνήτην θεὸν...ὕμνοις καὶ εὐδαιμονισμοῖς...ἀμείβεσθαι.

12. Jerome, *In Isaiam* 1, 1 (PL 24, 37): et super choros (qui in libro dierum plenius describuntur) Asaph, Iduthun et Eman, filii Chore constituti sunt, ut paulatim a sacrificiis victimarum ad laudes Domini transiret religio.

13. Apuleius, *Liber de Deo Socratis* 13, 148 (21 Thomas): Quippe, ut fine comprehendam, daemones sunt genere animalia, ingeiiio rationabilia, animo passiva, corpore aëria, tempore aeterna. Ex his quinque, quae commemoravi, tria principio eadem quae nobis(cum), quartum proprium, postremum commune cum diis immortalibus habent, sed differunt ab his passione. Quae propterea passiva non absurde, ut arbitror, nominavi, quod sunt iisdem, quibus nos, turbationibus mentis obnoxii. Unde etiam religionum diversis observationibus et sacrorum variis supliciis fides impertienda est, esse nonnullos ex hoc divorum numero, qui nocturnis vel diurnis, promptis vel occultis laetioribus vel tristioribus hostiis vel caeremoniis vel ritibus gaudeant, uti Aegyptia numina ferme plangoribus, Graeca plerumque choreis, barbara autem strepitu cymbalistrarum et tympanistrarum et choraularum.

14. Origen, *Contra Celsum* 8, 60 (GCS Orig. II 276 Koetschau): χρὴ γὰρ ἴσως οὐκ ἀπιστεῖν ἀνδράσι σοφοῖς, οἵ δή φασι διότι τῶν μὲν περιγείων δαιμόνων τὸ πλεῖστον γενέσει συντετηχὸς καὶ χροσηλωμένον αἵματι καὶ κνίσσῃ καὶ μελωδίαις καὶ ἄλλοις τισὶ τοιούτοις...

15. Porphyry, *De Abstinentia* II 34 (37 Hercher): Θεῷ μὲν τῷ ἐπὶ πᾶσιν, ὥς τις ἀνὴρ σοφὸς ἔφη, μηδὲν τῶν αἰσθητῶν μήτε θυμιῶντες μήτε ἐπονομάζοντες· οὐδὲν γάρ ἐστιν ἔνυλον, ὃ μὴ τῷ ἀύλῳ εὐθύς ἐστιν ἀκάθαρτον. Διὸ οὐδὲ λόγος τούτῳ ὁ κατὰ φωνὴν οἰκεῖος, οὐδ' ὁ ἔνδον, ὅταν πάθει ψυχῆς ᾖ μεμολυσμένος, διὰ δὲ σιγῆς καθαρᾶς καὶ τῶν περὶ αὐτοῦ καθαρῶν ἐννοιῶν θρησκεύσωμεν αὐτόν. *Ibid.* (37): Τοῖς δὲ αὐτοῦ ἐκγόνοις, νοητοῖς δὲ θεοῖς ἤδη καὶ τὴν ἐκ τοῦ λόγου ὑμνῳδίαν προσθετέον. *Ibid.* II, 58 (45): Ὅτι δὲ οὐ θεοῖς, ἀλλὰ δαίμοσι τὰς θυσίας τὰς διὰ τῶν αἱμάτων προσῆγον. Cf. also J. Bernays, *Theophrastos' Schrift über die Frömmigkeit*.

Ein Beitrag zur Religionsgeschichte (Berlin 1866), p. 33 and H. Koch, *Pseudo-Dionysius Areopagita in seinen Beziehungen zum Neuplatonismus und Mysterienwesen* (*Forschungen zur christlichen Literatur- und Dogmengeschichte* I 2–3) (Mainz 1900), p. 127.

16. Philodemos, *De musica* 28, 16 (98 Kemke): Cleanthes says: οὔτε γὰρ αἱ διάνοιαι μὲν οὐκ ὠφελοῦσιν, ὅταν δὲ μεληδηθῶσι ἐξ ἀμφοτέρων ἡ παρόρμησις γίνεται. καὶ γὰρ ὑπὸ διανοημάτων αὐτῶν γίνετ' οὐ μετρία, μετὰ δὲ τῶν μελῶν μείζων.

17. Philo, *De Plantatione* 126 (II 148 Cohn-Wendland): ἑκάστη μέν γετῶν ἀρετῶν ἐστι χρῆμα ἅγιον, εὐχαριστία δὲ ὑπερβαλλόντως· θεῷ δὲ οὐκ ἔνεστι γνησίως εὐχαριστῆσαι δι' ὧν νομίξουσιν οἱ πολλοὶ κατασκευῶν ἀναθημάτων θυσιῶν — οὐδὲ γὰρ σύμπας ὁ κόσμος ἱερὸν ἀξιόρχεων ἂν γένοιτο πρὸς τὴν τούτου τιμὴν —, ἀλλὰ δι' ἐπαίνων καὶ ὕμνων, οὐχ οὓς ἡ γεγωνὸς ἄσεται φωνή, ἀλλὰ οὓς ὁ ἀειδὴς καὶ καθαρώτατος νοῦς ἐπηχήσει καὶ ἀναμέλψει.

18. Philo, *De vita Moysis* II (III) 239 (256 Cohn): ὦ δέσποτα, πῶς ἂν σέ τις ὑμνήσειε ποίῳ στόματι, τίνι γλώττη, ποίᾳ φωνῆς ὀργανοποιίᾳ, ποίῳ ψυχῆς ἡγεμονικῷ; οἱ γὰρ ἀστέρες εἰς γενόμενοι χορὸς ἄσονταί τι μέλος ἐπάξιον;

19. Philo, *Legum allegoriarum* II 56 (101 Cohn): τοῦτο χάριν ὁ ἀρχιερεὺς εἰς τὰ ἅγια τῶν ἁγίων οὐκ εἰσελεύσεται ἐν τῷ ποδήρει. ἀλλὰ τὸν τῆς δόξης καὶ φαντασίας ψυχῆς χιτῶνα ἀποδυσάμενος καὶ καταλιπὼν τοῖς τὰ ἐκτὸς ἀγαπῶσι καὶ δόξαν πρὸ ἀληθείας τετιμηκόσι γυμνὸς ἄνευ χρωμάτων καὶ ἤχων εἰσελεύσεται σπεῖσαι τὸ ψυχικὸν αἷμα καὶ θυμιᾶσαι ὅλον τὸν νοῦν τῷ σωτῆρι καὶ εὐεργέτη θεῷ.

20. *Ibid.* III, 44 (122): ὅταν μέντοι διὰ πάντων ἡ ψυχὴ καὶ λόγων καὶ ἔργων ἐξαπλωθῇ καὶ ἐκθειασθῇ, παύονται τῶν αἰσθήσεων αἱ φωναὶ καὶ πάντες οἱ ὀχληροὶ καὶ δυσώνυμοι ἦχοι.

21. Porphyry, in Eusebius, *Praeparationes evangelicae* IV, 13, 2 (I 158 Heinichen): μόνῳ δὲ χρῶτο πρὸς αὐτὸν ἀεὶ τῷ κρείττονι λόγῳ· λέγω δὲ τῷ μὴ διὰ στόματος ἰόντι· καὶ παρὰ Τοῦ καλλίστου τῶν ὄντων διὰ τοῦ καλλίστου τῶν ἐν ἡμῖν αἰτοίη τ'ἀγαθά· νοῦς δέ ἐστιν οὗτος, ὀργάνου μὴ δεόμενος. Cf. E. Norden, *Agnostos Theos. Untersuchungen zur Formengeschichte religiöser Rede* (Leipzig 1913), p. 39.

Chapter Four

MUSIC AND SINGING IN THE CHRISTIAN LITURGY OF ANTIQUITY

1. CHRISTIAN "ADORATION IN SPIRIT."

O. Casel has already demonstrated the manner in which early Christianity adopted the concept of the "spiritual sacrifice" from pagan philosophy and applied it to its own liturgy.[1] The question now arises regarding the position taken by the early Christian Church with respect to music and singing. Jesus himself had proclaimed "adoration in spirit" as the new aspect of his teaching (Jn. 4:23). Consequently the use of instrumental music, as practiced in the pagan cults, was not an issue. Naturally, a more complex attitude toward music and singing developed only with the wider extension of Christianity.

The Apostolic Age bears witness to the joyful character of early Christianity, particularly as it was expressed in singing. In Eph. 5:19 Paul calls upon Christians to

address one another with psalms, hymns and spiritual songs, singing and making melody to the Lord in your heart.

Col. 3:16 also refers to singing "psalms and hymns and spiritual songs with thankfulness in your hearts to God." These words clearly express the Apostle's conviction that singing is a fitting way to honor God. There is at the same time, however, a certain reservation in what Paul says. In both passages he adds what seems to be a warning against a purely aesthetic pleasure in singing: such singing must take place "in your heart." This articulates well the primitive Christian position on liturgical singing. Only insofar as singing is the expression of an inner disposition of devotion does it have any meaning.

This attitude toward liturgical singing clearly approximated that held by the pagan philosophers previously mentioned. Still, it avoided the exaggerated spiritualistic tendency which regarded music as an obstacle to cultic action and portrayed the renunciation of music in liturgy as the higher ideal. Rather, the characteristics which Paul required of Christian song resulted in a highly spiritualized concept of divine worship. This prevailed to such an extent that Christians in the succeeding era often designated liturgical song as their sacrifice, thus distinguishing it from pagan sacrifice. In this respect the end of the eighth book of the *Oracula Sibyllina* is of interest to us. This work, according to J. Geffken, probably appeared before 180,[2] and it is marked by a Christian character. The text presents Christian song as a sacrifice "worthy of God," in sharp contrast to pagan sacrifice:

> We may not approach the interior of the temple or pour out libations to pictures of the gods or offer worship with vows, nor may we adorn [them] with fragrant flowers or with beaming lanterns or with magnificent votive gifts. Nor may we kindle the flames of the altars with the aroma of incense or, at the libations during the sacrifice of a bull, use the blood of an immolated sheep as a ransom to remove earthly punishment. We may not pollute ourselves with burning fat from flesh-consuming pyres or with the horrible smells of the ether. But, rejoicing in holy speech, with a happy heart, with the rich gift of love and generous hands, with psalms and hymns worthy of our God, we are encouraged to sing your praise, O eternal and unerring One.[3]

The whole aversion to pagan cultic music is expressed in these words:

> They do not pour out in libation upon the altar the blood of the victims; no kettle drum is heard, no cymbal, no many-holed flute, instruments full of senseless sounds, not the tone of the shepherd's pipe, which is like the curled snake, nor the trumpet, with its wild clamor.[4]

This repudiation of all instrumental music is also most apparent in Tertullian, when he gives a new interpretation to the sacrificial rite of the pagans in the sense of "spiritual sacrifice." In place of pagan cultic music, with which the sacrificial animal was led to the altar, he speaks of the singing of psalms and hymns:

> Accompanied by a procession of good works, singing psalms and hymns, we ought to lead this [victim] to the altar of God. Fully devoted from the heart, nourished on faith, guarded by truth, inviolate in innocence, pure in chastity, garlanded with love, [it] will obtain all things for us from God.[5]

2. PAGAN AND CHRISTIAN WORSHIP. THE STRUGGLE AGAINST PAGAN CULTIC MUSIC.

The more Christianity expanded among the pagans, the more difficult it became to hold fast to "adoration in spirit," as Christ had asked for. No longer did it suffice merely to offer the people a substitute for pagan sacrifice and cultic music in the λογική θυσία and in the singing of psalms and hymns. Now apologists had to work against the people's attraction for customs that they had grown to love. As early as the end of the second century Clement of Alexandria found himself called to take up the struggle against "the music of idols." In the *Paidagogos* he writes:

> When a man occupies his time with flutes, stringed instruments, choirs, dancing, Egyptian krotala and other such improper frivolities, he will find that indecency and rudeness are the consequences. Such a man creates a din with cymbals and tambourines; he rages about with instruments of an insane cult. . . . Leave the syrinx to shepherds and the flute to superstitious devotees who rush to serve their idols. We completely forbid the use of these instruments at our temperate banquet.[6]

The editor of the *Recognitions* offers his readers an explanation for the wide diffusion of the pagan religions. He notes that this was possible only on account of the sinister power of attraction that pagan cultic music had for men. In his opinion, unbelieving and pernicious men, after the Flood,

> introduced false and perverse religions and contrived banquets with food and drink. Led astray by feasts and festivities, the greater part of mankind gave itself over and followed the playing of flutes, shepherd's pipes, citharas and all sorts of musical instruments. . . . With this every error had its beginning.[7]

To their chagrin the ecclesiastical authorities of the time also learned to know the enticing artistry of the music to which many of their flock would succumb on the pagan feasts.

The incompatibility between the purposes which the pagans attributed to their liturgical music and the true concept of God served Arnobius as the starting point for an attack. He advises the pagans:

> You are convinced that the gods are pleased and influenced by the sound of brass and the blowing of flutes, by horse races and games in the theaters and that, as a result, the wrath which they have conceived at one time or another is quelled by such satisfaction. To us this seems out of place. In fact it is incredible that those who far transcend every kind of virtue should find pleasure and delight in things that a reasonable man laughs at and which no one appears to enjoy except little children or those who have been poorly and superficially brought up.[8]

He finds it ridiculous that the gods, as the pagans believe, would permit their judgments to be changed by the sound of bells, cymbals and drums and the music of choirs, that they feel honored by the rattling of castanets, and that they have to be sung to sleep and awakened by flute playing.[9] Arnobius is not totally and stubbornly opposed to a qualified recognition of music in general; he counts the cithara and the flute along with silver, bronze and books as part of the equipment which surrounds and sustains human life.[10] Still, music becomes hateful to him because of its sacral use in the pagan cult:

> Has he [God] sent souls [upon the earth] for this — that beings of a holy and most noble race should busy themselves with music and flute playing and should puff out their cheeks with blowing the flute?[11]

The struggle against pagan instrumental music still had far to go. Gregory Nazianzus had to impress continually upon his flock the fact that the playing of the tambourine had been replaced in Christian liturgy by hymnody, while the psalms took the place of other songs. He would contrast the pagan use of lights, flute playing and hand clapping with the spiritual joy and purity of those who participated in the service of the true God.[12]

3. The Conflict between Christianity and Jewish Temple Worship. Theodoret and Chrysostom on the Dependence of Israel's Liturgy on the Egyptian Cult of the Gods.

The entire campaign against instrumental music was made more difficult by the fact that even the Jews, God's chosen people, had made great use of this art in their liturgy.[12a] The Christian people were continually encouraged in the psalms which they sang to praise God with cymbal, tambourine and other instruments. Moreover, Christians also read in the Old Testament that the use of music was based on a divine command:

> The trumpets shall be to you a perpetual statute throughout your generations.... On the day of gladness, on your feast days and at the beginnings of your months you shall blow the trumpets over your burnt offerings and peace offerings, so that they may be to you a remembrance before your God (Num. 10:8, 10).

In the Temple at Jerusalem the Levites sang during the offering of the Paschal sacrifice to the accompaniment of flutes, which were sometimes played by non-Levites. In this regard the Talmudic description of the Feast of Tabernacles is very clear. At the liturgical celebration on the seven mornings of the feast those who participated chanted the Hosanna from Psalm 118:25 while they circled around the altar of holocaust, bending toward it the palm branches which they were holding in their hands. So too, as they retired from the altar at the sound of the trumpet, they cried out repeatedly: "Beauty be yours, O altar!" At eventide the most distinguished of the people assembled together. Pious men danced with torches in their hands before the people, singing songs and hymns, while the Levites, arranged upon the fifteen steps (corresponding to the fifteen gradual psalms) which led from the Court of the Men to the Court of the Women, accompanied them with harps, citharas and numerous other instruments. Two priests with trumpets stood at the upper gate between the Court of the Men and that of the Women. At the first cockcrow they blew the trumpets and continued to do so until they reached the east exit, which led out from the Court of the Women.[13]

A more elaborate musical embellishment of the liturgy can hardly be imagined. At times ecclesiastical writers would take the opportunity of contrasting the pagan dances with David's dance before the Ark of the Covenant,[14] a dance which had been pleasing to God. Christians rightly noted that in this dance the cithara, lyre, tambourine, sistrum and cymbals had also been used.[15] They had to realize, however, that in the Old Testament instrumental music had in fact been decreed by God. In 2 Chron. 29:24–28 we read:

> Then the priests killed the he-goats and spinkled their blood on the altar to make atonement for all of Israel. For the king had commanded that the burnt offering and the sin offering should be made for all of Israel. And he placed the Levites in the house of the Lord with cymbals, harps and citharas, according to the ordinance of King David, of Gad the seer and of Nathan the prophet; for so the Lord had commanded through his prophets. And the Levites stood there with David's stringed instruments, while the priests had the trumpets. Then Hezekiah commanded that the burnt offering be offered on the altar. And when the burnt offering was offered they began to sing praise to the Lord and to blow the trumpets and to make music with all the instruments that David, king of Israel, had established. While the whole assembly worshiped the singers sang and the trumpets played, until the burnt offering was consumed.

The rite based upon this text was very similar to the pagan sacrificial rite with its use of music during the act of sacrifice. In the face of the cult which is portrayed here it was the concern of the prophets to condemn any superficiality. As Amos 5:23 remarks:

> Away from me with the noise of your songs; the playing of your harps I do not wish to hear.

Now the Fathers of the Church made use of such passages to demonstrate that God was not pleased with instrumental music. Theodoret of Cyrus notes in one place that these words gave proof of the fact that God had permitted the Israelites a lesser evil in order to pre-

vent a greater one. During her long sojourn in Egypt, Israel had learned and adopted the wicked customs of the Egyptians. In order to draw
the Jews away from the service of idols God had permitted that they
offer to him alone the sacrifices and festivals with instrumental music
which they had previously offered in honor of the Egyptian idols. God
had not allowed musical instruments because he enjoyed their sound
but rather as a gradual replacement for the foolishness of idol worship.[16] In another passage Theodoret says:

> The Levites employed these instruments in times past in the Temple to
> praise God, not because God enjoyed the noise they made but because he
> approved the intention. We know that God takes no pleasure in songs
> and music because he says to the Jews: "Away from me with the noise of
> your songs; the sound of your instruments I do not wish to hear." But
> when this continued to happen he permitted it, since he wished to re-
> move them from the deception of idolatry. For since there were many
> devotees of sport and laughter, which took place in the temples of the
> idols, he permitted this in order to draw them to himself and so through a
> lesser evil to prevent a greater one.[17]

Chrysostom also regarded the instrumental music of the Jewish cult
as no more than a concession of God to the weakness of the Jews. God
wished thereby to incite their spirit to do gladly what was necessary
for them.[18] In order to give those who listened to their homilies on the
psalms no grounds for protest against the ecclesiastical prohibition of
instrumental music, most of the Fathers resorted to the use of allegory.
Clement of Alexandria, for instance, interpreted the psaltery to mean
the tongue of man and the cithara his mouth,[19] an exegesis which the
schools rapidly took up.[20] In contrast to such allegorical attempts,
Chrysostom explained the reason for the use of instrumental music in
Jewish liturgy in this way:

> A few say, to be sure, that the tambourine signifies the mortality of our
> flesh and that the psaltery means a heavenward gaze. For this instrument
> [the tambourine] is played with a downward motion, not with an up-
> ward one, as is the cithara. But I would prefer to say that they [the Jews]
> played these in times past on account of the dullness of their understand-
> ing and so that they might be drawn away from idols. As he [God] con-
> ceded sacrifices to them, so he also allowed them this, for he accom-
> modated himself to their weaknesses.[21]

Isidore of Pelusium also looked upon both sacrifice and music as an
expression of one and the same stupidity:

> If God received sacrifices and blood by reason of the foolishness of the

men of that time, why do you wonder that he should also have borne with the music of the cithara and the psaltery?[22]

Theodoret's opinion, that the Jews had brought back liturgical music from Egypt, is worthy of note. Philo reports that Moses learned "rhythm, harmony, meter and everything concerned with instrumental music" from the Egyptians.[23] Furthermore, he contended that during the apostasy to idol worship at Mount Sinai the Jews sang in the style of the Egyptian threnodies:

> Thus they made a golden bull, the image of an animal that was held to be the most sacred in that land; they offered unholy sacrifices, performed impious dances and sang hymns which differed in no way from the pagan mourning songs.[24]

This reference probably indicates the use of songs from the cult of Osiris. Despite the differences between the Mosaic and the Egyptian cults, it can hardly be denied that Egyptian influence on Jewish musical practices was quite significant. This would stand to reason because of the high quality of Egyptian cultic music. The tambourine or timbrel, a hoop of bells over which a white skin was stretched, came from Egypt. Miriam used this instrument to accompany the singing and dancing on the shores of the Red Sea (Ex. 15). The trumpet blown for decampment, at the gathering of the people and on different cultic occasions, especially during sacrifice (2 Chron. 30:21; 35:15; Num. 10:2), was the signaling instrument of the Egyptian army.[25] The sistrum, according to 2 Sam. 6:5, was used by the Israelites and bore the name *m^ena'an^e'im*. It was the same as the Egyptian *kemkem* that was employed in the cult of Isis. The solemnity celebrated on the occasion of the transferring of the Ark to Sion, as well as the dances of the daughters of Israel at the annual feast of the Lord at Shiloh (Judg. 21:21), were similar in their musical embellishment to Egyptian customs in the liturgy and at parades. As Herodotus reports, women sang the praises of Osiris while likenesses of the gods were borne about and, during the festival of Diana at Bubastis, choirs of men and women sang and danced to the beating of drums and the playing of flutes.[26]

The magnificent ceremonial of the pagan religions with which Israel was surrounded demanded some concessions to the sensuousness of the Jewish people so that there would be no danger of their giving in to an idol worhip more pleasing to the eye and ear than their own cult. Thus the explanations of Theodoret and Chrysostom appear to be fully justified.

4. UNA VOCE DICENTES: THE KOINONIA OF EARLY CHRISTIAN SINGING.

The question as to whether pagan antiquity was acquainted with singing in parts has never been sufficiently clarified since the necessary musical monuments are lacking.[27] There is, however, little doubt that the Greeks had knowledge of instrumental music arranged for several parts. The Greek myth of Hyganis, the father of Marsyas, recounts his creation of a musical harmony from high and low tones on his flute.[28] There is also the remark in which Plutarch states that the poet-composer Lasos of Hermione in Argos accompanied singing with flute music in several parts.[29]

In any event it may be accepted as reasonably certain that the instrumental accompaniment to the singing voice in Greek music did not carry the same part as the voice; instead it followed an independent part which was distinguished from the voice.[30] The lower instrumental part most probably followed the same line as the melody, while the others carried their own lines; hence the result was heterophonic or polyphonic. A comparison used by Plutarch in his *Laws of Marriage* is of importance in this respect. In order to explain the hegemony of the husband in his own home he uses as an example the arrangement of musical instruments. The instrument with the lower range always carries the melody:

> As when two [instrumental] lines are made to sound together and the lower one has the melody, so this fact also demonstrates the leadership and the will of the husband in his home.[31]

Stringed instruments and flutes alike were arranged for parts. Flutes were usually played in pairs. The right one, with the lower range, accompanied the singing, while the left one, which was generally shorter, pursued its own line and played the intermezzi. Both flutes were later joined together by a common mouthpiece, as paintings show. The left and higher-voiced flute thus had a line separate from the melody of the song. Its task was "succinere," as the Romans styled this particular form of accompaniment. Varro demonstrates this when he writes:

> Agricultura succinit pastorali vitae, quod est inferior, ut tibia sinistra a dextrae foraminibus.[32]

It has been shown in the preceding sections that Christianity, for purely cultic reasons, was obliged to prohibit instrumental music, which was so closely connected with idolatry. But there was still another reason why Christianity assumed a generally hostile position in this matter: the heterophony of instrumental music stood in sharp contrast to the primitive Christian idea of the divine unity and the communion of souls.

F.J. Dölger has demonstrated that the Neopythagorean concepts of unity-duality, good-evil, right-left, light-darkness, day-night and life-death were continued in Christian circles.[33] The Christians, like the Pythagoreans, considered unity as good and duality as evil, and they too compared the opposition of unity and duality to that of harmony and disharmony. Methodius of Olympus, for example, posits this group of oppositions: life-death, immortality-mortality, equality-inequality, harmony-disharmony, justice-injustice, wisdom-foolishness. In so doing he specifically emphasizes the strong relationship among the items in each series.[34]

With the understanding that unity and harmony stood in opposition to duality and disharmony the primitive Church rejected all heterophony and polyphony. The greatest possible harmony was pursued as the musical expression of the union of souls and of the community, as it prevailed in the early Christian liturgy.[34a] It is in this sense that the entire community of Christians, according to Clement of Alexandria, becomes a single συμφωνία:

> We want to strive so that we, the many, may be brought together into one love, according to the union of the essential unity. As we do good may we similarly pursue unity.... The union of many, which the divine harmony has called forth out of a medley of sounds and division, becomes one symphony, following the one leader of the choir and teacher, the Word, resting in that same truth and crying out: "Abba, Father."[35]

Here Clement uses singing in one voice as an image of the unity and harmony of all Christians. He also finds no more beautiful comparison for the harmony of the universe than that of the primitive Christian singing whose patron was David. In contrast to this stood profane music, represented by Jubal:

> And truly, this pure song, the key-note of the whole and the harmony of all things, extending from the center to the extremities and from the ends to the middle, has arranged all things harmoniously, not according to Thracian music, which follows Jubal, but according to the fatherly will of God, which fired the zeal of David.[36]

Accordingly Clement wished all chromatic music "with its colorful harmonies" to be banned by Christians. This referred to instrumental music which was particularly cultivated and which originated with the cithara.

But we shall choose temperate harmonies; we shall keep far away from our virile minds all liquid harmonies which by modulating tones lead to a dangerous art which trains to effeminacy and languor. Austere and temperate songs protect against wild drunkenness; therefore we shall leave chromatic harmonies to immoderate revels and to the music of courtesans.[37]

Thus the ideal of early Christian singing was unity or monophony. The most ancient evidence for this is probably found in the Prefaces of the Mass, which speak of the angels and archangels, cherubim and seraphim, *qui non cessant clamare quotidie una voce dicentes: Sanctus, Sanctus, Sanctus Dominus Deus Sabaoth.* J. Kroll and O. Casel see in these words a proof for singing in one voice, as this alone suited the spirit of early Christianity.[38] It was precisely because the heavenly hosts sang their praise of God in a single voice that the primitive Christians thought of this singing as so marvelous. In the *Ascension of Isaiah,* a second century work, a vision which the prophet saw is reproduced. He beholds his ascent into the sevenfold heaven, and in each of the seven heavens he encounters angels and saints praising God and singing in two choirs. The text stresses particularly each time that they are singing to God in a single voice.[39] Likewise, in the *Apocalypse of Peter* from the first half of the second century, we read:

> Those who lived there bore the same glory and, full of joy, praised the Lord with one voice in that place.[40]

In the *Acts of Perpetua,* dating from 203, Perpetua says exactly the same thing about her own vision. She beholds herself already in heaven with her companions in suffering,

> and we heard the united voice of some saying unceasingly: "Holy, holy, holy."[41]

Gregory Nazianzus describes the angelic choirs singing psalms and hymns, and he remarks that, despite many mouths, only one voice is heard.[42] Much more evidence might be given on this point, but it would disclose nothing new.

In the primitive Christian view the earthly liturgy was understood to be a replica of the heavenly ritual. Therefore Christian singing also had to sound out in a mighty harmony of voices. Clement of Rome already requires this of Christians at the close of his description of the angels' song of praise. After recalling the words of Is. 6:3 he writes:

> We too, assembled with one accord, should earnestly cry out without ceasing to him as with one voice.[43]

In fact the koinonia of singing went even further: the singing of the earthly Church was supposed to be united with that of the angels in heaven. According to Cyril of Jerusalem, it was only so that we might sing in unison with them that the triple *Sanctus* of the seraphim was revealed to us.[44]

Occasionally the earliest Fathers would intertwine this notion with the Pythagorean concept of the harmony of the spheres. Thus Origen answers Celsus' demand that Helios and Athena should be praised by saying:

We sing hymns only to God the Lord and to his only-begotten Son, just as do the sun, the moon, the stars and the whole heavenly array.[45]

So deeply penetrated is Origen with the idea of the koinonia of Christian singing that he says that God hears the singing of all Christian peoples as if they were calling on him with one voice, even though the Greeks approach him in Greek and the Romans in Latin.[46]

Before the time of Origen, Clement, his predecessor in the catechetical school of Alexandria, was exhorting the Christians to sing psalms while having their meals at home. He refers to the Greek usage customary at *symposia* — meals where guests were present; when the cups were filled, the "skolion" was sung. Clement expressly says that this song was performed in unison, in the style of Hebrew psalmody.[47] Here Clement probably has in mind a text from Plutarch which states that the guests at a banquet first sing the paean all together, as with a single voice.[48]

In his *Apology to the Emperor Constantius* Athanasius explains why so much importance was attached to this singing "as from a single mouth." In this work Athanasius had to defend himself against the complaints of the Eusebian party, which had denounced him to the emperor for conducting the liturgy in an Alexandrian church which was still partly under construction, just before its consecration. He speaks of the special difficulties concerning space, which occasioned what he had done, and then he continues:

Would it have been better for the people to have been divided, to have been forced into dangerous congestion or to have been gathered together in a space already available so that one and the same voice might rise in harmony from them? The latter was preferable. For this also permitted the people to appear as one heart and one soul, and thus God quickly gave them a favorable hearing. For, according to the Savior's promise, when two people unite their voices everything that they request will be granted. So it is also when, out of a multitude who have come together, a single voice is heard crying out "Amen" to God.[49]

According to this, Athanasius was seeking a more effective influence with God because of a greater number of Christians singing in one voice. Ambrose, on the other hand, envisioned the effect of this monophony on the singers themselves; he refers to it as

a pledge of peace and concord, like a cithara putting forth one song from different and equal voices.[50]

His contemporary, Basil of Caesarea, develops this idea still further:

Who can consider as an enemy one with whom he has sung God's praises with one voice? Hence singing the psalms imparts the highest good, love, for it uses communal singing, so to speak, as a bond of unity, and it harmoniously draws people to the symphony of one choir.[51]

It was precisely on account of this communion of souls, evoked and symbolized by the monophonic singing of psalms, that Chrysostom complained about gossiping in church. When this takes place the full notion of the mystical body of Christ, which lies at the basis of the Christian liturgy and receives its expression in such singing, is lost.[52] The entire Christian people becomes a single body, magnifying the Lord in song.

Cyprian of Antioch gives this impression when he describes the liturgy of the Church in Antioch:

Thereupon we went into the church, and [one could there] see the choir, which was like a choir of heavenly men of God or a choir of angels taking up a song of praise to God. To every verse they added a Hebrew word [as] with one voice, so that one might believe that there were not [a number of] men but rather one rational being comprehending a unity, which gave off a wonderful sound, which the dead prophets were announcing once more through the living.[53]

The monophonic koinonia of liturgical singing was also outwardly strengthened in certain areas. A letter of Acacius of Constantinople to Peter of Alexandria in the year 561 informs us that, while singing, the members of the community would hold each other's hands:

Therefore, with the same song of praise that the choirs of angels sang to the ears of the shepherds on earth in Bethlehem, the guardians and shepherds of the sheep together with the sheep (for in their unity and concord they hold one another's hands) praise God our Lord, who is the true head and the true shepherd of the flock.[54]

From the spirit of the early Church and its idea of the liturgy, which aimed at making "a unity out of the many who participate,"[55] there was room for nothing else than monophonic singing without instrumental accompaniment. The question now is whether the monuments of Christian music which have survived also corroborate this view. Unfortunately very few monuments of such extreme importance for the history of ecclesiastical music have come down to us. The oldest piece of Christian church music which can be dated is part of the Oxyrhynchus Papyrus XV 1786, discovered by the Egypt Exploration Society in Oxyrhynchos in a pile of papyrus strips and published in 1922. On one side of the papyrus is a grain invoice; on the other a Greek text and notes are inscribed.[56] The grain invoice renders a more precise dating possible. It stems from the first half of the third century, from the time following the *Constitutio Antoniniana.* The text and melody on the reverse are of a later date and belong to about the end of the third century.[57] The melody, as well as the style of notation, bears the mark of ancient Greek artistry. Thus the question must remain open as to whether or not this was a pagan melody to which a Christian text was later added. The fact that what we have is simply Greek vocal notation without any mixture of instrumental notation shows that the fragment is in complete agreement with the position that the ecclesiastical writers took on music. The instrumental notation which T. Reinach added in his translation is completely missing from the original.[58] Also, the diatonic scale demanded for Christian music by Clement of Alexandria in *Paidagogos* 2,4 is preserved. According to what is written, the notes produce the section of the scale ε ζ ι ξ o σ φ P—that is, as Bellermann holds, the purely diatonic series of f[1]–f.[59] The clear rejection of the chromatic scale with its many half-steps, which Clement wanted to leave to the "flower-bedecked music of courtesans," is plainly expressed here.

The text of the piece contains one of the most frequently mentioned ideas of the Church Fathers, namely the invitation to all God's creatures in heaven and on earth to praise him with hymns. It resembles the retort which Origen gives to Celsus in the passage already noted, where he says that Christians do not praise Helios and Athena in their songs but rather him whom the sun, moon and stars praise. The text reads:

all noble [creatures] of God together. . .shall not be silent, nor shall the light-bearing stars lag behind. . . . All the rushing rivers shall praise our Father and Son and Holy Spirit, all the powers shall join in saying: Amen, amen, power [and] praise. . .to the only giver of all good things. Amen, amen.[59a]

According to the text, it cannot be established as certain whether the hymn was used in private devotion or for liturgical worship. In any event both text and music conform to the spirit which was current in the early Christian communities, and thus it is a witness to the *una voce dicentes* of early Christian singing.[59b]

5. INSTRUMENTAL MUSIC IN THE LITURGY OF THE FIRST CHRISTIAN CENTURIES.

The strong opposition to instrumental music in both pagan and Christian liturgy, as well as pious belief in the *una voce dicentes*, made its exclusion from Christian worship obvious. Theory and practice, however, do not often go together; in carrying out any legislation the customs of the people present a factor that must not be overlooked. Moreover, every legal determination presupposes the existence of diverse possibilities which prove its necessity.

For the first two centuries the evidence for the vocal and musical form of the liturgy is meager. From the sources at our disposal we can assume that the cithara was used. The Book of Revelation may be cited in proof of the great antiquity of hymns to Christ; in several places (5:9, 14:3; 15:3) it speaks of a "new song" which will be sung in heaven to the Lamb. F. J. Dölger, *pace* W. Bousset, has rightly shown that the whole vision had for its model the earthly liturgy in which a hymn to Christ already had its place.[60] It is significant that John, in the sections where he speaks of this new song, expressly mentions that it is accompanied by the music of the cithara:

> ...the four living creatures and the twenty-four elders fell down before the Lamb, each holding a cithara...and they sang a new song... (5:8-9).

Furthermore, if, as Bousset holds, Ignatius of Antioch in his *Letter to the Ephesians* 4,1 probably has in mind a Christian liturgy,[61] it is most likely no mere accident that the cithara is mentioned along with the hymn to Christ, if only as a symbol of the koinonia of souls.

> Your presbytery...harmonizes as completely with the bishop as the strings with a cithara. Thus the praises of Jesus Christ are sung in your concord and the harmony of your love.[62]

Ignatius' symbolic use of the cithara was perhaps due to its connection with the hymn to Christ.

Along the same line of development, Clement of Alexandria in *Pai-*

dagogos 2,4 rejects every instrument but establishes a principle relative to the cithara and the lyre:

> But if you want to sing and praise God to the music of the cithara or the lyre it is not blameworthy. You are imitating the righteous King of the Hebrews, who was well-pleasing to God.[63]

The objection that Clement is speaking here only of meals to which guests are invited is verified by the chapter heading: Πῶς Χρὴ περὶ τὰς ἑστιάσεις ἀνίεσθαι. Along with these private meals, however, Clement primarily has in mind the community meal of the Christians, the agape, at which psalms were always sung. This idea is strengthened in light of the sharp contrast between the community meals of the pagans with all their abuses and those of the Christians with their temperate atmosphere. Since the lyre and the cithara were tolerated at the agape in Clement's time, the supposition that they were used in the liturgy appears justified, for in his time the liturgy was still very closely bound up with the agape.[64] The preferential place that the cithara and the lyre occupied is also stressed by Philo, who, in other respects, wished to have nothing to do with musical instruments. As a proof that the number seven is always the number of perfection he refers to the lyre:

> In music the seven-stringed lyre is indeed the best of all the instruments because the harmony, which is the noblest part of the song-poems, is made especially perceptible by it.[65]

The lyre remained comparatively unblemished by use in idol worship and was employed more frequently in private homes, while the flute, tambourine, cymbal and all the other instruments were much more closely associated with the pagan cults.

Yet the prohibition of instrumental music in early Christianity became ever more stringent. J.E. Häuser tells us that Basil introduced cithara accompaniment into the liturgy of Caesarea.[66] H. A. Köstlin, M. Hermesdorff, Krüll and P. Kleinert repeat this assertion, but it rests on a mistaken translation or a false reading.[67] In the same manner, the proofs adduced by J.N. Forkel and J. Combarieu from Pseudo-Justin are consistently weak.[68] J. Neumaier[69] maintains that musical instruments were used to accompany liturgical singing in the early Church, and he bases his proof on the misunderstood text of Basil and also on Prudentius.[70] The instruments which Prudentius mentions, however, were hardly ever used in the Christian liturgy; they only served his poetic fantasy as a means of praising God. Consequently this text cannot be taken as proof for an actual liturgical use of these instruments. Moreover, it is highly improbable that precisely these instruments, against which the repugnance of the ecclesiastical writers was directed, would later have found acceptance in the Christian cult.

Of greater significance for us, on the other hand, is a passage in Augustine's second discourse on Psalm 32 (33) where he asks his listeners:

> Has not the institution of those vigils in Christ's name caused the citharas to be banished from this place?[71]

As we learn from the context, Augustine gave this discourse in the memorial chapel of Saint Cyprian, where the saint was buried. It is quite clear from what Augustine says that vigils had taken place in this chapel and that citharas had been played at them. Whether Augustine was referring to the elimination of a long-standing custom or speaking out against a recent innovation is a question that cannot be answered from the discourse itself. Probably he was talking about a custom which the Christians had learned from the pagans' παννυχισμοί and their solemnities of the dead. The Christians thought they could continue these practices during the vigils and feasts of the martyrs — as, for instance, in the chapel of Saint Cyprian. Perhaps the ecclesiastical authorities had originally tolerated this in silence, as they did banquets in church, about which Augustine speaks in another place.[72] The discourse, though, can hardly refer to the actual use of instrumental music in the liturgy, but rather to popular religious feasts, such as those of the martyrs.

The *Quaestiones et responsiones ad orthodoxos* — one of the four pseudo-Justinian tracts which, according to J. Wittig, belong to the Antiochene school and were probably drawn up only after 400 during the Monophysite disturbances — present us with a rigid ecclesiastical decree against the use of all instruments.[73] The author is unknown. A. Harnack ascribed all four tracts, particularly the *quaestiones*, to Diodore of Tarsus,[74] but F.X. Funk has offered convincing arguments against this opinion.[75] The author, however, could not be Theodoret of Cyrus either, as Funk suggests.[76] *Quaestio* 107 is the one that concerns us: if it is a fact that unbelievers lead men astray with their songs and that the Jews were permitted to sing only on account of the hardness of their hearts, then why do Christians sing in church? The *responsio* follows:

> Singing of itself is not to be considered as fit only for the unclean, but rather singing to the accompaniment of soulless instruments and dancing

and the noise of the krotala. Therefore the use of such instruments with singing in church must be shunned, as well as everything else that is proper only for fools. Simple singing alone remains.... Paul calls it [singing] a sword of the spirit with which it [the spirit] outfits pious fighters for God against the invisible enemy. For it is and remains God's word, whether it is contemplated, sung or listened to, a protection against the demons.[77]

In another of the pseudo-Justinian tracts, the *Oratio ad Graecos,* these angry words are put in the mouth of God:

> I hate your feasts. The gluttony which takes place at them is unseemly, as are the lustful actions provoked by enticing flutes.[78]

The degree of concern to avoid the music of stringed instruments in the liturgy is shown by the so-called *Canons of Basil,* which were probably written shortly after the death of Athanasius in 373. Canon 74 contains this decree:

> If a lector learns to play the guitar he shall also be taught to confess it (?).
> If he does not return to it he shall suffer his penance for seven weeks. If he keeps at it he shall be excommunicated and put out of the church.[79]

The lectors referred to here also discharged the office of cantor, as canon 97 in the same collection presupposes.[80] Their musical vocation made it possible for them to be more easily led astray in the area of instrumental music than for others. But in order to forestall every danger of admitting such music into the church itself the canon forbids the lector to practice this art. H. Leclercq's attempt to deduce from the Greek grave inscription of El Doukheileh a proof that the cantor had the use of a musical instrument for his singing is mistaken.[81] A decree similar to that in the *Canons of Basil* is found later in the *Nomocanon* of Michael of Damietta:

> The lector may not wear a deacon's stole nor may he use a musical instrument.[82]

All these decrees demonstrate a concern to preserve ecclesiastical singing from every kind of instrumental music.

6. The Liturgical Singing of Women in Christian Antiquity. The Participation of Women in the Liturgy of the Heretics.

Christianity took a special position with regard to the liturgical singing of women. This position cannot be understood, however, without reference to its background in the pagan cults and among the Jews.[82a]

Women's singing played an important role in pagan worship. In Egypt at a comparatively early date women entered the ranks of the priestly singers of the gods. On a stele (Cairo 20026) dating from the time of the Middle Kingdom both "men and women singers of the temple" are mentioned.[83] In the New Kingdom women singers were found in large numbers in all the temples. Women and girls from the different ranks of society were proud to enter the service of the gods as singers or musicians. The understanding of this service was singular: these singers constituted the "harem of the gods."[84]

From the Greeks especially we hear of choirs of women in the processions held in honor of the gods. On the occasion of the spring sacrifice which took place on Delos choirs of women were present to sing the praises of the gods.[85] In the sanctuary of Eileithyia at Olympia virgins and matrons sang a hymn in honor of the goddess.[86] In preference to all other hymns these choirs generally sang the so-called epiphany hymns, which were intended to invite the gods to appear. Thus Plutarch writes:

> Why do the women of Elis call upon God in song to approach them with the bull's foot? Their song is the following:
> Come, Dionysos, Hero,
> into the holy temple of Elis,
> together with the Graces
> come violently into the temple with the bull's foot!
> Then they sing twice at the end: "Sacred Bull!"[87]

In Ionia and on the adjacent islands women dressed in festive clothing wandered about and begged, singing all the while, as Herodotus informs us, a song composed by the Lycian Olen that was supposed to call down the goddesses Opis and Arge.[88]

In Rome the choirs of women participating in the pagan cults were no less numerous. The Roman lexicographer Festus, in a description of the religious customs and rites of the Salians, speaks of a choir of young girls who officiated at the sacrifices and were clad in the ritual garments of dancers consecrated to the gods.[89] Choirs of women are mentioned almost always in descriptions of Roman processions, whether of expiation or petition.[90] On special occasions the Sibylline Books demanded that chosen virgins and chaste boys should sing the carmen to the gods. Thus Horace informs us in Carmen saeculare 4,8:

> Tempore sacro
> Quod Sibyllini monuere versus
> Virgines lectas puerosque castos

Dis, quibus septem placuere colles,
Dicere carmen.

According to Livy 27,37, the rite of the Sibyls prescribed that thrice nine virgins should sing the song of petition at the expiatory processions through the city of Rome.[91]

Choirs of women were no less active in the Jewish liturgy. At the thanksgiving service after the flight from Egypt Miriam led the choir of the women (Ex. 15:20–21),[92] and at the yearly solemnity of the Lord in Shiloh the daughters of Israel participated by singing and dancing (Judg. 21:21). Philo tells of a similar participation by women in the liturgical song of the communities of the Therapeutae. He describes the services conducted on vigils in the following way:

> After the meal they conduct the evening service thus: arising in unison they form two choirs in the center of the refectory, one of men and the other of women. The most esteemed and tactful is chosen as leader and cantor of each. Then they sing to God hymns composed in diverse meters and of various melodies, sometimes in unison, sometimes alternately. During this they move their hands rhythmically and dance and call on God in their songs — songs of festive processions and choral songs, alternating by choirs according to strophes and antistrophes.[93]

But what was the attitude of Christianity toward the singing of women in divine worship? In the first two centuries we hear little of any participation by women in the singing of the congregation, and yet women must have had a part in such singing. An exclusion of women would have stood in sharp contrast to the idea of the communion of souls which Ignatius of Antioch had emphasized so strongly and which was so important to the Fathers of the first centuries. This notion was embodied in congregational singing where "all sing as with one mouth," as it is stated repeatedly. It was precisely for the reason that all participated in it that this singing had special intercessory power in the sight of God. Ignatius writes in his *Letter to the Ephesians*:

> But all of you as individuals should become a choir so that, sounding together in harmony, singing the song of God in unison, you may with one voice sing praise to the Father through Jesus Christ, that he may hear you.[94]

At a much later time Chrysostom complained that this inner value of communal singing had been lost. In one of his homilies he says:

> Shall I name still another treasure chest that has been robbed of its original beauty? In times past all came together and sang the psalms as a

community. This we no longer do. Formerly there was one heart and one soul in everyone, but today we can no longer perceive such harmony of soul, and everywhere there is strong discord.

Then he speaks of gossiping in church and continues:

But can you not be silent? Then go outside so as not to disturb others, for in church only one voice should be heard, as though there were only one person. For that reason the lector alone speaks, and even the bishop sits and listens in silence. Thus the cantor sings alone, and when all join him in the response it is as though only one voice were sounding.[95]

It was on account of this koinonia of souls that Ambrose, Chrysostom's contemporary, defended the participation of women in liturgical singing. With reference to Paul's statement that "women should keep silent in the churches" he remarks:

The Apostle commands women to be silent in church, but they may sing the psalms; this is fitting for every age and for both sexes. In this singing, old men lay aside the rigor of age; downcast middle-aged men respond in the cheerfulness of their heart; younger men sing without peril of wantonness; youths sing without danger to their still impressionable age and without fear of being tempted to pleasure; tender maidens suffer not damage to the adornment of their chastity, and young widows let their rich voices ring out without endangering their modesty.

The explanation of this follows:

For it is a powerful bond of unity when such a great number of people come together in one choir. The strings of the cithara are of unequal length, yet they all sound in harmony. Even with the very small number of strings the virtuoso still sometimes mistakes his touch. But when all sing in community the Holy Spirit, as the Artist, permits no dissonance.[96]

The participation of women in the singing of the community is seen in the choirs of virgins which Ephraem founded to sing his hymns at the liturgy. A century earlier Paul of Samosata had introduced a similar innovation. Eusebius says of him:

The hymns in honor of our Lord Jesus Christ he set aside as too new and known by too few of the older men. But for his own glorification he had women sing hymns on the first day of Easter in the middle of the assembly. One would shudder to hear them.[97]

Of Ephraem almost the same is told:

In Edessa he instituted societies of women, taught the members the madrashe . . . and they gathered in church on the feasts of the Lord, on Sundays and on the feasts of the martyrs.[98]

It was because of the singing of hymns and the activity of their choirs of women that the heretics Bardesanes and Harmonius obtained so great a following. Ephraem was only able to combat this danger when he himself had hymns sung by women choirs. We are informed of this in an excerpt from an anonymous writer in Assemani's anthology:

> When the holy Ephraem saw how all were being torn away by the singing [of the heretics], and since he wanted to keep his own people away from dishonorable and worldly plays and concerts, he himself founded choirs of consecrated virgins, taught them the hymns and responses whose wonderful contents celebrated the birth of Christ, his baptism, fasting, suffering, resurrection and ascension, as well as the martyrs and the dead. He had these virgins come to the church on the feasts of the Lord and on those of the martyrs, as they did on Sundays. He himself was in their midst as their father and the citharist of the Holy Spirit, and he taught them music and the laws of song.[99]

Still another way in which women shared in liturgical singing has come down to us. It is well known that the singing of the psalms was diligently practiced in the convents of women.[100] Religious women, beginning from the time of the fourth century, took active part in the singing of the psalms in the city churches. Marûtâ of Maipherkat (second half of the fourth century) says:

> It is the will of the general synod that municipal churches should not be without this class of sisters. They shall have a diligent teacher and shall be instructed in reading and especially in psalmody. This is decreed by the synod without anathema.[101]

These sisters recited the psalms in common with the brothers in the municipal churches. Marûtâ gives this direction to the bishop:

> Let him attend closely to all that pertains to the liturgy. Let him see for himself how the brothers and sisters perform the external ceremonies of the temple, that they do not perform any heretical canons out of ignorance, that their service not become disreputable and disorderly, that they not hurry or swallow words, but that in their psalmody everything be fulfilled, and that they do not miss the services while they live from the *congrua* of the church.[102]

An even clearer testimony to this may be found in the report of the Gallican pilgrim Egeria (c. 386). She describes the morning service in the Church of the Holy Sepulcher in Jerusalem in these words:

> Every day before cockcrow all the gates of the Anastasis are opened and all the monks and virgins, or as they say here, the *monozantes* and *parthenae*, descend — not merely they but lay people, men and women, as well.... And from that hour until the break of day hymns and psalms are sung in alternate chant, and so too are the antiphons. And after each hymn a prayer is said.[103]

As late as the year 676, in a Nestorian synod of Mar George I, rules were set down for the clothes and headdress of these consecrated sisters. The ninth canon of this synod reads:

> The women who have set themselves apart for this vocation of virginity should be distinguished by their clothing and their style of hair. They should learn especially to recite the psalms, to care for divine worship and to take notice of the time for singing the *madrashe*.[104]

The singing of the *madrashe* or hymns seems to have been reserved to the sisters having vows. Whereas the brothers with vows learned merely the psalms, the sisters had to practice hymns too.[105] This was an innovation of Ephraem, a practice that quickly spread to all the larger municipal churches.

The singing of psalms by women is mentioned frequently. The Syrian poet Cyrillonas says in a hymn of petition written for the Feast of All Saints of the year 396:

> Behold, hymns are voiced by the tongues of children, and women sing your praises.[106]

In the *Church History* of Theodoret of Cyrus a certain Publia is mentioned:

> She had a choir of virgins who were praiseworthy for their lifelong virginity, and with them she ceaselessly worshiped God the creator and preserver of all things. At the time when the Emperor [Julian] died they sang more loudly than usual, for they considered the evildoer contemptible and ridiculous. They sang those songs most often which mocked the weakness of idols, and they said with David: 'The idols of the pagans are silver and gold, the works of human hands. Those who make them are like them, and so are all who trust in them."[107]

While the passage just quoted refers to the singing of women in conventual life, the so-called *Testament of Our Lord*, which in its present form dates back to the fifth century, clearly speaks of the singing of women in church. There we read:

> To the one who sings the psalms in church [probably as cantor] the virgins and the boys should reply in psalmody.[108]

Virgins did not only have a part in the common singing of the congregation but they also acted as cantors:

> They shall sing psalms and four canticles—one from Moses, one from Solomon, and the others from the prophets—with the children, two virgins, three deacons and three presbyters doing the singing.[109]

This practice becomes more understandable when we learn in the Arabic version of the *Canons of the Apostles* that the duties of the lectorate could be performed by women.[110] In this work we find the enumeration of deaconesses, subdeaconesses and lectresses. One and the same person very often performed the offices both of cantor and lector, as was quite natural in the smaller churches.[111] It is thus entirely plausible that the lectresses were also cantors, particularly since ecclesiastical singing in the earliest times approximated a recitative reading. Canon 52 of the Arabic *Canons of the Apostles*, which directs the children to the ambo at which the lectress exercises her office, is to be understood in this sense.[112] In the *Testament of Our Lord*, *pueruli* and *duae virgines* are also referred to as singing together, and they must have stood together, so that in both these references the same place is meant.

Nonetheless the singing of women in church did not enjoy the same good favor everywhere. The protests that forbade it became increasingly louder until such singing ceased completely. In the *Didascalia of the Three Hundred Eighteen Fathers* we already have a strong prohibition of the singing of women, but the struggle against their participation in liturgical communal singing must have begun long before this. In the above-mentioned *Didascalia* we read:

> Women are ordered not to speak in church, not even softly, nor may they sing along or take part in the responses, but they should only be silent and pray to God.[113]

According to P. Batiffol, this text dates back to about the year 375.[114] The same view is expressed by Cyril of Jerusalem (died 386). In his introductory *Catechesis* he speaks of the assignment of places in church and remarks:

> The virgins should sing or read the psalms very quietly during the liturgy. They should only move their lips, so that nothing is heard, for I do not permit women to speak in church. Women should therefore conduct themselves in this way: when they pray they should move their lips, but not so that they can be heard.[115]

Isidore of Pelusium (died 440) notes that

> perhaps women were originally permitted by the Apostles and presbyters to join in singing so as to prevent their gossiping in church. But later this permission was withdrawn since it was learned that they did not gain any salutory fruits of penance (κατάνυξις) from divine song, but used the sweetness of melody for disturbances of every kind, since they looked on it in exactly the same way as theater music.[116]

What were the reasons which led to the exclusion of women from singing in church? They were various. Of prime importance, though, was the fact that among the heretics women had prominent rank as prophetesses, lectresses, deaconesses and singers. The Gnostics began with such an arrangement, and we know that among the Marcionites women filled these same offices.[117] Tertullian expressed himself sharply more than once when writing of these innovations of the heretics:

> They are bold enough to teach, to dispute, to attempt exorcisms and cures, perhaps even to baptize.[118]

The practice which Ephraem adopted later as a measure to arrest the growth of heresy by permitting women to sing, sometimes even retaining the melodies of the heretical songs and simply replacing the words, was not a universal one.[119] The Church, at least from time to time, fought the singing of hymns, probably as a protest against the innovation of heretics.[120] So too, she took a negative position regarding this stronger attraction of women toward liturgical singing; in fact she abolished it altogether.

This development can be easily traced. Paul of Samosata was attacked on two points: first, in place of the usual hymns concerning Christ he substituted songs composed by himself; and second, he permitted these songs to be sung by women during the liturgy of Easter Sunday. Of particular importance for judging the grounds which led to the exclusion of women from singing in church is a passage in the *Contra Pelagianos* of Jerome. According to Gennadius,[121] Jerome is here attacking a work of Pelagius, written before 411, entitled *Eclogarum ex divinis scripturis liber unus, capitolorum indiciis in modum Cypriani praesignatus* (i.e., modeled on the *Testimonium libri* of Cyprian). Jerome quotes the *tituli* of a number of these *capitula* and then addresses Pelagius:

> Truly you are so gallant that, in order to win the favor of your amazons, you write in another place that "women also must have a knowledge of the law," although the Apostle teaches that women should be silent in church, and if they do not understand something they should ask their husbands at home. You are not satisfied merely to give the members of your party a knowledge of the Scriptures, but you also wish to enjoy their voices and their singing. So you continue with your prescriptions, that women too should sing praise to the Lord. Who does not know that women should sing the praises of the Lord — in their own chambers, far removed from the meetings of men and the assemblies of the multitude? But you permit what is not permissible, namely, that they do what should be performed by them secretly and without any witnesses as though they were lawfully constituted teachers.[122]

Thus, according to Jerome, there is an arrogance in the singing of women that cannot be harmonized with the Christian idea of the position of women. The whole complexity of this question is connected with the problem of the religious emancipation of women, which became very difficult on account of the attitude of the heretics toward the matter.

To understand the exclusion of women from singing at the liturgy, the attitude of Christianity with regard to the singing of women outside the liturgy, in private life, must also be considered. In antiquity women musicians and singers had a very bad reputation. The flutists, harpists and singers at banquets were courtesans. In Lucian of Samosata's *Dialogues of a Courtesan* we hear almost exclusively of women musicians and singers.[123] Sallust writes of Sempronia:

> She played the cithara and danced more elegantly than was becoming to an upright woman, and she could do many other things which minister to voluptuousness.[124]

It is little wonder, then, that Christianity showed a great aversion toward any participation of married women and virgins in profane music and song. Arnobius identifies the harpists and the courtesans with one another. He asks:

> Has God created souls for this, that women should become harlots, sambucists and harpists in order to surrender their bodies to lust?[125]

Commodian tells the Christian virgin: "You transgress the law when you go about among musicians."[126] Jerome, a prominent opponent of worldly song on the part of women, tells the young girl in his *Epistula ad Laetam* to be ignorant of *cantica mundi*.[127] The world of organ, flute, lyre and cithara should remain closed to the Christian maiden.[128] No pleasure should be taken in a friend "who limpidly sings a sweet song,"[129] for "the sweetness of the voice wounds the soul through the ear."[130] Basil of Caesarea thought it a pitiable sight for pious eyes to find a woman singing at the lyre rather than weaving.[131] This strictness lasted a long time. In the East a synod of 576 decreed that Christian parents from that time on should no longer permit their daughters to learn secular music.[132] In W. Riedel we read among the *Commandments of the Fathers, Superiors and Masters* that:

> Christians are not allowed to teach their daughters singing, the playing of instruments or similar things because, according to their religion, it is neither good nor becoming.[133]

All these passages, it is true, are concerned with worldly song and worldly music, to the practice of which pagan women attached excessive importance. Even in the time of Horace famous musicians such as Demetrius and Tigellius spent a great part of the day at the desks of their girl scholars.[134] In contrast to this the singing of the psalms was recommended again and again to Christian virgins precisely as a substitute for prohibited secular music. Tertullian writes:

> Let the two [spouses] sing psalms and hymns and incite each other to see who can sing better to his God.[135]

It was just this lack of singing of psalms and hymns by both partners that counted as one of the great losses of a marriage between a pagan and a Christian:

> What shall her husband sing to her or she to him? No doubt she will hear something from the stage.[136]

Jerome gives the practical advice to little Pacatula: *Psalmos mercede decantet*.[137] And in his letter to Laeta he writes concerning the young Paula: "While it is still tender, her tongue must be filled with the sweetness of the psalms."[138] He strongly suggests to this girl in her teens that she sing hymns early in the morning and also at the third, sixth and ninth hours of the day.[139] In the so-called *Canons of Basil* the thirty-sixth canon prescribes: "A virgin must use her tongue frequently in singing the psalms."[140]

But even in this extra-liturgical singing of psalms by women moderation and prudence had to be exercised. In the pseudo-Clementine *De virginitate*, which dates from about the first half of the third century,[141] the unmarried of both sexes are forbidden to sing Christian hymns or psalms at pagan banquets. It says:

> We do not cast holy things to dogs or pearls to swine, but we celebrate the praises of God with all modesty and discretion, with fear of God and devotion. We do not practice the sacred cult in the places where the pagans carouse, nor at banquets where they mock God in their impiousness with unchaste tongues. For this reason we do not sing any of the psalms in the presence of the pagans, nor do we read the Scriptures to them, lest we become like the flutists and the singers and the soothsayers, as many are doing when they act thus. For, so as to sate themselves with a bite of bread and a little wine, they sing the songs of the Lord in a foreign land—that of the pagans. Such things cannot be allowed.[142]

Gregory Nazianzus wished that virgins knew how to sing the divine canticles (οεῖα ᾄσματα) with the heart rather than with the voice.[143] The singing of the psalms in private life was to be performed by male rather than female voices. Of Arsilios, the ruler of the Iberians (in present-day Georgia), it was said:

And although many great ones of the earth, those in search of pleasure
and the insouciant, customarily provide men and women singers to
escape the nothingness of this world and to derive some passing enjoy-
ment from song, he, like King David, procured men to sing sacred songs.
These men sang the holy words of God at meals and throughout the day,
so that his palace differed in no way from a church.[144]

Here too there was a complete exclusion of female singing in the national customs.

According to some of the Fathers, there was a sensuous quality to a
woman's singing. Isidore of Pelusium says in the passage mentioned
previously that women did not derive any true penitential fruit from
their singing: κατάνυξιν ἐκ τῶν ὑείων ὕμνων οὐχ ὑπομένουσι. This hinder-
ing of the κατάνυξις, the *compunctio cordis*, contrition of heart, was attributed to the singing of women. The same objection was also largely
responsible for the aversion toward the development of song in the
monasteries of the time. This is clear in the sharp struggle of the Abbots Nilus and Pambo against any innovation in singing in monastic
worship which threatened to invade the monastic liturgy from the
municipal churches.[145]

The question still remains whether the singing of women in pagan
worship was not a reason for opposition to their singing in the Christian liturgy. The answer is in the negative, for the struggle against the
participation of women in liturgical singing was not uniform enough
and was too limited to particular places. Moreover, this exclusion of
women occurred only at a later date. According to the citations that
have been made, the development is rather the following: women
commonly and universally took part in liturgical singing in earliest
Christian times on account of the notion of the spiritual koinonia,
which expressed itself in community singing. Special choirs of women
separated from the rest of the congregation and corresponding to the
choirs of the pagan cults seem to have been unknown in the first two
centuries of Christianity, so far as can be judged from the extant
sources. Hence no complaints are heard against the singing of women
in the first two centuries. The struggle for or against the liturgical singing of women broke out when some heretics, from the time of Paul of
Samosata, began to establish choirs of women separated from the rest
of the congregation to perform the singing at the liturgy. The example
of these heretics led some of the Fathers, chief among whom was
Ephraem, to imitate them for tactical reasons and likewise use such
choirs of women in order to deprive their opponents of this weapon of

attack. Other Fathers, however, sharply resisted this practice of the heretics. Thus it was that conflict arose concerning the singing of women in church. As opposition grows harsher particularly when it fails to prevail, so a number of the Fathers went so far as to forbid women to take any part in the communal singing. For all this, then, pagan idol worship did not furnish the reason for abolishing the singing of women in the Christian liturgy.

It was otherwise, though, with the pagan cult of the dead. We know of the participation of women as mourners at pagan funerals.[146] At burial services choirs of women often sang. Herodian relates that at the funeral rites of a Roman emperor a choir of distinguished women would sing hymns and paeans in honor of the deceased.[147] The memorial services for the dead were celebrated with great banquets, music, dancing and singing. This practice also set in on the vigils of the feasts of the martyrs, despite every prohibition.[148] We know from the letter of Augustine to Alypius of Tagaste and from his *Enarratio II in Ps. 32* how difficult it was to eradicate this remnant of paganism.[149] He tells how banquets were held in the church with dancing and cithara music. It is easy to understand, then, why Jerome gave the Christian maiden the advice to visit the basilicas of the martyrs only in the company of her mother.[150] On another occasion he told the virgin never to leave her mother's immediate presence during the celebration of the vigil.[151] The 99th canon of the *Canons of Father Athanasius* says that a virgin should not be in church at night, but that she should be in the monastery.[152] The Council of Auxerre (573/603) at a later time decreed in this respect:

> It is not permitted for choirs of virgins to sing in church or to prepare banquets in church.[153]

How long this abuse lasted may be seen from a passage in a homily of Pope Leo IV (847-855) in which he orders:

> Forbid the singing of choirs of women in the church or in the vestibule of the church. Forbid those diabolical songs which the people are accustomed to sing over the dead during the hours of the night.[154]

At about this time in the East the ecclesiastical canons of the Patriarch John III enjoined an excommunication on all women going to the graves of their dead to play the tambourine and to dance.[155] Certainly the pagan cult of the dead with all its popular practices was the reason why the singing of women was forbidden in many places at the vigils. How widespread this was, however, is seen from the fact that Gregory

Nazianzus, in the eulogy for his sister Gorgonia, praises her diligence in attending the vigil celebrations and stresses that she sang psalms at night.[156] Again, according to the testimony of Egeria, women were present during the Easter vigil in Jerusalem.[157] And in the so-called *Testament of Our Lord* the *laus nocturna viduarum* is mentioned at various times.[158] Practice was not uniform everywhere. While some places forbade the singing of women, or even their participation in vigil celebrations, an Eastern synod of 676 decreed that the professed sisters

> on the day of burial shall sing the *madrashe* while following the coffin, and on the memorial days and on the vigils they shall recite the *madrashe*.[159]

Thus there were various causes that furnished the reasons in different localities for the prohibition of the singing of women in church until, with the cessation of communal singing at the liturgy, it ceased everywhere.

7. The Development of Boys' Singing in the Christian Liturgy. Lectores infantuli.

Parallel to the development of the liturgical singing of women in the first two centuries was that of boys' singing. The singing of boys, however, was accorded an entirely different position in the liturgy than that of women.

The pagans frequently used boys' choirs in their worship, especially on festive occasions. This custom may be explained in the first place by the musical quality of boys' voices; their individuality and beauty, which could not be matched by either men's or women's voices, was greatly valued in antiquity. Thus Lucian of Samosata calls the boy's voice "perfectly delicate, not so deep as to be called masculine nor so fine as to be effeminate and lacking in power, but falling soft, mild and lovely upon the ear."[160] The chief reason, though, for the participation of boy's choirs in cultic celebrations is to be found in the fact that the innocence of young boys was expected to have a particularly strong influence upon the divinity.[161] So it was, as can be seen repeatedly, that "an innocent boy, whose parents are both still living," was employed at pagan sacrifices and oracles as a medium between god and man.

In the sacrifices of the Greeks boys who were ἀμφιθαλεῖς were necessary, and in Rome *quatuor pueri praetextati patrimi et matrimi* were used in the service of the Fratres Arvales, twelve priests who made annual offerings to the field Lares.[162] Boys were readily employed also in the pagan supplicatory processions, during which they would sing the entreaties of all the people to the gods. Pausanias describes the procession to the river Sythas with two choirs of youths who were sent there to bid the gods Apollo and Artemis to come to the acropolis of the city.[163] In the Eiresione procession on Samos, in which harvest wreaths were carried, a choir of boys, each one with a twig of blessings in his hand, sang πλοῦτος ἔσεισι.[164] In Delos, at the solemn sacrifices, choirs of boys who danced and sang to the cithara and the flute were always in attendance.[165] Similarly we find that thirty chosen boys sang the hymns in honor of Hecate on Stratonikeia.[166] In fact in many areas it appears that regular singing schools for such boys were founded. There the boys lived and daily sang the praise of the god. The scoffer Lucian pours out his sarcasm in a passage in which he speaks of the fraudulent prophet Alexander of Abonouteichos, who kept choir boys in the service of his god with him:

> To all others he forbade pederasty as shameful. In order not to admit his own guilt in this matter, however, the admirable fellow devised the following scheme: he proposed to the cities in Paphlagonia and Pontus that every three years they should send him choir boys who would sing hymns of praise with him to the god. Moreover, only the noblest, fairest and most charming boys were to be sent — after a previous careful examination. These he confined with himself, slept with and abused with every possible lechery.[167]

At the sacrifices of the Salii in Rome a choir of boys was present. On the *Saeculares*, in a temple of Apollo on the Palatine, twenty-seven boys and an equal number of girls of noble rank, whose parents were both still living, sang hymns and paeans in Greek and Latin for the protection of the Roman cities. This same custom also prevailed in the supplicatory processions in honor of the god of the city, Zeus Sosipolis.[168]

In the first Christian centuries we hear nothing of special boy choirs taking part in the Christian liturgy. Probably a certain power was ascribed to the singing of children, based on the commonly held view that the innocent had great influence with God. For this reason the ecclesiastical writers continually asked for the zealous participation of children in the liturgy. F.J. Dölger has shown that, according to the *Clementine Recognitions*, in the third century already children were calling upon God to send down rain during a time of drought and bad harvest.[169] Gregory Nazianzus recommends the participation of children in ecclesiastical singing because their youth "excites compassion and is most worthy of the divine mercy."[170] In his commentary on Matthew's Gospel Chrysostom enumerates the prayers that are said in the liturgy and says:

> The third [prayer is] for ourselves, when innocent children appear before the congregation to implore God's mercy.[171]

The children's diligent participation in singing the psalms is recorded by Basil of Caesarea, who contrasts their devotion with the interior lack of fervor of many adults during the liturgical singing.[172]

None of these citations makes any mention of special boy choirs. We probably have an intimation of them, though, in the Gallic pilgrim Egeria's description of the liturgical singing in Jerusalem. There it is no longer simply children who are spoken of but rather boys, *pisinni*, who do the singing; whenever the deacon would name a person to be prayed for, they would answer him with *Kyrie eleison*.[173] The efforts of the Emperor Julian in this regard are also interesting. He sought to revive in his time the ancient liturgical music of the pagans — probably in conscious opposition to the Christians. Julian demanded that religious hymns be sung not only in the temples but also in private homes, most likely because he saw how great a role the psalms and Christian hymns played in the private life of the Christians. In order to promote his aims he offered prizes to boys who practiced religious singing and sacred music.[174] It is uncertain whether this was only a resumption of former pagan customs or whether at the same time it provided a counterweight to the singing activity of Christian youth in the church, the school and at home. In any case, the position that the boy choir gradually attained in the Christian liturgy became increasingly important.

The so-called *Testament of Our Lord* shows a significant development here. The boys still responded to the cantor together with the virgins[175] and sang the psalms in the Office alternately with the virgins,[176] yet for that very reason the choir of boys stood out ever more in opposition to the singing of the people at large. Thus the four canticles were sung by the boys, two virgins, three deacons and three priests.[177] The canticles at vespers were sung by the boys alone, while the people replied in common with Alleluia.[178] So we see that the boy choir eventually relieved the cantor of his position; the word *re-*

spondeat already points to this. There was a similar development in the West, which we learn by way of a remark of Germanus of Paris (died 576). He states that at the beginning of Mass three children sing in one voice the threefold *Kyrie eleison*.[179] Jacob of Edessa probably also refers to choir boys when he forbids boys in general to enter the sanctuary outside of the time for the liturgy but makes an exception if the boy is one of those "who has been assigned in the church."[180] Since the boy singers had to go into the sanctuary during the liturgy the reason for the exception is obvious. Even today among the Syrian Jacobites the boy singers crouch before the altar with the cantor, clad in their ecclesiastical garb.[181]

The development of boy choirs is very closely linked with the employment of boys as lectors in the church.[181a] As the boy choir superseded the cantor, so individual boys from the choir gradually took the place of the lector, whose office was often connected with that of the cantor. We read in the epitaph of Pope Liberius (died 366):

Parvulus ut que loqui coepisti dulcia verba,
Mox scripturarum lector pius indole factus,
Ut tua lingua magis legem, quam verba sonaret.[182]

A decretal of Pope Siricius (died 398) determines that whoever dedicates himself to the service of the Church from his childhood must begin as a lector.[183] A law of Justinian dating from 546 decrees that a person could exercise the lectorate beginning in his eighth year.[184] Ennodius, speaking of Epiphanius, his second predecessor in the episcopal seat of Pavia, agrees with this: *annorum ferme octo lectoris ecclesiastici suscepit officium*.[185] An African inscription from the sixth century even speaks of a five year old lector, called to this holy office when he hardly *loqui coeperat dulcia verba*.[186] These youthful lectors also formed the boy choir. That such was the case appears in the story which Gregory of Tours tells about a lector from the church of Saint Maurice in Agaunum who died at an early age.[187] Saint Maurice showed himself in a vision to the youth's disconsolate mother and told her to go to the church the next day; there she would hear the voice of her son among the choir boys. The lectorate thus passed more and more into the hands of the young singers. This explains why the office of acolyte had precedence over the more ancient office of lector.

The choir boys and young lectors were later educated in their own school. On an inscription from Lyons the head of one of these schools is mentioned:

> Here rests Stephen, the servant of God, head of the school of lectors,
> who carried out his service in the Church at Lugdunum...[188]

It was the task of this *primicerius* to train the boys in reading and singing. From just such a school there developed in Rome the famous
schola cantorum.[188a] We may therefore assume that in training boys
for the office of lector the first step was to form special choirs of boys.

Inasmuch as the heretics often used boy choirs to popularize their
songs, an intensified use of them was highly recommended in ecclesiastical circles, so that the Church might not abandon to her opponents such an effective means of propaganda. The *Acta Ephraemi* tells us
that Bardesanes taught choir boys to sing to the accompaniment of the
cithara:

> A group of boys came to Bardesanes; these he taught to sing to the
> cithara and in various other ways.[189]

Ephraem himself mentions that boys would sing the psalms in the
liturgy. He speaks of the splendor of Nisan, the month of Easter,
which adorns the Church with its array of flowers, and he compares
the magnificently colored image of the spring month with the liturgical celebration: the flowers are the Scriptures, which the voices of the
boys and the virgins seem to strew over the congregation, as if the sun
were shining on it. These flowers will be mingled with those that
bloom on earth. The bishop will offer his homilies, the priests their en-
comia, the deacons their readings, the youths their shouts of joy, the
boys their psalms and the virgins their songs.[190] From this it appears
that Ephraem was acquainted with the singing of boys in the liturgy.
But since we hear nothing to the effect that Ephraem introduced boy
choirs into the liturgy to counteract Bardesanes we may surmise that
boys' singing was a liturgical custom before Ephraem's time. Despite
this we cannot lightly dismiss the influence that the heretics had on the
development of boys' singing in the Church. Indeed, O. Braun has
suggested polemical reasons for the practice of ecclesiastical singing in
the Oriental elementary schools.[191]

We know that the Nestorians used boy choirs to spread their songs
and hymns. The Jacobite Maphrian Denhâ reports in the biography of
his predecessor Marûtâ (died 649) that

> the Nestorians of the East carefully instituted schools in all their villages,
> which were regularly visited by them. There they introduced songs,
> hymns, antiphons and the singing of psalms. Thus they led the simple in-
> to error and sought to bewitch the ears of lay people, who are easily led
> astray by hymns and melodies.[192]

The monasteries which were dedicated to the instruction of boys in psalm and hymn singing in schools specially set up by them demonstrate that such schools were probably primarily concerned with ecclesiastical singing and not merely with influencing domestic life.[193]

Yet the institutions of the heretics were not able to dilute the joy which the faithful took in boys' singing, and what happened here was quite other than it was with the singing of women. The Church made use of boys' singing and gave it a liturgical character. The employment of choir boys as lectors, moreover, strengthened this development and gave the young singers an ecclesiastical consecration.

8. SINGING AS DIVINE WORSHIP IN THE FOURTH AND FIFTH CENTURIES. LITURGY AND ART.

The earliest of the Church Fathers frequently emphasized the beauty and euphony of the human voice, which no instruments could surpass, in contrast to the cultic music of the pagans. Instruments were considered lifeless and soulless, whereas the human voice was a living means of glorifying God. This was a thought to which Clement of Alexandria in particular gave expression.[194] Chrysostom explains:

> No cithara, no flute, or any other musical instrument produces such a [lovely] sound, which one can perceive, than when those holy ones [the monks] sing in deepest silence and solitude.[195]

In contrast to the Christian people's joy in singing and the growing melodic development of liturgical song, many ecclesiastical writers of the fourth and fifth centuries began to fear that the prayerful character of singing could suffer because of too great an artistic elaboration. They were concerned lest the aesthetic predominate in the liturgy to the detriment of souls. Chrysostom, alluding to this, remarks that God has absolutely no need of singing but that he only permits it as a concession to men's weakness:

> For as he accepted sacrifices without needing them (as he says: "If I were hungry I would not tell you") but rather because he wished to give men the opportunity of praising him, so he also accepts hymns, not because he needs beautiful sounds but because his wish is our salvation.[196]

And again:

> Since God saw the frivolity of many men, their aversion to reading spiritual things and their disinclination for the effort that goes with it, he wished to make this effort more pleasant and less perceptible and [therefore] he joined melody to the Word of God so that they [men], being

spiritually influenced by the rhythm of the melody, would send up holy hymns to him with great willingness. For nothing at all so edifies and gives wings to the soul, looses it from the earth and the body's fetters and makes it so contemplative and contemptuous of earthly things as the melody of music and a godly and rhythmic song.[197]

According to this view, singing and melody were conceived of as concessions to man's weaknesses. This is a further development of the idea which Chrysostom expresses in regard to instrumental music in his exposition of Psalm 150.[198] The same notion is found in the pseudo-Justinian *Quaestiones et responsiones ad orthodoxos.*[199]

In the West it was primarily Augustine who was intent on not letting melodic beauty become the main concern in ecclesiastical singing. He permitted singing only for the sake of the text. In his *Confessions* he tells how powerfully the liturgical singing in Milan had struck him:

> I confess now that in melodies which your words enliven and which are sung with a sweet and practiced voice I find a little rest, not such that I cling to them but that I may leave off when I wish. Yet with those words by which they are enlivened, so that they gain entry with me, they look for a place of honor in my heart, and I can hardly show them a worthy one. For sometimes it seems to me that I give them more honor than they deserve—when I feel our spirits moved to flaming devotion more piously and ardently by those same holy words when they are sung than when they are not sung, and when I feel that all the affections of our spirit have, according to their diversity, proper modes of voice and song which are stirred up by I know not what strange relationship. But the pleasure of my flesh, which must not be permitted to enervate the spirit, often causes me to fall.... Sometimes, however, being too cautious of this very danger, I err by overmuch severity—so greatly in fact that I wish all the melodies of the sweet chants with which David's psalter is accompanied would be banished from my ears and from the Church herself. Then the safer course seems to me to be what I remember was often told me about Athanasius, Bishop of Alexandria, who made the reader of the psalm utter it with so slight an inflection that it was nearer to speaking than to singing. But when I recall the tears that I shed upon hearing the singing of the Church in the first days of my recovered faith, and that now I am moved not by the singing but by what is sung when it is sung with a clear voice and the proper modulation, I again acknowledge the great utility of this institution. So I waver between the danger of sensual pleasure and the experience of wholesomeness, but I rather approve of the custom of singing in Church, although I do not offer an irrevocable opinion on it, so that by what pleases the ears the weaker spirit may rise to the feelings of devotion.

Hence, according to Augustine, ecclesiastical singing is only to be borne with out of consideration for men. That the artistic aspect is no concern of God's is expressed in his words:

> Voce cantamus, ut nos excitemus,
> Corde cantamus, ut illi [Deo] placeamus.[201]

What has been said above proves that this was not merely an individual point of view. It was a position which, according to Augustine, Athanasius was able to impose on the Alexandrian liturgy. Most significant for us, though, is the fact that in the Orient, about the year 400, this idea was embodied in a canon. In the so-called *Canons of Basil* we read in canon 97 that

> those who sing psalms at the altar shall not sing with pleasure but with wisdom; they shall sing nothing but psalms.[202]

9. The Doctrine of Katanyxis. Oriental Monasticism as Inimical to Artistic Singing. The Character of Oriental Piety.

Augustine's reference to the fact that Athanasius opposed any melodic elaboration in Alexandrian liturgical singing and allowed only a recitative delivery of the psalms and hymns[203] suggests that the struggle between the conservative and the progressive camps regarding liturgical singing was still not conclusively terminated. Augustine himself expressly noted that he did not wish to make a final judgment on whether artistically arranged liturgical music should be approved or disapproved over against a recitative execution. It is important now to see how representatives of the opposing opinions clashed almost daily in the East and produced a cleavage between monastic and popular piety.

In the *Apophthegmeta Patrum*, an ancient collection of sayings of primitive abbots and patriarchs, we read of the opposition of Pambo, an abbot of the Nitrian desert (whose death, according to C. Butler, fell between the years 385 and 390[204]), to the introduction of musical innovations which were practiced in the Church of Alexandria:

> The Abbot Pambo sent his disciple to Alexandria to sell their [the monks'] handiwork. This disciple spent sixteen days in the city, as he told us. At night he slept in a room in the church,[205] in the aisle of the holy Apostle Mark. After he had observed the liturgy of the church he returned to the elder [Pambo]. But he had also learned *troparia* [in Alexandria]. The elder spoke to him [after his return]: "Son, I see that you are disturbed. Were you beset by a temptation in the city?" The brother

answered: "Father, we spend our days here serenely and we sing neither canons nor *troparia*. But when I came to Alexandria I saw the choirs in the church and how they sing, and I became very sad that we do not sing canons and *troparia*." Then the elder said to him: "Woe to us, my son! The days have come when monks turn away from the enduring nourishment which the Holy Spirit gives them and surrender themselves to singing. What kind of contrition (κατάνυξις) is that? How can tears come from the singing of *troparia*? How can a monk possess contrition if he stays in the church or in his cell and raises his voice like the lowing of the cattle? For when we stand in God's sight we must be most contrite and not presumptuous. Monks have not come into this desert to place themselves before God in pride and presumption, to sing melodic songs and make rhythmic tunes, to shake their hands and stamp their feet. Our duty is to pray to God in holy fear and trembling, with tears and sighing, with devotion and vigilance, with modesty and a humble voice. See, I tell you, my son, the days will come when Christians will destroy the books of the holy Evangelists, the holy Apostles and the inspired Prophets, and they will rip up the Holy Scriptures and compose *troparia* in their place.[206]

This text is very important for the history of liturgical music. It demonstrates the use of *troparia* and canons in the liturgy of the Alexandrian Church. However, such a highly developed situation appears rather early for Pambo's time, so that we are justified in having doubts about the early dating of the text. The daily opposition between the monastic ideal of piety and the worship of the ordinary Christians, though, is significant. Pambo was resolutely opposed to melodic singing because it hindered katanyxis, the spirit of contrition and penance. Tears were the duty of monks. This basic idea is also expressed in the name which the Persian monks were given — *abîlê*, or "the weeping ones."[207] John of Ephesus speaks of the same conception of piety among the Monophysite monks.[208] John the Nasirean, at the end of his work, would pass the rest of the day and night in an unbroken vigil, praying with such unceasing tears and violent weeping that his eyelids disappeared.[209]

The singing of the psalms was perfectly suited to bring about sentiments like these, as the Fathers of the Church frequently remarked. Basil, for example, notes that the psalms could draw tears even from a person with a heart of stone.[210] Gregory Nazianzus narrates that the Emperor Valens was deeply moved when he attended Basil's liturgy in Caesarea, and the singing of the psalms struck his ear like thunder.[211] But in Pambo's view the elaborate and melodically adorned singing presented an obstacle to katanyxis. Isidore of Pelusium fought against the singing of women for the same reason, because it produced no feeling of contrition but only succeeded in arousing the passions.[212]

Such views had already made an appearance in the first century with Philo:

> And when the sense of hearing surrenders to a beautiful voice, is the spirit able to think anything becoming?[213]

The musical-aesthetic doctrines of Neoplatonism had the same tendency. Porphyry, for example, sharply attacks the music which is connected with spectacles and dances because the sensual fascination which it exerts on man hinders the mind in its thinking.[214] Augustine's point of view, as it was portrayed in the previous chapter, was closely related to this opinion. The man who gives in to the beauty of singing or of any other kind of music thereby falls into the power of sensuality and abandons true spiritual interiority. The ideas which are attributed to the Abbot Pambo in the *Apophthegmata* were not purely personal but rather represented the common position in Oriental monastic circles.

In the so-called *Plerophoria* of Bishop John of Maiûma, a writing which, according to A. Baumstark,[215] appeared about 515, we read:

> A brother asked the Abbot Silvanus: "Father, how do I begin to acquire katanyxis? I am much plagued by acedia and sleep. And when I rise at night I have to struggle a great deal and can say no psalm without singing *echoi* [melodies], nor can I overcome my weariness." And the elder answered: "My son, your praying of the psalms with *echoi* is presumptuous and dangerous, for that is as much as saying that you sing. But [the true] brother does not sing, for singing stiffens and hardens the heart and does not permit the soul to experience katanyxis. Thus, if you wish to achieve katanyxis, do not sing, and when you are ready to pray your spirit should search out the power of the verse and you should reflect that you are standing in the presence of God, who searches out the heart and the loins. And when you rise up from sleep you should first praise God with your mouth and not immediately begin the canon. But when you come out from your cell pray the Creed and the Lord's Prayer; and when you go into it begin with the canon slowly and deliberately, while considering with sighs your sins and the punishment that you must suffer for them."
>
> Then the brother said: "Father, since I am alone I sing the office of the canons and the hours and the *oktoëchos*." And the elder replied: "This is why katanyxis and sorrow flee from you. Consider the great Fathers, how they began unlearned and without the knowledge of anything but a few psalms. They knew neither *echoi* nor *troparia* and yet they shone like stars in the cosmos because of their virtue. The Abbot Paul, and An-

thony, and Paul the Simple, the Abbot Pambo and Apollo and all who came after are witnesses to my words. They who even brought the dead to life and possessed power over the demons had nothing to do with songs, *troparia* and *echoi*, but they passed their time in prayer and fasting. For man cannot be saved by beautiful singing but only by the fear of God and the observance of the commands of Christ. Singing, on the contrary, has already dragged many down to the baser things of the world. And it has stirred up not only wordly people to unchastity and the passions but even priests. My son, singing is a thing for people of the world, and that is also why the people come together in the churches. See, my son, how many choirs there are in heaven, but nowhere does it stand written of them that they sing the *oktoëchos*, but only that one choir sings the Alleluia unceasingly and the other the *Holy, holy Lord Sabaoth.* . . . Therefore be of a simple spirit and God will give you katanyxis."[216]

We have still another text from eastern Syrian monasticism. When Mar Isho'jahb III became patriarch in 647 (or 650) he wanted to build a school in the vicinity of the monastery of Abbot Rabban Kamisho', in which children also could be instructed in singing. Rabban Kamisho' thereupon assembled the monks, went with them to Mar Isho'jahb and said to him:

> It is not for us ascetics to be disturbed as we sit in our cells by the singing of Alleluias, psalms, antiphons and the hymns of children and night-watchers. We have neither heard nor read that this ever happened in any monastery of the Fathers. Our vocation is what we have learned from the Scriptures and received from our Father, Mar Jacob — to weep and be sorrowful, sitting in our cells. For neither in his life nor in his death did he command us to teach each other singing or recitation. Cease from making us school children again. We wish to sit alone in our cells and read. If you want to build schools, behold: all the cities and towns and their territory, the whole country of Persia is under your jurisdiction. Build where you wish. But in this monastery no school will be built, or else we will all depart.[217]

Since the patriarch would not give up his plan the monks took their relics and left.

How long such views held sway in the Orient is made clear from a text published by A. Mingana.[218] The Nestorian metropolitan of Amida, Barsalibi (died 1171), was asked by the monk Rabban Ishô', who had been reconciled to Greek theology and the Greek rite, to join the Melchites. Barsalibi answered with a treatise in ten chapters in which, among other things, he told Rabban Ishô', who had alluded to the melodic songs, canons, *kathismata*, *stichera* and the *oktoëchos* of the Greek liturgy, that one does not enter heaven by *kathismata* or *stichera* but by good works; that at the time of the Apostles there were no musical modes; and that the Greeks had borrowed their melodies, which are of little value for believers and merely amuse those who sing them, from the pagans.[219]

Thus we have an example of the fact that the views of the monks also won support in the episcopacy. They refused to favor any elaboration of ecclesiastical music because of their conception of piety and worship. Despite this, in the struggle for the further development of Church music on the one hand or the cessation of such development on the other, the practice of the Church emerged victorious, and the monks later accepted the innovations into their liturgy.[220]

In the text cited above from the *Apophthegmata*[221] Pambo judges hand-clapping and foot-stamping during liturgical singing very severely. This recalls a report of Theodoret concerning the Meletians who had settled in Egypt:

> They also devised those ridiculous [usages], daily purifying their bodies with water to the accompaniment of hand-clapping and a kind of dance, during which they sang hymns and shook little bells that were fastened on a piece of wood and did other such things. Therefore the great Athanasius was continually fighting with them.[222]

The custom of hand-clapping during singing remained a primitive substitute for rhythmical instruments such as the tambourine or the drum among the Orientals. Fulcherius of Chartres, who was present at the Holy Saturday solemnity of lights in the Church of the Holy Sepulchre in Jerusalem, noted that the participants in the liturgy began to accompany the singing of the clergy by clapping their hands as soon as the light appeared.[223] According to A. v. Maltzew, the custom of clapping while singing is still practiced in the Ethiopian Church.[224] The Greeks in Jerusalem also use this kind of accompaniment to the singing on certain feasts.[225]

In general it was in the East that the varying notions about the musical elaboration of the liturgy conflicted most sharply with one another, whereas in the West instrumental music was assigned some part in worship. In fact instrumental music is found today even in those places which had previously been most unfavorable to any kind of music — among the Copts, for instance. A. J. Butler, describing his travels in Egypt, said that the singing in the monastery of Deir el-Baramûs was accompanied by cymbals and triangles.[226] Duke Johann

Georg of Saxony attended a liturgy in the same monastery, and the singing was accompanied by cymbals. From the monastery of Deir es-Suriani he reported that at communion time the monks joined in a festive song, to the accompaniment of cymbals and triangles.[227] According to Butler, this instrumental music is customary in all the old Egyptian churches.

Butler feels that this instrumental music came from pagan liturgy, and there is much to be said for that opinion.[228] The action of Athanasius in Alexandria as well as the fact that the Meletians even in Theodoret's time practiced music which was taken over from the pagans makes it easy to believe that this music came from pagan liturgy. Even the sistrum of the cult of Isis found its way into the Ethiopian Christian liturgy.[229] Popular tradition thus showed itself more powerful than the inflexibility of the monastery.

NOTES

1. O. Casel, "Die λογικὴ θυσία der antiken Mystik in christlich-liturgischer Umdeutung," in *Jahrbuch für Liturgiewissenschaft* 4 (1924), 37 ff. On Christian "adoration in spirit" cf. A. Dohmes, "Der pneumatische Character des Kultgesanges nach frühchristlichen Zeugnissen," in *Vom christlichen Mysterium. Gesammelte Arbeiten zum Gedächtnis von O. Casel* (Düsseldorf 1951), pp. 35–53. R. Schönig, "Zur Theologie des christlichen Kultgesanges," in *Musicus Magister. Festgabe für Th. Schrems* (Regensberg 1963), pp. 16–43. F.J. Basurco, *El canto cristiano en la tradición primitiva* (Madrid 1966). O. Söhngen, *Theologie der Musik* (Kassel 1967), pp. 12–25. W. Arlt, "Sakral und Profan in der Geschichte der abendländischen Musik," in *Archiv für Liturgiewissenschaft* 10 (1968), 376–377.

2. J. Geffken, "Komposition und Entstehungszeit der Oracula Sibyllina," in TU NF 8, 1 (Leipzig 1902), 38.

3. *Oracula Sibyllina* 8, 496 (GCS 173 Geffken): ἀλλ' ἁγναῖς πραπίδεσσι γεγηθότες εὔφρονι θυμῷ / — — μειλιχίοις ψαλμοῖσι θεοπρεπέεσσί τε μολπαῖς / ἄφθιτον ἐξυμνεῖν σε καὶ ἄψευστον κελόμεσθα.

4. *Ibid.* 8, 113 (GCS 147): οὐ θυσιῶν σπονδαῖς ἐπὶ βωμοῖς αἷμα χέουσιν· τύμπανον οὐκ ἠχεῖ, οὐ κύμβαλον...οὐκ αὐλὸς πολύτρητος, ἔχοντα φρενοβλάβον αὐδήν, οὐ σκολιοῦ σύριγμα φέρον μίμημα δράκοντος. οὐ σάλπιγξ πολέμων ἀγγέλτρια βαρβαρόφωνος.

5. Tertullian, *De oratione* 28 (CSEL 20, 198 Reifferscheid-Wissowa): hanc [scil. hostiam] de toto corde devotam, fide pastam, veritate curatam, innocentia integram, castitate mundam, agapen coronatam cum pompa operum bonorum inter psalmos et hymnis deducere ad dei altare debemus omnia nobis a deo impetraturam.

6. Clement of Alexandria, *Paidagogos* 2, 4 (GCS Clem. I 181 Stählin): οἱ δὲ ἐν αὐλοῖς καὶ ψαλτηρίοις καὶ χοροῖς καὶ ὀρχήμασιν καὶ κροτάλοις Αἰγυπτίων καὶ τοιαύταις ῥαθυμίαις σάλοι ἄτακτοι καὶ ἀπρεπεῖς καὶ ἀπαίδευτοι κομιδῇ γίγνοιντο ἂν κυμβάλοις καὶ τυμπάνοις ἐξηχούμενοι καὶ τοῖς τῆς ἀπάτης ὀργάνοις περιφοφούμενοι. *Ibid.* (GCS Clem. I 182): Σύριγξ μὲν οὖν ποιμέσιν ἀπονενεμήσθω, αὐλὸς δὲ ἀνθρώποις δεισιδαίμοσιν εἰς εἰδωλολατρείας σπεύδουσιν. καὶ γὰρ ὡς ἀληθῶς ἀποπεμπτέα τὰ ὄργανα ταῦτα νηφαλίου συμποσίου.

7. *Recognitiones* 4, 13 (120 Gersdorf): Sed processu temporis, Dei quidem cultus et iustitia ab infidelibus et impiis corrumpitur, sicut paulo post apertius ostendemus. Perversae autem et erraticae religiones introducuntur, quibus se plurima pars hominum per occasionem feriarum et solemnitatum dederunt, potus instaurantes et convivia, tibiasque ac fistula et citharas ac diversa genera musicorum sectantes, et semetipsos per omnia temulentiae ac luxuriae propinantes. Hinc omnis error accepit originem.

8. Arnobius, *Adversus nationes* 7, 36 (CSEL 4, 270 Reifferscheid): Vos aeris tinnitibus et tibiarum sonis, vos equorum curriculis et theatralibus ludis persuasum habetis deos et delectari et adfici irasque aliquando conceptas eorum ista satisfactione molliri: nos inconveniens ducimus, quinimmo incredibile iudicamus, eos qui gradibus mille genus omne virtutum perfectionis transierint summitate in voluptatibus habere atque in deliciis res eas quas homo sapiens rideat et quae non aliis videantur continere aliquid gratiae quam infantibus parvulis et trivialiter et populariter institutis.

9. *Ibid.* 7, 32 (CSEL 4, 265): ...irae numinum offensionesque placentur...etiamne aeris tinnitibus et quassationibus cymbalorum? etiamne tympanis? etiamne symphoniis? quid? Efficiunt crepitus scabillorum, ut cum eos audierint numina, honorifice secum existiment actum et ferventes animos irarum oblivione deponant?

10. *Ibid.* 2, 23 (CSEL 4, 67): Quid si cithara, tibia, argentum aes aurum codex radius liber? Quid instrumenta si cetera quibus vita succingitur et continetur humana?

11. *Ibid.* 2, 42 (CSEL 4, 82): Idcirco animas misit, ut res sancti atque augustissimi nominis symphoniacas agerent et fistulatorias hic artes, ut inflandis bucculas distenderent tibiis.

12. Gregory Nazianzus, *Oratio* 5, 25 (PG 35, 708/709): μηδὲ πρόθυρα καλλωπίσωμεν· μὴ τῷ αἰσθητῷ φωτὶ καταλαμπέσθωσαν οἱ οἰκίαι, μηδὲ συναυλίαις καὶ κρότοις περιηχείσθωσαν. οὗτος μὲν γὰρ Ἑλληνικῆς ἱερομανίας ὁ νόμος· ἡμεῖς δὲ μὴ τούτοις τὸν θεὸν γεραίρωμεν, μηδὲ τὸν παρόντα καιρὸν ἐπαίρωμεν, οἷς οὐκ ἄξιον, ἀλλὰ ψυχῆς καθαρότητι, καὶ διανοίας φαιδρότητι, καὶ λύχνοις τοῖς ὅλον τὸ σῶμα φωτίζουσι τῆς Ἐκκλησίας, θείοις λέγω θεωρήμασι καὶ νοήμασι, ἐπί τε τὴν ἱερὰν λυχνίαν ἐγειρομένοις, καὶ πᾶσαν τὴν οἰκουμένην καταλάμπουσι...Ἀναλάβωμεν ὕμνους ἀντὶ τυμπάνων, ψαλμῳδίαν ἀντὶ τῶν αἰσχρῶν λυγισμάτων τε καὶ ᾀσμάτων.

12a. On music in the Jewish liturgy cf. D. Wohlenberg, *Kultmusik in Israel* (Diss. Hamburg 1967). There is still considerable discussion concerning the influence of Jewish liturgical music on the music of the Christian liturgy. Cf. N.H. Emanuel, *The Influence of Ancient Hebrew Music on Gregorian Chant* (Diss. Rochester 1935), who holds for a dependence on the part of Christian music, as well as E. Werner, *The Sacred Bridge. The Interdependence of Liturgy and Music in Synagogue and Church during the First Millenium* (London-New York 1959) and S. Corbin, *L'Église à la conquête de sa musique* (Paris 1960). On the other hand G. Wille, *Musica Romana. Die Bedeutung der Musik im Leben der Römer* (Amsterdam 1967), opposes the notion that the music of the early Church in the West derived from the Synagogue; he appeals to the Oxyrhynchos Papyrus 1786 as demonstrating the organic development of ecclesiastical music from Greek music of the classical era.

13. Cf. F.J. Dölger, *Sol Salutis* (Münster ² 1925), p. 19, n. 2.

14. Gregory Nazianzus, *Oratio* 5, 25 (PG 35, 709): Εἰ γὰρ ὀρχήσασθαι δεῖ σε, ὡς πανηγυριστὴν καὶ φιλέορτον, ὄρχησαι μέν, ἀλλὰ μὴ τὴν Ἡρωδιάδος ὄρχησιν τῆς ἀσχήμονος, ἧς ἔργον Βαπτιστοῦ θάνατος· ἀλλὰ τὴν Δαβὶδ ἐπὶ τῇ καταπαύσει τῆς κιβωτοῦ, ἣν ἡγοῦμαι τῆς εὐκινήτου καὶ πολυστρόφου κατὰ θεὸν πορείας εἶναι μυστήριον.

15. Cf. Introduction, n. 1.

16. Theodoret, *Graecorum affectionum curatio* 7, 16 (185 Raeder): Ἐν γὰρ δὴ τῇ Αἰγύπτῳ πλεῖστον ὅσον τὸν Ἰσραὴλ διατρίψαντα χρόνον καὶ τὰ πονηρὰ τῶν ἐγχωρίων εἰσδεξάμενον

ἔθη καὶ θύειν εἰδώλοις καὶ δαίμοσι παρ' ἐκείνων μεμαθηκότα καὶ παίζειν καὶ χορεύειν καὶ ὀργάνοις μουσικοῖς ἐπιτέρπεσθαι, τούτων ἐν ἕξει γενόμενον ἐλευθερῶσαι θελήσας, θύειν μὲν ξυνεχώρησεν, ἀλλ' οὐ πάντα θύειν, οὐδέ γε τοῖς ψευδωνύμοις τῶν Αἰγυπτίων θεοῖς, ἀλλ' αὐτῷ μόνῳ τοὺς Αἰγυπτίων προσφέρειν θεούς. *Ibid.* 7, 21 (186): τὰ τῶν εὐήχων ὀργάνων ἠνέσχετο, οὐ τῇ τούτων ἁρμονίᾳ τερπόμενος, ἀλλὰ κατὰ βραχὺ παύων τῶν εἰδώλων τὸν πλάνον. *Ibid.* 7, 34 (190): "Α γὰρ δὴ περὶ τούτων ἐν τῷ νόμῳ προσετέταχει, τῆς ἐκείνων ἦν ἀναισθησίας, οὐ τῆς αὐτοῦ χρείας τε καὶ βουλήσεως. Ταῦτα καὶ ἑτέρωθι λέγει: »Τὰ ὁλοκαυτώματα ὑμῶν οὐκ ἔστι δεκτά. καὶ αἱ θυσίαι ὑμῶν οὐχ ἡδυνάν μοι« καὶ αὖ πάλιν βοᾷ: »ἀπόστησον ἀπ' ἐμοῦ ἦχον ᾠδῶν σου, καὶ φωνῆς ὀργάνων σου οὐκ ἀκούσομαι« Καὶ ἄλλα δὲ πάμπολλα τοιαῦτα ἔστιν εὑρεῖν, δηλοῦντα σαφῶς, ὡς οὐ δεόμενος θυσιῶν ὁ Θεὸς οὐδὲ καπνῷ καὶ κνίση καὶ τοῖς μουσικοῖς ὀργάνοις ἐπιτερπόμενος ταῦτα τελεῖσθαι προσέταξεν, ἀλλὰ τῆς ἐκείνων προμηθούμενος ἰατρείας.

17. Theodoret, *In Ps.* 150 (PG 80, 1996): Τούτοις οἱ Λευῖται πάλαι τοῖς ὀργάνοις ἐχρῶντο ἐν τῷ θείῳ νεῷ τὸν θεὸν ἀνυμνοῦντες· οὐκ ἐπειδὴ θεὸς ἐτέρπετο τῇ τούτων ἠχῇ, ἀλλ' ἐπειδὴ τῶν γιγνομένων τὸν σκοπὸν ἀπεδέχετο. Ὅτι γὰρ ᾠδαῖς καὶ κρούμασι τὸ θεῖον οὐκ ἐπιτέτερπται, ἀκούομεν αὐτοῦ λέγοντος Ἰουδαίοις: »Ἀπόστησον ἀπ' ἐμοῦ ἦχον ᾠδῶν σου, καὶ φωνῆς ὀργάνων σου οὐκ ἀκούσομαι.« Ταῦτα τοίνυν γίνεσθαι συνεχώρησε, τῆς τῶν εἰδώλων αὐτοὺς πλάνης ἀπαλλάξαι θελήσας. Ἐπειδὴ γὰρ φιλοπαίγμονές τινες ἦσαν, καὶ φιλογέλωτες, ταῦτα δὲ ἅπαντα ἐν τοῖς εἰδώλων ἐπετελεῖτο ναοῖς, συνεχώρησε ταῦτα, διὰ τούτων αὐτοὺς ἐφελκόμενος, καὶ τῇ ἐλάττονι βλάβῃ κωλύων, τὴν μείζονα, καὶ διὰ τῶν ἀτελῶν προπαιδεύων τὰ τέλεια.

18. Chrysostom, *Homil. in Ps.* 150 (PG 55, 497): καὶ τὰ ὄργανα δὲ ἐκεῖνα διὰ τοῦτο ἐπετέτραπτο τότε, διά τε τὴν ἀσθένειαν αὐτῶν, καὶ διὰ τὸ χυρνᾶν αὐτοὺς εἰς ἀγάπην καὶ συμφωνίαν, καὶ ἐγείρειν αὐτῶν τὴν διάνοιαν μεθ' ἡδονῆς ποιεῖν τὰ τὴν ὠφέλειαν παρεχόμενα, καὶ εἰς πολλὴν βούλεσθαι αὐτοὺς ἄγειν σπουδὴν διὰ τῆς τοιαύτης ψυχαγωγίας. Τὸ γὰρ βάναυσον αὐτῶν καὶ ῥάθυμον καὶ ἀναπεπτωκὸς σοφιζόμενος ὁ θεός, ἀφυπνίζειν αὐτοὺς ταύτῃ μεθώδευσε τῇ σοφίᾳ ἀνακεράσας τῷ πόνῳ τῆς προσεδρίας τὸ ἡδὺ τῆς μελωδίας.

19. Clement of Alexandria, *Paidagogos* 2, 4 (GCS Clem. I 182 Stählin): τοῦ κώμου τούτου τὴν λειτουργίαν τὴν θεϊκὴν διαχωρίζον ψάλλει τὸ πνεῦμα »αἰνεῖτε αὐτὸν ἐν ἤχῳ σάλπιγγος« καὶ γὰρ ἐν ἤχῳ σάλπιγγος ἀναστήσει τοὺς νεκρούς. »αἰνεῖτε αὐτὸν ἐν ψαλτηρίῳ« ὅτι ἡ γλῶττα τὸ ψαλτήριον κυρίου. »καὶ ἐν κιθάρᾳ αἰνεῖτε αὐτόν«, κιθάρα νοείσθω τὸ στόμα.

20. Cf. Eusebius, *In Ps.* 91 (PG 23, 1172 ff). Ambrose, *De Elia et ieiunio* 15 (55) (PL 14, 716). Idem, *Expositio evangelii Lucae* 7, 237 (CSEL 32, 388 Schenkel). Cassiodorus, *Expositio in Ps.* 97 (Maurist ed. 312): Quid est hoc quod instrumenta musica frequenter posita reperimus in psalmis, quae non tam videntur mulcere aurium sensum, sed provocare potius cordis auditum? Sed quoniam ille sonus et modulatio tibiarum a sacris mysteriis nostra nihilominus aetate discessit, restat ut intelligentiam huius rei spiritualiter perquirere debeamus . . . ut dubium non sit haec instrumenta dulcisona probabilium actuum nobis indicare concordiam.

21. Chrysostom, *Homil. in Ps.* 149, 2 (PG 55, 494): Τινὲς μὲν καὶ τούτων τῶν ὀργάνων τὸν λόγον κατὰ ἀναγωγὴν ἐλαμβάνοντες, λέγουσιν ὅτι τὸ μὲν τύμπανον τὴν νέκρωσιν τῆς σαρκὸς ἡμῶν ἐπιζητεῖ, τὸ δὲ ψαλτήριον τὸ πρὸς τόν οὐρανὸν βλέπειν. Καὶ γὰρ ἄνωθεν τὸ ὄργανον τοῦτο κινεῖται, οὐ κάτωθεν ὥσπερ ἡ κιθάρα. Ἐγὼ δὲ ἐκεῖνο ἂν εἴποιμι, ὅτι τὸ παλαιὸν οὕτως ἤγοντο διὰ τῶν ὀργάνων τούτων, διὰ τὴν παχύτητα τῆς διανοίας αὐτῶν, καὶ τὸ ἄρτι ἀπεσπάσθαι ἀπὸ τῶν εἰδώλων. Ὥσπερ οὖν τὰς θυσίας συνεχώρησεν, οὕτω καὶ ταῦτα ἐπέτρεψε, συγκαταβαίνων αὐτῶν τῇ ἀσθενείᾳ. Ἀπαιτεῖ τοίνυν ἐνταῦθα, τὸ μεθ' ἡδονῆς ᾄδειν, τοῦτο γὰρ ἐστι τὸ Αἰνεσάτωσαν τὸ ὄνομα αὐτοῦ ἐν χορῷ, τὸ μετὰ συμφωνίας, τὸ μετὰ βίου καθαροῦ.

22. Isidore of Pelusium, *Epist.* II 176 (PG 78, 628): εἰ θυσιῶν καὶ αἱμάτων ἠνέσχετο τὸ θεῖον διὰ τῶν ἀνθρώπων τὸ τηνικάδε νηπιότητα, τί θαυμάζεις, εἰ καὶ μουσικῆς διὰ κιθάρας καὶ ψαλτηρίου τελουμένης;

23. Philo, *De vita Moysis* I 23 (125 Cohn): ἀριθμοὺς μὲν οὖν καὶ γεωμετρίαν τήν τε

ῥυθμικὴν καὶ ἁρμονικὴν καὶ μετρικὴν θεωρίαν καὶ μουσικὴν τὴν σύμπασαν διά τε χρήσεως ὀργάνων καὶ λόγων τῶν ἐν ταῖς τέχναις καὶ διεξόδοις τοπικωτέραις Αἰγυπτίων οἱ λόγιοι παρεδίδοσαν.

24. Philo, *De specialibus legibus* III 125 (185 Cohn-Wendland): ταῦρον δὲ κατασκευασάμενοι χρυσοῦν, Αἰγυπτιακοῦ μίμημα τύφου, θυσίας ἀνῆγον ἀθύπτους καὶ ἑορτὰς ἀνεόρτους καὶ χοροὺς ἀχορεύτους ἐπετέλουν σὺν ᾠδαῖς καὶ ὕμνοις ἀντὶ θρήνων.

25. Cf. J. Weiss, *Die musikalischen Instrumente des Alten Testamentes* (Graz 1895), p. 94.

26. Herodotus 2, 48 (I 134 Stein): προηγέεται δὲ αὐλός. αἱ δὲ ἕπονται ἀείδουσαι τὸν Διόνυσον. *Ibid.* 2, 60 (I 138): Ἐς μέν νυν Βούβαστιν πόλιν ἐπεὰν κωμίζωνται, ποιεῦσι τοιάδε. πλέουσι τε γὰρ δὴ ἅμα ἄνδρες γυναιξί, καὶ πολλόν τι πλῆθος ἑκατέρων ἐν ἑκάστῃ βάρι. αἱ μέν τινες τῶν γυναικῶν κρόταλα ἔχουσαι κροταλίζουσι, οἱ δὲ αὐλέουσι κατὰ πάντα τὸν πλόον. αἱ δὲ λοιπαὶ γυναῖκες καὶ ἄνδρες ἀείδουσι καὶ τὰς χεῖρας κροτέουσι.

27. Cf. F. Vaněk, "War die griechische Musik mehrstimmig?" in *Festschrift für J. Krâl* (Prague 1913), pp. 215 ff and M. Vogel, "Zum Ursprung der Mehrstimmigkeit," in *Kirchenmusikalisches Jahrbuch* 49 (1965), 57–64.

28. Apuleius, *Florida* III (3 Krüger): Rudibus adhuc musicae saeculis – Hyganis acuto tinnitu et gravibombo concentum musicum miscuit.

29. Plutarch, *De musica* 29, 1141 (VI 514 Bernardakis): Λᾶσος δὲ ὁ Ἑρμιονεὺς εἰς τὴν διθυραμβικὴν ἀγωγὴν μεταστήσας τοὺς ῥυθμοὺς καὶ τῇ τῶν αὐλῶν πολυφωνίᾳ κατακολουθήσας, πλείοσί τε φθόγγοις καὶ διερριμμένοις χρησάμενος εἰς μετάθεσιν τὴν προϋπάρχουσαν ἤγαγε μουσικήν.

30. Cf. H. Abert, *Die Lehre vom Ethos in der griechischen Musik* (Leipzig 1899), p. 58.

31. Plutarch, *Coniugalia praecepta* 11, 139 (I 340 Bernardakis): Ὥσπερ ἂν φθόγγοι δύο σύμφωνοι ληφθῶσι, τοῦ βαρυτέρου γίγνεται τὸ μέλος, οὕτω πᾶσα πρᾶξις ἐν οἰκίᾳ σωφρονούσῃ πράττεται μὲν ὑπ' ἀμφοτέρων ὁμονοούντων, ἐπιφαίνει δὲ τὴν τοῦ ἀνδρὸς ἡγεμονίαν καὶ προαίρεσιν.

32. Varro, *Rerum rust.* 1, 2, 16 (13 Goetz). In general cf. also J. Jéannin, *Mélodies liturgiques syriennes et chaldéennes* (Paris 1922), p. 276. On the use of the flute in antiquity cf. A. Schneider, *Zur Geschichte der Flöte im Altertum* (Zurich 1890), pp. 34 f.

33. Cf. F.J. Dölger, *Die Sonne der Gerechtigkeit und der Schwarze* (Münster 1919), p. 42.

34. Methodius, *Symposium* 3, 7, 67 (GCS 34 Bonwetsch): δύο γὰρ τὰ εἰς ἄκρον ἀλλήλοις ἐναντία ζωὴ καὶ θάνατος, ἀφθαρσία καὶ φθορά. ἰσότης μὲν γάρ ἐστιν ἡ ζωή, ἀνισότης δὲ ἡ φθορά, καὶ ἁρμονία μὲν ἡ δικαιοσύνη καὶ ἡ φρόνησις, ἀναρμοστία δὲ ἡ ἀδικία καὶ ἡ ἀφροσύνη. Cf. Dölger, *ibid.*, pp. 92 f.

34a. Cf. A. Dohmes, "Die Einstimmigkeit des Kultgesanges als Symbol der Einheit," in *Liturgie und Mönchtum* 1 (1948), 67–72.

35. Clement of Alexandria, *Protrepticos* 9 (GCS Clem. I 65 Stählin): εἰς μίαν ἀγάπην συναχθῆναι οἱ πολλοὶ κατὰ τὴν τῆς μοναδικῆς οὐσίας ἕνωσιν σπεύσωμεν. ἀγαθοεργούμενοι ἀναλόγως ἑνότητα διώκωμεν, τὴν ἀγαθὴν ἐκζητοῦντες μονάδα. ἡ δὲ ἐκ πολλῶν ἕνωσις ἐκ πολυφωνίας καὶ διασπορᾶς ἁρμονίαν λαβοῦσα θεϊκὴν μία γίνεται συμφωνία, ἑνὶ χορευτῇ καὶ διδασκάλῳ τῷ λόγῳ ἑπομένη, ἐπ' αὐτὴν τὴν ἀλήθειαν ἀναπαυομένη »᾿Αββᾶ« λέγουσα »ὁ πατήρ«.

36. *Ibid.* 1. (GCS Clem. I 6): καὶ δὴ τὸ ᾆσμα τὸ ἀκήρατον, ἔρεισμα τῶν ὅλων καὶ ἁρμονία τῶν πάντων, ἀπὸ τῶν μέσων ἐπὶ τὰ πέρατα καὶ ἀπὸ τῶν ἄκρων ἐπὶ τὰ μέσα διαταθέν, ἡρμόσατο τόδε τὸ πᾶν, οὐ κατὰ τὴν Θράκιον μουσικήν, τὴν παραπλήσιον Ἰουβάλ, κατὰ δὲ τὴν πάτριον τοῦ θεοῦ βούλησιν, ἣν ἐζήλωσε Δαυίδ.

37. Clement of Alexandria, *Paidagogos* 2, 4 (GCS Clem. I 184 Stählin): καὶ γὰρ ἁρμονίας παραδεκτέον τὰς σώφρονας, ἀπωτάτω ὅτι μάλιστα ἐλαύνοντας τῆς ἐρρωμένης ἡμῶν

διανοίας τὰς ὑγρὰς ὄντως ἁρμονίας, αἵ περὶ τὰς καμπὰς τῶν φθόγγων κακοτεχνοῦσαι εἰς θρύψιν καὶ βωμολοχίαν ἐκδιαιτῶνται· τὰ δὲ αὐστηρὰ καὶ σωφρονικὰ μέλη ἀποτάσσεται ταῖς τῆς μέθης ἀγερωχίαις. καταλειπτέον οὖν τὰς χρωματικὰς ἁρμονίας ταῖς ἀρχρώμοις παροινίαις καὶ τῇ ἀνθοφορούσῃ καὶ ἑταιρούσῃ μουσικῇ. On popular singing in the primitive Christian liturgy cf. J.A. Jungmann, *Liturgisches Erbe und pastorale Gegenwart* (Innsbruck-Munich 1960), pp. 451-464.

38. Cf. J. Kroll, "Die Lehren des Hermes Trismegistos," in *Beiträge zur Geschichte der Philosophie des Mittelalters* 12, 2-4 (Munster 1914), 308 and O. Casel, "Das Gedächtnis des Herrn in der altchristlichen Liturgie," in *Ecclesia Orans* 2 (Freiburg 1922), 31.

39. *Ascensio Isaiae* 7, 15 (107 Charles): et cantabant una voce. *Ibid.* 9, 28 (124): et adoraverunt eum una voce cantantes.

40. *Apocalypsis Petri* (fragment from Akhmin) 19 (85 Preuschen): ἴση δὲ ἦν ἡ δόξα τῶν ἐκεῖ οἰκητόρων καὶ μιᾷ φωνῇ τὸν κύριον θεὸν ἀνευφήμουν εὐφραινόμενοι ἐν ἐκείνῳ τῷ τόπῳ.

41. *Passio SS. Perpetuae et Felicitatis* 12 (81 Gebhardt): καὶ ἠκούσαμεν φωνὴν ἡνωμένην λεγόντων· Ἅγιος, ἅγιος, ἅγιος, ἀκαταπαύστως.

42. Gregory Nazianzus, *Carmina* II 1, 1, 280 (PG 37, 991): Ἀγγελικοί τε χοροὶ ψαλμοῖς θεὸν οἵ γ' ἐρέθουσιν, Ἰστάμενοι, ψυχάς τε θεῷ πέμποντες ἐν ὕμνοις, Πόλλων ἐκ στομάτων ξυνήν ὄπα γηρύοντες.

43. Clement of Rome, *Epist. I ad Corinthios* 34, 5 (53 Funk-Bihlmeyer): καὶ ἡμεῖς οὖν ἐν ὁμοίᾳ ἐπὶ τὸ αὐτὸ συναχθέντες τῇ συνειδήσει ὡς ἐξ ἑνὸς στόματος βοήσωμεν πρὸς αὐτὸν ἐκτενῶς.

44. Cyril of Jerusalem, *Catechesis mystagog.* 5, 6 (PG 33, 1113): Διὰ τοῦτο γὰρ τὴν παραδοθεῖσαν ἡμῖν ἐκ τῶν σεραφὶμ θεολογίαν ταύτην λέγομεν, ὅπως κοινωνοὶ τῆς ὑμνῳδίας ταῖς ὑπερκοσμίοις γενόμεθα στρατιαῖς. On the earthy liturgy as an image of the heavenly and on the singing of the angels cf. R. Hammerstein, *Die Musik der Engel. Untersuchungen zur Musikanschauung des Mittelalters* (Bern-Munich 1962).

45. Origen, *Contra Celsum* 8, 67 (GCS Orig. II 283 Koetschau): ὕμνους γὰρ εἰς μόνον τὸν ἐπὶ πᾶσι λέγομεν θεὸν καὶ τὸν μονογενῆ αὐτοῦ θεὸν λόγον. καὶ ὑμνοῦμεν γε θεὸν καὶ τὸν μονογενῆ αὐτοῦ ὡς καὶ »ἥλιος καὶ σελήνη« καὶ »ἄστρα« καὶ πᾶσα ἡ οὐρανία στρατιά. On the music of the spheres cf. P.R. Coleman-Norton, "Cicero and the Music of the Spheres," in *Classical Journal* 45 (1950), 237-241.

46. Origen, *ibid.* 8, 37 (GCS Orig. II 252): ἀλλ' οἱ μὲν Ἕλληνες Ἑλληνικοῖς οἱ δὲ Ῥωμαῖοι Ῥωμα(ν)ϊκοῖς, καὶ οὕτως ἕκαστος κατὰ τὴν ἑαυτοῦ διάλεκτον εὔχεται τῷ θεῷ καὶ ὑμνεῖ αὐτὸν ὡς δύναται. καὶ ὁ πάσης διαλέκτου κύριος τῶν ἀπὸ πάσης διαλέκτου εὐχομένων ἀκούει ὡς μιᾶς, ἵν' οὕτως ὀναμάσω, φωνῆς, τῆς κατὰ τὰ σημαινόμενα ἀκούων, δηλουμένης ἐκ τῶν ποικίλων διαλέκτων.

47. Clement of Alexandria, *Paidagogos* 2, 4 (GCS Clem. I 184 Stählin): ἀλλὰ καὶ ἐν τοῖς παλαιοῖς Ἕλλησι παρὰ τὰς συμποτικὰς εὐωχίας καὶ τὰς ἐπιφεκαζούσας κύλικας Ἑβραϊκῶν κατ' εἰκόνα ψαλμῶν ᾆσμα τὸ καλούμενον σκολιὸν ᾔδετο, κοινῶς ἁπάντων μιᾷ φωνῇ παιανιζόντων, ἔσθ' ὅτε δὲ καὶ ἐν μέρει περιελιττόντων τὰς προπόσεις τῆς ᾠδῆς· οἱ δὲ μουσικώτεροι αὐτῶν καὶ πρὸς λύραν ᾖδον.

48. Plutarch, *Quaestiones convivales* 1, 5, 615 (IV 9 Bernardakis): πρῶτον μὲν ᾖδον ᾠδὴν τοῦ θεοῦ κοινῶς ἅπαντες μιᾷ φωνῇ παιανίζοντες, δεύτερον δ'ἐφεξῆς ἑκάστῳ μυρσίνης παραδιδομένης, ἣν αἴσακον οἶμαι διὰ τὸ ᾄδει τὸν δεξάμενον ἐκάλουν· ἐπὶ δὲ τούτῳ λύρας περιφερομένης, ὁ μὲν πεπαιδευμένος ἐλάμβανε καὶ ᾖδεν ἁρμοζόμενος.

49. Athanasius, *Apologia ad imperatorem Constantium* (PG 25, 616): καὶ πῶς ἦν βέλτιον κατὰ μέρος καὶ διηρημένως τὸν λαὸν μετ' ἐπικινδύνου συνοχῆς, ἤ ὄντος ἤδη τόπου τοῦ δυναμένου δέξασθαι πάντας, ἐν αὐτῷ συνελθεῖν καὶ μίαν καὶ τὴν αὐτὴν μετὰ συμφωνίας τῶν λαῶν

γενέσθαι τὴν φωνήν; Τοῦτο βέλτιον ἦν· τοῦτο γὰρ καὶ τὴν ὁμοψυχίαν ἐδείκνυε τοῦ πλήθους· οὕτω καὶ ταχέως ὁ θεὸς ἐπακούει. Εἰ γὰρ κατὰ τὴν αὐτοῦ Σωτῆρος ἐπαγγελίαν, ἐὰν δύο συμφωνήσαιεν περὶ παντός, οὗ ἂν αἰτήσωνται, γενήσεται αὐτοῖς· τί, ἐὰν τοσούτων λαῶν συνελθόντων μία γένηται φωνή, λεγόντων τῷ θεῷ τὸ 'Ἀμήν; On the acclamation ἐξ ἑνὸς στόματος cf. E. Peterson, ΕΙΣ ΘΕΟΣ. Epigraphische, formgeschichtliche und religionsgeschichtliche Untersuchungen (Forschungen zur Religion und Literatur des Alten und Neuen Testaments herausgegeben von Bultmann und Gunkel N. F. 24) (Göttingen 1926), 192, n. 1. When Peterson explains the fact that the characteristics of the acclamatory calls and the hymns merged into one another by noting that this was the age of the prose hymn, we may see in the ἐξ ἑνὸς στόματος still more evidence for ecclesiastical singing in one voice.

50. Ambrose, Enarratio in Ps. 1 (PL 14, 924): pignus pacis atque concordiae, citharae modo ex diversis et disparibus vocibus unam exprimens cantilenam.

51. Basil, Homilia in Ps. 1, 2 (PG 29, 212): Τίς γὰρ ἔτι ἐχθρὸν ἡγεῖσθαι δύναται μεθ' οὗ μίαν ἀφῆκε πρὸς θεὸν τὴν φωνήν; ῞Ωστε καὶ τὸ μέγιστον τῶν ἀγαθῶν τὴν ἀγάπην ἡ ψαλμῳδία παρέχεται οἰονεὶ σύνδεσμόν τινα πρὸς τὴν ἕνωσιν τὴν συνῳδίαν ἐπινοήσασα, καὶ εἰς ἑνὸς χοροῦ συμφωνίαν τὸν λαὸν συναρμόζουσα.

52. Chrysostom, Homilia 36 in Epist. I ad Corinthios (PG 61, 313): Ἀλλ' οὐ δύνασαι σιγᾶν; Οὐκοῦν ἔξιθι, ἵνα μὴ καὶ ἑτέροις γένη βλάβη. Καὶ γὰρ μίαν ἐν ἐκκλησίᾳ δεῖ φωνὴν εἶναι ἀεί, καθάπερ ἑνὸς ὄντος στόματος.

53. Confessio Cypriani 17, in S. Cypriani opera (Maurist ed.), CCCX: Εἶθ' οὕτως ἀπήειμεν εἰς τὴν ἐκκλησίαν, καὶ ἰδεῖν τὸν χόρον οὐρανίων ἐοικότα θεοῦ ἀνθρώπων ἢ χορῷ ἀγγέλων θεῷ ἀναμέλποντι. Ἑβραϊκήν τε λέξιν ἑκάστῳ στίχῳ ἀπαγαγόντες μιᾷ φωνῇ, ὡς πείθεσθαι αὐτὸς μὴ εἶναι ἀνθρώπους, ἀλλὰ φύσιν λογικὴν σύγκλυδον ἀπηχοῦσαι θαυμάσιον ἦχον, ὃν οἱ προφῆται θανόντες διὰ τῶν ζώντων πάλιν προεφήτευον. Cf. F.J. Dölger, Sol Salutis (Münster ² 1925), p. 132.

54. K. Ahrens and G. Krüger, Die sogenannte Kirchengeschichte des Zacharias Rhetor (Scriptores sacri et profani III) (Leipzig 1899), p. 83. The custom of holding hands while singing a hymn was practiced among the Manichaeans and may be seen in Gnostic literature (e.g., Acta Joh. 94). Cf. Peterson, ΕΙΣ ΘΕΟΣ 139, n. 2. As I have been informed by Prof. R. Stapper, a similar custom of holding hands while praying exists today among the Mennonites.

55. Chrysostom, In Joannem homilia 79 (PG 59, 426): Διὰ τοῦτο καὶ ἐν τοῖς μυστηρίοις ἀσπαζόμεθα ἀλλήλους, ἵνα οἱ πολλοὶ γενώμεθα ἕν.

56. Published by the Egypt Exploration Society, The Oxyrhynchos Papyrus Part XV, ed. with translation and notes by B.P. Grenfell and A.S. Hunt (London: 1922), no. 1786, pp. 21–25. The hymn is also printed with modern notation according to the paraphrase of H. Stuart Jones in C. Wessely, Les plus anciens monuments du Christianisme écrits sur papyrus (PO XVIII 3) (1924), pp. 506–508.

57. Cf. O. Ursprung, "Der Hymnus aus Oxyrhynchos, das älteste Denkmal christlicher (Kirchen?) Musik," in Bulletin de la Société "Union Musicologique" 3 (1923), 129 and idem, "Der Hymnus aus Oxyrhynchos (Ende des III. Jahrh.; ägyptischer Papyrusfund) im Rahmen unserer kirchenmusikalischen Frühzeit," in Theologie und Glaube 18 (1926), 390.

58. T. Reinach, "Un ancêtre de la musique de l'église," in Revue musicale III (1922), 9.

59. Cf. O. Ursprung, "Der Hymnus aus Oxyrhynchos, das älteste Denkmal...," 129.

59a. ὁμοῦ πᾶσαί τε θεοῦ λόγιμοι α...αρ...π(ρ)υτανηω σιγάτω μηδ' ἄστρα φαεσφόρα λ(ειπ)ε[σ]θων...ποταμῶν ῥοθίων πᾶσαι ὑμνούντων δ'ἡμῶν πατέρα χ' υἱὸν χ' ἅγιον πνεῦμα πᾶσαι δυνάμεις ἐπιφωνούντων ἀμὴν ἀμὴν ἀμὴν κράτος αἶνος...δωτῆρι μόνῳ πάντων ἀγαθῶν ἀμὴν ἀμήν.

59b. On the hymn, which continues to arouse controversy, cf. also H. Abert, "Ein neuentdeckter frühchristlicher Hymnus mit antiken Musiknoten," in *Zeitschrift für Musikwissenschaft* 4 (1922), 524 ff. Idem, "Das älteste Denkmal der christlichen Kirchenmusik," in *Antike* 2 (1926), 282-290. R. Wagner, "Der Oxyrhynchos-Notenpapyrus XV Nr. 1786," in *Philologus* 79 (1923), 201-221. C. del Grande, "Inno cristiano antico," in *Revista Indo-Greco-Italica* 7 (1923), 173-179. Literary parallels and demonstrations are adduced in N. Terzaghi, "Sul POxy. 1796," in *Raccolta di scritti in onore di Giacomo Lumbroso* (Milan 1925), pp. 229ff. E. Wellesz, "The Earliest Example of Christian Hymnody," in *Classical Quarterly* (1945), 34-35, labels the hymn Byzantine and connects it with the Syrian origin of primitive Christian song. However, R.P. Winnington-Ingram, "Ancient Greek Music," in *Lustrum* 3(1958), 10, writes: "This may be correct. His transcription, however, disregards the fact that the rhythmical notation is Greek and should be interpreted in the light of other Greek evidence." But Wellesz, in *A History of Byzantine Music and Hymnography* (Oxford ² 1964), p. 129, remains convinced that this hymn is generally unrelated to ancient Greek music despite its Greek notation. K.G. Fellerer, in dependence on S. Lauffer, *Abriss der antiken Geschichte* (Munich ² 1964), sees in the hymn an attempt to Christianize the forms of Greek music. E. Werner, *The Sacred Bridge. The Interdependence of Liturgy and Music in Synagogue and Church during the First Millenium* (London-New York 1959), p. 355, finds elements of Jewish psalmody in the hymn, although not only the notation but also the melody and structure appear Hellenistic. E. Pöhlmann, *Griechische Musikfragmente. Ein Weg zur altgriechischen Musik* (Nuremberg 1960), p. 24, is of another opinion: "On the whole, one receives the impression that the composer of the hymn is following Greek examples, although he really has no ear for the Greek language. This would explain the metrical mistakes as well as the fact that the accentuation of words is frequently ignored in favor of following the melody. The striving for a rich melody line without regard for quantity and accent probably indicates the influence of Hebrew liturgical music." Cf. also A.W. Hollemann, "The Oxyrhynchus Papyrus 1786 and the Relationship between Ancient Greek and Early Christian Music," in *Vigiliae Christianae* 26 (1972), 1-17.

60. Dölger, *Sol Salutis*, p. 128.

61. W. Bousset, *Kyrios Christos* (Göttingen 1913), p. 287.

62. Ignatius of Antioch, *Epist. ad Ephesios* 4, 1 (83 Funk-Bihlmeyer): Τὸ γὰρ ἀξιονόμαστον ὑμῶν πρεσβυτέριον, τοῦ θεοῦ ἄξιον, οὕτως συνήρμοσται τῷ ἐπισκόπῳ, ὡς χορδαὶ κιθάρᾳ. διὰ τοῦτο ἐν τῇ ὁμονοίᾳ ὑμῶν καὶ συμφώνῳ ἀγάπῃ Ἰησοῦς Χριστὸς ἄδεται. Cf. Dölger, *Sol Salutis*, p. 125.

63. Clement of Alexandria, *Paidagogos* 2, 4 (GCS Clem. I 283 Stählin): ἂν πρὸς κιθάραν ἐθελήσῃς ἢ λύραν ἄδειν τε καί ψάλλειν, μῶμος οὐκ ἔστιν, Ἑβραῖον μιμήσῃ δίκαιον βασιλέα εὐχάριστον τῷ θεῷ.

64. Cf. H. Achelis, "Die ältesten Quellen des orientalischen Kirchenrechtes," in TU 6, 4 (Leipzig 1891), 202. Of course this applies only to Alexandria. In *Apologia* I 67 Justin witnesses to the break of the union of agape and Eucharist, which is also suggested in *Apologia* I 26 and II 12. Cf. also the article "Agape" by H. Leclercq in DACL I 1, 775.

65. Philo, *Legum allegoriarum* I 5, 14 (I 64 Cohn): κατά τε τὴν μουσικὴν ἡ ἑπτάχορδος λύρα πάντων σχεδὸν ὀργάνων ἀρίστη, διότι τὸ ἐναρμόνιον, ὅ δὴ τῶν μελῳδουμένων γενῶν ὀργάνων ἐστὶ τὸ σεμνότατον, κατ᾽ αὐτὴν μαλιστά πως θεωρεῖται.

66. J.E. Häuser, *Geschichte des christlichen, insbersondere des evangelischen Kirch-*

engesanges und der Kirchenmusik von Entstehung des Christentums bis auf unsere Zeit. Ein historischaesthetischer Versuch (Leipzig 1834), p. 14.

67. A.W. Ambros, *Geschichte der Musik* (Breslau 1864) II 19. H.A. Köstlin in the *Realencyklopädie für protestantische Theologie* X 450. M. Hermesdorff in F.X. Kraus, RE II 458: "When the day breaks, then all join in the praise of God to the sound of the harp, as it were with one mouth." In Kraus, *ibid.*, Krüll cites Ambros uncritically: "...to the sound of the cithara...." Γ. Kleinert, *Musik und Religion, Gottesdienst und Volksfeier* (Leipzig 1908), p. 21: "According to this, Basil had sought to concede a place to the citharas...."

The place mistakenly translated by these historians of music is in Basil, *Epist.* 107 (PG 32, 764): ἡμέρας ἤδη ὑπολαμπούσης, πάντες κοινῇ ὡς ἐξ ἑνὸς στόματος καὶ μιᾶς καρδίας, τὸν τῆς ἐξομολογήσεως ψαλμὸν ἀναφέρουσι τῷ κυρίῳ. The Latin text employs *velut ex uno ore et uno corde* for the Greek ὡς ἐξ ἑνὸς στόματος καὶ μιᾶς καρδίας. Thus Ambros, Häuser, Köstlin, Hermesdorff, Krüll and Kleinert substitute *corda* (= string) for *corde* (= heart).

68. J.N. Forkel, *Allgemeine Geschichte der Musik* II (Leipzig: 1801), p. 18 and J. Combarieu, "La musique et la magie," in *Études de philologie musicale* III (Paris 1909), 9 both read in Ps.-Justin, *Quaestiones et responsiones ad orthodoxos* 107 (PG 6, 1354) the faulty text ἐστὶ θεοῦ καὶ ἐνθυμούμενον καὶ ἀδόμενον καὶ ανακρουόμενον instead of ἀκουόμενον and thus understand the participation of instruments in the Christian liturgy, whereas the context demands ἀκουόμενον. Cf. *infra*, n. 77.

69. J. Neumaier, *Geschichte der christlichen Kunst* (Schaffhausen 1856), I, 267.

70. Prudentius, *Apotheosis* 386 (99 Dressel):

> Quidquid in aere cavo reboans tuba curva remugit.
> Quidquid ab arcano vomit ingens spiritus haustu,
> Quidquid casta chelis, quidquid testudo resultat,
> Organa disparibus calamis quod consona miscent;
> Aemula pastorum, quod reddunt vocibus antra:
> Christum concelebrat, Christum sonat, omnia Christum,
> Muta etiam fidibus sanctis animata loquuntur.

71. Augustine, *Enarratio II in Ps.* 32, 5 (PL 36, 279): Nonne id egit institutio in nomine Christi vigiliarum istarum, ut ex isto loco citharae pellerentur?

72. On pagan and Christian vigils cf. *infra*, Chapter 6, section 7.

73. G. Rauschen and J. Wittig, *Patrologie* (Freiburg ⁸⁻⁹ 1921), p. 272. Cf. Dölger, *Sol Salutis*, p. 243, n. 2.

74. A. Harnack, "Diodor v. Tarsus," in TU NF 6, 4 (Leipzig 1901), 33 ff.

75. F.X. Funk, *Kirchengeschichtliche Abhandlungen und Untersuchungen* 3 (Paderborn) 1907), pp. 323 ff.

76. Dölger, *Sol Salutis,* p. 243, n. 2, places the anonymous author c. 400.

77. Ps.-Justin, *Quaestiones et responsiones ad orthodoxos* 107 (PG 6, 1354): Οὐ τὸ ἆσαι ἁπλῶς ἐστὶ τοῖς νηπίοις ἁρμόδιον, ἀλλὰ τὸ μετὰ τῶν ἀψύχων ὀργάνων ἆσαι, καὶ μετὰ ὀρχήσεως καὶ κροτάλων· διὸ ἐν ταῖς ἐκκλησίαις προαίρεται ἐκ τῶν ᾀσμάτων ἡ χρῆσις τῶν τοιούτων ὀργάνων, καὶ τῶν ἄλλων τῶν νηπίοις ὄντων ἁρμοδίων, καὶ ὑπολέλειπται τὸ ᾆσαι ἁπλῶς. Ἡδύνει γὰρ τὴν ψυχήν...Μάχαιραν τοῦ Πνεύματος τοῦτο ὁ Παῦλος ὀνομάζει, ἐν ᾧ κατὰ τῶν ἀοράτων πολεμίων ὁπλίζει τοὺς ὁπλίτας τῆς εὐσεβείας. Ῥῆμα γὰρ ἐστι θεοῦ καὶ ἐνθυμούμενον καὶ ᾀδόμενον καὶ ἀκουόμενον, δαιμόνων γίνεται ἀπελατικόν. On singing as a protection against the demons cf. M. Schneider, "Die Bedeutung der menschlichen Stimme in den alten Kulturen," in *Tribus* 2/3 (1952/1953), 9–29.

78. *Ps.-Justin, Oratio ad Graecos* 4 (PG 6, 236): Καὶ τὰς πανηγύρεις ὑμῶν μεμίσηκα. Ἄμετροι γὰρ ἐκεῖ πλησμοναί, καὶ αὐλοὶ γλαφυροί, ἐκκαλούμενοι πρὸς οἰστρώδεις κινήσεις. καὶ μύρων περίεργοι χρίσεις, καὶ στεφανῶν περιθέσεις.

79. Riedel, *Die Kirchenrechtsquellen des Patriarchats Alexandrien* (Leipzig 1900), p. 267. [This represents a translation from Arabic into German, which employs the word "guitar." Whether the original Arabic used "guitar" is highly unlikely, since the guitar was not developed before the Middle Ages. Probably the Arabic, which was unavailable to me, intended a cithara or other such stringed instrument. — Tr.]

80. *Ibid.,* p. 273: "If the deacons read well they shall read the psalms, and if the priests read well they shall read the Gospel. If they do not read well the oldest lectors shall read the psalms and the deacons the Gospel."

81. In order to show that about the year 500 the cantor used a musical instrument, at least of one string, while singing, Leclercq in DACL III 1, 357 draws attention to a grave inscription from El Doukheileh, which is presently in the Museum in Alexandria:

+ ΕΚΟΙΜΗΘΗ ΕΝ
ΚΩ Ο ΜΑΚΑΡΙΟΣ
ΑΒΒΑ ΔΩΡΟΘΕΟΣ
Ο ΨΑΛΤΗΣ ΜΗΝΙ
ΦΑΡΜΟΥΘΙ ΙΣ ΙΝΔ Η
ΔΙΟΚΛΗΤΙΑΝ ΣΜΣ

Leclercq resolves the inscription correctly: ἐκοιμήθη ἐν Κυρίῳ ὁ μακάριος ὁ ἀββᾶ Δωρόθεος ὁ ψάλτης μηνί φαρμουθί ις ἰνδ(ικτιῶνος) ἡ Διοκλητιαν(οῦ) σνς, i.e., "Here rests in the Lord the holy Abbot Dorotheos, the cantor, on the 16th day of the month of Pharmouti, the 8th indiction, in the 246th year according to the Diocletian enumeration 530 A.D." But Leclercq's own translation of ψάλτης as *harpiste*, by which he demonstrates that it was customery for cantors to use a musical instrument, is incorrect; in the Orient ψάλτης was the official designation of the cantor, as canon 15 of the Council of Laodicea in Hefele-Leclercq I 2, 1007 shows: περὶ τοῦ μὴ δεῖν, πλὴν τῶν κανονικῶν ψαλτῶν, τῶν ἐπὶ τὸν ἄμβωνα ἀναβαινόντων καὶ ἀπὸ διφθέρας ψαλλόντων, ἑτέρους τινὰς ψάλλειν ἐι Ἐκκλησίᾳ. Leclercq's argumentation is also faulty.

82. Canon 35 of the *Nomocanon* of Michael of Damietta in Riedel, *Die Kirchenrechtsquellen . . .*, p. 104.

82a. On the sacral and communitarian functions of the woman in Christian and non-Christian antiquity cf. A. Oepke in G. Kittel, *Theological Dictionary of the New Testament* I, trans. and ed. by G.W. Bromiley (Grand Rapids, Mich. 1964), pp. 776–789.

83. Cf. F. Zimmerman, *Die ägyptische Religion nach der Darstellung der Kirchenschriftsteller und die ägyptischen Denkmäler* (Paderborn 1912), p. 151.

84. A. Erman and H. Ranke, *Ägypten und ägyptisches Leben in Altertum* (Tübingen ² 1923), p. 335.

85. *Hymni Homerici* 1, 156 (8 Baumeister): πρὸς δὲ, τόδε μέγα θαῦμα, ὅου κλέος οὔποτ' ὀλεῖται, κοῦραι Δηλιάδες Ἑκατηβελέταο θεράπναι· αἵ ἐπεὶ ἄρ πρῶτον μὲν Ἀπόλλων ὑμήσωσιν.

86. Pausanias 6, 20, 3 (II 146 Spiro): παρθένοι δὲ ἐν τῷ τῆς Εἰλυθίας ὑπομένουσαι καὶ γυναῖκες ὕμνοι ἄδουσι, καθαγίζουσ[α]ι δὲ καὶ θυμιάματα παντοῖα αὐτῷ ἐπισπένδειν οὐ νομίζουσιν οἶνιν.

87. Plutarch, *Quaestiones graecae* 36, 299 (II 339 Bernardakis): Διὰ τί τὸν Διόνυσον αἱ τῶν Ἠλείων γυναῖκες ὑμνοῦσι παρακαλοῦσι βοέω ποδὶ παραγίνεσθαι πρὸς αὐτάς· ἔχει δ' οὕτως ὁ ὕμνος· Ἐλθεῖν, ἥρω Διόνυσε, Ἀλείων ἐξ ναὸν Ἁγνὸν σὺν Χαρίτεσσιν ἐς ναὸν Τῷ βοέῳ ποδὶ θύων·

εἶτα δὶς ἀπᾴδουσιν· ἄξιε ταῦρε. Cf. Diodorus Siculus, *Bibliotheca historica* 4, 3, 2 f. On the song cf. L. Weniger, *Das Kollegium der sechzehn Frauen und der Dionysosdienst in Elis* (*Jahresbericht des Gymnasiums zu Wiemar*) (1883), p. 8 and F. Schwenn, *Gebet und Opfer. Studien zum griechischen Kultus* (*Religionswissenschaftliche Bibliothek* 8) (Heidelberg 1927), p. 8.

88.   Herodotus 4, 35 (I 295 Stein): καὶ γάρ ἀγείρειν σφι τὰς γυναῖκας ἐπονομαζούσας τὰ ὀνόματα ἐν τῷ ὕμνῳ τόν σφι Ὠλὴν ἀνὴρ Λύκαιος ἐποίησε, παρὰ δὲ σφέων μαθόντας νησιώτας τε καὶ Ἴωνας ὑμνέειν Ὦπίν τε καὶ Ἄργην ὀνομάζοντάς τε καὶ ἀγείροντας (οὗτος δὲ ὁ Ὠλὴν καὶ τοὺς ἄλλους παλαιοὺς ὕμνους ἐποίησε ἐκ Λυκίης ἐλθὼν τοὺς ἀειδομένους ἐν Δήλῳ).

89.   Festus, *De verborum significatu: Salias virgines* (439 Lindsay): Salias virgines Cincius ait esse conducticias, quae ad Salios adhibeantur cum apicibus paludatas, quas Aelius Stilo scripsit sacrificium facere in Regia cum pontifice paludatas cum apicibus in modum Saliorum. Cf. R. Cirilli, *Les prêtres danseurs de Rome. Étude sur la corporation sacerdotale des Saliens* (Paris 1913), p. 78 and J. Moreau, "A propos de la danse des Saliens," in *Latomus* (1947), 85–89.

90.   Macrobius, *Saturnaliorum* 1, 6, 14 (25 Eyssenhardt): Acta igitur obsecratio est pueris ingenuis itemque libertinis sed et virginibus patrimis matrimisque pronuntiantibus carmen: ex quo concessum ut libertinorum quoque filii, qui ex iusta dumtaxat matrefamilias nati fuissent, togam praetextatam et lorum in collo pro bullae decore gestarent. Cf. Livy 27, 37, 7 f.; 31, 12, 9 f.

91.   Cf. Dölger, *Sol Salutis*, pp. 88 and 95.

92.   Philo, *De vita Moysis* I 180 (163 Cohn): τὸ μέγα τοῦτο καὶ θαυμαστὸν ἔργον Ἑβραῖοι καταπλαγέντες ἀναιμωτὶ νίκην οὐκ ἐλπισθεῖσαν ἤραντο καὶ κατιδόντες ἐν ἀκαρεῖ φθορὰν ἀθρόαν πολεμίων δύο χόρους, τὸν μὲν ἀνδρῶν, τὸν δὲ γυναικῶν, ἐπὶ τῆς ἠϊόνος στήσαντες εὐχαριστικοὺς ὕμνους εἰς τὸν θεὸν ᾖδον, ἐξάρχοντος Μωυσέως μὲν τοῖς ἀνδράσιν, ἀδελφῆς δὲ τούτου ταῖς γυναιξίν· ἡγεμόνες γὰρ οὗτοι τῶν χορῶν ἐγεγένηντο. Thus, according to Philo, there was antiphonal singing here between the choir of the men and that of the women.

93.   Philo, *De vita contemplativa* 11, 83 (VI 68 Cohn-Reiter): Μετὰ δὲ τὸ δεῖπνον τὴν ἱερὰν ἄγουσι παννυχίδα. ἄγεται δὲ ἡ παννυχὶς τὸν τρόπον τοῦτον· ἀνίστανται πάντες ἀθρόοι, καὶ κατὰ μέσον τὸ συμπόσιον δύο γίνονται τὸ πρῶτον χοροί, ὁ μὲν ἀνδρῶν, ὁ δὲ γυναικῶν· ἡγεμὼν δὲ καὶ ἔξαρχος αἱρεῖται καθ' ἕτερον ἐντιμότατός τε καὶ ἐμμελέστατος. εἶτα ᾄδουσι πεποιημένους ὕμνους εἰς τὸν θεὸν πολλοῖς μέτροις καὶ μέλεσι, τῇ μὲν συνηχοῦντες, τῇ δὲ καὶ ἀντιφώνοις ἁρμονίαις ἐπιχειρονομοῦντες καὶ ἐπορχούμενοι, καὶ ἐπιθειάζοντες τοτὲ μὲν τὰ προσόδια, τοτὲ δὲ τὰ στάσιμα, στροφάς τε τὰς ἐν χορείᾳ καὶ ἀντιστροφὰς ποιούμενοι. On the relationship of the Therapeutae to the ancient prophetic guilds of Israel, in which similar activity took place, cf. H. Junker, *Prophet und Seher in Israel* (Trier 1927), pp. 19 f.

94.   Ignatius of Antioch, *Epist. ad Ephesios* 4, 2 (83 Funk-Bihlmeyer): καὶ οἱ κατ' ἄνδρα δὲ χορὸς γίνεσθε, ἵνα σύμφωνοι ὄντες ἐν ὁμονοίᾳ, χρῶμα θεοῦ λαβόντες ἐν ἑνότητι, ᾄδετε ἐν φωνῇ μιᾷ διὰ Ἰησοῦ Χριστοῦ τῷ πατρί, ἵνα ὑμῶν καὶ ἀκούσῃ.

95.   Chrysostom, *Homilia 36 in Epist. I ad Corinthios* (PG 61, 313): Εἴπω καὶ ἄλλην θήκην κεχενωμένην τοῦ πατρῴου κόσμου; συνῇσαν τὸ παλαιὸν ἅπαντες, καὶ ὑπέψαλλον κοινῇ. Τοῦτο ποιοῦμεν καὶ νῦν· ἀλλὰ τότε μὲν ἐν ἅπασι μία ψυχὴ ἦν, καὶ καρδία μία· νυνὶ δὲ οὐδὲ ἐν μιᾷ ψυχῇ τὴν ὁμόνοιαν ἐκείνην ἴδοι τις ἄν, ἀλλὰ πολὺς ὁ πόλεμος πανταχοῦ... Ἀλλ' οὐ δύνασαι σιγᾶν; Οὐκοῦν ἔξιθι, ἵνα μὴ καὶ ἑτέροις γένῃ βλάβη. Καὶ γὰρ μίαν ἐν ἐκκλησίᾳ δεῖ φωνὴν εἶναι ἀεί, καθάπερ ἑνὸς ὄντος σώματος. Διὰ τοῦτο καὶ ὁ ἀναγινώσκων μόνος φθέγγεται· καὶ αὐτὸς ὁ τὴν ἐπισκοπὴν ἔχων ἀνέχεται σιγῇ καθήμενος· καὶ ὁ ψάλλων ψάλλει μόνος· κἂν πάντες ὑπηχῶσιν, ὡς ἐξ ἑνὸς στόματος ἡ φωνὴ φέρεται.

96.   Ambrose, *Enarratio in Ps.* 1 (PL 14, 925): Mulieres Apostolus in ecclesia tacere iubet: psalmum etiam bene clamant: hic omnes dulcis aetati, hic utrique aptus est sexui.

Hunc senes rigori senectutis deposito canunt, hunc veterani tristes in cordis sui iucunditate respondent, hunc iuvenes sine invidia cantant lasciviae, hunc adolescentes sine lubricae aetatis periculo et tentatmento concinunt voluptatis, iuvenculae ipsae sine dispendio matrimonialis psallunt pudoris, puellulae sine prolapsione verecundiae cum sobrietate gravitatis hymnum Deo inflexae vocis suavitate modulantur.... Magnum plane unitatis vinculum, in unum chorum totius numerum plebis coire! Dispares citharae nervi sunt, sed una symphonia. In paucissimis chordis saepe errant digiti artificis; sed in populo spiritus artifex nescit errare.

On Ambrose and the singing of psalms cf. H. Leeb, *Die Psalmodie bei Ambrosius* (*Wiener Beiträge zur Theologie* 18) (Vienna 1967). Leeb considers Ambrose's references to the use of psalmody and proves once again what Augustine (*Conf.* 9, 6) and Ambrose's biographer Paulinus (*Vita Ambrosii* 13) said concerning his introduction from the Orient of a new method of singing the psalms. He is of the opinion that it was probably not an alternate singing of the psalms which was introduced, as had always been supposed, but rather a responsorial type of psalm singing, theretofore unknown in the West. One must concede to the author that, in many places in which Ambrose speaks of the people's participation in the psalmody, he always has in mind the singing of an individual which is interrupted by the congregation's response and never the alternate singing of two choirs.

However, B. Fischer, in a discussion of Leeb's study in *Theologische Revue* 68 (1972), 379, feels that it is most improbable that Ambrose would have been the first to have introduced a responsorial singing of the psalms—such as their text itself suggests—into the West. The *genus consolationis et exhortationis* which the Milanese Christians, in the words of Augustine, introduced *magno studio fratrum concinentium* for the first time according to the Oriental model could refer to the alternate singing of the refrain: "If one section of the congregation sang the refrain and then it was sung to it in return, then the term *genus consolationis*, in the sense of Eph. 5:9 and Col. 3:16, would be understandable in a milieu in which the alternate singing of the psalms was precluded, inasmuch as there were no books and it is unlikely that the simple Milanese Christians of the fourth century would have known the psalms by heart." Fischer then turns to our passage from Ambrose and continues: "One would have to pursue the question as to whether the groups which would thus have sung the refrain to one another were divided into men and women. In any event Ambrose is among those Church Fathers who (at the beginning of the explanation to Psalm 1), contrary to Paul's words on the silence of women in church (1 Cor. 14:34), expressly declares himself in favor of female participation in the liturgical singing of the psalms." Fischer then proposes a hypothesis which, in my opinion, has a lot to be said for it: "There would accordingly have been three stages in the development of psalm singing. The most ancient would be that a single individual sang the psalm, while the listening congregation came in with a response from time to time. Perhaps from about the year 386 the custom spread from Milan throughout the West that these responses would be sung first by one part of the congregation (the men?) and then repeated by the other part (the women?). Only much later, with the monks, was the third stage reached—that of alternating the singing of the psalms between two choirs."

97. Eusebius, *Hist. eccles.* 7, 30, 10 (GCS Eus. II 2, 710 Schwartz): ψαλμοὺς δὲ τοὺς μὲν εἰς τὸν κύριον ἡμῶν Ἰησοῦν Χριστὸν παύσας ὡς δὴ νεωτέρους καὶ νεωτέρων ἀνδρῶν συγγράμματα, εἰς ἑαυτὸν δὲ ἐν μέσῃ τῇ ἐκκλησίᾳ τῇ μεγάλῃ τοῦ πάσχα ἡμέρᾳ ψαλμῳδεῖν γυναῖκας παρασκευάζων, ὧν καὶ ἀκούσας ἄν τις φρίξειεν. Cf. also Mansi I 1095 on the Third Synod of Antioch and *History of the Patriarchs* (PO 1, 194).

98. O. Braun, *Das Buch der Synhados* (Stuttgart 1900), p. 341. On *madrashe*

(songs) as opposed to *memre* (metric discourses) cf. O. Bardenhewer, *Geschichte der altkirchlichen Literatur* IV (Freiburg 1924), p. 344.

99. Assemani, *Bibliotheca Orientalis* I (Rome 1720), 47–48: Videns beatus Ephraem quantum omnes cantu caperentur, illosque a profanis et inhonestis lusibus choreisque evocare cupiens, choros virginum Deo sacrarum instituit docuitque hymnos et scalas et responsoria, sublimibus et spiritualibus sententiis referta de Christi nativitate, baptismo, ieiunio, actibus, passione, resurrectione et ascensione, de martyribus, de paenitentia, de defunctis; effecit ut virgines Deo sacrae ad ecclesiam convenierent cunctis solemnibus Domini festis et martyrum solemnitatibus atque diebus dominicis. Ille vero, velut pater et spiritus cithaeredus, in medio aderat, docebatque modos musicos et modulandi carminis leges. Cf. also Bedjan, *Acta Martyrum* III (Paris 1893), p. 653. According to J. Jéannin, *Mélodies liturgiques syriennes et chaldéennes* (Paris 1922), p. 144, Assemani's translation "inhonestis lusibus choreisque" is incorrect; the original text was: "dances to the accompaniment of tambourines."

100. Cf. S. Schiwietz, *Das morgenländische Mönchtum* II (Mainz 1913), p. 179.

101. O. Braun, *Maruta von Maipherkat, De sancta Nicaena synodo* (*Kirchengeschichtliche Studien* IV 3) (Münster 1898), p. 87.

102. *Ibid.*, p.101.

103. *Peregrinatio Aetheriae* 24, 1 (CSEL 39, 71 Geyer): Nam singulis diebus ante pullorum cantum aperiuntur omnia hostia Anastasis et descendent omnes monazontes et parthenae, ut hic dicunt, et non solum hii, sed et laici praeter viri et mulieres, qui tamen volunt maturius vigilare. Et ex ea hora usque in lucem dicuntur hymni et psalmi responduntur, similiter et antiphonae: et cata singulos ymnos fit oratio. On the present dating of the *Peregrinatio* cf. G.E. Gingras, *Egeria. Diary of a Pilgrimage* (*Ancient Christian Writers* 38) (New York 1970), pp. 12–15.

104. J. Chabot, *Synodicon orientale ou Recueil des Synodes Nestoriens* (Paris 1902), p. 486.

105. C. Kayser, *Die Canones Jakobs von Edessa* (Leipzig 1886), p. 111.

106. Bickell-Landesdorfer, *Ausgewählte Schriften der syrischen Dichter* (BKV 6) (Kempten 1913), p. 20.

107. Theodoret, *Hist. eccles.* 3, 19, 2 (GCS 197 Parmentier): Αὕτη χορὸν ἔχουσα παρθένων τὴν διὰ βίου παρθενίαν ἐπηγγελμένων, ἀεὶ μὲν ὕμνει τὸν πεποιηκότα καὶ σεσωκότα θεόν· τοῦ δὲ βασιλέως παριόντος γεγωνότερον κοινῇ ἔψαλλον, εὐκαταφρόνητον ἡγούμεναι καὶ καταγέλαστον τὸν ἀλάστορα. ᾖδον δὲ μάλιστα ἐκεῖνα τὰ ᾄσματα, ἃ τῶν εἰδώλον κωμῳδεῖ τὴν ἀσθένειαν, καὶ μετὰ τοῦ Δαβὶδ ἔλεγον: Τὰ εἴδωλα τῶν ἐθνῶν ἀργύριον καὶ χρυσίον ἔργα χειρῶν ἀνθρώπων.

108. *Testamentum Domini Nostri Jesu Christi* 2, 22 (143 Rahmani): Ei, qui in ecclesia psallit, virgines et pueri respondeant psallentes.

109. *Ibid.* 1, 26 (55): Psallant psalmos et cantica quatuor, unum quod ex Moyse, [alia] ex Salomone et ex Prophetis alia sic: psallentes pueruli, duae virgines, tres diaconi, tres presbyteri.

110. Canon 53 in *Les Canons des Apôtres* (PO 8, 639 Perier): "As for the deaconesses, subdeaconesses and lectresses, we have already expressed ourselves on that subject."

111. Cf. Sozomen, *Hist. eccles.* 4, 3 (PG 67, 1113): ὁ δὲ Μαρκιανὸς ψάλτης καὶ ἀναγνώστης τῶν θείων Γραφῶν. Cf. also Athanasius, *Ad Marcellinum* 12 (PG 27, 24). Cf. F. Wieland, *Die genetische Entwicklung der sog. Ordines minores in den drei ersten Jahrhunderten* (7. Suplementheft der Römischen Quartalschrift) (Rome 1897), p. 165.

112. *Les Canons des Apôtres* (PO 8, 635 Perier): "The children shall go to the ambo and another deacon shall oversee them and reprimand them if they are disobedient."

113. *Didascalia CCCXVIII patrum* 8 (18 Batiffol): γυναιξὶ δὲ παραγγέλλεσθαι ἐν ἐκκλησίαις μὴ λαλεῖν, μηδὲ ἐν ψιθυρισμῷ, μῆτε συμφάλλειν, μῆτε συνυπακούειν, εἰ μὴ μόνον σιγᾶν, καὶ εὔχεσθαι θεῷ δὲ ἐντεύξεως καὶ σεμνῆς πολιτείας.

114. P. Batiffol, *Studia Patristica* (Paris 1889), p. 138.

115. Cyril of Jerusalem, *Procatech.* 14 (PG 88, 356): Καὶ ὁ σύλλογος πάλιν ὁ παρθενικὸς οὕτω συνειλέχθω ἢ ψάλλων ἢ ἀναγινώσκων ἡσυχῇ. ὥστε λαλεῖν μὲν τὰ χείλη, μὴ ἀκούειν δὲ τὰ ἀλλότρια ὦτα· γυναικὶ γὰρ λαλεῖν ἐν ἐκκλησίᾳ οὐκ ἐπιτρέπω. Καὶ ἡ ἔγγαμος δὲ ὁμοίως μιμείσθω. καὶ προσευχέσθω καὶ τὰ χείλη κινείσθω, φωνὴ δὲ μὴ ἀκουέσθω.

116. Isidore of Pelusium, *Epist.* 1, 90 (PG 78, 244): Τὰς ἐν ἐκκλησίαις φλυαρίας καταπαῦσαι βουλόμενοι οἱ τοῦ Κυρίου ἀπόστολοι, καὶ τῆς ἡμῶν παιδευταὶ καταστάσεως, ψάλλειν ἐν αὐταῖς τὰς γυναῖκας συνετῶς συνεχώρησαν. Ἀλλ᾽ πάντα εἰς τουναντίον ἐτράπη τὰ θεοφόρα διδάγματα καὶ τοῦτο εἰς ἔκλυσιν καὶ ἁμαρτίας ὑπόθεσιν τοῖς πλείοσι γέγονε. Καὶ κατάνυξιν μὲν ἐκ τῶν θείων ὕμνων οὐχ ὑπομένουσι. τῇ δὲ τοῦ μέλους ἡδύτητι εἰς ἐρεθισμὸν παθημάτων χρώμενοι, οὐδὲν αὐτὴν ἔχειν πλέον τῶν ἐπὶ σκηνῆς ἀσμάτων λογίζονται. Χρὴ τοίνυν, εἰ μέλλοιμεν τὸ τῷ θεῷ ἀρέσκον ζητεῖν..., παύειν ταύτας καὶ τῆς ἐν ἐκκλησίᾳ ᾠδῆς.

117. Irenaeus, *Adversus haereses* I 13, 2 (PG 7, 580): Πάλιν δὲ γυναιξὶν ἐπιδοὺς ἐκπώματα κεκραμένα, αὐτὰς εὐχαριστεῖν ἐγκαλεύεται, παρεστῶς αὐτοῦ. Jerome, *Epistula* 133 (*Ad Ctesiphontem*) (CSEL 56, 248 Hilberg). Cf. also Th. Schermann, *Ein Weiherituale der römischen Kirche am Schlusse des ersten Jahrhunderts* (Munich-Leipzig 1913), p. 36 and A. v. Harnack, *Die Mission und Ausbreitung des Christentums in den ersten drei Jahrhunderten* (Leipzig ⁴ 1924), II 601 ff.

118. Tertullian, *De praescriptione* 41 (II 39 Oehler). Cf. also *De baptismo* 17. Tertullian's opinion did not change in his Montanistic period, for according to *De exhortatione castitatis* 10 and *De ieiunio* 1, he considered Prisca, Priscilla and Maximilla to be holy prophetesses. However, he remarks expressly in *De virginibus velandis* 9 (I 895 Oehler): Non permittitur mulieri in ecclesia loqui, sed nec docere, nec tinguere, nec offerre, nec ullius virilis muneris, nedum sacerdotalis officii sortem sibi vindicare. Th. Schermann writes in "Die allgemeine Kirchenordnung, frühchristliche Liturgie und kirchliche Überlieferung," in *Studien zur Geschichte und Kultur des Altertums*, Ergänzungsband III, 2 (Paderborn 1915), p. 204, that Chapter 26 of the so-called *Apostolic Church Order*, which contains decrees prohibiting women's participation in the liturgy, was drawn up in opposition to certain liberties among the Gnostics. F. Leitner, *Der gottesdienstliche Volksgesang im jüdischen und christlichen Altertum* (Freiburg 1906), p. 263, also suggests that the later decree of Emperor Licinius forbidding women to visit the house of God and to hold worship in common with men was a countermeasure to the activity of women in the Gnostic liturgy. But this supposition is incorrect. In fact the decree gave women more rights than it took from them, and it could hardly have served as a defensive measure since it forbade bishops to instruct women in the mysteries of salvation and set down the number of those who might teach women. Cf. Eusebius, *Vita Constantini* I 53 (GCS Eus. I 32 Heikel): Διὸ δὴ δεύτερον νόμον ἐτίθει, μὴ δεῖν προστάττων ἄνδρας ἅμα γυναιξὶν ἐπὶ τὰς τοῦ θεοῦ παρεῖναι εὐχάς, μηθ᾽ ἐπὶ τὰ σέμνα τῆς ἀρετῆς διδασκαλεῖα φοιτᾶν τὸ γυναικῶν γένος, μηδ᾽ ἐπισκόπους καθηγεῖσθαι γυναιξὶ θεοσεβῶν λόγων γυναῖκας δ᾽ αἱρεῖσθαι γυναικῶν διδασκάλους.

119. Theodoret, *Hist. eccles.* 4, 29 (GCS 269 Parmentier): Καὶ ἐπειδὴ Ἁρμόνιος ὁ Βαρδησάνου ᾠδάς τινας συντεθείκει πάλαι, καὶ τῇ τοῦ μέλους ἡδονῇ τὴν ἀσέβειαν κεράσας κατεκήλει τοὺς ἀκούοντας, καὶ πρὸς ὄλεθρον ἦργευε, τὴν ἁρμονίαν τοῦ μέλους ἐκεῖθεν λαβών, ἀνέμιξε τὴν εὐσέβειαν, καὶ προσενήνοχε τοῖς ἀκούουσιν ἥδιστον ὁμοῦ καὶ ὀνησιφόρον φάρμακον. ταῦτα καὶ νῦν

τὰ ἄσματα φαιδροτέρας τῶν νικηφόρων μαρτύρων τὰς πανηγύρεις ποιεῖ. Cf. also Sozomen, *Hist. eccles.* 3, 16 and Cassiodorus, *Hist. tripartita* 8, 6.

120. The heresy was manifested, according to the contemporary view, by the substitution of hymns for psalms. Cf., e.g., O. Braun, *Maruta von Maipherkat, De sancta Nicaena synodo (Kirchengeschichtliche Studien* IV 3) (Münster 1898), p. 47: "Instead of Peter they have set up Marcion for themselves as [head] of the Apostles, [and instead of psalms they have composed] hymns [for themselves]."

121. Gennadius, *De viris inlustribus* 43 (77 Richardson).

122. Jerome, *Contra Pelagianos* 1, 25 (PL 23, 519): Verum tu trantae es liberalitatis, ut favorem tibi apud Amazonas tuas concilies, ut in alio loco scripseris, scientiam legis etiam feminas habere debere, cum Apostolus doceat esse tacendum mulieribus in ecclesia, et si quid ignorant, domi suos viros debere consulere. Nec sufficit tibi dedisse agmini tuo scientiam Scripturarum, ut earum voce et canticis delecteris. Jungis enim et poenis in titulo quod et feminae Deo psallere debeant. Quis enim ignorat, psallendum esse feminis in cubiculis suis, et absque virorum frequentia et congregatione turbarum? Verum tu donas, quod non licet; ut quod verecunde facere debeant, et absque ullo arbitro, magistri auctoritate proclament.

123. Lucian, *Dialogi meretricii* 12, 1, 311 (III 407 Jakobitz): ἄρτι δὲ σὺν ἐμοὶ κατακείμενος ἐπήνεις Μαγίδιον τὴν ψάλτριαν·...καὶ ἡ αὐλητοῖς Κυμβάλιον.

124. Sallust, *De coniuratione Catilinae* 25 (20 Ahlberg): psallere et saltare elegantius quam necesse est probae, multa alia, quae instrumenta luxuriae sunt. Sed ei cariora semper omnia quam decus atque pudicitia fuit...lubido sic accensa, ut saepius peteret viros quam peteretur.

125. Arnobius, *Adversus nationes* 2, 42 (CSEL 4, 82 Reifferscheid): Idcirco animas mismit, ut in maribus exsoleti, in feminis fierent meretrices sambucistriae psaltriae, venalia ut prosternerent corpora.

126. Commodian, *Instructiones* 2, 7, 11–12 (CSEL 15, 82 Dombart): Transgrederis legem, cum te facis musicis inter *Ibid.* 2, 29, 17 ff (CSEL 15, 86) the poet speaks to Christian women:

> Quid memorem vestes aut totam Zabuli pompam
> Resputis legem, mavultis mundo placere
> Saltatis in domibus, pro psalmis cantatis amores.

127. Jerome, *Epistula* 107 (*Ad Laetam de institutione filiae*) 4, 1 (CSEL 55, 294 Hilberg).

128. *Ibid.* 8, 3 (CSEL 55, 299): Surda sit ad organa; tibia, lyra et cithara, cur facta sint, nesciat.

129. *Ibid.* 9, 3 (CSEL 55, 300): Placeat ei comes non compta atque formonsa, quae liquido gutture carmen dulce moduletur.

130. Jerome, *Epistula* 128 (*Ad Pacatulam*) 4, 3 (CSEL 56, 160 Hilberg): vocis dulcedines per aurem animam vulnerantes.

131. Basil, *Comment. in Isaiam* 5, 158 (PG 30, 378): 'Ελεεινὸν θέαμα σώφροσιν ὀφθαλμοῖς, μὴ ἱστουργεῖν γυναῖκα, ἀλλὰ λυρῳδεῖν.

132. Canon 37 of the Synod of Mar Ezekiel in J.B. Chabot, *Synodicon orientale ou Recueil des Synodes Nestoriens* (Paris 1902), p. 386.

133. W. Riedel, *Die Kirchenrechtsquellen* ... p. 191

134. Martial, *Epigrammaton* 3, 63, 7 (74 Heraeus): inter feminas tota qui luce

cathedras desidet. Horace, *Saturae* 1, 10, 91 (153 Kiessling-Heinze): Discipularum inter iubeo plorare cathedras.

135. Tertullian, *Ad uxorem* 2, 9 (I 697 Oehler): Sonant inter duos [coniuges] psalmi et hymni et mutuo provocant, quis melius deo suo cantet.

136. *Ibid.* 2, 6 (I 692): Quid maritus suus illi, vel marito quid ipsa cantabit? Audiet sane aliquid dei coenas de taberna.

137. Jerome, *Epistula* 128 (*Ad Pacatulam*) 1, 3 (CSEL 56, 157 Hilberg).

138. Jerome, *Epistula* 107 (*Ad Laetam de institutione filiae*) 4, 1 (CSEL 55, 294 Hilberg): Adhuc tenera lingua Psalmis dulcibus imbuatur.

139. *Ibid.* 9, 3 (CSEL 55, 300): mane hymnos canere, tertia, sexta, nona hora quasi bellatricem Christi stare in acie.

140. Riedel, *Die Kirchenrechtsquellen...*, p. 256.

141. O. Bardenhewer, *Geschichte der altkirchlichen Literatur* II (Freiburg ² 1914), p. 303.

142. Ps.-Clement, *De virginitate* 2, 6, 3 (PG 1, 432): nec proicimus sanctum canibus nec margaritas ante porcos, sed Dei laudes celebramus cum omnimoda disciplina et cum omni prudentia et cum omni timore Dei atque animi intentione. Cultum sacrum non exercemus ibi, ubi inebriantur gentiles et verbis impuris in conviviis suis blasphemant in impietate sua. Propterea non psallimus gentilibus neque scripturas illis praelegimus, ut ne tibicinibus aut cantoribus aut hariolis similes simus sicut multi, qui ita agunt et haec faciunt, ut buccella panis saturent sese, et propter modicum vini eunt et cantant cantica Domini in terra aliena gentilium ac faciunt quod non licet.

143. Gregory Nazianzus, *Carmina* I 3, 2 (PG 37, 603):

Κερκίς σοι γε μέλοι, καὶ εἴρια, καὶ μελεδῶναι
Θείοις ἐν λογίοις, σοφίη, καὶ ᾄσματα θεῖα,
Λεπταλέης φωνῆς ἔμφρων θρόος, οὐ ἐπίδεικτος,
Ἧς πλέον ἐν πραπίδεσσι, μικρὸν δ' ἐπὶ χείλεσι κείσθω.

144. R. Raabe, *Petrus der Iberer* (Leipzig 1895), p. 19.

145. Cf. *infra,* Chapter 4, section 9.

146. On music and singing in the pagan and Christian cults of the dead cf. *infra,* Chapter 6.

147. Herodian 4, 2, 5 (110 Stavenhagen): ἑκατέρωθεν δὲ βάθρα τινὰ σύγκειται ἐν κλίμακος σχήματι, καὶ ἐπὶ μὲν θατέρου μέρους τῶν εὐγενεστάτων καὶ εὐπατριδῶν χορὸς ἕστηκε παίδων, ἐν δὲ τῷ ἀντικειμένῳ γυναικῶν τῶν ἐν ἀξιώσει εἶναι δοκουσῶν. ᾄδουσι δὲ ἑκάτεροι ὕμνους τε καὶ παιᾶνας ἐς τὸν τετελευτηκότα, σεμνῷ μέλει καὶ θρηνώδει ἐρρυθμισμένους.

148. On pagan and Christian vigils cf. *infra,* Chapter 6, sec. 7.

149. Cf. *ibid.* and *supra,* n. 71.

150. Jerome, *Epistula* 107 (*Ad Laetam de institutione filiae*) 9, 2 (CSEL 55, 300 Hilberg): basilicas martyrum et ecclesias sine matre non adeat.

151. *Ibid.*: Vigiliarum dies et sollemnes pernoctationes sic virguncula nostra celebret, ut ne transversum quidem unguem a matre discedat.

152. Riedel, *Die Kirchenrechtsquellen...*, p. 58.

153. Canon 9 of the Council of Auxerre in Hefele-Leclercq III 1, 216.

154. Leo IV, *Homilia* (*XIV* 895 Mansi): *Cantus et choros mulierum in ecclesia vel in atrio ecclesiae prohibite. Carmina diabolica quae nocturnis horis super mortuos vulgus facere solet et cachinnos quos exercet, sub contestatione Dei omnipotentis vitate.*

155. F. Nau, *Les canons et les resolutions canoniques* (Paris 1906), p. 96: "Women who go to the grave to grieve over their dead with tambourines and dancing shall not have access to church or to communion, and it is not permitted for priests to be present when they do this [dancing]."

156. Gregory Nazianzus, *Oratio* 8 (PG 35, 805): Ὦ νυκτῶν ἀΰπνων, καὶ ψαλμῳδίας, καὶ στάσεως ἐξ ἡμέρας εἰς ἡμέραν ἀποληγούσης! Ὦ Δαβὶδ ταῖς πισταῖς μόνον ψυχαῖς οὐ μακρὰ μελῳδήσας.

157. *Peregrinatio Aetheriae* 24, 12 (CSEL 39, 74 Geyer): De laicis etiam viris aut mulieribus si qui volunt, usque ad lucem loco sunt, si qui nolunt, revertuntur in domos suas et reponent dormito.

158. *Testamentum Domini Nostri Jesu Christi* 1, 43 (101 Rahmani): laus nocturna viduarum. *Ibid.* (103): laus aurorae viduarum habentium praecedentiam sessionis. On widows in the *Testamentum* cf. A. Kalsbach, "Die altkirchliche Einrichtung der Diakonissen bis zu ihrem Erlöschen," in *Supplementheft der Römischen Quartalschrift* 22 (Freiburg 1926), 41.

159. Canon 9 of the Synod of Mar George I in Chabot, *Synodicon orientale...*, p. 486.

160. Lucian, *Imagines* 13 (II 2, 35 Sommerbrodt): πᾶς δὲ ὁ τόνος τοῦ φθέγματος οἷος ἀπαλώτατος, οὔτε βαρὺς ὡς εἰς τὸ ἀνδρεῖον ἡρμόσθαι, οὔτε πάνυ λεπτὸς ὡς θηλύτατός τε εἶναι καὶ κομιδῇ ἔκλυτος, ἀλλ᾽ οἷος γένοιτ᾽ ἂν παιδὶ μήπω ἡβάσκοντι, ἡδὺς καὶ προσηνὴς καὶ πράως παραδυόμενος ἐς τὴν ἀκοήν.

161. Cf. E. Fehrle, *Die kultische Keuschheit im Altertum* (RVV 6) (Giessen: 1910), 112 f. and A.D. Nock, "Eunuchs in Ancient Religion," in ARW 23 (1925), 30.

162. Cf. M.P. Nilsson, *Griechische Feste von religiöser Bedeutung mit Ausschluss der Attischen* (Leipzig 1906), p. 148.

163. Pausanias 2, 7, 8 (I 144 Spiro): Καὶ γὰρ ἐπὶ τὸν Σύθαν ἴασιν οἱ παῖδες τῇ ἑορτῇ τοῦ Ἀπόλλωνος, καὶ ἀγαγόντες δὴ τοὺς θεοὺς ἐς τὸ τῆς Πειθοῦς ἱερὸν αὖθις ἀπάγειν ἐς τὸν ναὸν φασι τοῦ Ἀπόλλωνος.

164. M.P. Nilsson, "Die Prozessionstypen im griechischen Kult," in *Jahrbuch des kaiserlichen deutschen archäologischen Instituts* 31 (1916), 321.

165. Lucian, *De saltatione* 16 (II 1, 133 Sommerbrodt): Ἐν Δήλῳ δέ γε οὐδὲ αἱ θυσίαι ἄνευ ὀρχήσεως, ἀλλὰ σὺν ταύτῃ καὶ μετὰ μουσικῆς ἐγίγνοντο. παίδων χοροὶ συνελθόντες ὑπ᾽ αὐλῷ καὶ κιθάρᾳ οἱ μὲν ἐχόρευον, ὑπωρχοῦντο δὲ οἱ ἄριστοι προκριθέντες ἐξ αὐτῶν. τὰ γοῦν τοῖς χοροῖς γραφόμενα τούτοις ᾄσματα, ὑπορχήματα ἐκαλεῖτο καὶ ἐμπέπληστο τῶν τοιούτων ἡ λύρα.

166. F. Poland, *Geschichte des griechischen Vereinswesens* (Leipzig: 1909), p. 49.

167. Lucian, *Alexander* 41, 247 (II 1, 119 Sommerbrodt): προλέγων δὲ πᾶσιν ἀπέχεσθαι παιδίου συνουσίας, ὡς ἀσεβές ὄν, αὐτὸς τοιόνδε τι ὁ γεννάδας ἐτεχνάσατο. ταῖς γὰρ πόλεσι ταῖς Ποντικαῖς καὶ ταῖς Παφλαγονικαῖς ἐπήγγειλε θεηκόλους πέμπειν ἐς τριετίαν ὑμνήσοντας παρ᾽ αὐτῷ τὸν θεόν. καὶ ἔδει δοκιμασθέντας καὶ προκριθέντας τοὺς εὐγενεστάτους καί ὡραιοτάτους καὶ κάλλει διαφέροντας, οὓς ἐγκλεισάμενος ὥσπερ ἀργυρωνήτοις ἐχρήσατο καὶ συγκαθεύδων καὶ πάντα τρόπον ἐμπαροινῶν.

168. F.J. Dölger, *Sol Salutis* (Münster ² 1925), p. 95.

169. *Ibid.*, p. 88.

170. Gregory Nazianzus, *Oratio* 16, 13 (PG 35, 952): ναὶ, τέκνα ἀγαπητά, ναί, θείας κοινωνοὶ καὶ νουθεσίας καὶ φιλανθρωπίας... ἡλικίαν ἐλεεινήν, καὶ μάλιστα τῆς τοῦ θεοῦ φιλανθρωπίας ἀξίαν.

171. Chrysostom, *In Matthaeum homilia* 71, 4 (PG 58, 666): καὶ ἡ τρίτη δὲ πάλιν, ὑπὲρ

ἡμῶν αὐτῶν, καὶ αὕτη τὰ παιδία τὰ ἄμωμα τοῦ δήμου προβάλλεται, τὸν θεὸν ἐπὶ ἔλεον παρακαλοῦντα... ὑπὲρ δὲ ἡμῶν αὐτῶν οἱ παῖδες, ὧν τῆς ἁπλότητος τοὺς ζηλωτὰς ἡ βασιλεία τῶν οὐρανῶν μένει.

172. Basil, *In famen et siccitatem homilia* 3 (PG 31, 309): Ὀλίγοι λοιπὸν μετ' ἐμοῦ καὶ τῆς προσευχῆς, καὶ οὗτοι ἰλιγγιῶντες, χασμώμενοι, μεταστρεφόμενοι συνεχῶς, καὶ ἐπιτηροῦντες, πότε τοὺς στίχους ὁ ψαλμῳδὸς συμπληρώσει, πότε, ὡς δεσμωτηρίου, τῆς ἐκκλησίας, καὶ τῆς ἀνάγκης τῆς προσευχῆς ἀφαιρεθήσονται. Οἱ δὲ δὴ παῖδες οἱ σμικρότατοι οὗτοι, οἱ τὰς δέλτους ἐν τοῖς διδασκαλείοις ἀποθέμενοι, καὶ συμβοῶντες ἡμῖν, ὡς ἄνεσιν μᾶλλον καὶ τέρψον τὸ πρᾶγμα μετέρχονται, ἑορτὴν ποιούμενοι τὴν ἡμετέραν λύπην, ἐπειδὴ τῆς ἐπαχθείας τοῦ παιδευτοῦ, καὶ τῆς φροντίδος τῶν μαθημάτων πρὸς ὀλίγον ἐλευθεροῦνται.

173. *Peregrinatio Aetheriae* 24, 5 (CSEL 39, 72 Geyer): Et diacono dicente singulorum nomina semper pisinni plurimi stant respondentes semper: Kyrie eleyson, quod dicimus nos: miserere Domine, quorum voces infinitae sunt. Cf. also F.J. Dölger, *Sol Salutis* (Munster ² 1925), p. 64.

174. Julian, *Epistula* 56 (566 Hertlein): ὑπὲρ μὲν οὖν τῶν παίδων τοσαῦτα. τοὺς δὲ νῦν ἀκροωμένους τοῦ μουσικοῦ Διοσκόρου ποίησον ἀντιλαβέσθαι τῆς τέχνης προθυμότερον, ὡς ἡμῶν ἑτοίμων ἐπὶ ὅπερ ἂν ἐθέλωσιν αὐτοῖς συνάρασθαι. Cf. also G. Feischauer, "Zur Geschichte des Knabengesangs im ausgehenden Altertum," in *Festschrift M. Schneider* (Leipzig 1955), pp. 11-15.

175. Cf. *supra*, n. 108.

176. *Testamentum Domini Nostri Jesu Christi* 2, 4 (167 Rahmani): ut virgines alternatim cum puerulis in officio sacro canant.

177. Cf. *supra*, n. 109.

178. *Testamentum Domini Nostri Jesu Christi* 2, 11 (135 Rahmani): Dicunt pueruli et cantica ad ascensionem lucernae. Universus populus psallens voce consona respondeat Alleluia.

179. Cf. Dölger, *Sol Salutis*, p. 93. On Germanus of Paris and his liturgy cf. A. Wilmart in DACL VI 1049 and J. Quasten, "Oriental Influence in the Gallican Liturgy," in *Traditio* 1 (1943), 55-78. An edition of the text with emendations on the text in Migne is in J. Quasten, *Expositio antiquae Liturgiae Gallicanae Germano Parisiensi ascripta* (*Opuscula et Textus. Series Liturgica* fasc. 3) (Münster 1934). A new critical edition of the text is in E.C. Ratcliff, *Expositio antiquae Liturgiae Galicanae* (London 1971).

180. C. Kayser, *Die Canones Jakobs von Edessa* (Leipzig 1886), p. 11.

181. H. Petermann, *Reisen im Orient* I (Leipzig 1860), p. 109.

181a. On *lectores infantuli* cf. E. Peterson, "Das jugendliche Alter der Lektoren," in *Ephemerides Liturgicae* 48 (1934), 437-442. Cf. also the remark in A. Olivar, "Preparación e improvisación en la predicación," in *Kyriakon. Festschrift J. Quasten* (Münster 1970), p. 748, n. 49.

182. J.B. de Rossi, *Bolletino di archeologia cristiana* 4, 2 (1883), 8 and 21 ff.

183. Siricius, *Epistula I ad Himerium* 13 (634 Constant): Quicumque itaque se Ecclesiae vovit obsequiis a sua infantia, ante pubertatis annos baptizari et lectorum debet ministerio sociari. Cf. J.B. de Rossi, *Bolletino di archeologia cristiana* 4, 2 (1883), 17.

184. Cf. A. de Waal, *Sänger and Gesang auf altchristlichen Inschriften Roms vom 4. bis 9 Jahrhundert* (Mainz 1895), p. 300.

185. Ennodius, *Vita Epiphanii* 8 (CSEL 6, 332 Hartel).

186. CIL VIII 453: Vitalis lector in pace, vixit annis V, depositus s(ub) d(i)e III nonas Maias ind(ictione) prima.

187. Gregory of Tours, *Miraculorum lib.* I 76 (PL 71, 771): Verum cum iam

spiritalibus eruditus esset in literis et cum reliquis clericis in choro canentium psalleret, modica pulsatus febre, spiritum exhalavit.... Surge crastina die ad matutinum, et audies vocem eius inter choros psallentium.

188. E. LeBlant, *Inscriptions chrétiennes de la Gaule* I (Paris 1856), p. 142, nr. 65 = CIL XIII 2385 f.:

✝IN HOC LOCO REQVIESCIT
FAMOLVS DI STEFANVS PRIMICIRIVS
SCOLAE LECTORVM SERVIENS ECL
LVGDVNINSI VIXIT ANNOS LXVI
OBIIT VIIII KL DECEMBRIS DVODECIES PC
IVSTINI INDICTIONE XV

188a. Cf. S.J.P. Van Dijk, "Gregory the Great, Founder of the Urban 'Schola Cantorum,'" in *Ephemerides Liturgicae* 77 (1963), 335–356 and J. Smits van Waesberghe, "Das gegenwärtige Geschichtsbild der mittelalterlichen Musik II," in *Kirchenmusikalisches Jahrbuch* 47 (1963), 11–38.

189. *Acta Ephraemi*, in *Ephraemi Syri Opera Omnia* 3, syr.-lat. (Rome: 1743), p. LI: Ingressi sunt ad Bardesanem coetus puerorum, quos ille docuit ad citharam et varios canticorum modos canere.

190. *S. Ephraemi Syri Hymni et Sermones* II, ed. by T.J. Lamy (Mechlin 1886), p. 751. Cf. T. Michels, "Das Frühjahrssymbol in östlicher Liturgie, Rede und Dichtung des christlichen Altertums," in *Jahrbuch für Liturgiewissenschaft* 6 (1926), 6.

191. O. Braun, *Ostsyrisches Mönchsleben* (BKV 22) (Kempten 1915), p. 22.

192. *Ibid.*, p. 28.

193. Cf. V. Ryssel, *Georgs des Araberbischofs Gedichte und Briefe* (Leipzig 1891), p. 2: "Observe and consider with the eyes of the spirit—and give glory to God's great power—how little children with stammering tongues are occupied with the songs of King David."

194. Clement of Alexandria, *Protrepticos* 1, 5, 3 (GCS Clem. I 6 Stählin): τὰ ἄψυχα ὄργανα ὑπεριδών.

195. Chrysostom, *In Epist. I ad Timoth.* 4 homilia 14 (PG 62, 576): Εἶτα διαναστάντες, εὐθέως ἑστήκασιν, ὕμνους ᾄδοντες προφητικοὺς μετὰ πολλῆς τῆς συμφωνίας, μετ' εὐρύθμων μελῶν. Οὔτε κιθάρα, οὔτε σύριγγες, οὔτε οὐδὲν ἄλλο ὄργανον μουσικὸν τοιαύτην ἀφίησι φωνήν, οἵαν ἐστιν ἀκοῦσαι ἐν ἡσυχίᾳ βαθείᾳ, καὶ ἐν ἐρημίᾳ τῶν ἁγίων ᾀδόντων ἐκείνων.

196. Chrysostom, *Homilia in Ps.* 7, 15 (PG 55, 104): Ὥσπερ γὰρ θυσίας ἔλαβεν, οὐχὶ δεόμενος θυσιῶν ('Ἐὰν γὰρ πεινάσω, φησίν, οὐ μή σοι εἴπω Ps. 49, 12) ἀλλ' ἐνάγων τοὺς ἀνθρώπους εἰς τὴν αὐτοῦ τιμήν, οὕτω καὶ ὕμνους δέχεται, οὐ δεόμενος τῆς παρ' ἡμῶν εὐφημίας, ἀλλ' ἐπιθυμῶν τῆς ἡμῶν σωτηρίας.

197. Chrysostom, *Homilia in Ps.* 49 (PG 55, 156): Πολλοὺς τῶν ἀνθρώπων κατιδὼν ὁ θεὸς ῥαθυμοτέρους ὄντας, καὶ πρὸς τὴν τῶν πνευματικῶν ἀνάγνωσιν δυσχερῶς ἔχοντας, καὶ τὸν ἐκεῖθεν οὐχ ἡδέως ὑπομένοντας κάματον. ποθεινότερον ποιῆσαι τὸν πόνον βουλόμενος, καὶ τοῦ καμάτου τὴν αἴσθησιν ὑποτεμέσθαι, μελῳδίαν ἀνέμιξε τῇ προφητείᾳ, ἵνα τῷ ῥυθμῷ τοῦ μέλους ψυχαγωγούμενοι πάντες, μετὰ πολλῆς τῆς προθυμίας τοὺς ἱεροὺς ἀναπέμπωσιν αὐτῷ ὕμνους. Οὐδὲν γὰρ, οὐδὲν οὕτως ἀνίστησι ψυχήν, καὶ πτεροῖ, καὶ τῆς γῆς ἀπαλλάτει, καὶ τῶν τοῦ σώματος ἀπολύει δεσμῶν, καὶ φιλοσοφεῖν ποιεῖ, καὶ πάντων καταγελᾶν τῶν βιωτικῶν, ὡς μέλος συμφωνίας, καὶ ῥυθμῷ συγκείμενον θεῖον ᾆσμα.

198. Cf. *supra*, n. 18.

199. Cf. *supra*, n. 77.

200. Augustine, *Confessiones* 10, 33 (CSEL 33, 263 Knöll): Nunc in sonis, quos ani-

mant eloquia tua, cum suavi et artificiosa voce cantantur, fateor, aliquantulum adquiesco, non quidem ut haeream, sed ut surgam, cum volo. Attamen cum ipsis sententiis quibus vivunt ut admittantur ad me, quaerunt in corde meo nonnullius dignitatis locum, et vix eis praebeo congruentem. Aliquando enim plus mihi videor honoris eis tribuere, quam decet, dum ipsis sanctis dictis religiosius et ardentius sentio moveri animos nostros in flammam veritatis, cum ita cantantur, quam si non ita cantarentur, et omnes affectus spiritus nostri pro sui diversitate habere proprios modos in voce atque cantu, quorum nescio qua occulta familiaritate excitentur. Sed delectatio carnis meae, cui mentem enervandam non oportet dari, saepe me fallit.... Aliquando autem hanc ipsam fallaciam immoderatius cavens erro nimia severitate, sed valde interdum, ut melos omnes cantilenarum suavium, quibus Daviticum psalterium frequentatur, ab auribus meis removeri velim atque ipsius ecclesiae, tutiusque mihi videtur, quod de Alexandrino episcopo Athanasio saepe dictum mihi conmemini, qui tam modico flexu vocis faciebat sonare lectorem psalmi, ut pronuncianti vicinior esset quam canenti. Verumtamen cum reminiscor lacrimas meas, quas fudi ad cantus ecclesiae in primordiis recuperatae fidei meae, et nunc ipsum quod moveor non cantu, sed rebus quae cantantur, cum liquida voce et convenientissima modulatione cantantur, magnam instituti huius utilitatem rursus agnosco. Ita fluctuo inter periculum voluptatis et experimentum salubritatis magisque adducor non quidem inretractibilem sententiam proferens cantandi consuetedinem approbare in ecclesia, ut per oblectamenta aurium infirmior animus in affectum pietatis adsurgat.

201. Augustine, *Enarratio in Ps.* 147, 5 (PL 37, 1917).

202. W. Riedel, *Die Kirchenrechtsquellen des Patriarchats Alexandrien* (Leipzig 1900), p. 274. On the continuation of this view in the Middle Ages cf. A. Schmid, *Der Kirchengesang nach den Liturgikern des Mittelalters* (Kempten 1900), p. 9. On the singing of the psalms in Christian worship cf. A. Arens, *Die Psalmen im Gottesdienst des Alten Bundes. Eine Untersuchung zur Vorgeschichte des christlichen Psalmengesanges* (Trier 1961).

203. Cf. the foregoing paragraphs.

204. C. Butler, *The Lausiac History of Palladius* II (Cambridge 1904), pp. 29–32 and 129 ff. Cf. also R.T. Meyer, *Palladius. The Lausiac History (Ancient Christian Writers* 34) (Westminster, Md. 1965).

205. The ξενοδοχεῖον is indicated here. Cf. canon 47 of Rabbula in F. Nau, *Les canons et les résolutions canoniques* (Paris 1906), p. 88: "Visitators, priests and deacons shall not live in hostelries or inns when they come to the city, but they shall live in the ξενοδοχεῖον of the church or in the monasteries outside [the city]."

206. Paulos Euergetinos, Συναγωγὴ τῶν θεοφθόγγων ῥημάτων καὶ διδισκαλιῶν τῶν θεοσόφων καὶ ἁγίων πατέρων (Venice 1783), p. 371. Since this edition is very rare the text has been reproduced below in extenso. I am grateful to Prof. Dr. A. Rücker for indicating to me Christ-Paranikas *Anthologia graeca carminum Christianorum. Beiträge zur kirchlichen Literatur der Byzantiner* (Leipzig 1871), p. XXIX, where the text has been printed with a few variations, which I have placed in parentheses.

Ὁ Ἀββᾶς Παμβὼ ἀπέστειλε τὸν μαθητὴν αὐτοῦ (ἐν Ἀλεξανδρείᾳ) πωλῆσαι τὸ ἐργόχειρον αὐτοῦ. ποιήσας δὲ ἡμέρας ἓξ καὶ δέκα (ἐν τῇ πόλει) ὡς ἔλεγεν ἡμῖν, τὰς νύκτας ἐκάθευδεν ἐν τῷ νάρθηκι τῆς ἐκκλησίας ἐν τῷ Ναῷ τοῦ ἁγίου Ἀποστόλου Μάρκου. καὶ ἰδὼν τὴν ἀκολουθίαν τῆς (ἁγίας) Ἐκκλησίας, ἀνέκαμψε πρὸς τὸν γέροντα. ἔμαθε δὲ καὶ τροπάρια. λέγει οὖν αὐτῷ ὁ γέρων. ὁρῶ σε τέκνον τεταραγμένον· μή τις πειρασμός σοι συνέβη ἐν τῇ πόλει; ἀποκρίνεται ὁ ἀδελφός (γέροντι). φύσει Ἀββᾶ, ἐν ἀμελείᾳ δαπανῶμεν τὰς ἡμέρας ἡμῶν ἐν τῇ ἐρήμῳ ταύτῃ. καὶ οὔτε κανόνας, οὔτε τροπάρια ψάλλομεν. ἀπελθὼν γὰρ ἐν Ἀλεξανδρείᾳ, εἶδον τὰ τάγματα τῆς ἐκκλησίας τῶς ψάλλουσι, καὶ ἐν λύπῃ γέγονα πολλῇ, διότι οὗ ψάλλομεν καὶ ἡμεῖς κανόνας καὶ τροπάρια. λέγει οὖν αὐτῷ ὁ γέρων. οὐαὶ ἡμῖν τέκνον. ὅτι ἔφθασαν αἱ ἡμέραι, ἐν αἷς ὑπολείψουσιν οἱ Μοναχοὶ τὴν στερεάν τροφὴν τὴν διὰ (τοῦ) Ἁγίου Πνεύματος ῥηθεῖσαν, καὶ ἐξακολουθήσωσιν ἄσμασι (ἄσματα) καὶ ἤχοις (ἤχους). ποία γὰρ κατάνυξις; ποία δάκρυα τίκτονται ἐκ τῶν τροπαρίων; ὅτε ἐν Ἐκκλησίᾳ τίς ἵσταται ἢ ἐν κελλίῳ, καὶ ὑφοῖ τὴν φωνὴν αὐτοῦ ὡς οἱ βόες; εἰ γὰρ ἐνώπιον τοῦ θεοῦ παριστάμεθα, ἐν πολλῇ κατανύξει ὀφείλομεν παρίστασθαι, καὶ οὐχὶ ἐν μετεωρισμῷ. καὶ γὰρ οὐκ ἐξῆλθον οἱ Μοναχοὶ ἐν τῇ ἐρήμῳ ταύτῃ, ἵνα παρίστανται τῷ θεῷ καὶ μετεωρίζονται καὶ μελεδῶσιν ἄσματα, καὶ ῥυθμίζουσιν ἤχους καὶ σείουσι χεῖρας, καὶ μεταβαίνουσι πόδας. ἀλλ' ὀφείλομεν ἐν φόβῳ θεοῦ (πολλῷ) καὶ τρόμῳ δακρυσί τε καὶ στεναγνοῖς μετὰ εὐλαβοῦς (εὐλαβείας) καὶ εὐκατανύκτου καὶ μετρίας καὶ ταπεινῆς φωνῆς τὰς προσευχὰς τῷ θεῷ προσφέρειν. ἰδοὺ γὰρ φθείρουσιν οἱ Χριστιανοὶ τὰς βίβλους τῶν Ἁγίων Εὐαγγελίων, καὶ τῶν Ἁγίων Ἀποστόλων καὶ τῶν θεσπεσίων Προφητῶν, λειαίνοντες τὰς Ἁγίας Γραφὰς καὶ γράφοντες τροπάρια.

O. Wessely, "Die Musikanschauung des Abtes Pambo," in *Anzeiger der Oesterreichischen Akademie der Wissenschaften. Philos.-Hist. Klasse* 89 (1953), 42–62, deals with more aspects of Pambo's thoughts on music.

On katanyxis cf. also Gregory Nazianzus, *Epistula* 163. Chrysostom, *De statuis* 17, 1. **Mark the Hermit**, *Opusculum* 1, 15. John Moschus, *Pratum spirituale* 50. John Climacus, *Scala paradisi* 7. On the notion in the West cf. P. Régamy, "La componction du coeur," in *La Vie Spirituelle* 44 (1935), 1–16, 65–84.

207. Cf. J.A. Wensinck, "Über das Weinen in den monotheistischen Religionen Vorderasiens," in *Festschrift Eduard Sachau z. 70. Geburtstag gewidmet* (Berlin 1915), p. 26.

208. *Ibid.*

209. *Ibid.* There was a similar notion of piety in the West. Augustine, John Cassian, Prudentius and the *Rule* of St. Benedict all indicate that praying with tears is a valuable gift. Cf. J. Balogh, "Unbeachtetes in Augustins Konfessionen," in *Didaskaleion* N.S. 4 (1926), 5–21. M. Lot-Borodine, "Le mystère du 'don des larmes' dans l'Orient chrétien," in *La Vie Spirituelle* 48 (1936), 65–110. B. Steidle, "Die Tränen, ein mystisches Problem in alten Mönchtum," in *Benediktinische Monatsschrift* 20 (1938), 181–187. K. Holl, *Enthusiasmus und Bussgewalt beim griechischen Mönchtum* (Leipzig 1898). J. Hausherr and G. Horn, "Vie de Symeon le nouveau theologien," in *Oriens Christianus* 12 (1928), 31. H. Graef, "The Spiritual Director in the Thought of Symeon the New Theologian," in *Kyriakon. Festschrift J. Quasten* (Münster 1970), p. 613.

210. Basil, *Homilia in Ps.* 1, 2 (PG 29, 213): ψαλμός γὰρ καὶ ἐκ λιθίνης καρδίας δάκρυον ἐκκαλεῖται.

211. Gregory Nazianzus, *Oratio* 43, 52 (PG 36, 561): Ἐπειδὴ γὰρ ἔνδον ἐγένετο καὶ τὴν ἀκοὴν προσβαλούσῃ τῇ ψαλμῳδίᾳ κατεβροντήθη.

212. Cf. *supra*, n. 116.

213. Philo, *Legum allegoriarum* II, 26 (96 Cohn): τί δ' ὅταν ἡ ἀκοὴ προσέχῃ φωνῆς ἐμμελείᾳ, δύναται ὁ νοῦς λογίζεσθαί τι τῶν οἰκείων; οὐδαμῶς.

214. Porphyry, *De abstinentia* 1, 34 (13 Hercher): Αἱ δὲ διὰ τῶν ἀκοῶν ἐμπαθεῖς οὖσαι κινήσεις ἔκ τε ποιῶν ψόφων καὶ ἤχων, αἰσχρορρημοσύνης τε καὶ λοιδορίας, ὡς τοὺς μέν πολλοὺς τέλεον τοῦ λογισμοῦ ἐκδεδυχότος φέρεσθαι ποιοῦσι οἰστρουμένους, τοὺς δ' αὖ θηλυνομένους παντοίας στροφὰς ἐλίττεσθαι.

215. A. Baumstark, *Festbrevier und Kirchenjahr der syrischen Jakobiten* (Paderborn 1910), p. 4. Cf. also J. Nau, "Les Plérophories de Jean évèque de Maiouma," in *Revue de l'Orient Chrétien* 3 (1898), 232 ff. and PO 8, 179 f.

216. John of Maiuma, *Plerophoria* (PO 8, 180). The variations of Paulos Euergetinos (cf. n. 206) have been placed in parentheses.

Ἀδελφὸς ἠρώτησε τὸν ἄββαν Σιλουανὸν λέγων· »Τί ποιήσω, ἀββᾶ, πῶς κτήσομαι τὴν κατάνυξιν, πάνυ γὰρ πολεμοῦμαι (ὀχλοῦμαι) ὑπὸ τῆς ἀκηδίας καὶ τοῦ ὕπνου (καὶ τοῦ μυσταγμοῦ). Καὶ ὅτε ἀνίσταμαι τῇ νυκτὶ (ἐκ τοῦ ὕπνου), πολλὰ πυκτεύω (ἐν τῇ ψαλμῳδίᾳ), καὶ χωρὶς τοῦ ἤχου ψαλμὸν οὐ λέγω, καὶ οὐ δύναμαι περιγένεσθαι τοῦ ὕπνου (μυσταγμοῦ, οὔτε ψαλμὸν ἄνευ ἤχου λέγω).« Καὶ ἀπεκρίθη (αὐτῷ) ὁ γέρων· »Τέκνον, τὸ λέγειν σε τοὺς ψαλμοὺς μετὰ ἤχου πρώτη ὑπερηφανία ἐστὶ καὶ ἔπαρσις, τουτέστιν ἐγὼ ψάλλω (ὑποβάλλοι σοι γὰρ ὅτι ἐγὼ ψάλλω). Ὁ ἀδελφὸς οὐ ψάλλει, τὸ γὰρ ᾆσμα (δεύτερον δὲ, καὶ) σκληρύνει (σου) τὴν καρδίαν καὶ πωρώνει, καὶ οὐκ ἐᾷ τὴν ψυχὴν κατανυγῆναι. Εἰ οὖν θέλεις εἰς (τὴν) κατάνυξιν ἐλθεῖν, ἄφες τὸ ᾆσμα, καὶ ὅτε ἵστασαι τὰς εὐχὰς ποιῶν, ὁ νοῦς σου τὴν δύναμιν τοῦ στίχου ἐρευνάτω, καὶ λογίζου ὅτι ἐνώπιον τοῦ θεοῦ παρίστασαι, τοῦ ἐτάζοντος καρδίας καὶ νεφρούς. Καὶ ὅτε ἀναστῇς ἐκ τοῦ ὕπνου, πρὸ πάντων δοξάσει (δοξασάτω) τὸν θεὸν τὸ στόμα σου, καὶ μὴ ἄρξῃ τοῦ κανόνος εὐθύς· ἀλλ᾽ ἐξελθὼν ἔξω τοῦ κελλίου (εἶτα), στιχολόγησον τὴν πίστιν, καὶ τὸ πάτερ ἡμῶν ἐν τοῖς οὐρανοῖς. Καὶ τότε εἰσελθών, ἄρξαι τοῦ κανόνος (σου) ἀνετῶς ἀνετῶς, στενάζων καὶ ἐνθυμούμενος τὰς ἁμαρτίας σου, καὶ τὴν κόλασιν, ἐν ᾗ μέλλεις βασανίζεσθαι ἐν αὐτῇ.« Καὶ λέγει ἀδελφός· »Ἐγώ, ᾿αββᾶ, ἐξ ὅτε (ἐξότου) ἐμόνασα, τὴν ἀκολουθίαν τοῦ κανόνος καὶ τὰς ὥρας, καὶ τὰ τῆς (κατὰ τὴν ὀκτώηχον) ὀκταήχου ψάλλω;« Καὶ λέγει (ἀπεκρίθη) ὁ γέρων· »(Καὶ) Διὰ τοῦτο καὶ ἡ κατάνυξις καὶ τὸ πένθος φεύγει ἀπὸ σοῦ. Ἐννόησον (γὰρ) τοὺς μεγάλους πατέρας πῶς ἰδιῶται ὑπῆρχον (ὑπάρχοντες), καὶ μὴ (μήτε ἤχους μήτε τροπάρια) ἐπιστάμενοι, εἰ μὴ ὀλίγους ψαλμούς. Καὶ οὔτε ἤχους οὔτε τροπάρια ἐγίνωσκον, καὶ δίκην φωστήρων ἐν κόσμῳ ἔλαμψαν. Καὶ μαρτυρεῖ μοῦ τῷ λόγῳ (οἷος ἦν) ὁ ἀββᾶς Παῦλος (ὁ ἁπλοῦς), καὶ ὁ Ἀββᾶς Ἀντώνιος, καὶ Παῦλος ὁ ἁπλοῦς καὶ ὁ ἀββᾶς Παμβώ, καὶ ὁ ἀββᾶς Ἀπολλώ, καὶ οἱ καθ᾽ ἑξῆς (λοιποὶ θεοφόροι Πατέρες), οἵτινες καὶ νεκροὺς ἤγειραν (καὶ μεγάλας δυνάμεις ἐποίησαν), καὶ κατὰ δαιμόνων τὴν ἐξουσίαν ἐδέξαντο, καὶ οὐκ ἐν ᾄσμασι καὶ τροπαρίοις καὶ ἤχοις, ἀλλ᾽ ἐν προσευχῇ (τῇ μετὰ συντετριμμένης καρδίας) καὶ νηστείᾳ. Οὐ γὰρ ἡ καλλιεπία τοῦ ᾄσματος ὑπάρχει ἡ σῴζουσα τὸν ἄνθρωπον, ἀλλ᾽ ὁ φόβος τοῦ θεοῦ καὶ ἡ τήρησις τῶν τοῦ Χριστοῦ ἐντολῶν (δι᾽ ὧν καὶ ὁ τοῦ θεοῦ φόβος τῇ καρδίᾳ ἐγγίνεται ἀδιαλείπτως· καὶ τὸ πένθος κρατύνεται τὸ πάσης ἁμαρτίας ἐκκαθαίρον τὸν ἄνθρωπον. καὶ τὸν νοῦν λευκότερον καὶ χιόνος ἀπεργαζόμενον). Τὸ γὰρ ᾆσμα πολλοὺς εἰς τὰ κατώτατα τῆς γῆς κατήγαγε, καὶ οὐ μόνον κοσμικούς, ἀλλὰ καὶ ἱερεῖς (ἐκθηλύναν αὐτοὺς) εἰς πορνείας καὶ εἰς πάθη (ἕτερα πάθη αἰσχρὰ καταχρημνίσαν αὐτούς) πολλὰ αὐτοὺς ἐβόθρισε[ν], καὶ τὸ ᾆσμα, τέκνον, τῶν κοσμικῶν ἐστι, διὰ τοῦτο γὰρ καὶ συναθροίζεται ὁ λαὸς ἐν ταῖς ἐκκλησίαις. Ἐννόησον, τέκνον, πόσα τάγματά εἰσιν ἐν τῷ οὐρανῷ, καὶ οὗ γέγραπται περὶ (τινος) αὐτῶν ὅτι μετὰ τῆς ὀκταήχου ψάλλουσιν, ἀλλὰ τάγμα ἓν ἀκαταπαύστως τὸ ἀλληλούϊα ᾄδει, ἕτερον τάγμα τὸ ἅγιος ἅγιος Κύριος Σαβαώθ... ἀλλ᾽ ἔσω ταπεινόφρων, καὶ ὁ θεὸς παρέχει σοι τὴν κατάνυξιν.

The *oktoëchos* mentioned frequently above was the official hymnal of the Syrian Church which contained hymns of a non-Biblical character, ordered according to the eight modes in which they were composed. Cf. E. Wellesz, *Aufgaben und Probleme auf dem Gebiete der byzantinischen und orientalischen Kirchenmusik* (*Liturgiewissenschaftliche Quellen und Forschungen* 18) (Münster 1923), p. 101.

217. O. Braun, *Ostsyrisches Mönchtum* (BKV 22) (Kempton 1915), p. 25.

218. A. Mingana, *Editions and Translations of Christian Documents in Syriac and Garshuni* with an introduction by Rendel Harris. I. "A treatise of Barsalibi against the Melchites," in *Bulletin of the John Rylands Library* 2 (1927), 110–204.

219. *Ibid.*, 140 f. One often sees in the literature of the time an attempt to show, on apologetic grounds, the dependence of Byzantine ecclesiastical music on ancient Greek music; according to present day research, however, such a dependence does not seem to have existed. Cf. E. Wellesz, *Aufgaben and Probleme . . .*, p. 102 and C. Hoeg, "Les rapports de la musique chrétienne et de la musique de l'antiquité," in *Byzantion* 25/27 (1955/1957) 383–412.

220. On the stance of the monks with regard to the liturgy cf. E. Dekkers, "Les anciens moines cultivaient-ils la liturgie?" in *Vom christlichen Mysterium. Gessamelte*

Arbeiten zum Gedächtnis von O. Casel (Düsseldorf 1951), pp. 97–114. For a related problem on liturgy in transition cf. H. Hucke, "Die Entwicklung des christlichen Kultgesanges zum Gregorianischen Gesang," in *Römische Quartalschrift* 48 (1953), 147–194.

221. Cf. n. 206.

222. Theodoret, *Haereticarum fabularum compendium* 4, 7 (PG 83, 425): Ταύτῃτοι, ὡς αὐτόνομοι, καὶ τὰ καταγέλαστα ἐκεῖνα προσεπενόησαν, τὸ παρ᾽ ἡμέραν μὲν ὕδατι τὸ σῶμα καθαίρειν, μετὰ δὲ κρότου χειρῶν, καὶ τινος ὀρχήσεως, τὰς ὑμνῳδίας ποιεῖσθαι, καὶ κώδωνας πολλοὺς κάλου τινὸς ἐξηρμημένους κινεῖν, καὶ τὰ ἄλλα ὅσα τούτοις ἐστὶ παραπλήσια. Οὗ δὴ χάριν αὐτοῖς ὁ μέγας ἐκεῖνος Ἀθανάσιος πολεμῶν διετέλεσεν.

223. Fulcherius of Chartres: Per totam exemplo civitatem laus iucunda..., sonant signa, populus manibus plaudit, clerus laetus cecinit. Cited in G. Klameth, *Das Karsamstagsfeuerwunder in der Grabeskirche zu Jerusalem nach dem Bericht des Fulcherius von Chartres* (Vienna 1913), p. 7.

224. A. v. Maltzew, *Die Sakramente der orthodox-katholischen Kirche des Morgenlandes* (Berlin 1898), p. 38. Cf. also the remark on Ethiopian singing in C. Conti Rossini, *Acta Sancti Jared (Corpus script. christ. orient.)* Ser. II, T. 17, p. 6; Jared was considered the founder of Ethiopian church music. The Ethiopian priests would accompany the singing of hymns composed by Jared with so loud a clapping that their hands would be injured. This same ecstatic type of singing with the clapping of hands and the accompaniment of drums is practiced even today among the Ethiopians. Cf. E. Wellesz, *Aufgaben und Probleme...*, p. 107. An Ethiopian liturgical Marian hymn sung by two choirs to the accompaniment of tambourine and sistrum on Marian feasts may be found in A. Roman, "Une hymne du Nagara Maryam," in *Revue de l'Orient chrétien* 23 (1923), 416 ff.

225. H. Petermann, *Reisen im Orient* I (Leipzig 1860), p. 247.

226. A.J. Butler, *Ancient Coptic Churches of Egypt* I (Oxford 1884), p. 327.

227. Johann Georg, Herzog zu Sachsen, *Streifzüge durch die Kirchen und Klöster Ägyptens* (Leipzig 1914), pp. 29 and 32.

228. A.J. Butler, *Ancient Coptic Churches of Egypt* II 82. "The wild and somewhat barbaric clash of cymbals, which accompanies the chanting in every ancient church of Egypt, is probably a relic of pagan rather than of Jewish tradition." Butler then recalls the music in the cults of Dionysus and Cybele.

229. Cf. C. Sachs, "Altägyptische Musikinstrumente," in *Der alte Orient* 21, 3/4 (Leipzig 1920), 3.

Chapter Five

MUSIC AND SINGING IN CHRISTIAN PRIVATE LIFE

1. CHRISTIAN DOMESTIC PRAYER SERVICES.

The close relation between domestic and public cult in pagan antiquity has already been noted.[1] It was for this reason that music in private homes was considered by Christians to be connected with idol worship. In fact the portrayals of pagan domestic sacrifices show that the accompaniment of flute music was as normal there as in public sacrifices. Thus on the Pompeian murals a flutist is always present at the offering to the Lares.[2] A wall painting of just such an offering, presently in the Casa di Pansa in Pompeii, depicts the *genius* in the middle, to the right of the altar, and a flute player standing to the left.[3] A mural with a similar subject may be found in the National Museum in Naples.[4] To the right of the altar stands the *genius familiaris* with a cornucopia and a bowl of libation; to the left of the altar, and portrayed somewhat smaller, is the flute player, who touches a scabellum (a castanet-like instrument played with the foot) with his left foot. Behind the *genius* and the flutist are slaves with sacrificial gifts. On either side of the mural a Lar is painted, of larger stature than the other figures; each is clothed in tunic and pallium and holds a drinking horn and a small bucket.

In the primitive Church there was a great interest in house devotions. The element of song in these domestic celebrations was the psalms and hymns, which were meant to displace the pagan songs. Clement of Alexandria alludes to the Greek custom of singing the *skolion* at meals in order to recommend that Christians sing the psalms at that time:

> But if you want to sing and praise God to the music of the cithara or the lyre it is not blameworthy. You are imitating the righteous King of the Hebrews, who was well-pleasing to God. . . . Among the ancient Greeks also a song called a *skolion* was sung, in the style of the Hebrew psalms, at banquets and feasts, and the guests sang it together with a single voice. Sometimes they also sang it in turns when drinking, while the more musical of them sang to the lyre.[5]

Tertullian emphasized with pride the variety and richness of Christian singing, so that no one needed for the sake of art to pursue the pernicious corruptions of the pagans.[6] "If you want hymns," we read in the Syrian *Didascalia*, "you have the psalms of David."[7]

This strong opposition to secular songs arose because they frequently contained the names of the gods, which Christians were forbidden to pronounce. Thus the *Apostolic Constitutions* command:

> A believing Christian may sing no pagan song...for it could happen that in singing he might mention the demonic names of the idols, and he would give an opportunity to the evil one rather than to the Holy Spirit.[8]

The proscription of pagan songs, then, occurred with good reason. In place of the hero-songs which, according to Cicero, were often sung in domestic life,[9] there appeared songs about martyrs, while hymns to God replaced love songs. Even the pagan children's song had to give way to the Alleluia. Thus we find Jerome demanding of a very young girl:

> When she sees her grandfather she should leap upon his breast, hold him around the neck and, whether he is willing or not, sing Alleluia to him.[10]

Relatively few archeological monuments portraying scenes of Christian domestic prayer services still remain. A sarcophagus in the Palazzo Corsini in Rome shows in the left corner a young woman playing a lyre and surrounded by other women and children.[11] To the right four men are sitting, one of whom is holding a scroll. F. Münter[12] concludes that this has reference to Christian domestic prayer as Tertullian described it:

> Let the two [spouses] sing psalms and hymns and incite each other to see who can sing better to his God.[13]

F.X. Kraus, drawing attention to the scroll, recalls the primitive record of Christian hymns recorded by Eusebius.[14] But if this really pertains to a scene from life, for which the evidence is very weak,[15] it is hardly in keeping with what we know of Christian domestic prayer. The bearing of the people who are portrayed is inappropriate. The significance of the scroll, as it has been adduced, does not merit credence; a lyre in a woman's hand and a scroll in a man's were favorite and common images on pagan sarcophagi.[16]

The use of lyre and cithara in Christian domestic prayer services is not at all inconceivable, since both these instruments were excluded from the comprehensive prohibition of musical instruments. Aside from the reference which has already been made to the *Paidagogos* of

Clement of Alexandria,[17] there is a remark of Synesius of Cyrene in which he boasts of having conceived and composed a hymn to Christ with cithara accompaniment.[18] In general Synesius appears to permit the Christian use of the lyre and the cithara. In a letter to his brother regarding the hymn to Nemesis composed by Mesomedes about 140 A.D. he quotes three verses, adding: "Nemesis, to whom we sing on the lyre."[19] In fact no uniform measures appear to have been taken with respect to the toleration of the lyre. Chrysostom, in his exposition of Psalm 41 (42), speaks of singing psalms at mealtime. Everyone is to join in, young or old, whether his voice is harsh or delicate:

> You need no cithara, no tightly-strung strings, no plectrum and no artfulness, nor any instruments except, if you wish, that you make yourself into a cithara, destroying the melodies of the flesh and composing with your body a συμφωνία for your soul.[20]

These words could well mean that Chrysostom did not ultimately stand in opposition to the use of the cithara. Nonetheless, in another text he does not hold it exempt from the condemnation of instrumental music, for he calls the songs which are sung to stringed instruments diabolical.[21]

Here the question arises about the significance of the lyre and lute players on the early Christian sarcophagi. C.M. Kaufmann simply calls them space-fillers.[22] An example of such a sarcophagus, probably belonging to the third century, may be found in the Lateran Museum.[23] In the center of the sarcophagus is a framed surface with the portrait of the deceased, an old woman. Her face is turned slightly to the left, and she holds in her left hand a scroll upon which she rests the fingers of her right hand. The style of her coiffure, plain and unparted, with the hair falling closely behind the ears, appears to be from the time of Julia Domna. To the right and left of this section there are winged cupids holding baskets of fruit. Next to them on either side are shepherds, each standing between two pines. The one of the left is beardless and youthful; he is supporting himself with a staff, and at his feet a dog sits looking up at him. The shepherd on the right is bearded, with his face turned toward the left; he is carrying a lamb on his shoulders, while at his feet a goat and a ram are visible. C.M. Kaufmann suggests that he is the Good Shepherd.[24] At either end of the monument are two female musicians. The one to the right seems to be younger than the other. Her hair is in plaits bound about the head and she is clothed in a gown which leaves her neck and right shoulder

free. She is seated on a high-backed chair of woven reeds and is playing a musical instrument with a long fret-board, the four strings of
which are fastened above and below to button-like pegs. The woman
to the extreme left is wearing a hair style similar to that of the central
figure. She is sitting on a stool, clothed in the same manner as her
counterpart. In her left hand she holds an instrument resembling a lute
with a thick resonance base, and in her right hand is a heavy club.

There is reason to think that the three women thus portrayed depict
the deceased woman at different stages of her life, particularly since
the facial expression of the figure to the left closely resembles that of
the center figure. Consequently the deceased person appears in the
center in her later years, while on either end she is portrayed as
younger.

The musical instruments, like the scroll which the center figure
holds, could be signs of a cultivated upbringing following similar
depictions on pagan sarcophagi. They may also have accorded with
actual customs in Christian circles, which tended to be more liberal
than is suggested by the strict prohibitions of the ecclesiastical writers;
both Clement of Alexandria and Synesius of Cyrene, as we have seen,
did in fact concede the use of lyre and cithara by way of exception. In
spite of that, however, this position is not tenable. Since we very frequently find a lyre or a lute player on pagan sarcophagi[25] an interpretation of their appearance on Christian sarcophagi must not be
limited to texts from Christian writers but must also consider non-
Christian monuments. H. Dütschke's explanation that the lyre in the
woman's hand is a sign of her education is not satisfactory.[26] The ancient portrayals of the hereafter, which depict life after death in a
richly musical way,[27] suggest that in the lyre or lute player the dead
person is shown as one of the blessed. This hypothesis gains in pro-
bability when one realizes that the lyre appeared as a votive offering
to the dead in antiquity.[28] It was particularly in the embellishment of
sarcophagi that Christians received a major heritage from the pagans.
So it was that the lyrist appeared on the Christian sarcophagi. The
mere adaptation of such an image as a "space-filler" is out of the question; Christian portrayals of heaven were rich enough to fill this symbol of the hereafter with new meaning. We need only recall the
description of the liturgy of the heavenly Jerusalem in the Book of
Revelation.[29]

The side surface of a sarcophagus from Saint-Maximin depicts Tabitha's restoration to life (Acts 9:36ff).[30] Tabitha, who is supporting herself on her pallet, has just raised herself at the word of the Apostle, who stands at her feet. In front of the bed three smaller persons, whose gestures recall a mourning ritual, are kneeling or sitting.[31] In the background we can see two women, their veiled heads turned to Tabitha. In the entrance on the side there stands an organ with eight pipes. H. Leclercq is reminded by this scene of the hymns and psalms which the Christians sang at wakes, and he considers the organ to be the accompanying instrument which the artist anachronistically portrayed.[32] But this opinion is questionable, given the negative attitude of the Christian writers to every kind of instrumental funeral music.[33] Furthermore, precisely in the fourth century, to which time Leclercq dates this sarcophagus, Jerome spoke out very sharply against the organ, saying that the Christian virgin must be deaf to its music.[34] It seems rather that the artist wished to use the organ in a contemporary way to indicate the type of music which was played at pagan and Jewish funerals. His basis for this representation would have been found in Mt. 9:23, where it is mentioned that flutists were present in the house of Jairus.

2. THE CHRISTIAN REJECTION OF MUSIC IN PRIVATE LIFE. THE EXCLUSION OF MUSICIANS FROM THE CHURCH ACCORDING TO THE OLDEST ECCLESIASTICAL LAW.

Christianity did not stand alone in its rejection of music in the liturgy but shared this idea with a great number of pagan philosophers. Before the appearance of Christianity many voices were raised in pagan circles against the growing musical extravagance in secular life. Among the Romans music, particularly instrumental music performed as an art, was not really appreciated outside the cult. In contrast to the Greeks, the Roman priestly nobility, with its ideal of *gravitas*, considered music and dancing to be vices, as Cornelius Nepos reports.[35] As in cultic matters, however, so also here, Roman *modestia* succumbed finally to the Asiatic influences to which the city was exposed through her own conquests. Livy complains harshly of these symptoms of decline:

> The first instances of foreign extravagance were introduced into the city by the Asiatic army [of Scipio Africanus]. They first brought to Rome ornate couches, valuable rugs, hangings and other cloth furnishings which were considered very precious for household goods at that time, console

tables and sideboards. Then women citharists and sambuca players and [other] diversions were added to the banquets and amusements.[36]

The decline of music was marked especially by the vulgar role which it played in pantomime. Lucian of Samosata writes that Krato made himself the spokesman for many serious-minded persons when he called such music unworthy of an educated man:

> My dear fellow, can a man who has had the benefit of an education as well as a little traffic with philosophy, who strives after the better things and has familiarity with the ancients — can such a man sit down and listen to flute music and watch an effeminate man strutting about in woman's clothes, imitating amorous females with his lewd singing?[37]

The excessive accumulation of musical frivolities provided the occasion for Ammianus Marcellinus' bitter remark in the second half of the fourth century that, while libraries stood empty, hydraulic organs, lyres and flutes were being manufactured everywhere.[38]

However, between the pagan opposition and the rigorism with which the Christians opposed this type of music there was a great difference. The reasons for which Christians passed their sharp judgment were other than those of the pagans. It is true that Christians also held music in contempt because it promoted moral decay. Thus Clement of Alexandria condemned flute music because it was "a chain in a bridge of sensual love and idle impulses," and he rejected the noise of cymbal and tambourine because it made one forget propriety and morality.[39] But the most important reason for Clement's condemnation of profane music in private life, which all other Christian writers shared with him, was the close relationship between music and the pagan cult of the idols. Therefore all the music of that time, as far as Christians were concerned, constituted one great worship of idols. Consequently Clement wanted to leave the flute to the idolaters,[40] while Gregory Nazianzus adduced as the reason for his rejection of the same instrument its use in the cult of Cybele — "the madness of the Phrygian flutes, the sound of a castrated man."[41] Only from this basic position can we understand the strong resistance to this music, as well as the comparison which Epiphanius of Salamis could make between the flute and the serpent through whom the devil led Eve astray. This writer draws a parallel between the gestures of the flutist when he is playing and the devil, who casts his glance on high so that he might blaspheme the heavenly beings.[42]

Later even the cithara and the lyre no longer enjoyed the privileged position which Clement had accorded them.[43] Basil included the playing of these instruments among the arts whose end was perdition.[44] The blame for this development lay with the utterly disreputable women citharists and lyrists who were drawn to the pagan banquets. Jerome gives the Christian widow Furia the advice:

> Drive out the singer like a criminal. Cast from your house all women lyrists and harpists, the devil's choir whose songs are the deadly ones of sirens.[45]

Augustine too, who in the *De doctrina christiana* strives after the most extensive use of all the arts in the Christian life, only permits an acquaintance with the cithara and other instruments if it serves to help grasp spiritual things and to understand Scripture:

> We may not flee music on account of pagan superstitions if we are able to derive from it something useful for understanding the holy Scriptures. Neither may we concern ourselves with their theatrical nonsense if we have something to say about citharas and other instruments that might advance our knowledge of spiritual things.[46]

The intolerance of early Christianity for music in private life appears in a very special way in the ecclesiastical canons, which excluded every practicing professional musician from the Christian community. In the so-called *Canons of Hippolytus*, dating from the end of the fourth century, the twelfth canon reads:

> Whoever performs in a theater or is a wrestler or a runner or a music teacher or a comic actor...(?) or who teaches savagery or is a hunter or an animal trainer or an animal fighter or a priest of the idols — none of these may be permitted to attend a sermon until they have been purified from these unclean works. After forty days they may hear a sermon. When they prove themselves worthy they will be baptized.[47]

The *Canons of Basil*, written about 400, which forbid the lector to practice any instrumental music,[48] also prescribe the exclusion of women singers of ill repute:

> If anyone is a chorus dancer (χορευτής) he shall either give up his profession or be excommunicated and banned from the mysteries. Likewise if he is a dancer.... An actor shall cease or be cast out. A woman who dances in taverns and allures people by her beautiful singing and her deceitful melody, which is full of temptation, shall, if she renounces her profession, wait forty days before she communicates; then she may receive the mysteries.[49]

The *Apostolic Constitutions* expressly number cithara and lyre playing among the forbidden professions:

> If an actor or an actress wishes to be received, or a charioteer or a gladiator or a runner or a fencing master or an athlete or a flutist or a

citharist or a lyrist or a public dancer, he shall either discontinue these things or be turned away.[50]

The lengthy duration of these laws is shown by the *Nomocanon* of Michael of Damietta, which contains this ordinance:

If anyone plays a cithara or an instrument which is blown he shall either cease or be cast out.[51]

The same may be seen in canon 70 of Gabriel ben Turiek, who considered musical instruments reprehensible.[52]

The extant sources do not show that ecclesiastical laws were as sharply directed against the manufacturers of musical instruments. In fact one receives the opposite impression from a tombstone, preserved in Saint Paul's in Rome, which comes from a cemetery nearby on the Via Ostiensis (cf. the illustration). According to A. de Waal, it belongs to the fourth century and has a Christian character.[53] On it an organ with twelve pipes is portrayed,[54] while the base shows the head of Medusa. Above the organ the following inscription may be read: RVSTICVS SE VIBV FECIT. Thus this seems to be the epitaph of a Christian organ maker.

3. PAGAN AND CHRISTIAN TABLE CUSTOMS. THE TABLE OF DEMONS AND THE TABLE OF CHRIST IN DOMESTIC LIFE.

The difficulties which Christianity encountered in its opposition to domestic music can be judged if one considers pagan table customs. It was the custom to play music not only at luxurious and licentious feasts and banquets, where Andalusian women danced their infamous dances to the beat of castanets and the music of flutes while bawdy numbers were sung and Greek singers of both sexes rendered the songs of Sappho and Anacreon, but at simpler meals as well. Usually hired musicians or musically educated slaves took care of this part of the entertainment.[55] Thus Martial, who rented a room on the third floor of a tenement, promised a friend that he would season the very meager meal to which he had invited him with at least the playing of the short flute.[56] Pliny the Younger permitted the single guest whom he had invited to a simple meal to choose among a reading, a comic scene and a lute performance.[57] The archeological monuments also bear witness to an extravagant love of music.[58]

The accumulation of musical delights often actually turned into a torment for the guests. Martial himself answers the question as to which is the best kind of banquet by saying: "The one with no flute players."[59] So too the pagan Claudian, in the year 400, praised the banquets at which no cithara was heard.[60]

Christians must have detested all the more the table practices of a civilization doomed to die, as Clement of Alexandria shows in the fourth chapter of the second book of the *Paidagogos*, which is concerned with banquets.[61] The poet Commodian, a contemporary of Constantine, addresses the pagans:

> However often you may have eaten with flutists, if you have not adored the crucified Lord you have perished.[62]

In reference to Is. 5:12 ("They have lyre and harp, timbrel and flute and wine at their feasts, but they do not regard the deeds of the Lord or see the works of his hands"), Basil of Caesarea attacks the playing of the lyre at meals. For him this instrument adorned with gold and ivory was like an idol that was also plated with the same precious metals. Lyre and idol are the same in that they both lead man to perdition.[63] Psaltery and cithara, in his opinion, only increase the intemperance that wine causes, and thus they hinder any association with the works of God. Trumpet, syrinx, cithara, sambuca and psaltery were the means by which Nebuchadnezzar brought about the downfall of the Jews and induced them to worship idols.[64] Basil develops in dramatic rhetoric the manner in which cithara, flute and cymbal are commonly used to bewail the dead, but how revelers employ these same instruments to evoke passionate feelings during a banquet.[65] Chrysostom is opposed to all instrumental music at mealtime for the same reason, for whatever stupefying drunkenness does, music also does: it renders the soul less vigorous and disposes it to debauchery.[66] In fact, for Christian homilists instrumental music during meals became symbolic of the sinner and of the pagan, just as the singing of psalms and hymns symbolized the Christian. Ambrose preached forcefully against some of his flock who had taken part in drinking

parties which lasted until dawn, and he contrasted their behavior with
that of other Christians:

> Are hymns sung, and do you take the cithara? Are psalms sung, and do
> you take the psaltery or the tambourine? Woe to you, for you are aban-
> doning salvation and choosing death.[67]

Certainly the demoralizing character of dinner music, as it was
practiced at that time, was greatly responsible for the prohibitive attitude that the ecclesiastical writers took toward it. But the most basic
reason for this attitude was the worship of idols. Christians were forbidden to sing pagan songs because by them they were inviting demons rather than Christ to the meal. In the Christian literature of that
time it was frequently emphasized that pagan songs had somewhat the
same effect as an epiclesis: they were able to summon the demons.
Chrysostom in particular stresses this: ᾄσματα πορνικά attract demons,
while ᾄσματα πνευματικά invite Christ to the table. He speaks about this
in his exposition of Psalm 41 (42):

> I say this not so that you may sing praise alone, but that you may also
> teach your children and your wives such songs, to sing not only while
> weaving and doing other work but especially at table. For at the ban-
> quets the devil is waiting in ambush, since there he has drunkeness and
> gluttony, laughter, idleness and licentiousness as companions. Thus it is
> particularly necessary before and after eating to erect a fortress of
> psalms, so to speak, against him, and when leaving the table to sing holy
> hymns to God together with your wife and children. . . . For just as those
> who invite actors, dancers and lewd women to their banquets also invite
> demons and the devil and fill their house with numberless enemies, so
> those who invite David with the cithara through him invite Christ into
> their home.[68]

In his first homily on the Epistle to the Colossians Chrysostom expresses the same sentiment at greater length:

> Let us look at what follows [i.e., at a banquet]. There one hears pipes,
> citharas and flutes; here there is no noisy music, but rather the singing of
> psalms and hymns. There songs sound to the praise of demons; here to
> the praise of God, Lord of the universe. Do you see what gratitude there
> is here, while there ingratitude and crudity predominate? Tell me then,
> what sort of behavior is this, that instead of thanking God who has
> nourished us with his gifts you invite in demons? For the songs accom-
> panied by stringed instruments are nothing but the devil's songs. Instead
> of saying: "Praise to you, O Lord, for having fed me with your gifts," do
> you behave like a worthless dog and never think of God, but sing to the
> demons? Dogs fawn upon the members of the household whether they
> receive anything or not, but not you. A dog continues to fawn upon his

master even if he receives nothing, but you bark at your Lord even after having received his gifts. Moreover, however well a stranger may treat a dog, the animal does not abandon his guard but refuses his friendship; you, however, even though you continually suffer unspeakable harm from the demons, invite them to your feasts. So you are even worse than a dog.[69]

Such harsh words can only be understood in the context of religious history. In fact the invitation of the god to the table was especially practiced in the comunity meals of the cults, as Aelius Aristides reports with reference to the cult of Serapis:

Only with this god do men take part in their offerings in a special way in complete community, for they invite him [the god] to table and set him in the first place as their guest and table companion.[70]

But non-religious meals also had a certain religious consecration, for during them offerings were made to the Lares.[71] Accordingly hymns, such as the paeans of the Greeks, were often sung in praise of the gods. Secular songs, too, contained invocations of the gods. Lucian of Samosata writes that dancing songs were dedicated to Aphrodite:

The song which is sung while dancing is an invitation to Aphrodite and the gods of love to help in the dancing and jumping.[72]

The Christian singing of psalms and hymns at mealtime thus had the important task of replacing the pagan hymns and as Chrysostom says, of inviting Christ to table. Even in Clement of Alexandria's time the singing of psalms had an established place at Christian meals.[73] Tertullian seems to know of the singing of hymns at table (at an agape) when in his *Apology* he concedes a place to the improvised song:

After eating it is expected that everyone sing God's praises, however he is able, whether from the holy Scriptures or out of his own talent.[74]

Thus singing at table was responsorial, as it was in church, or it was purely solo, although Clement of Alexandria and Chrysostom speak of singing in unison. One is reminded of Tertullian in Cyprian's letter to Donatus, in which he writes that mealtime should also be a time of grace:

A modest meal should sound with psalms, and if you have a good memory and a pleasant voice you should take upon yourself the singer's office.[75]

In this way Christianity wholly retained the customs of antiquity, which made use of solo singing at meals. In fact Christian psalm singers so completely took the place of pagan singers that they were even invited by pagans to sing at their banquets.[76] It was in this way that the singing of psalms and hymns reformed pagan table customs in a Christian sense.

4. CHRISTIANITY'S OPPOSITION TO PAGAN WEDDING CUSTOMS. LICENTIA FESCENNINA. POMPA DIABOLI.

The singing of psalms and hymns was particularly important in supplanting pagan wedding customs with their highly objectionable fertility rites, as they were expressed in the so-called *licentia Fescennina*. These were the mocking verses sung by boys and girls at weddings and at harvest feasts. The name *Fescenninus* has customarily been derived from Fescenninum in Etruria, where these verses were said to have been especially used. M. Schanz[77] has pointed out, however, that a connection is far more probable with the word *fascinum*, the symbol of procreative power which played an important role in pagan wedding ceremonies and which Augustine mentions.[78] The scandalous pagan wedding ceremonies employed singing and music extensively,[79] and one can see, then, how the Fathers of the Church would condemn music and dancing when they spoke of wedding celebrations.[79a]

With respect to Eph. 5:32 ("This is a great mystery; I refer to Christ and the Church") Chrysostom writes concerning wedding festivities:

If then, someone asks, since neither maidens nor married women may dance, who shall dance? No one. What need is there of dancing? Dances take place in the pagan mysteries, but in ours there is silence and decency, modesty and peacefulness. A great mystery is being celebrated. Out with the harlots, out with the unclean! How much of a mystery is it? Two come together and form one. When the bride enters why is there no dancing, why no cymbals, but rather profound silence and calm? Rather, when they come together, making not a lifeless image or the image of an earthly creature but the image of God himself, why do you introduce such a pagan uproar, disturbing those present and filling their souls with shame and confusion? . . . Tell me, do you celebrate the mystery of Christ and invite the devil? . . . Where flutists are, there Christ is not; but even if he should enter he first casts them out and only then works wonders. What can be more disagreeable than such Satanic pomp?[80]

For Chrysostom, music and dancing belong to the devil's pomp, which Christians had renounced in baptism.

In a homily on Gen. 29 he addresses his flock:

You see how worthily weddings were celebrated in times past. People who hide behind Satan's pomp and from the very beginning drag marriage into the mud should listen, for then there were no flutes, no cymbals, no devilish dances.[81]

The *hymenaios*, the wedding song sung to the music of cithara and flute by those who escorted the bride into the bridegroom's house, was quite well-liked in Christian circles, and Chrysostom had to take strong measures against it.[82] In another text he attacks the hymns to Aphrodite which were sung during the wedding dance:

> But flutes, syrinxes and cymbals, drunken leapings-about and the rest of present-day shamelessness was foreign to them [then]. But with us the dancers sing hymns to Aphrodite . . . and filthy songs on that day [of the wedding].[83]

The struggle against the ancient practices was a hard one. "I know well," Chrysostom says at one time,

> that people laugh at me when I reproach them and that I seem foolish to many when I dare to speak against the old customs, for custom wreaks a powerful deception. Nonetheless I will continue to declare these things.[84]

He describes the entire *licentia Fescennina*, which consisted in bringing the bride and groom by night with torches and flute music to the market place, while the participants were inflamed "with a certain diabolical rivalry" to excel each other in mockery and lewd songs, poured out on the bridal couple. And even if this were not to result in unchastity,

> the devil is satisfied with the horrible speeches and songs and with the fact that the bride is put on public exhibition and taken to the market place with the bridegroom. Although everything happens at night, darkness does not draw a veil over this atrocious scene. Many torches are used, so that the shameful deed does not remain hidden. Why the great crowd of people? Why the drunkenness? Why the flute playing? Does all this take place in the open so that even those who are sleeping in their homes may know about it and, roused by the sound of the flutes, look down on this comedy from their windows? What shall one say of the songs that breathe forth nothing but sensuality, dishonorable passions, forbidden relationships and the downfall of families?[85]

All these pagan wedding ceremonies belong to the pomp of the devil, especially the music:

> Cymbals, flutes, lewd and adulterous songs — these are the devil's pomp.[86] The devil is present [at these weddings], summoned by demonic pomp. But you renounced this pomp and entered the service of Christ on the day when you were initiated into the sacred mysteries.[87]

The thought which Chrysostom always puts into the foreground in relation to Eph. 5:32 is that marriage is a mystery and that the wedding day is the day of initiation into this mystery. This became even clearer when one considers that the pagans designated their mysteries as ἱεροὶ γάμοι and also likened marriage to a mystery.[88]

Chrysostom was not alone in his condemnation of music and dancing at wedding festivities. In canon 53 of the Council of Laodicea (c. 380) we read:

> It is not permitted for Christians to go to weddings and dance, but only in all propriety to eat or take a light collation, as is fitting for Christians.[89]

Indeed, canon 54 of the same Council presupposes more laxity in practice when it does not suppress shows at weddings but only forbids clerics to view such things:

> Members of the hierarchy or clerics may not look at shows at weddings or banquets but must get up and leave before the actors come.[90]

Gregory Nazianzus wishes all these pagan customs to be banned from Christian weddings and desires only one thing:

> May Christ be present at the weddings and change the water into wine, that is, may everything be changed into the better, so that what cannot be mixed will not be mixed, and bishops and buffoons, prayers and noise, psalmody and the music of flutes will not all collide together.[91]

And if Chrysostom had said: "Where dancing is, there is the devil,"[92] Commodian before him had already reckoned it all as the devil's pomp. Addressing Christian women he remarks:

> What shall I say of the pomp of the devil? You look down on the law and prefer to be pleasing to the world; you dance in your homes and sing love songs instead of psalms.[93]

Ephraem expresses himself similarly:

> Let us come before his presence with praise and rejoice before him with psalms! With psalms, he [the psalmist] says, and not with ribaldry, with psalms and not with diabolical songs. He says: "Come, let us fall down and worship and weep before him!" Not: "Let us dance and play the cithara," but rather: "Let us weep with psalms and hymns...." Where there is the singing of psalms with contrition, there God is present with his angels. But where the songs of our adversaries are heard, there is God's anger and woe and requital for laughter.... Where cithara playing and dancing and hand-clapping take place, there is the deluding of men and the ruin of women and the sorrow of angels and a feast for the devil. O the devil's spitefulness! How he beguiles everyone!... Today they seem to sing the psalms, as God has prescribed, and tomorrow they dance passionately, as the devil teaches.... Today they are Christians

and tomorrow pagans. . . . Do not sing psalms today with the angels so as to dance tomorrow with the demons. Far be it from you to be today one who loves Christ and listens to the Scriptures as they are read and tomorrow is a traitor who despises Christ and listens to cithara music.[94]

With regard to all of this one must bear in mind that dancing, like music, was considered idolatrous because of its use in pagan cult.[95] Only thus can the sharp contrast between Christ and the devil, which appears in all the citations, be understood.

5. CHRISTIANITY AND THEATER MUSIC.

Christians believed that the theater and the music heard there were part of the *pompa diaboli.* Just as the most ancient ecclesiastical laws kept music teachers from the Church, so they also forbade Christians to take part professionally in any theatrical activity.[96] Cyril of Jerusalem provides this commentary to the words of abrenunciation:

> And then you say: "And from all his pomp." To this pomp of the devil belong the mania of the theater, horse races, hunting and all vanities of that kind. . . . Do not wish greedily to be concerned with the passions of the theater, where obscene shows with actors are shamelessly presented, as well as the frantic dances of effeminate men. . . . All that belongs to the pomp of the devil.[97]

Tertullian adduces theatrical music as a means by which one can recognize that the theater is idolatrous: the theater and pagan liturgy

> resemble each other in their devices, having the same procession to the place of display from temples and altars with their wretched incense and blood, the same accompaniment of flutes and trumpets, both under the direction of the designator and the haruspex, the arrangers of funeral processions and games.[98]

Therefore he reproaches the music and singing of the theater as cultic-ly infected:

> That which pertains to the voice, melody, instruments and writing belongs to Apollo, the Muses, Minerva and Mercury. Hate, O Christian, the things whose authors you must hate.[99]

So theater music is clearly branded as a service of the idols. For this reason Pseudo-Cyprian, in his treatise *De spectaculis*, designates it a crime if a Christian occupies himself with such theater music, for it is consecrated to idols.[100] For Chrysostom the melodies of the theater are the songs of the devil and of the demons.[101] Yet it was precisely these theater tunes that the people most enjoyed singing. On account of the absolutely public character of the theatrical productions of that time such tunes became popular more quickly than they do today. In the Antonine period, for example, it was customary for people to go daily to the theater or to the odeum.[103] On the streets and in public places one would hear nothing but the singing of theater tunes.

Hence it is not to be wondered at that the Emperor Julian, in his reorganization of pagan religion, later permitted the priests to attend only "sacred tournaments" but forbade them to form friendships with musicians or charioteers:

> Under no circumstances shall a priest be present at immoral plays, nor shall he bring them into his house, for this is not at all proper for him to do. And if it had been possible to drive them all out of the theater so that, purified again, they could have been given back to Dionysos, I would certainly have made the attempt to carry it through. But since I am of the opinion that this was neither possible nor useful had it been possible, I renounced this ambition completely. Nevertheless I demand that the priests keep far away and leave the immorality of the theater to the people. Thus no priest may enter a theater, nor make friends with a musician or a charioteer, nor shall a dancer or an actor come into his house. But whoever wishes may attend the sacred tournaments, which women are forbidden both to take part in and to view.[104]

Julian's attitude toward the theater of the time shows us that it was probably not excessive rigorism that led Christianity, for reasons of morality, to forbid its adherents to attend the shows. But with this there was, as already noted, the far more important consideration for Christians that everything connected with the theater, even the "sacred tournaments," was dedicated to the gods.

Julian's failure to carry out a reform of the theater, a task to which he did not feel himself adequate, also explains why Christianity's struggle against theater music lasted for centuries. Even here the only substitute for theater music was the singing of psalms and hymns. Thus Tertullian played off psalms against theater tunes.[105] Hilary,[106] Ambrose[107] and Augustine[108] all recommended Christian songs as substitutes for the music of the stage. Gaudentius of Brescia warned of the use of lyre, flute and cymbals, since through their use a Christian home could become a theater and a dwelling of the devil:

> Unhappy those houses where lyre and flute are heard, where all sorts of music sounds with the cymbals of the dancers, for they are no different than theaters. I beg, then, that all these things be cast out. Let the house of a Christian and a baptized person be undisturbed by the devil's choir .... Let it be sanctified by diligent prayer and the frequent singing of psalms, hymns and spiritual songs.[109]

In the last analysis, then, theater music was a service of the gods, and therefore for Christians the practice of this music was equivalent to a violation of the baptismal vows.

6. Musical Education of Pagan and Christian Youth.

Since the pagans considered music as a subject to be taught and as part of a child's upbringing, Christians also had to arrive at a judgment concerning the instruction of children in music and singing. For the pagans of antiquity it was Plato above all who had laid down the principles of pedagogy, and he stressed the advantages of a good musical education:

> Children should grow up in a healthy atmosphere, and their feeling for harmony should be nourished from their youth on up. For this reason a musical education is very important, because cadence and harmony generally penetrate into the interior of the soul, influence it strongly, create well-being and, when one has been properly reared, make a person well-mannered—although the opposite occurs when there has been no proper upbringing.[110]

Thus the question arose as to what music children should learn. Plato prohibited the use of many-stringed and rich sounding instruments such as the different kinds of harps (πηκτίς, τρίγωνον, μάγαδίς) and the flute, and he retained only the lyre and the cithara.[111] Girls should learn music as well as boys, although it was important that only those types of singing should be chosen which conformed more to the feminine character. Music should make a woman mild and modest, just as a woman's whole bearing in relation to her husband, her children and her servants should be marked by mildness and modesty.[112] The first things that children learn to sing should be hymns to the gods and songs about the heroes.[113] Thus instruction in singing also had a religious aim. According to Lucian of Samosata, music and arithmetic were the subjects with which a child's education should begin.[114]

Christianity inherited antiquity's appreciation for good music in children's upbringing. Clement of Alexandria remarked that music was used for the ornamentation and ordering of manners. But music which aroused sadness or violent emotions should be scorned.[115] According to him, music belonged to the so-called "liberal sciences," even if only as a handmaid of philosophy.[116]

As close as Plato's conception was to Clement's, the way in which music was taught in the declining years of pagan antiquity was far removed from this ideal. Instruction in instrumental music took first place, while the text and melody of what was sung was considered of less account. It was precisely with regard to the upbringing of children that Commodian found fault with the practice of secular music:

> Et choros historicos et cantica musica quaeris
> Nec tali subolem insanire licentia curas?[117]

Basil of Caesarea broached the question as to what attitude Christian youth should maintain toward the music of the time. His own position he supported by citing David and Pythagoras when he asserted that it all depended on whether one should lend his ear to healthy or harmful melodies, and he advised Christian youth to avoid those songs which could destroy the soul:

> For passions, unfree and base, are wont to arise from this kind of music. But we must seek out the other kind of music, which is better and which leads to the good, which David, the composer of holy songs, made use of to free the king from his melancholy. Pythagoras also, when he had fallen among drunken revelers, is said to have commanded the flutist who was leading the carousing to change the melody and to play in the Doric mode. This melody was supposed to have produced such a sobering effect that they all threw away their crowns and went home ashamed. Others rave and bluster like Corybantes and Bacchantes when they hear flute music. So much depends upon whether one listens to healthy or to harmful tunes. Therefore you should have as little to do with music as it is now practiced as you would with any other disgraceful act.[118]

In general, however, Basil was convinced that children should be instructed in music.[119] He was thinking primarily of religious songs, which he felt should accompany the Christian throughout his entire life, for in his eyes the psalms were

> a safeguard for children, an ornament for the mature and a consolation for the elderly.[120]

He put so much trust in spiritual songs that he could write:

> No matter how brutal a man may be, as soon as he hears the psalms being sung the wildness departs from his soul and the melody seems to make him fall into a slumber.[121]

For every stage of growth in virtue such singing would be excellent, providing instruction for beginners, a means of advancement for those making progress and a support for the perfect.[122] Basil wished the psalms to be sung at home, since they were "a refreshment in the cares of the day."[123]

Jerome also considered the psalms part of a child's upbringing. A little girl should know the Psalter by heart by the age of seven.[124] Her mouth should be closed to frivolous, worldly songs, but she should seek delight in the songs of the Church.[125] How diligently the singing of psalms was practiced in the schools of the Orient has already been noted.[126] Secular music, on the other hand, was eventually forbidden to children, even in synodal statutes.[127]

NOTES

1. Cf. *supra*, Chapter 1, n. 27.

2. W. Helbig, *Wandgemälde der vom Vesuv verschütteten Städte Campaniens* (Leipzig 1868), nos. 51–56, 58, 60.

3. *Ibid.*, no. 53.

4. Cf. Plate 2 and also A. de Marchi, *Il culto privato* I (Milan 1896), p. 92.

5. Cf. n. 47 and n. 63. On the lyre cf. L. Eizenhöfer, "Die Siegelbildvorschläge des Clemens von Alexandria und die älteste christliche Literatur," in *Jahrbuch für Antike und Christentum* 3 (1960), 66–67.

6. Tertullian, *De spectaculis* 29 (CSEL 20, 28 Reifferscheid-Wissowa): Satis nobis litterarum est, satis versuum est, satis sententiarum, satis etiam canticorum. J. Kroll, *Die christliche Hymnodik bis zu Klemens von Alexandria* (*Programm der Akademie von Braunsberg*, 1921/1922), p. 24, remarks that, for Tertullian, *versus* and *cantica* could only mean hymns.

7. H. Achelis, *Didaskalie* II in TU NF 10, 2, 5.

8. *Constitutiones Apostolorum* V 10, 2 (265 Funk): Ὁ γὰρ τοι Χριστιανὸς ὁ πιστὸς οὐδὲ ᾠδὴν ἐθνικὴν ὀφείλει λέγειν, οὔτε ᾆσμα πορνικόν· ἐπεὶ συμβήσεται αὐτῷ διὰ τῆς ᾠδῆς, εἰδώλων μνημονεύειν ὀνόματα δαιμονικά, καὶ ἀντὶ τοῦ ἁγίου Πνεύματος, εἰσφρήσει ἐν αὐτῷ τὸ πονηρόν.

9. Cf. *supra*, Chapter 1, n. 30.

10. Jerome, *Epistula* 107 (*Ad Laetam de institutione filiae*) 4, 8 (CSEL 55, 295 Hilberg): Cum avum viderit, in pectus eius transiliat, e colo pendeat, nolenti alleluia decantet.

11. There is a reproduction in R. Garrucci, *Storia dell' arte cristiana* V (Prato 1879), table 296, 4 and C.M. Kaufmann, *Handbuch der christlichen Archäologie* (Paderborn³ 1922), p. 491. Cf. H. Dütschke, *Ravennatische Studien* (Leipzig 1909), p. 188.

12. F. Münter, *Sinnbild und Kunstvorstellung der alten Christen* (Altona 1825), I 84.

13. Tertullian, *Ad uxorem* 2, 9 (I 697 Oehler).

14. F.X. Kraus, RE II 292.

15. Cf. Dütschke, *Ravennatische Studien*, p. 188.

16. Opinions differ as to the meaning of these symbols — whether they refer to the education of the deceased or to their activity in the afterlife.

17. Cf. Origen, *De oratione* 2, 4 (GCS Orig. II 301 Koetschau): οὐδὲ γὰρ δύναται ἡμῶν ὁ νοῦς προσεύξασθαι, ἐὰν μὴ πρὸ αὐτοῦ τὸ πνεῦμα προσεύξηται οἱονεὶ ἐν ὑπηκόῳ αὐτοῦ,

ὥσπερ οὐδὲ ψάλαι καὶ εὐρύθμως καὶ ἐμμελῶς, καὶ ἐμμέτρως καὶ συμφώνως ὑμνῆσαι τὸν πατέρα ἐν Κριστῷ, ἐὰν μὴ ,,τὸ πνεῦμα'' τὸ ,,πάντα'' ἐρευνῶν, ,,καὶ τὰ βάθη τοῦ θεοῦ'' πρότερον αἰνέσῃ καὶ ὑμνήσῃ τοῦτον. Despite the accumulation of musical terms in this passage it is hardly a proof for the use of stringed instruments in Christian private life, for by this time ψάλλειν already had the weaker sense of "to sing" – which is the way Clement of Alexandria uses it in the passage just mentioned, when he writes: πρὸς κιθάραν . . . ἢ λύραν ἄδειν τε καὶ ψάλλειν. Likewise ψάλτης was the official designation of the cantor. Cf. *supra*, Chapter 4, n. 81. Consequently the translation of Origen by P. Koetschau in BKV 48 (1926), p. 13 ("wie er auch den Vater in Christus nicht mit dem Saitenspiel besingen . . . kann"), is incorrect.

18. Synesius, *Hymni* 7, 1 (PG 66, 1612): Πρῶτος νόμον εὑρόμαν Ἐπὶ σοί, μάκαρ, ἄμβροτε,. Γόνε κύδιμε Παρθένου Ἰησοῦ Σολυμήϊε, Νεοπηγέσιν ἁρμογαῖς Κρέξαι κιθάρας μίτους. *Ibid.* 8, 1 (PG 66, 1612): Ὑπὸ Δώριον ἁρμογὰν Ἐλεφαντοδέτων μίτων λύρας Στάσω λιγυρὰν ὄπα Ἐπὶ σοί, μάκαρ, ἄμβροτε, Γόνε Κύδιμε Παρθένου.

19. Synesius, *Epist.* 94 (PG 66, 1464): Ἐῶ τὰ κατὰ τὸν ἑταῖρον Δισκουρίδην, ὅτι μετρίως ἐπράχθη, καὶ οὐχ ὡς ἂν κινῆσαι θεοῦ τε καὶ ἀνθρώπων νέμεσιν. Αὕτη μέντοι σαφῶς ἐστι περὶ ἧς πρὸς λύραν ἄδομεν.

20. Chrysostum, *Homilia in Ps.* 41 (PG 55, 158): Ἐνταῦθα οὐ χρεία κιθάρας, οὐδὲ νεύρων τεταμένων, οὔτε πλήκτρου καὶ τέχνης, οὐδὲ ὀργάνων τινῶν, ἀλλ' ἐὰν θέλῃς, σὺ σαυτὸν ἐργάσῃ κιθάραν, νεκρώσας τὰ μέλη τῆς σαρκός, καὶ πολλὴν τῷ σώματι πρὸς τὴν ψυχὴν ποιήσας τὴν συμφωνίαν.

21. Chrysostom, *Homilia 1 in Epist. ad Coloss. I* (Maurist ed. 11, 330): Ἀλλὰ δὴ τὰ μετὰ ταῦτα ἴδωμεν. Ἐκεῖ μὲν αὐλοὶ καὶ κιθάραι καὶ σύριγγες, ἐνταῦθα δὲ οὐδὲν ἀπηχὲς μέλος. ἀλλὰ τί; ὕμνοι, ψαλμῳδίαι. Ἐκεῖ μέν οἱ δαίμονες ἀνυμνοῦνται, ἐνταῦθα δὲ ὁ πάντων Δεσπότης Θεός· Ὁρᾶς πόσης μὲν αὕτη χάριτος, πόσης δὲ ἀγνωμοσύνης ἐκείνη καὶ ἀναισθησίας γέμει; Εἰπὲ γάρ μοι· ὁ θεός σε ἔθρεψεν ἐκ τῶν ἀγαθῶν αὐτοῦ, καὶ δέον αὐτῷ εὐχαριστεῖν μετὰ τὸ τραφῆναι, σὺ δὲ τοὺς δαίμονας ἐπεισάγεις; τὰ γὰρ διὰ τῶν πηκνίδων οὐδὲν ἄλλο ἢ δαιμόνων ἄσματα. Δέον εἰπεῖν, εὐλογητὸς εἶ Κύριε, ὅτι ἐθρεψάς με ἐκ τῶν ἀγαθῶν σου, σὺ δὲ καθάπερ τις κύων ἄτιμος, οὐδὲ μέμνησαι, ἀλλὰ τοὺς δαίμονας ἐπεισάγεις; Μᾶλλον δὲ οἱ μὲν κύνες λαβόντες, καὶ μὴ λαβόντες σαίνουσι τοὺς οἰκείους, σὺ δὲ οὐδὲ τοῦτο.

22. Cf. Kaufmann, *Handbuch . . .*, pp. 253 and 493, illustration 242, 3.

23. Cf. Plate 28, 2. There is a detailed description in J. Ficker, *Die altchristlichen Bildwerke im christlichen Museum des Laterans* (Leipzig 1890), p. 74.

24. Kaufmann, *Handbuch . . .*, p. 493, illustration 242, 3. On the significance of the Good Shepherd on sarcophagi cf. Th. Klauser, "Gibt es in der Sarkophagplastik Schaftträger-Figuren, mit denen Jesus gemeint ist?" in *Jahrbuch für Antike und Christentum* 8/9 (1965/1966), 129–135.

25. Cf., e.g., the sarcophagus in S. Vittore in Ravenna, of which there is a reproduction in Dütschke, *Ravennatische Studien*, p. 65. Another example is the sarcophagus cover in the Palazzo dei Conservatori reproduced in Plate 28, 1 of the present work. In the two recumbent figures two spouses are intended. The husband holds an open scroll in his left hand, while his wife plays the lute.

26. Dütschke, *ibid.*, p. 189. Cf. also J. Quasten, "Die Leierspielerin auf heidnischen und christlichen Sarkophagen," in *Römische Quartalschrift* 37 (1929), 1–13.

27. Cf. *infra*, Chapter 6, Sec. 2.

28. Cf. *ibid.*

29. Cf. *supra*, Chapter 4, Sec. 5.

30. Cf. Plate 29, 1.

31. On sitting as a gesture of mourning cf. Th. Klauser, *Die Cathedra im Totenkult der heidnischen und christlichen Antike* (*Liturgiegeschichtliche Quellen und Forschungen* 21) (Münster 1927), pp. 13 f. and 23. f.

32. H. Leclercq, DACL VII 1, 1190.

33. Cf. *infra*, Chapter 6, Sec. 4.

34. Cf. *infra*, Chapter 4, n. 128.

35. Cornelius Nepos, *Vita* 15, *Epaminondas* 1, 2 (60 Halm): Scimus enim musicen nostris moribus abesse a principis persona, saltare etiam in vitiis poni: quae omnia apud Graecos et grata et laude digna ducuntur.

36. Livy 39, 6, 7 (IX 12 Weissenborn): Luxuriae enim peregrinae origo ab exercitu Asiatico invecta in urbem est. Ii primum lectos aeratos, vestem stragulam pretiosam, plagulas et alia textilia et, quae tum magnificae supellectilis habebantur, monopodia et abacos Romam advexerunt. Tunc psaltriae sambucistriaeque et convivalia (alia) ludorum oblectamenta addita epulis.

37. Lucian, *De saltatione* 2 (140 Sommerbrodt): Ἀνὴρ δέ τις ὤν, ὦ λῷστε, καὶ ταῦτα παιδείᾳ σύντροφος καὶ φιλοσοφίᾳ τὰ μέτρια ὡμιληκώς, ἀφέμενος, ὦ Λυκῖνε, τοῦ περὶ τὰ βελτίω σπουδάζειν καὶ τοῖς παλαιοῖς συνεῖναι, κάθησαι καταυλούμενος, θηλυδρίαν ἄνθρωπον ὁρῶν ἐσθῆσι μαλακαῖς καὶ ᾄσμασι ἀκολάστοις ἐναβρυνόμενον καὶ μιμούμενον ἐρωτικὰ γύναια.

38. Ammianus Marcellinus, *Rerum gestarum* 14, 6, 18 (16 Carolus-Clark): Quod cum ita sint, paucae domus studiorum seriis cultibus antea celebratae, nunc ludibriis ignaviae torpentis exundant, vocabili sono, perflabili tinnitu fidium resultantes, denique pro philosopho cantor, et in locum oratoris doctor artium ludicrarum accitur et byblio- thecis sepulchrorum ritu in perpetuum clausis, organa fabricantur hydraulica, et lyrae ad speciem carpentorum ingentes, tibiaeque et histrionici gestus instrumenta non levia.

39. Clement of Alexandria, *Paidagogos* 2, 4 (GCS Clem. I 183 Stählin).

40. Cf. *supra*, Chapter 4, n. 6.

41. Gregory Nazianzus, *Carmina* II 2, 7, 260 (PG 37, 1571): αὐλῶν τε Φρυγίων μανιητόκος ἔκτομος ἤχη.

42. Epiphanius, *Panarion haer.* 25, 4 (GCS Ep. I 272 Holl): Καὶ γὰρ καὶ αὐτὸς ὁ αὐλὸς μίμημά ἐστι τοῦ δράκοντος, δι' οὗ ἐλάλησεν ὁ πόνηρος καὶ ἠπάτησε τὴν Εὖαν. Ἀπὸ τοῦ τύπου γὰρ ἐκείνου κατὰ μίμησιν ὁ αὐλὸς τοῖς ἀνθρώποις εἰς ἀπάτην κατεσκευάσθη. Καὶ ὅρα τὸν τύπον ὅν αὐτὸς ὁ αὐλῶν ἐν τῷ αὐλῷ ποιεῖται. Αὐλῶν γὰρ ἄνω ἀνανεύει, καὶ κάτω κατανεύει, δεξιά τε κλίνει καὶ εὐώνυμα ὁμοίως, ἐκείνῳ. Τούτοις γὰρ καὶ ὁ διάβολος τοῖς σχήμασιν κέχρηται, ἵνα κατὰ τῶν ἐπουρανίων ἐνδείξηται τὴν βλασφημίαν.

43. Cf. *supra*, Chapter 4, n. 63.

44. Basil, *Comment. in Isaiam* 5, 158 (PG 30, 377): τῶν δὲ ματαιοτεχνῶν, οἷον κιθαριστικῆς, ἢ ὀρχηστικῆς, ἢ αὐλητικῆς, ἢ ἄλλων τοιούτων, παυσαμένης τῆς ἐνεργείας, τὸ ἔργον συναφανίζεται. καὶ ὄντως, κατὰ τὴν ἀποστολικήν φωνήν, τὸ τέλος τούτων ἀπώλεια.

45. Jerome, *Epistula* 54 (*Ad Furiam de viduitate servanda*) 13 (CSEL 54, 479 Hilberg): Cantor pellatur ut noxius; fidicinas et psaltrias et istius modi chorum diaboli quasi mortifera sirenarum carmina proturba ex aedibus tuis.

46. Augustine, *De doctrina christiana* 2, 18 (PL 34, 49): Nos tamen non propter superstitionem profanorum debemus musicam fugere, si quid inde utile ad intelligendas sanctas scripturas rapere potuerimus; nec ad illorum theatricas nugas converti, si aliquid de citharis et de organis, quod at spiritualia capienda valeat, disputemus.

47. W. Riedel, *Die Kirchenrechtsquellen des Patriarchats Alexandrien* (Leipzig 1900), p. 206.

48. Cf. *supra*, Chapter 4, Sec. 5.

49. Riedel, *Die Kirchenrechtsquellen*..., p. 257.

50. *Constitutiones Apostolorum* VIII 31, 9 (534 Funk): τῶν ἐπὶ σκηνῆς ἐάν τις προσίη ἀνὴρ ἢ γυνὴ ἢ ἡνίοχος ἢ μονομάχος ἢ σταδιοδρόμος ἢ λουδεμπιστὴς ἢ χοραύλης ἢ κιθαριστὴς ἢ λυριστὴς ἢ ὁ τὴν ὄρχησιν ἐπιδεικνύμενος ἢ πάπηλος, ἢ παυσάσθωσαν ἢ ἀποβαλλέσθωσαν.

51. Riedel, *Die Kirchenrechtsquellen*..., p. 176.

52. *Ibid.*, p. 63.

53. A. de Waal, "Le chant liturgique dans les inscriptions romains du IVe à IXe siècle," in *Compte rendu du Congrès scientifique international des catholiques* (Brussels 1895), 2, 313.

54. The instrument which is pictured is quite similar to that on the sarcophagus of Saint-Maximin (cf. Plate 29, 1); both depictions may date from the same century. A terracotta fragment with another similar portrayal of an organ likewise belongs to the fourth century; it is preserved in the Museum of the Campo Santo Tedesco. (Cf. Plate 29, 2.) It shows a young singer in festal clothing, accompanied by an organist at an organ pictured to the right. The fragment was found in 1890 in the excavations in the Villa Ludovisi. On the dating and on the dress of the singer cf. J. Wilpert, "Un capitolo di storia del vestriario," in *L'Arte* 1 (1898), 104. The two organs in the socle relief on the south side of the Obelisk of Theodosius in Istanbul are of the same type. There one may see a dance performed before the emperor to the accompaniment of organ and flute. There is a reproduction in E. Wellesz, *Byzantinische Musik* (Breslau 1927), p. 82. On the early history of the organ cf. the instruments discovered in Pompeii and reproduced in Plate 26 of the present work. For portrayals of organs on ancient monuments cf. H. Leclercq, "Instruments de musique," in DACL VII 1, 1181 ff. One not shown there is a graffito which was discovered in 1928 under S. Sebastiano in Rome. A gladiatorial combat is depicted. Behind his instrument the organist is visible, and in the foreground four persons are occupied in pumping air for the organ. This reminds me of a scene on the reverse of a medal of Valentinian, published in J.H. Sabatier, *Description générale des medaillons contorniates* (Paris 1860), table X. On the construction of the hydraulic organ cf. Tertullian, *De anima* (II 576 Oehler): Spectra portentosissimam Archimedes munificentiam, organum hydraulicam dico, tot membra, tot partes, tot compagines, tot itinera vocum, tot compendia sonorum, tot commercia modorum, tot acies tibiarum, et una moles erunt omnia. *Idem, De baptismo* 8 (I 626 Oehler): Sane humano ingenio licebit spiritum in aquam arcessere et concorporationem eorum accommodatis desuper manibus alio spiritu tantae claritatis animare, deo autem in suo organo non licebit per manus sanctas sublimitatem modulari spiritalem? For more on the hydraulic organ cf. J. Moreau, "Die Wasserorgel auf dem romischen Mosaik von Nennig an der Mosel," in *Saarbrucker Hefte* 4 (1956), 44!49.

On the question as to when the Church changed her position and permitted musical instruments in the liturgy cf. D. Schuberth, *Kaiserliche Liturgie. Die Einbeziehung von Musikinstrumenten, insbesondere Orgel, in den frühmittelalterlichen Gottesdienst* (Göttingen 1968).

55. Cf. H. Blümner, *Die römischen Privataltertumer* (*Handbuch der klassischen Altertumswissenschaft* 4, 2) (Munich 1911), p. 411.

56. Martial, *Epigrammaton* 5, 78, 22 (126 Heraeus):

> Parva est cenula (quis potest negare)
> Nec de Gadibus improbis puellae
> Vibrabunt sine fine prurientes

Lascivos docili tremore lumbos;
Sed quod non grave sit nec infacetum
Parvi tibia condyli sonabit.

57. Pliny, *Epistularum* 9, 17, 3 (249 Kukula): cum lector aut lyristes aut comoedus inductus est.

58. There is a reproduction of a meal at which a female lutenist, a lyre-playing boy and a flutist are present in F.J. Dölger, ΙΧΘΥΣ III (Münster 1922), tables LIII and LV. Cf. also the depiction of the sarcophagus in the Vactican Museum reproduced in Dölger, ΙΧΘΥΣ IV (Münster 1927), tables 250, 2 and 252.

59. Martial, *Epigrammaton* 9, 77, 5 (219 Heraeus): Quod optimum sit quaeritis convivium? In quo choraules non erit.

60. Claudian, *De consulatu Stilichonis* 2, 141 (155 Koch):

nullo citharae convivia cantu
non pueri lasciva sonant.

61. Cf. *supra*, Chapter 4, Sec. 2.

62. Commodian, *Instructiones* 1, 32, 7 (CSEL 15, 43 Dombart):

Auro licet cenes cum turba choraulica semper,
Cruciarium Dominum si non adorasti peristi.

63. Basil, *Comment. in Isaiam* 5, 158 (PG 30, 376): Σοὶ δὲ χρυσῷ καὶ ἐλέφαντι πεποικιλμένη ἡ λύρα ἐφ' ὑψηλοῦ τινος βωμοῦ ὥσπερ τι ἄγαλμα καὶ εἴδωλον δαιμόνων ἀνάκειται. καὶ γυνή τις ἀθλία, ἀντὶ τοῦ τὰς χεῖρας ἐρείδειν πρὸς ἄτρακτον διδαχθῆναι, διὰ τὴν ἐκ τῆς δουλείας ἀνάγκην ἐπὶ λύραν ἐκτείνειν ἐδιδάχθη παρὰ σοῦ, ἴσως καὶ μισθοὺς τελέσαντος, τάχα καὶ προαγωγῷ τινι γυναικὶ παραδόντος ἢ μετὰ τὸ πᾶσαν ἀσέλγειαν ἐν τῷ ἰδίῳ σώματι ἀπαθλῆσαι, ταῖς νέαις προκάθηται τῶν ὁμοίων διδάσκαλος.

64. *Ibid.* 5, 160/161 (PG 30, 381): Ἀλλὰ κιθάρα καὶ ψαλτήριον τὴν μέθην αὐτοῖς συνεπιτείνει, τὰ εὑρήματα τοῦ Ἰουβάλ, ... Ἀλλ' ἀπεδίδρασκεν ὁ πατριάρχης, ὡς ἐμπόδιον οὖσαν πρὸς τὸ ἐμβλέπειν τοῖς ἔργοις κυρίου.... Ἀλλὰ καὶ τοῦ Ναβουχοδονόσορ ἐπὶ τοῦ ἐγκαινισμοῦ τῆς εἰκόνος, σάλπιγγος καὶ σύριγγος καὶ κιθάρας, καὶ σαμβύκης, καὶ ψαλτηρίου, συμφωνίας καὶ παντὸς γένους μουσικῶν συνηχούτων. οἱ μὲν λαοί, καὶ αἱ φυλαί, καὶ αἱ γλῶσσαι κατέπιπτον.

65. *Ibid.* 5, 155 (PG 30, 372): Εἶτα πόρρω προϊόντος τοῦ πότου, αὐλοὶ καὶ κιθάραι καὶ τύμπανα, κατὰ μὲν τὴν ἀλήθειαν ἀποθρηνοῦνται τοὺς ἀπολλυμένους, κατὰ δὲ τὴν ἐπιτήδευσιν τῶν μεθυόντων, ὥστε αὐτοῖς πάσας τῆς ψυχῆς τὰς ἡδονὰς τῇ μελῳδίᾳ διεγερθῆναι.

66. Chrysostom, *In Isaiam* 5, 5 (Maurist ed. 6, 57): Ὅπερ καὶ ἡ μέθη ποιεῖ σκοτοῦσα, τοῦτο ἡ μουσικὴ μαλάττουσα τὸ εὔτονον τῆς διανοίας, καὶ κατακλῶσαι τῆς ψυχῆς τὴν ἀνδρείαν, καὶ ἐπὶ μείζονας ἐξάγουσα ἀσελγείας.

67. Ambrose, *De Elia et ieiunio* (PL 14, 716): Vae illis qui mane ebrietatis potum requirunt, quos conveniebat Deo laudes referre, praevenire lucem et occurrere oratione soli iustitiae, qui suos visitat et exsurgit nobis, si nos Christo, non vinae et sicerae surgamus. Hymni dicuntur, et tu citharam tenes? Psalmi canuntur, et tu psalterium sumis aut tympanum? Merito vae quia salutem relinquis, mortem eligis.

68. Chrysostom, *Homilia in Ps.* 41 (PG 55, 157): Τοῦτα λέγω, οὐχ ἵνα ἐπαινῆτε μόνον, ἀλλ' ἵνα καὶ **παῖδας** καὶ γυναῖκας τὰ τοιαῦτα διδάσκητε ᾄσματα ᾄδειν, οὐχ ἐν τοῖς ἱστοῖς μόνον, οὐδὲ ἐν τοῖς ἄλλοις ἔργοις, ἀλλὰ μάλιστα ἐν τραπέζῃ. Ἐπειδὴ γὰρ ὡς τὰ πολλὰ ἐν συμποσίοις ὁ διάβολος ἐφεδρεύει μέθην καὶ φαγίαν ἔχων αὐτῷ συμμαχοῦσαν, καὶ γέλωτα καὶ ἄτακτον, καὶ ψυχὴν ἀνειμένην, μάλιστα τότε δεῖ καὶ πρὸ τραπέζης, καὶ μετὰ τράπεζαν, ἐπιτειχίζειν αὐτῷ τὴν ἀπὸ τῶν ψαλμῶν ἀσφάλειαν, καὶ κοινῇ μετὰ τῆς γυναικὸς καὶ τῶν παίδων ἀναστάντες ἀπὸ τοῦ συμποσίου, τοὺς ἱεροὺς ᾄδειν ὕμνους τῷ θεῷ...ὥσπερ γὰρ οἱ μίμους, καὶ ὀρχηστάς, καὶ πόρνας γυναῖκας εἰς τὰ συμπόσια εἰσάγοντες, δαίμονας καὶ τὸν διάβολον ἐκεῖ καλοῦσι, καὶ μυρίων

πολέμων τὰς αὐτῶν ἐμπιπλῶσιν οἰκίας, οὕτως οἱ τὸν Δαυὶδ καλοῦντες μετὰ τῆς κιθάρας, ἔνδον τὸν Χριστὸν δι' αὐτοῦ καλοῦσιν...

69. Cf. n. 21.

70. Cf. F.J. Dölger, ΙΧΘΥΣ II (Münster 1922), p. 503, n. 4.

71. Ibid., P. 503, n. 1.

72. Lucian, De saltatione 11 (II 1, 132 Sommerbrodt): τοιγαροῦν καὶ τὸ ᾆσμα, ὃ μεταξὺ ὀρχούμενοι ᾄδουσιν, Ἀφροδίτης ἐπίκλησίς ἐστι.

73. CF. supra, Chapter 4, Sec. 4.

74. Tertullian, Apologeticum 39 (266 Oehler): ut quisque de scripturis sanctis vel de proprio ingenio potest, provocatur in medium deo canere.

75. Cyprian, Ad Donatum 16 (CSEL 3, 16 Hartel): Sonet psalmos convivium sobrium: ut tibi tenax memoria est, vox canora, adgredere hoc munus ex more. Cf. E. Schweitzer, "Fragen der Liturgie in Nordafrika zur Zeit Cyprians," in Archiv für Liturgiewissenschaft 12 (1970), 75–76.

76. Cf. supra, Chapter 4, n. 142.

77. M. Schanz, Geschichte der römischen Literatur 3 (Handbuch der klassischen Altertumswissenschaft 8, 3) (Munich ² 1905), p. 21. Against this derivation cf. G. Wissowa, "Fescennini versus," in RE VI 2223.

78. Augustine, De civitate Dei 6, 9 (CSEL 40, 1, 292 Hoffmann): Sed quid hoc dicam, cum ibi sit et Priapus nimius masculus, super cuius immanissimum et turpissimum fascinum sedere nova nupta iubeatur, more honestissimo et religiossimo matronarum?

79. Cf. Cicero, Auctor ad Herennium 4, 33, 44 and Plutarch, Quaestiones convivales 3, 6, 4, 2.

79a. On pagan and Christian wedding customs cf. K. Ritzer, Formen, Riten und religiöses Brauchtum der Eheschliessung in den christlichen Kirchen des ersten Jahrtausends (Liturgiewissenschaftliche Quellen und Forschungen 38) (Münster 1962).

80. Chrysostom, Homilia 12, 5 in Epist. ad Coloss. IV (Maurist ed. 11, 486): "Ἂν τοίνυν, φησί, μήτε παρθένοι μήτε γεγαμημέναι, τις ὀρχήσεται; Μηδείς· ποία γὰρ ὀρχήσεως ἀνάγκη; Ἐν τοῖς τῶν Ἑλλήνων μυστηρίοις αἱ ὀρχήσεις, ἐν δὲ τοῖς ἡμετέροις σιγὴ καὶ εὐκοσμία, αἰδὼς καὶ καταστολή. Μυστήριον τελεῖται μέγα· ἔξω αἱ πόρναι, ἔξω οἱ βέβηλοι. Πῶς μυστήριόν ἐστι; Συνέρχονται, καὶ ποιοῦσιν οἱ δύο ἕνα. Διὰ τί, ὅτε μὲν εἰσήει, οὐκ ὄρχησις, οὐ κύμβαλα, ἀλλὰ πολλὴ σιγή, πολλὴ ἡσυχία.... ὅπου γὰρ μέθη, ἀκολασία, ὅπου αἰσχρολογία, ὁ διάβολος πάρεστι τὰ παρ''ἑαυτοῦ εἰσφέρων. Τούτοις ἑστιώμενος, εἰπέ μοι, μυστήριον Χριστοῦ τελεῖς, καὶ τὸν διάβολον καλεῖς; Τάχα με φορτικὸν εἶναι νομίζετε..." Ἔνθα αὐληταί, οὐδαμοῦ ὁ Χριστός. ἀλλὰ κἂν εἰσέλθῃ, τὸ πρῶτον ἐκβάλλει τούτους, καὶ τότε θαυματουργεῖ. Τί τῆς σατανικῆς πομπῆς ἀηδέστερον;

81. Chrysostom, Homilia 56, 1 in Genesim 29 (Maurist ed. 4, 623): Εἶδες τὸ πάλαιον μεθ' ὅσης σεμνότητος τοὺς γάμους ἐπετέλουν; Ἀκούσατε οἱ περὶ τὰς σατανικὰς πόμπας ἐπτοημένοι, καὶ ἐξ αὐτῶν προοιμίων τὰ σεμνὰ τοῦ γάμου καταισχύνοντες. Μή που αὐλοί; μή που κύμβαλα; μή που χορεῖαι σατανικαί;

82. Chrysostom, De non iterando coniugio 4 (PG 48, 615): καὶ τὸν κρότον, καὶ τὸν ὑμέναιον.

83. Chrysostom, In illud, Propter fornication. uxor. (Maurist ed. 3, 235): αὐλοί δέ, σύριγγες καὶ κύμβαλα, καὶ τὰ οἰνώδη σκιρτήματα καὶ ἡ λοιπὴ ἡ νῦν ἀσχημοσύνη πᾶσα ἐκ ποδῶν ἦν. Οἱ δὲ ἐφ' ἡμῶν καὶ ὕμνους εἰς τὴν Ἀφροδίτην ᾄδουσι χορεύοντες... καὶ αἰσχύνης γέμοντα ᾄσματα κατ' ἐκείνην ᾄδουσι τὴν ἡμέραν. On the Christian rejection of dancing cf. C.

Andresen, "Altchristliche Kritik am Tanz. Ein Ausschnitt aus dem Kampf der alten Kirche gegen Heidnische Sitte," in *Zeitschrift für Kirchengeschichte* 72 (1961), 217-262.

84. Chrysostom, *Homilia 12, 5 in Epist I ad Corinthios* (PG 61, 103): Καὶ οἶδα μὲν ὅτι δόξω καταγέλαστος εἶναι τούτων ἐπιλαμβανόμενος, καὶ πολλὴν ὀφλήσω παρὰ τοῖς πολλοῖς ἄνοιαν τοὺς παλαιοὺς νόμοις μετανικῶν· ὅπερ γὰρ ἔφθην εἰπώ, πολὺς τῆς συνηθείας ὁ παραλογισμός. ἀλλ' ὅμως οὐ παύσομαι λέγων.

85. *Ibid.* 12, 6 (PG 61, 103): Τί γὰρ ὁ πολὺς ὄχλος βούλεται; τί δὲ ἡ μέθη; τί δὲ αἱ σύριγγες; οὐχ εὔδηλον ὅτι ἵνα μηδὲ οἱ ἐν ταῖς οἰκίαις ὄντες, καὶ βαπτιζόμενοι ὕπνῳ βαθεῖ, ταῦτα ἀγοῶσιν, ἀλλ' ὑπὸ τῆς σύριγγος διεγειρόμενοι, καὶ ἄνωθεν ἀπὸ τῶν δρυφάκτων κατακύπτοντες, μάρτυρες γένωνται τῆς κωμῳδίας ἐκείνης; Τί ἄν τις εἴποι τὰς ᾠδὰς αὐτάς. . .καὶ μεταξὺ νέων ἀκολάστων ἀσχημονοῦσαι τοῖς ἀτάκτοις ᾄσμασι, τοῖς αἰσχροῖς ῥήμασι, τῇ σατανικῇ συμφωνίᾳ. The portrayal of wedding processions on pagan monuments is fully in accord with this text. A flutist was always present, and generally there was a citharist also. Vase pictures are particularly instructive in this area. Cf. S. Eitrem, *Beiträge zur griechischen Religionsgeschichte* III (*Videnskapsselskapets Skrifter II. Hist.-Filos. Klasse* 1919, 2) (Kristiania 1920), pp. 70 ff and A. Rumpf (*Die Religion der Griechen* (*Bilderatlas zur Religionsgeschichte*, ed. by H. Haas, 13/14) (Leipzig 1928), no. 176. Eitrem, p. 73, ascribes an apotropaic significance to music at the wedding procession: 'The apotropaic music prepared the way, which the torches also showed in the darkness of the night."

86. Chrysostom, *In Acta Apostolorum homilia* 42, 3 (Maurist ed. 360): ἐκεῖ τοῦ διαβόλου ἡ πομπή, κύμβαλα, αὐλοί, καὶ ᾄσματα πορνείας γέμοντα καὶ μοιχείας. On the *pompa dioboli* cf. H. Rahner, "Pompa diaboli," in *Zeitschrift für katholische Theologie* 55 (1931), 239-273. J.H. Waszink, "Pompa diaboli," in *Vigiliae Christianae* 1 (1947), 13-41. J. Kirsten, *Abrenuntiatio diaboli. Eine Untersuchung zur Bedeutungsgeschichte des altkirchlichen Taufrituals* (Diss. Heidelberg 1952).

87. Chrysostom, *Homilia in Julianianum martyrem* 4 (Maurist ed. 2, 809): καὶ γὰρ πάρεστιν (ὁ διάβολος) ὑπὸ τῶν πορνικῶν ᾀσμάτων, ὑπὸ τῶν αἰσχρῶ ῥημάτων, ὑπὸ τῆς δαιμονικῆς πομπῆς καλούμενος Σὺ δὲ ἀπετάξω πάσῃ ταύτῃ τῇ πόμπῃ, καὶ τῇ τοῦ Χριστοῦ λατρείᾳ συνετάξω κατὰ τὴν ἡμέραν ἐκείνην, καθ' ἣν τῶν ἱερῶν κατηξιώθης μυστηρίων.

88. Cf. H.G. Pringsheim, *Archäologische Beiträge zur Geschichte des eleusinischen Kults* (Munich 1905), p. 28.

89. Hefele-Leclercq I 2, 1023: "Ὅτι οὐ δεῖ χριστιανοὺς εἰς γάμους ἀπερχομένους βαλλίζειν ἢ ὀρχεῖσθαι, ἀλλὰ σεμνῶς δειπνεῖν ἢ ἀριστᾶν, ὡς πρέπει χριστιανοῖς.

90. *Ibid.*: "Ὅτι οὐ δεῖ ἱερατικοὺς ἢ κληρικούς τινας θεωρίας θεωρεῖν ἐν γάμοις, ἢ δείπνοις, ἀλλὰ πρὸ τοῦ εἰσέρχεσθαι τοὺς θυμελικούς, ἐγείρεσθαι αὐτοὺς καὶ ἀναχωρεῖν ἐκεῖθεν.

91. Gregory Nazianzus, *Epist.* 232 (PG 37, 376): Ἐν δὲ τῶν καλῶν παρεῖναι Χριστὸν τοῖς γάμοις καὶ τὸ γενέσθαι οἶνον τὸ ὕδωρ, τὸ δέ ἐστι, πάντα μεταποιεῖσθαι εἰς τὸ βέλτιον. οὕτως, ὡς μὴ τὰ ἄμικτα μίγνυσθαι, μήτε εἰς ταὐτὸν ἄγειν ἐπισκόπους καὶ γελωτοποιούς, εὐχὰς καὶ κρότους, ψαλμῳδίας καὶ συναυλίας.

92. Chrysostom, *In Matthaeum homilia* 48 (PG 57, 491): Ἔνθα γὰρ ὄρχησις, ἐκεῖ διάβολος.

93. Commodian, *Instructiones* 2, 29, 17 (CSEL 15, 86 Dombart):

> Quid memorem vestes aut totam Zabuli pompam?
> Respuitis legem, mavultis mundo placere
> Saltatis in domibus, pro psalmis cantatis amores.

94. Ephraem, *Über die Enthaltung von weltlichen Lustbarkeiten* 5 (BKV, Kempten 1870, Zingerle I, 414).

95. On dancing cf. *infra*, Chapter 6, sec. 7.

96. Cf. *supra*, Chapter 5, sec. 2.

97. Cyril of Jerusalem, *Catecheses* 19, 6 (PG 33, 1069): Εἶτα λέγεις, καὶ πάσῃ τῇ πομπῇ αὐτοῦ. Πομπὴ δὲ διαβόλου ἐστὶ θεατρομανίαι καὶ ὑποδρομίαι, κυνηγησία, καὶ πᾶσα τοιαύτη ματαιότης... Μὴ περισπούδαστός σοι ἔστω ἡ θεατρομανία, ἔνθα τὰς ἀσελγείας τῶν μίμων ὄψῃ, ὕβρεσι πεπραγμένας καὶ πάσῃ ἀσχημοσύνῃ, ἐκτεθηλυσμένων τε ἀνδρῶν ἐμμανεῖς ὀρχήσεις ...ταῦτα γὰρ πάντα πομπή ἐστι τοῦ διαβόλου.

98. Tertullian, *De Spectaculis* 10 (CSEL 20, 11 Reifferscheid-Wissowa): Apparatus etiam ex ea parte consortes, qua ad scaenam a templis et aris et illa infelicitate turis et sanguinis inter tibias et tubas itur duobus inquinatissimis arbitris funerum et sacrorum, designatore et haruspice. A relief on a Pompeian grave (reproduced in Daremberg-Saglio II 1593) shows a circus parade led by trumpeters.

99. *Ibid.* (CSEL 20, 12): Quae vero voce et modis et organis et litteris transiguntur, Apollines et Musas et Minervas et Mercurios mancipes habent. Orderis, Christiane, quorum auctores non potes non odisse.

100. Ps.-Cyprian, *De spectaculis* (CSEL 3.3, 10 Hartel): Quid nervos cum clamore commissos? Haec etiamsi non essent simulacris dicata, obeunda tamen et spectanda non essent christianis fidelibus; quoniam etsi non habebant crimen, habent in se maximam et parum congruentem fidelibus vanitatem.

101. Chrysostom, *Homilia in Ps.* 8, 1 (PG 55, 106).

102. Cf. J. Burckhard, *Die Zeit Constantins des Grossen* (Leipzig ³ 1898), p. 461.

103. Cf. F. Leitner, *Der gottesdienstliche Volksgesang im jüdischen und christlichen Altertum* (Freiburg 1906), p. 253.

104. Julian, *Epistula* 89 b (144 Bidez-Cumont): Τοῖς ἀσελγέσι τούτοις θεάτροις τῶν ἱερέων μηδεὶς μηδαμοῦ παραβαλλέτω μηδὲ εἰς τὴν οἰκίαν εἰσαγέτω τὴν ἑαυτοῦ· πρέπει γὰρ οὐδαμῶς. Καὶ εἰ μὲν οἶόν τε ἦν ἐξελάσαι παντάπασιν αὐτὰ τῶν θεάτρων, ὥστε αὐτὰ πάλιν ἀποδοῦναι τῷ Διονύσῳ καθαρὰ γενόμενα, πάντως ἂν ἐπειράθην αὐτὸ προθύμως κατασκευάσαι· νυνὶ δὲ οἰόμενος τοῦτο οὔτε δύνατον οὔτε ἄλλως, εἰ καὶ δυνατὸν φανείη, συμφέρον ἂν γενέσθαι, ταύτης μὲν ἀπεσχόμην **παντάπασι τῆς Φιλοτιμίας·** ἀξιῶ δὲ τους ἱερέας ὑποχωρῆσαι καὶ ἀποστῆναι τῷ δήμῳ τῆς ἐν τοῖς θεάτροις ἀσελγείας. Μηδεὶς οὖν ἱερεὺς εἰς θέατρον ἐξίτω, μηδὲ ποιείσθω φίλον θυμελικὸν μηδὲ ἁρματηλάτην, μηδὲ ὀρχηστὴς μηδὲ μῖμος αὐτοῦ τῇ θύρᾳ προσίτω. Τοῖς ἱεροῖς ἀγῶσιν ἐπιτρέπω μόνον τῷ βουλομένῳ παραβάλλειν, ὧν ἀπηγόρευται μετέχειν οὐκ ἀγωνίας μόνον ἀλλὰ καὶ θέας ταῖς γυναιξίν. The letter is probably directed to the high priest of the province of Asia.

105. Tertullian, *De spectaculis* 25 (CSEL 20, 25 Reifferscheid-Wissowa): inter effeminati tibicinis modos psalmum secum comminiscetur.

106. Hilary, *Tractatus in Ps.* 118, 14 (CSEL 22, 408 Zingerle).

107. Ambrose, *Hexaëmeron* 3, 1 (CSEL 32, 161 Schenkl).

108. Augustine, *Enarratio in Ps.* 39, 9 (PL 36, 439).

109. Gaudentius of Brescia, *Sermo* 8 (PL 20, 890): Ubi lyra sonat et tibia, ubi omnia postremo genera musicorum inter cymbala saltantium concrepant, infelices illae domus sunt, quae nihil discrepant a theatris. Auferantur, quaeso, universa ista de medio. Sit domus christiani ac baptizati hominis immunis a choro diaboli, sit plane humana, sit hospitalis; orationibus sanctificetur assiduis; psalmis, hymnis, canticisque spiritualibus frequentetur; sit sermo Dei et signum Christi in corde, in ore, in fronte, inter cibos, inter pocula, inter colloquia, in lavacris, in cubilibus....

110. Plato, *Politeia* 3 (401 d, e, 402 a Burnet): Ἆρ' οὖν, ἦν δ' ἐγώ, ὦ Γλαύκων, τούτων ἕνεκα κυριωτάτη ἐν μουσικῇ τροφή, ὅτι μάλιστα καταδύεται εἰς τὸ ἐντὸς τῆς ψυχῆς ὅ τε ῥυθμὸς καὶ ἁρμονία, καὶ ἐρρωμενέστατα ἅπτεται αὐτῆς φέροντα τὴν εὐσχημοσύνην, καὶ ποιεῖ εὐσχήμονα, ἐάν τις

ὀρθῶς τραφῇ εἰ δὲ μή, τοὐναντίον; καὶ ὅτι αὖ τῶν παραλειπομένων καὶ μὴ καλῶς δημιούργη θέντ-
ων ἢ μὴ καλῶς φύντων ὀξύτατ' ἂν αἰσθάνοιτο ὁ ἐκεῖ τραφεὶς ὡς ἔδει.

111. *Ibid.* (399 c, d): Ἀλλ', ἢ δ' ὅς, οὐκ ἄλλας αἰτεῖς λείπειν ἢ ἃς νυνδὴ ἐγὼ ἔλεγον. Οὐκ
ἄρα, ἢν δ' ἐγώ, πολυχορδίας γε οὐδὲ παναρμονίου ἡμῖν δεήσει ἐν ταῖς ᾠδαῖς τε καὶ μέλεσιν. Οὔ
μοι, ἔφη φαίνεται. Τριγώνων ἄρα καὶ πηκτίδων καὶ πάντων ὀργάνων ὅσα πολύχορδα... δημιουρ-
γοὺς οὐ θρέψομεν.

112. Plato, *De legibus* 8 (829 e Burnet): ἀλλ' ὅσα τε ἱερὰ κριθέντα ποιήματα ἐδόθη τοῖς
θεοῖς, καὶ ὅσα ἀγαθῶν ὄντων ἀνδρῶν ψέγοντα ἢ ἐπαινοῦντά τινας ἐκρίθη μετρίως δρᾶν τὸ τοιοῦτον.
τὰ αὐτὰ δὲ λέγω στρατείας τε πέρι καὶ τῆς ἐν ποιήσεσι παρρησίας γυναιξί τε καὶ ἀνδράσιν ὁμοίως
γίγνεσθαι δεῖν.

113. Plato, *Euthydemos* 276 c. *Idem, Protagoras* 338 e–339 a. *Idem, Politeia* 10 (607
a Burnet): ὕμνους θεοῖς καὶ ἐγκώμια τοῖς ἀγαθοῖς.

114. Lucian, *Anarchasis* 21 (73 Jakobitz): τὴν μὲν τοίνυν ψυχὴν μουσικῇ τὸ πρῶτον καὶ
ἀριθμητικῇ ἀναρριπίζομεν.

115. Clement of Alexandria, *Stromata* 6, 11, 90 (GCS Clem. II, 477 Stahlin): περιττὴ
δὲ μουσικὴ ἀποπτυστέα ἡ κατακλῶσα τὰς ψυχὰς καὶ εἰς ποικιλίαν ἐμβάλλουσα τοτὲ μὲν θρηνώδη,
τοτὲ δὲ ἀκόλαστον καὶ ἡδυπαθῆ, τοτὲ δὲ ἐκβακχευομένην καὶ μανικήν.

116. *Ibid.* 6, 10, 80 (GCS Clem. II 471): παρ' ἑκάστου μαθήματος τὸ πρόσφορον τῇ
ἀληθείᾳ λαμβάνων, τῆς μὲν μουσικῆς ἐν τοῖς ἡρμοσμένοις...

117. Commodian, *Instructiones* 2, 16, 20 (CSEL 15, 80 Dombart).

118. Basil, *De legend. libr. gentil.* 7 (PG 31, 583): Ἀνελευθερίας γὰρ δὴ καὶ ταπεινότη-
τος ἔκγονα πάθη ἐκ τοῦ τοιοῦδε τῆς μουσικῆς εἴδους ἐγγίνεσθαι πέφυκεν. Ἀλλὰ τὴν ἑτέραν
μεταδιωκτέον ἡμῖν, τὴν ἀμείνω τε καὶ εἰς ἄμεινον φέρουσαν, ᾗ καὶ Δαβὶδ χρώμενος, ὁ ποιητὴς τῶν
ἱερῶν ἀσμάτων, ἐκ τῆς μανίας, ὥς φασι, τὸν βασιλέα καθίστη. Λέγεται δὲ καὶ Πυθαγόραν, κωμας-
ταῖς περιτυχόντα μεθύουσι, κελεῦσαι τὸν αὐλητὴν τὸν τοῦ κώμου κατάρχοντα, μεταβαλόντα τὴν
ἁρμονίαν, ἐπαυλῆσαί σφισι τὸ Δώριον· τοὺς δὲ οὕτως ἀναφρονῆσαι ὑπὸ τοῦ μέλους, ὥστε τοὺς
στεφάνους ῥίψαντας, αἰσχυνομένους ἐπανελθεῖν. Ἕτεροι δὲ πρὸς αὐλὸν κορυβαντιῶσι καὶ ἐκβακχ-
εύονται. Τοσοῦτόν ἐστι τὸ διάφορον ὑγιοῦς ἢ μοχθηρᾶς μελῳδίας ἀναπλησθῆναι. Ὥστε, τῆς νῦν δὴ
κρατούσης ταύτης ἧττον ὑμῖν μεθεκτέον ἢ οὑτινοσοῦν τῶν αἰσχίστων. παντοδαποὺς ἡδονήν...

119. Basil, *Homilia in Ps.* 1, 1 (PG 29, 212): ἵνα οἱ παῖδες τὴν ἡλικίαν, ἢ καὶ ὅλως οἱ
νεαροὶ τὸ ἦθος, τῷ μὲν δοκεῖν μελῳδῶσι, τῇ δὲ ἀληθείᾳ τὰς ψυχάς ἐκπαιδεύωνται.

120. *Ibid.* 2 (PG 29, 212): (ψαλμὸς) νηπίοις ἀσφάλεια, ἀκμάζουσιν ἐγκαλλώπισμα,
πρεσβυτέροις παρηγορία, γυναιξὶ κόσμος ἁρμοδιώτατος. Τὰς ἐρημίας οἰκίζει, τὰς ἀγορὰς
σωφρονίζει.

121. *Ibid.* 1 (PG 29, 212): καὶ πού τις τῶν σφόδρα ἐκτεθηριωμένων ὑπὸ θυμοῦ, ἐπειδὰν ἄρ-
ξηται τῷ ψαλμῷ κατεπάδεσθαι ἀπῆλθεν εὐθύς, τὸ ἀργιαῖον τῆς ψυχῆς τῇ μελῳδίᾳ κατακοιμίσας.

122. *Ibid.* (PG 29, 213): εἰσαγομένοις στοιχείωσις, προκοπτόντων αὔξησις, τελειουμένων
στήριγμα.

123. *Ibid.* 2 (PG 29, 212): Ψαλμὸς δαιμόνων φυγαδευτήριον, τῆς τῶν ἀγγέλων βοηθείας
ἐπαγωγή... ἀνάπαυσις κόπων ἡμερινῶν.

124. Jerome, *Epistula* 128 (*Ad Pacatulam*) 4, 2 (CSEL 56, 160 Hilberg): cum autem
virgunculam et rudem edentulam septimus aetatis annus exceperit...discat memoriter
psalterium.

125. Jerome, *Epistula* 107 (*Ad Laetam de institutione filiae*) 12, 1 (CSEL 55, 302
Hilberg): discat primum Psalterium, hisce canticis avocet.

126. Cf. *supra*, Chapter 4, sec. 7.

127. Cf. *supra*, Chapter 4, sec. 6.

Chapter Six
MUSIC AND SINGING IN THE PAGAN AND CHRISTIAN CULTS OF THE DEAD

1. THE CEREMONIES OF WAKING, OF THE FUNERAL PROCESSION AND OF INTERMENT AMONG THE PAGANS.

Great as was the significance of music in the pagan cult of the gods, still greater was the role it played in the cult of the dead. And as difficult as Christianity's struggle was to prohibit all pagan music from its liturgy, so much more difficult was it to give the ceremonies of the dead a character appropriate to the Christian spirit, free of all pagan mourning customs which were irreconcilable with the Christian concept of death.

If we review the different stages of the pagan mourning ritual, the prominent position which music occupied can be plainly seen. When death occurred the corpse was laid out and the wake began in its presence. This ceremony was accompanied by words (θρῆνος = naenia) and gestures (κοπετός = planctus) of lamentation. Such mourning extended for the whole time of the wake. Originally it was carried out by relatives and friends who had gathered in the place of mourning, but later hired women mourners were employed. The words of lamentation were sung in a particular mourning tone, and almost everywhere they were sung in alternation. This fashion prevailed as early as the time of the Babylonians. An unpublished fragment from Ashurbanipal's library which describes a royal entombment carries these words on the reverse side: "The wives lament and the friends answer."[1] Thus responsorial singing between men and women seems to have been customary at Babylonian funerals.

A similar custom prevailed in Greece. From time to time the women mourners would raise a wild cry, following a determined rhythm, and all the while they would strike their breasts, pull out their hair and scratch their cheeks until the blood came. Friends and relatives who were present joined in occasionally in the lament with the expression of sorrow — αἰεί, αἰεί.[2] The contents of the song of lamentation stressed

the spiritual and corporeal qualities of the deceased. So Festus explained the word *naenia* as a "song of praise sung at a funeral to flute accompaniment."[3] The flute, then, was an indispensable instrument at a
ceremony of mourning. The Greeks also used the lyre or the cithara to
accompany the lament,[4] but the specific instrument of lamentation
among all peoples was the flute. Even among the Assyrians and Babylonians it performed this service. In the dirge reproduced by P. Haupt
we read:

> A cry sounds from his breast; like a flute he breaks into lamentation.[5]

At the close of the narration of Ishtar's journey to the nether world
there is reference to flute playing during mourning.[6] In a prayer
directed to the goddess A — the consort of the sun god — we find the expression:

> On his breast, which laments like a flute, he mourns for you.

In Egypt, too, the flute was used in lamentation, In the funeral rite
for Adonis the double flute was blown. Consequently it was quite
natural that the Israelites should also make use of it in their ceremonies for the dead. Jeremiah has the Lord say:

> Therefore my heart mourns for Moab like a flute, and my heart cries like
> the sound of a flute for the men of Kir-heres.[7]

Matthew 9:23 shows clearly that flute playing was customary at
wakes: when Jesus entered the house of Jairus the flute players had
already begun the dirge.[8] Flavius Josephus reports that flutists were
hired to play the dirges for those fallen at the city of Jotapa.[9] The
Talmud, in the section on the Sabbath, decrees:

> If a gentile has brought flutes on the Sabbath no Israelite may play
> mourning music with them unless they have been brought from nearby.[10]

It was even prescribed that everyone, including the poorest, should
have at least two flutists and one female mourner at a funeral.[11]

As in the orient, so it was among the Greeks and Romans. The sarcophagus from Hagia Triada (1300 B.C.) attests to the Greeks' use of
the double flute and the cithara at sacrifices for the dead.[12] On a Cor-
inthian urn in the Louvre,[13] which depicts in painting the laying-out of
Achilles' body, a female citharist appears among the mourning
women.[14] From the Etruscan era of the fifth century before Christ we
have the portrayal of a wake on a tombstone in the Museo Baracco in
Rome.[15] The persons standing about the corpse are in mourning. The
one to the left of the corpse holds his hands raised in the position of
the mourning ceremony (*planctus*). On the right another person bears

a sash to place on the deceased. At the foot of the corpse is a flutist blowing the double flute; around his mouth is the so-called capistrum, a leather band used to prevent the unpleasant distension of the cheeks and concentrate the breath of the player on the two mouthpieces of the instrument.[16] Thus flute playing here accompanied the rite of mourning in the presence of the corpse.[17] On the other hand, the upper part of the relief fragment, to judge by the movement of the persons, probably portrays a scene from the grave dances that were held in honor of the deceased at his interment and which the lyrist visible on the left is accompanying.[18]

In the Roman ritual for the dead music was performed at the wake and, in fact, very shortly after death. A relief in the Museo delle Terme in Rome, which was found on the Via Latina, is of special interest here.[19] A woman with the expression of death lies upon a bed. At the foot of the bed two musicians are portrayed, one of whom blows a flute and the other a curved horn. Under the scene is the inscription, MORITUR, which leads one to conclude that the moment of death itself is shown here.[20] This portrayal recalls the Roman proverb, "to send for the trumpeters," which was used to indicate approaching death.[21]

In the year 1847 several reliefs were found on the Via Labicana in the vicinity of Rome. They come from the mausoleum of the Haterii and belong to about the first century after Christ. One of the reliefs, presently in the Lateran Museum, gives a remarkably clear depiction of the lamentation in the presence of the corpse.[22] A dead women lies in solemn state on her bier. The man at the head of the bier, who is bringing a garland to adorn the deceased, may be the pollinctor, whose duty it was to prepare the corpse. The other people standing about the bier are striking their breasts with their hands as a sign of mourning. To the left at the foot of the bed is a woman flutist, seated on a stool, accompanying the mourning with the double flute.[23]

Although music was essential in mourning at home it played an even more important role in the funeral procession. In Egypt the sistrum accompanied the dirges of the solemn procession to the grave.[24] In Greece Solon had to speak out against too great an expenditure for burials; he abolished the libations and sacrifices of propitiation before the funeral or at the place of interment. However, the dirges with flute accompaniment remained, as Lucian of Samosata bears witness.[25] The funeral procession began to the sound of flutes, which played a dirge in the mournful Lydian mode.[26] In Rome the Law of the Twelve Tables reduced the number of the flute players in the funeral procession to ten and forbade women to join in the lamentations and to lacerate their cheeks.[27] Yet these efforts of the law to put a stop to excessive manifestations of grief remained without success. The people believed firmly that the gods of the nether world demanded these public shows of sorrow and would receive the dead person in a more friendly way in proportion to the clamor of the lamentation at his burial.[28] But the ritual of the dead among the Greeks ultimately became an empty ceremony without any deeper meaning, and as such it began to be disparaged in the eyes of thoughtful men.[29] This attitude was promoted by the fact that frequently the most unworthy people had the most splendid funerals. For example, the greatest musicians in all of Greece were summoned to the funeral of the concubine of Harpalos, the disloyal treasurer of Alexander the Great.[30]

It was no different in Rome. Cicero was obliged to invoke the Law of the Twelve Tables. The rite of the funeral procession in Greece was similar to that of the Romans insofar as a trumpeter led both. The testimony for Greece is given in Plutarch's description of the procession to the grave of those who had fallen at Plataeae.[31] According to Persius, the following order prevailed in the Roman funeral procession — first the trumpet player, then the torch bearers, and then the corpse with its attendants.[32] Seneca mocks the frivolities and the too infrequent seriousness of demeanor in a Roman funeral procession when he describes the funeral of the Emperor Claudius:

> So many trumpeters, horn players and musicians of all kinds were present that even Claudius was able to hear them. Everybody was gay and cheerful.... The dirge was sung by a mighty choir in anapaests: *Fundite fletus/Edite planctus* ....[33]

According to Propertius, there was no trumpet at the burial of a poorer person, for he states that he himself would be content with a simple funeral, without a retinue, the sound of the trumpet or a procession with bowls of incense, as was the case with the funeral of a simple man.[34] Servius declares that there was no trumpet either when children were buried.[35]

An interesting monument from Roman times illustrates the written descriptions in a remarkable way.[36] The monument, a relief on a block of stone 1.66 meters long, .68 meter high and .30 meter wide, was found in 1879 in Preturi (ancient Amiternum) in Italy and is currently in the museum at Aquila. Inscriptions found at the same time in that place date it to the end of the Republic or during the reign of Augustus.[37] The relief portrays a funeral procession. At the head of the procession is a man blowing a lituus, or curved cavalry trumpet, two horn players and four flutists playing double flutes. Two female mourners with lively gestures of lamentation follow. The catafalque occupies the center of the relief. It is borne by eight people, and on it is a bier on which the deceased lies. The women who follow the bier are perhaps relatives of the deceased. The total impression of the relief supports C. Huelsen's belief that this is a funeral procession of an important person.[38]

The ceremonies of lamentation were naturally repeated as soon as the procession arrived at the grave site.[39] At the *lustratio rogi* music seems to have had a more apotropaic role. A triple procession around the funeral pile accomplished its purification, and during this time the flutists and trumpeters played their instruments.[40]

2. The Meal of the Dead and the Cult of the Grave. Depictions on Greek Ointment Jars. Music and Singing in Ancient Portrayals of the Hereafter.

Just as in other ceremonies of the dead, music was also used at the meal of the dead. This meal, which was held from time to time at the grave, was marked by a cheerful character. In the original view of the ancients, the purpose of the meal was to refresh the dead, and when it took place the gravestone was crowned with a wreath and anointed. Thus, in Lucian, Charon asks Hermes:

> Why do you crown the gravestone there and anoint it? Others also erect a funeral pile before the grave, dig a hole and burn these costly meals and seem to pour out wine and a mixture of honey into the hole.

Hermes replies:

> I do not know, ferryman, how this benefits the one who is in Hades. Nonetheless, they are convinced that the smoke and incense swirl about the souls that are below and that as many as possible of them eat of it and drink the mixture of honey from out of the hole.[41]

Naturally, most of the meal was consumed by those who participated in it, and only the part which fell to the dead who had been invited was burned. Sometimes it would seem that people were satisfied simply to crown the gravestone and adorn it, since the meal of the dead was entirely for the benefit of the living. Lucian finds this particularly amusing:

> However, you will grant that nothing can be more ridiculous than to be well anointed and crowned with roses but perishing of hunger and thirst. Thus is it at a funeral meal when the gravestone of one recently deceased is anointed and crowned, while the funeral guests keep the wine and meal for themselves.[42]

It was the same with regard to music at the meal of the dead. When at the end of the meal the funeral guests would resort to their own pleasures, to playing and dancing, it was because music was originally supposed to have offered comfort to the dead. The Egyptians believed this, as we see, for example, in the paintings of Neferhotep's grave at Thebes, where the relatives and friends of the dead man are sitting in festal clothing and adorned with flowers. They are eating and drinking, watching the dancers and listening to the song of the harpist, who addresses the dead man himself:

> Celebrate the beautiful day! Set forth ointments and fine oil for your nostrils and wreaths and lotus blossoms for the body of your dear sister, who is seated at your side. Let there be singing and music before you; cast everything sad behind you and think only of joy.[43]

A similar situation existed among the Greeks, the Etruscans and the Romans. A Greek relief of a meal of the dead, dating from the fifth century before Christ and presently in the Museo Baracco in Rome, depicts a husband and wife reclining at a meal, looking at a lyrist who attends them with his playing.[44] The portrayals of banquets on Etruscan sepulchral monuments are well known, and music is rarely missing on them. The upper relief of a gravestone in the museum in Fiesole shows a meal of the dead, while the lower relief portrays a flutist and two dancing figures.[45] The museum's inscription notes that this is a representation of the activities of the blessed in Elysium. On the upper relief the figure who is eating is pictured in a reclining position. Since the living usually sat while the deceased were thought to recline, this clearly represents a meal of the dead.[46] The music and dancing portrayed on the lower relief, like the meal, serve to refresh the dead person.

From the Roman circle of culture there are sarcophagi with scenes of meals of the dead which portray the deceased at table, as they had been in life, accompanied by elaborate musical entertainment. A sarcophagus in the Lateran Museum in Rome shows a meal of the dead in which the dead man is at table.[47] From both sides food is being brought to him. To the left, at the foot of the couch on which he reclines, a lutenist and, in the background, a flutist proffer him musical entertainment.

A question arises here concerning the significance of musical instruments which are seen on Greek tombstones and ointment jars (λήκυθοι) used in the Greek cult of the dead. It is often said that in these portrayals the relatives of the deceased are depicted coming to the grave to entertain him with music. But we must first distinguish between the portrayals in which the dead person has a musical instrument in his hand and those in which the persons visiting the deceased are carrying musical instruments. In the first case the musical instrument in the dead person's hand — usually a lyre or a tambourine — is meant to signify that the deceased no longer leads an earthly life but is already taken up with the affairs of the other world. An ointment jar at Oxford illustrates this point.[48] Judging from her demeanor, the seated woman can be none other than the dead person. In her hand she holds a lyre, and she has just stopped playing so as to receive an offering from a relative or a friend. There is a similar portrayal on a mixing jar from Campagna in the Berlin Museum (no. 3053 B).[49] Here the dead person is sitting on a gravestone while in his hand he holds a beribboned tambourine with a gesture which suggests that he had just received it as a gift.

The explanation of the second group of portrayals, in which persons who are visiting the deceased carry a lyre, a tambourine or an Apuleian sistrum, is more difficult. In opposition to the previously mentioned explanation, namely, that relatives are coming to entertain the deceased with music, the fact remains that the persons depicted as approaching the deceased on Greek ointment jars are never playing their instruments. A picture on ointment jar no. 2458 in the Berlin Museum brings us a step closer to a more acceptable explanation.[50] Here the person bearing the cithara is stretching out his hands toward the gravestone on which the dead man is sitting as if he wished to offer the latter the instrument. The cithara is thus a votive offering for the deceased. Ointment jar no. 3262 in the same museum carries a very good portrayal of a similar scene.[51] In the center is the gravestone, with five vessels on one of its steps. On top of the stone stands a large lyre, with a *cathedra* next to it. To the right of the gravestone is a person with his right hand in the gesture of offering, while a second person coming from the left (probably the deceased) stretches out his hand toward the lyre.

Why, then, were musical instruments offered to the dead and why are the dead pictured as playing the lyre? In antiquity singing and instrumental music, playing and dancing were considered to be the chief occupation and pastime of the blessed. This notion can be found in numerous remarks of ancient writers. Lucian, in his description of a journey to the Isle of the Blessed, speaks of hearing from afar the music which was being played at their banquet:

> Now and then one could also hear very clearly different sounds — not noisy, but such as would come from a banquet when a few people are playing the flute or the cithara.[52]

The popular religions of the time, especially Orphism and the mystery cults, portrayed the life of the blessed as a continual banquet. Such views were popularized by the rites of initiation into these mysteries. That of Eleusis, for example, included a journey through the afterlife. A passage from Plutarch's book *On the Soul* compares dying to the great initiations. The text preserved by Stobaios reads in part:

> Then the soul experiences what those who have been initiated into the great mysteries have known. Therefore both events are spoken of as completions [τελευτᾶν—τελεῖσθαι]. First a wandering and a weary running about. Paths full of danger, ending in darkness. Then, before the end, all that is frightful and horrible, along with shaking, sweat and astonishment. But then there appears a wondrous light. Pure places and meadows receive him, where sounds are heard and dancing is held, and noble words and exalted visions are had. Among these the initiated walks freely, henceforth totally perfected, with his head crowned, celebrating his feasts.[53]

It is thus quite possible that this life of the blessed is intended by the portrayal of musical instruments. This would be so especially since the lyre, tambourine and sistrum played an important role in the mystery religions and their initiation rites and were designated as the instruments which the blessed used — particularly the lyre.[54]

In this regard it is noteworthy that the siren on grave paintings is very often pictured with a tambourine, flute or lyre. Above the inscription on the gravestone of Metrodoros of Chios, for example, a siren in the left corner is shown striking a tambourine, while one in the right corner plays a flute.[55] G. Weicker has demonstrated that the depiction of sirens playing music on graves cannot be explained by a simple adaptation of the type created for the portrayal of the adventures of Odysseus.[56] The numerous musical sirens on graves have a deeper significance.[57] They are portrayals of human souls enjoying music in the afterlife. The blessed used these instruments at the mystical banquet and in the eternal mysteries which, according to the mystery religions, constituted life in the Elysian Fields.

The portrayals on ointment jars and graves consequently show only that the deceased was indulging in the specific occupation of the blessed. They attest that he has been taken up by the gods. The relatives of the deceased found consolation in this belief, as the depictions prove. The custom of offering a lyre or tambourine to the dead by placing it on his grave was meant to express the conviction of his relatives that the deceased had attained a happy fate. In the grave on the sacred street of Eleusis we find two customs in conjunction with one another: a lyre is being offered to the dead man, whose head is adorned with a golden wreath. Both details show that this dead man was considered to be a hero.[58] This belief is the same as the one expressed in the mausoleum of Marsala in the National Museum in Palermo, which contains such inscriptions as ΔΙΟΔΩΡΟΣ ΗΡΩΣ ΑΓΑΘΟΣ.[59] Again and again in the decorative paintings tambourines, cymbals, mirrors and ribbons are presented as offerings to the hero. It was probably thought originally that the offering of musical instruments, like every other gift to the dead, would make their life easier in Hades, since they would be able to join the blessed in singing and playing.

The portrayals on Greek ointment jars and gravestones indicate a link between the tradition of art in religious imagery and the winged music-making cupids on Roman gravestones, which supposedly symbolize life in the hereafter. They are found, for example, on an octagonal ash urn currently in the Capitoline Museum. According to its inscription, this urn was given by the freedman Decimus Lucilius Soter to his patron Lucius Lucilius Felix.[60] This theme recurs on the tombstone of the soldier Marcinus in the Provincial Museum in Bonn.[61] The cymbal-playing, dancing Maenad on the front of the monument has no other purpose than to symbolize the ecstatic joy of the dead man in the hereafter.

3. The Purpose of Music in the Cult of the Dead. The Adjuration of the Dead.

The religious-historical fact of the extraordinarily elaborate use of music in the pagan cult of the dead raises the question regarding the purpose of this music. An apotropaic character has frequently been ascribed to it. Thus, allusion has been made to the Egyptian burial rite which, besides the clapping of the sistrum, also prescribed beating with palm fronds. These measures, it has been said, were intended to drive away from the corpse the wicked demons who, according to ancient belief, would try to seize possession of the dead person.[62] This opinion, however, is unacceptable. Although the music of the dead most likely had an apotropaic character, the question concerning the object of these apotropaic measures remains: was the dead person supposed to be kept away from the living so that he could not return and work harm? Such was the case with the Roman paterfamilias who, at a banquet for the dead, made a clatter with bronze vessels and scattered black beans for the souls of those who were visiting the house of their descendents so that they would leave.[63] Or was it meant, as was keeping watch by the corpse, to protect the dead person from the dangers that pressed in upon him?[64] It may be that the second view became the dominant one, although it was not so originally. The music of the dead envisioned the deceased himself as its object. It was, in fact, supposed to be a means of making the spirit of the deceased docile, so that it could be led wherever his survivors wished. Thus it had the aspect of an adjuration of the deceased.

The Babylonians had already understood this interpretation. In the final lines of *Ishtar's Journey to the Underworld*, for example, we read:

> In the days of Tamuz play me the crystal-like flute, on the...instrument play me his lament, you men and women who mourn, so that the dead may arise and breathe the fragrance of the sacrifice.[65]

Here the spirits of the dead are summoned by music. This was the essential purpose of music in the cult of the dead among the Mediterranean peoples. Statius also mentions it in his *Thebais* when he says:

> Then the first tones of the curved flute, with which the Phrygians are wont to adjure the tender spirits of the departed, gave the signal to mourn.[66]

In this vein, the story that Orpheus had called the spirit of his wife back from the nether world by his music was not far-fetched to the ancients, for in general they were convinced of the uncanny influence that music exercised over the dead. So Virgil notes that, by the power of the brightly-sounding strings of his Thracian cithara, Orpheus was able to summon the shade of his wife.[67] Martianus Capella represents music as declaring to the gods:

Through me men call down your help, and they placate the wrath of those who dwell below by songs of mourning.[68]

These passages all show that, according to ancient belief, music had an adjuratory effect on the spirits of the departed and that by it they were rendered tractable to the living. Furthermore, we are able to understand why the music of the dead during mourning had to be performed in the presence of the corpse only if we recall that the spirit of the deceased remained in the vicinity of the body. At the interment music served to lead the spirit to the grave. Without a doubt, the original significance of the music of the dead was probably known to only a few people. Actions performed frequently often lose their meaning, which consequently falls into oblivion. An example of this is a custom which is reported by Herodotus. He tells how the Egyptians would clash cymbals at the death of their king.[69] Herodotus believed that this was done to announce the king's death, while Apollodoros gave the original meaning when he saw this action as an apotropaic measure.[70] Later, when this custom was no longer understood, the clashing of cymbals was explained as a sign of the king's death. But the fact that women were obliged to carry out this rite permits Herodotus' report to be seen in another light. Even in the most primitive times there were figures of women holding tambourines depicted on Greek and Phoenician graves.[71] These tambourines were beaten by women during the mourning, as we see on the Sarcophagus of the Mourning Women from Sidon. There two women, leading a section of female mourners, are stiking tambourines[72] — a custom which, like all the music of the dead, was basically supposed to have had an adjuratory and preventive effect on the dead.

Only gradually did fear of the return of the dead and the adjuratory attitude consequent on it yield to a sense of piety. In ceremonies for the dead this took the form of a wish to assist the helpless soul to overcome the dangers which surrounded it. For instance, a bell whose sound could be heard from afar whenever the wind moved it was hung at the top of Porsenna's pyramidal grave. This was intended to preserve the deceased from the harmful influences which emanated from the wicked demons.[73] In a similar manner, Alexander the Great's funeral car was encircled with bells.[74] The popular belief in the power of bells to drive demons away and break magic spells was so great that they were even placed in the graves with the dead. In Christian graves also whole sets of bells have been found — a sign of how deeply this belief was embedded in the cultural world of the time.[75] Here too the original significance was later lost, for pious men who were considered to be free of any guilt were accompanied to their graves with music in order to show that their souls had been received into the higher spheres.[76] So it is that Macrobius explains all the music of the dead by remarking that men make use of it to indicate that the soul of the departed has returned to the source of all beautiful music, that is, to heaven.[77]

4. The Christian Transformation of Pagan Death Customs. Christian Mourning Ritual in the House of the Dead.

It has already been pointed out that the pagan cult of the dead with its excessive manifestation of grief and its musical extravagance was rejected by the more thoughtful pagans. In the consolatory writings of the philosophers principles which were in opposition to the customs of the time were frequently set down. The Academic Krantor from Soloi in Cicilia (c. 330–270 B.C.), in his book *On Suffering*, recommends metriopathy for the wise man. This middle course between too great a show of grief and a total absence of feeling was the only attitude befitting him. In the Judaeo-Hellenistic world Philo presented Abraham's attitude at the death of Sarah as an ideal worthy of imitation by his readers:

> When the most distinguished men of that place came to take part in his mourning and saw nothing that was customary with them, no moaning, no lamentation, no striking of the breast, not of men or of women, but only a quiet and moderate sorrow in the whole house, they wondered not a little.[78]

Such philosophic considerations, however, held weight only among a relatively small number of people, and they were never very influential outside their own circle.

Christianity, for its part, was compelled to suppress completely the cult of the dead as it had been handed down. This necessity arose not only from the fact that very many of the usages and customs of the ritual of the dead fell under the ban which was attached to idolatry but also from the essentially different conception which Christianity had of death.[79] The fear of incurring the guilt of idolatry probably explains, for example, the prohibition of setting a wreath of flowers on the head of the deceased, as Minucius Felix and Tertullian report.[80]

Both the fear of idolatry and the Christian idea of death worked together to the disfavor of pagan music of the dead. The relationship between music and cult in general has already been discussed. Now the
struggle which the young Church had to take up against the notion of
death which faced her will be delineated. This struggle led to her condemnation of pagan music of the dead.

The mourning ceremonies of the pagans which have been previously discussed can be understood more clearly when one realizes that the
pagans looked on death as an evil. In this respect pagan grave inscriptions are very revealing. The gravestone of a twenty year old girl
named Prokope bears these terrible words:

> MANVS LEBO CONTRA DEVM
> QVI ME INNOCENTEM SVSTVLIT

"I raise my hands against God, who has taken me away in my innocence."[81]

It was otherwise with Christianity, which viewed death not as an
evil but as a deliverance and a blessing from God. Therefore primitive
Christian grave inscriptions often contain exhortations to abstain
from all signs of grief. In his grave inscription one child makes this request of his parents:

> NE PECTORA TVNDITE VESTRA
> O PATER ET MATER—

Do not beat your breasts, O father and mother.
This point of view introduced a complete transformation of the
mourning ceremonies.

The Christians replaced lamentations and dirges sung in alternation
with the antiphonal singing of the psalms. Chrysostom shows clearly
that a different concept of death necessarily implies a change in the
songs about death. Death, he says, has its mournful side, which is
manifest in θρῆνος and κοπετός, but it also has its joyful aspect, which is
apparent in the singing of psalms and hymns. It is only through Christianity that this joyful aspect has been made known to the world. On
account of this "we sing psalms for the dead."[83] In his *Confessions*
Augustine relates that, on the death of his mother Monica, Evodius
seized the Psalter and began the words of Psalm 101: "I will sing of
mercy and of judgment to you, O Lord," and all those present responded. Said Augustine:

> It did not seem appropriate to us to celebrate the funeral with tearful
> lamentations and with mourning, for so it is that men are accustomed to

bewail what they feel to be the miserable fate of the dead, as if it were complete extinction. But her death was not miserable, nor was she completely dead.[84]

Gregory of Nyssa says that at the death of his sister Macrina, psalms were sung the whole night through as at the vigil of a martyr.[85] Jerome sharply distinguishes between the pagan and the Christian wake. He relates that, at the death and burial of the saintly Paula in Bethlehem, psalms were sung throughout the week in Greek, Latin and Syriac while the body was laid out in the Church of the Redeemer, but there was

no lamenting and beating of the breast as men in the world are used to doing.[86]

In the monastery of Shenute of Atripe in Egypt monks from all the communities would gather around the deceased as he lay on his pallet and sing psalms. Five selections from the Scriptures were read in honor of the dead monk and five psalms were sung.[87] When Peter the Iberian died the Christians washed his body, put on it the stole in which he used to celebrate the sacred mysteries and laid it out with pious modesty and reverence. And the text continues,

we lit many lanterns and candles and spent the whole night watching, to the singing of psalms, hymns and spiritual songs.[88]

To be sure, the pagan cult of the dead was too much a part of the past lives of many Christians, formerly pagans, for them simply to be able to replace the pagan dirges and funeral music with psalmody. Therefore Chrysostom, homilizing on the awakening of the daughter of Jairus, takes his hearers seriously to task because they were not able to refrain from such customs. He points out that Jesus, in performing his miracle, had cast out the flute players, and he continues:

If the Lord sent such people away then, so much the more now. Then it was not yet known that death is merely a sleep; now it is clearer than the sun.... Thus in the future no one should mourn and lament any longer and bring the saving work of Christ into discredit. For he has conquered death. Why then do you mourn unnecessarily? Death has become sleep. Why do you wail and weep? It is ridiculous when the pagans do it. But when even a believing Christian is not ashamed of such conduct, what excuse does he have? What pity do those people deserve who are so foolish and now, after so much time, have such clear proofs of the resurrection? But you, as if you took special pains to increase your guilt, even bring in pagan women as mourners so as to make the grief greater and enkindle the spark of sorrow, and you do not listen to Paul who says: "What has Christ to do with Belial?"[89]

In another place Chrysostom compares the outcries of lamentation, the gestures of sorrow and the dirges with the activities of the Bacchantes, and he claims that they are unworthy of Christians, who live in the hope of the resurrection.[90]

The synods also took up the struggle against these remnants of paganism. In the *Commandments of the Fathers, Superiors and Masters* we read:

> It has come before our assembly that some men who are confounded by death think of the universal rule of the almighty God as the hypocrites do. They are like the pagans and others who do not acknowledge the resurrection of the dead, like foolish and insensitive men. They know nothing of God and the sisters of faith — patience, gratitude, peaceableness and calm — but publicly manifest the magnitude of their grief. Women especially pull out their hair, rip their clothing, lacerate their cheeks, make music with castanets, drums and flutes, cut down trees, palms and other growing things, lament for a long time and do similar things which are opposed to faith. Now the synod commands that those who have met with an occasion of sorrow should remain in churches or monasteries or in their houses, as those do who dwell in the land quietly, peacefully and seriously, as those who do believe in the truth, who have faith in the resurrection and are convinced of it and who console themselves with that with which the priests and true believers console themselves. Whoever does otherwise the entire synod puts under the ban and forbids to enter the church.[91]

If Chrysostom was concerned about drawing Christians away from the custom of introducing pagan women as mourners, this synodal decree indicates very clearly that even Christian women dared to engage in pagan lamentations at the death of a Christian, and that thus the pagan customs remained virtually undisturbed.

The use of music for mourning was similar to that which accompanied the cult of the dead. Eusebius heard it among the pagans of his time who, in their grief over relatives struck down by the plague, were playing dirges and funeral music in every street and public place.[92] Basil of Caesarea was also familiar with flutes, citharas and tambourines as instruments of ritual mourning. In an attempt to dissuade his flock from playing them at meal time he insisted: "These instruments are for those who mourn the dead."[93]

The prohibitions of excessive lamentation and of the music of the dead grew continually more stringent. They were directed, as one would expect, particularly to women, who most held the pagan ceremonies and gave way to immoderate manifestations of sorrow. This explains Shenute of Atripe's regulation that the burials of nuns might be carried out only by monks.[94] Women were excluded from participation in funerals or at least were forbidden entrance to houses of mourning, since the danger of extravagant manifestations of grief was greatest there. The Nestorian synod of 576 determined in its fourth canon that, instead of cutting their hair, rending their clothing, howling, lamenting, beating drums, singing and cutting branches, women should remain quietly in the churches or monasteries or in their own houses on days of mourning.[95] In canon 17 of Mar George (seventh century) the lamentation which some women would carry on in the house of mourning was forbidden, and it was decreed that women might accompany the bier only to the place where the hymn of consolation (būyā) was sung. "Further they may not go,"[96] probably because they would thus not have the opportunity of indulging in pagan lamentations at the grave. However, nuns who were following the bier were permitted to sing madrashe, even though they might not enter the house of mourning and sing there.[97] Patriarch Cyriacus of Antioch (793–817) threatens with interdict any house where lamentation for the dead has taken place:

> The clergy and the faithful, for the course of a month, may not enter a house in which there have been lamentations and the singing of dirges, not even to bring communion to a dying person.[98]

The centuries-long struggle of Christianity against the pagan wake perhaps explains the custom which exists today among the Melchites: a woman mourner in dark veils takes her place near the head of the person who has just died; the women of the house, as well as other female relatives, sit about the corpse and respond with sobbing and lamentation to the threnody of the mourner. Then one or more priests come and drive her out.[99]

5. The Christian Funeral Procession.

Christianity asserted its influence not only in the laying out of the dead but also in the matter of the procession to the grave. In his book *De corona militis* Tertullian demonstrates the relentless efforts of Christianity to do away with pagan customs in this area. He asks if it is fitting for a Christian to become a soldier, and his answer is in the negative. As one of his reasons he declares that it is unfitting for a dead Christian to be disturbed by the music of the trumpeter when he expects to be awakened by an angelic trumpet.[100] This text is invaluable for the history of Christianity's struggle against the use of music in the cult of the dead. It has been shown above that the pagans sought to adjure and placate the spirits of the dead with their music of lamentation. Tertullian does not at all deny music's influence on these spirits, but he asserts that music disturbs the dead and is harmful to them. The word *inquietabitur* which he uses recalls a canon of the Council of Elvira (c. 300) against the pagan custom of lighting candles at the grave:

> Candles shall not be lit in the cemetery during the day, for the spirits of the saints must not be disturbed (*inquietandi*). Let whoever does not observe this be excommunicated.[101]

This also, then, refers to a custom which, in the pagan view, was supposed to be useful to the dead but which Christians considered as disturbing and therefore harmful to them. The difference between these two points of view indicates to some extent the sharpness with which the struggle against the custom in question was conducted. It is important for the history of religion, however, that Tertullian does not gainsay music's influence on the spirits of the deceased but, in contrast to the pagans' belief in its usefulness,[102] ascribes to it a harmful and disturbing influence on the departed soul.

Commodian is more moderate than Tertullian in his rejection of the ceremonies of the funeral procession.[103] He seeks primarily to dispose of the opinion that pagan rites help the dead, and he says that people who permit such things at a funeral commit a grave sin.

In the procession to the grave, just as at the laying-out, the alternate singing of dirges was replaced by the singing of psalms. A number of tomb inscriptions expressly mention psalm and hymn singing during the time that the deceased was borne to the grave. Such is, for example, the following fourth-century inscription from the Cemetery of Saint Cyriaca:

HYMNIS EST A NOBIS
AD QUIETEM PACIS TRANSLATA.[104]

In the same century the *Apostolic Constitutions* prescribed that believers who had fallen asleep in death should be accompanied to their graves with the singing of psalms.[105] Gregory Nazianzus writes of the burial of his brother Caesarius, who had died in his prime, that

> his honorable and precious remains were accompanied to rest by ceaseless singing, borne in solemn procession to the place of the martyrs,

adorned by the holy hands of his parents, honored by his mother, who put on festal garments and substituted pious devotion for mourning, wisely checking the flow of her tears.[106]

In his fourth homily on the Epistle to the Hebrews Chrysostom instructs us regarding the choice of psalms to be sung at burials. He explains that these psalms and hymns should be joyful, and thus totally unlike the dirges of the pagans, which many of his listeners still sang along with the psalms:

Tell me then, what do the shining lamps mean? Do we not accompany them [believers] as fighters [to their graves]? What do the hymns mean? Do we not praise and thank God because he has crowned the departed and released him from his pains, because he has taken him away from fear and has him with himself? Is that not why there are hymns and psalms? All of this is an expression of joy, for if one is happy, so it is written, then let him sing songs of praise.

He reprimands the many Christians who still practice pagan mourning customs and indicates that they should bear in mind the words of the psalms which they sing in the funeral procession:

Consider what you sing then: "Turn back, my soul, to your rest, for the Lord has done good things for you." And again: "I will fear no evil, for you are with me." And again: "You are my refuge in the affliction that has encircled me." Ponder the meaning of the psalms. But you pay no heed; you are drunk with grief...But if bitter death should occur...and somebody should hire these mourning women — believe my words, for I speak as I think, and whoever wants to get angry may do so — I will cast him out of the Church as an idolater....[107]

From this we learn that Psalms 23, 32 and 116, songs of trust and hope in God, were sung at funerals. Even Alleluias were heard; according to Jerome, both young and old joyfully sang Alleluia at Fabiola's burial.[108] It was a kind of congratulation, so to speak, for the victory that had been attained after the battle. This persisted in the Old Gallican and Mozarabic funeral rites, and to this day the Alleluia at funerals is customary in the Greek Church.[109]

Yet, in spite of these exhortations and practices, many often succumbed to human weakness. Gregory of Nyssa speaks of the crowd of men and women who had gathered from everywhere for his sister Macrina's funeral. He admitted that, when the procession began, great lamentation broke out during the singing of the psalms, for she had been well-loved on account of her good deeds.[110]

Originally only psalms were sung at funerals; later the singing of hymns was added. We know that Ephraem composed threnodies for his choirs of virgins.[111] In the account of his sister Macrina's funeral Gregory of Nyssa reports that a choir of virgins, led by a deaconess named Lampadia, took part in the procession.[112] The synodal decree of 676, which permitted — or rather ordered — the performance of *madrashe* by consecrated sisters, proves that the singing of hymns by virgins was later permitted at burials.[113] Justinian mentions the participation of *feminae canonicae et ascetriae*, who also sang hymns, at burials.[114] Later, at least in many places, there was mòre care in choosing hymns, and they were restricted again to the psalms, since there were attempts to sing pagan dirges along with the psalms. With this in mind one can understand the decision of the Third Council of Toledo in 589 that only psalms should be sung at burials and that funeral songs as well as the custom of striking the breast were forbidden. Wherever possible, the bishop was supposed to enforce this among all the faithful, at least among clerics.[115] The qualification in these last words suggests the difficulties inherent in carrying out the canon and reveals the compromising position of many clerics.

6. The Singing of Psalms and Hymns at the Christian Commemorations of the Dead.

Christianity, like paganism, also had its commemorations of the dead. F. J. Dölger has shown that Christians and pagans used the same word for these commemorations — ’αναμνησις or *memoria*.[116] In fact Christianity also retained in part the time schedule followed by the pagans.

Yet the contrast between the contents of the commemorations was most strong. In place of the meal of the dead which the pagans ate at the grave on the third day the Christians celebrated the Eucharist with an agape of the dead, and in place of pagan music and singing the Christians sang psalms.

It is important for the history of religion, however, that both pagan and Christian commemorations had in view the well-being of the dead. In Christianity this concern for the dead was considerably deepened, for the Eucharistic meal, with its greater value, was substituted for the funeral repast: the "fish of the living" was served in place of the "fish of the dead."[117] The singing of psalms was also intended to be useful to the dead. So it is that we often find engraved on tombstones the plea to sing psalms for the deceased. An inscription from

the year 373 from Umbria mentions the perpetual singing of psalms
which the soul of the departed, Aurelia, should receive from the
relatives gathered by her grave:

SANCTIVQE · TVI · MANES
NOBIS · PETENTIBVS · AD · SINT
VT · SEMPER · LIBENTERQVE
SALMOS · TIBIQVE · DICAMVS
AVRELIA · YGVIA[118]

The *Apostolic Constitutions* also express concern for the dead when
they decree that psalms should be sung for the deceased in churches
and cemeteries[119] and that the third day of death should be com-
memorated by the singing of psalms, the reading of the Scriptures and
prayers.[120] Among the *Canons of Father Athanasius*, canon 100 forbids mourning for the dead; instead the relatives of the dead are
ordered to read and sing the psalms if the deceased was a believer.[121]
From the day of burial until the commemoration of the third day
psalms and hymns were sung occasionally at the grave. A letter of
Evodius to Augustine concerning the death of a young ecclesiastical
clerk shows this:

> We honored his memory with obsequies worthy of such a soul, because
> for three days we praised the Lord with hymns over his grave, and on the
> third day we offered the sacraments of redemption.[122]

When the inhabitants of Majûma and Gaza came to the funeral of
Peter the Iberian they found him already laid to rest:

> For the next seven days, gathered together in all joy and with expressions
> of praise, they held meetings and vigils over him with hymns and services
> and spiritual songs, while they celebrated and kept festival for the praise
> of God and the honor of the blessed one.[123]

7. THE CHRISTIAN COMMEMORATION OF THE MARTYRS. THE PAGAN *Pervigilium* AND THE CHRISTIAN VIGIL. THE MOST ANCIENT SYNODAL DECISIONS AGAINST DANCING IN CHURCH.

The Christian cult of the martyrs was naturally very closely related
to the cult of the dead. Consequently the Christian commemoration of
the dead had a very strong similarity to the celebration of the martyrs'
feasts.

> The commemoration of a martyr is a commemoration of the dead
> elevated from the realm of the commonplace.[124]

In fact the rite of both commemorations had originally been the same. The three essential components of the Christian commemoration of the dead which have been discussed above are also found in the celebrations for the martyrs. They are the celebration of the Eucharist, the holding of meals at the grave and the singing of psalms. These served as a substitute for the sacrifice of the dead, the meal of the dead, singing and dancing. The graveside meals were a common phenomenon, at least in Augustine's time. In the fourth century Eusebius attests to the hymns and psalms, the Eucharistic sacrifice and the meal as characteristics of the feasts of martyrs.[125]

We have already had evidence from Tertullian (c. 200) concerning singing at the feast of a martyr and the use of hymns at such an event.[126] According to Theodoret, the antiphonal singing of psalms was introduced into the vigils and feasts of martyrs by Flavian of Antioch and Diodore of Tarsus.[127] Augustine mentions the singing of Psalm 116 at the feast of a martyr.[128] Maximus of Turin, in one of his sermons, refers to Psalm 32, which had been sung shortly before.[129] The singing of psalms and hymns was so closely associated with the cult of the martyrs that Peter the Iberian, when he spent some time in his twelfth year as a hostage in Constantinople at the court of Theodosius the Younger, honored the martyrs of his homeland privately in his bedroom with hymns:

> For he had bones of holy martyrs who were Persian and who had suffered a martyr's death in those times, whose names we know from the tradition of the saint and from correspondence with him, whose memories we celebrate and whose martyrologies we read. These he had placed in a shrine...in his room with every mark of reverence. And there he slept before them on the floor and celebrated the divine service with lights and incense, hymns and prayers. And when he was offering them every honor he clearly saw many times how they would sing and watch and pray with him.[130]

The hymns of the martyrs were especially loved by the people. That is why Ephraem and others, such as Marûtâ of Maipherkat,[131] composed songs which were sung at the commemorations and processions in honor of the martyrs.

However, the commemorations of the martyrs became a matter of concern for many persons of authority in the Church. Not only were the pagan ceremonies continued in them with their great pomp, but the people also saw in them a substitute for the all-night vigils in honor of the gods, to which converts from paganism were still deeply attached. These nocturnal celebrations — παννυχίδες or *pervigilia* —

were very popular among the pagans. They were essentially a Greek custom. Juvenal, writing of the *lectisternium* and *pervigilium* in Egypt, informs us of their existence there in connection with the Greek cult of the gods.[132] The mystery cults made these nocturnal celebrations popular. In Greece the Bacchic solemnities involving women were often celebrated at night. In the cult of the gods at Delphi, Sikyon and Patraea, this was already customary at quite an early time.[133] From the Greeks the Romans also became acquainted with this mode of celebration. Tacitus writes in his *Annales* that, after Rome was burned in the year 64 under Nero, a means of propitiating the angry gods was sought; the Sibylline Books gave the information that *sellisternia* — banquets offered specifically to female deities — and *pervigilia* should be celebrated by matrons in honor of Vulcan, Ceres, Proserpina and Juno.[134] Only women were permitted to participate in the *pervigilium* in the annual nocturnal sacrificial celebration for the Bona Dea, a goddess of fertility and chastity whose feast was May 1st.[135] This celebration was arranged by the Roman women in honor of the goddess and it took place in the consul's home in the presence of the Vestal Virgins, through the agency of the wife or the mother of the consul.[136] Cicero mentions *Pervigilia* in the cult of Iacchus:

> Quid ergo aget Iacchus Eumolpidaeque et augusta illa mysteria, si quidem sacra nocturna tollimus?[137]

In every one of these *pervigilia* music and dancing were more the custom than at any other cultic occasion. E. Rohde describes the all-night vigils in the cult of Sabazios among the Thracians:

> The celebration took place on the top of the mountains in the dark of night, by the wavering light of torches. There was loud music, the resounding clash of brass cymbals, the heavy beat of large drums and, in the midst of all this, the "madness-inducing melody" of the deep-sounding flutes, whose soul Phrygian flutists had awakened. Aroused by this wild music, the company of those celebrating danced while uttering shrill shouts.[138]

The Roman *pervigilia* were no different. Livy gives the following description of the beginnings of these nocturnal mystery celebrations in Rome:

> At first there were mysteries in which only a few participated, but afterwards they began to spread among men and women. The joys of the banquet and of wine were included in the divine worship so that the spirits of more might be enticed. When the wine had produced its inflaming effect and the night and the mixture of men and women of delicate age with

those already mature had removed all sense of shame, then temptations of every kind began, since everyone found delights to which nature had given him a compelling attraction. . . . They did much with malice and cunning, but most of what they did was done by violence. The violence remained hidden because no sound of protest during the rapes and murderous deeds could be heard on account of the noise of cymbals and drums.[139]

In this regard a remark of Suetonius is interesting. In his biography of the Emperor Caligula he stresses how enraptured the emperor was by dancing, music and singing, so that he himself appeared as a singer and dancer. Suetonius continues:

It also seems that on the day he was murdered he had announced a *pervigilium* for no other reason than that of making, at a favorable time, his first appearance on stage.[140]

At the *pervigilium* in honor of the Bona Dea there was no lack of music. Plutarch tells us that

Clodius, a man of noble descent, but very young and inwardly shameless, fell in love with Caesar's wife Pompeia and sneaked in [to the *pervigilium*] in the guise of a female citharist; for the women just then were celebrating in Caesar's dwelling a famous mystery sacrifice, closed to the eyes of all men, and so no man was present.[141]

As late as the fourth century Epiphanius pictures for us, from his own perspective, an all-night vigil from the 5th to the 6th of January which was held in the Temple of Kore in Alexandria:

The whole night they celebrated with singing and the sound of flutes to honor the idol. When the vigil was at an end they went at cockcrow, lamps in their hands, into a certain underground room and brought up an unclothed wooden idol, sitting upon a litter, a cross-shaped seal upon her forehead, two on her hands and two on her knees — in all, five golden seals. They bore this idol seven times about the innermost temple to the sound of flutes, tambourines and hymns, and then back into the underground room. In answer to the question as to what kind of mystery this was they replied: Today at this hour the virgin Kore gave birth to the Aion.[142]

It is easy to see why such all-night vigils were so popular. Consequently the Church's struggle against them was all the more difficult. Here also she sought to conquer form by way of content, inasmuch as she gave the people a substitute in the Christian vigil.[143] The most ancient ecclesiastical celebration of this type is the Paschal Vigil. Tertullian already bears witness to it when he advises Christian maidens not to marry pagans because they would hinder them in the duties of their religion, for who would let his wife leave his side and go to the evening devotions when it is demanded?. . . Who would rest easy when she would be away for the whole night during the Paschal solemnities?[144]

According to Augustine, the Paschal Vigil is the *mater omnium vigiliarum*.[145] As a substitute for the numerous *pervigilia* of the pagan gods, however, the Paschal Vigil alone was not enough for pagan converts. An attempt was made to add distinction to the greater feasts of the martyrs also with vigils.

The predilection of the people in orthodox ecclesiastical circles for the pagan *pervigilia* was one reason for introducing the vigils of the martyrs. This is evident in what Augustine tells us about the feasts of the martyrs and how they were celebrated with particular splendor. In a letter written in 395 to his friend, Bishop Alypius of Tagaste, Augustine relates that, after much trouble, his preaching had restrained the people from their accustomed banquets in church on the feast of Saint Leontius, an earlier bishop of Hippo. His Christians had asked heatedly: "Why just now? Those who did not forbid it before were also Christians!" Augustine continues:

When I heard this I really did not know what means I could use to influence them. . . . But that it might not seem as if we wished to reproach our forebearers, who had either tolerated or did not dare to forbid such excesses of an unthinking people, I explained to them by what necessity this bad custom seemed to have arisen in the Church. For, when peace came after many violent persecutions, crowds of pagans wishing to become Christians were prevented from doing this because of their habit of celebrating the feast days of their idols with banquets and carousing; and, since it was not easy for them to abstain from these dangerous but ancient pleasures, our ancestors thought that it would be good to make a concession for the time being to their weakness and permit them, instead of the feasts which they had renounced, to celebrate other feasts in honor of the holy martyrs — not with the same profanity but with a similar self-indulgence.[146]

From this letter of Augustine it can be clearly seen that the form of the feasts of the martyrs was shaped by the determination to draw the people away from the feasts of the gods and to offer them a substitute.

The Christian commemorations and vigils of martyrs were thus intended to meet a need of the newly-converted in two ways: they were supposed to be a commemoration of the dead which could also be celebrated with external splendor and joy.[147] In this way they served as a substitute for the wanton commemorations of the pagans. Further, they were meant to supplant the pagan feasts and *pervigilia*. Therefore a great task was imposed on these celebrations. The enormity of the task may be understood from the fact that, in their manner of acting, the people did not sufficiently observe a distinction between the pagan *pervigilia* and the Christian vigils, between the pagan feasts of the gods and the Christian feasts of the martyrs. Herein lay the danger of the Christian celebrations.

The chief concern of the rite of the Christian vigil regarding singing was set down in the *Didascalia* in the first half of the third century. It refers to the Paschal Vigil:

> Gather together, remain without sleep and be watching the whole night with prayers and supplications, the reading of the Prophets, the Gospels and the Psalms, in fear and trembling and with diligent weeping until the third hour of the night which follows the Saturday, and then break your fast.[148]

About this time, Aphraat, Bishop of Mar Matthai near Mossul, also mentions fasting, praying and the singing of psalms as essential components of the Paschal Vigil.[149]

In a letter of 375 to the clerics of Neocaesarea Basil describes the way psalms are sung in his church at Caesarea at the celebration of the vigil. He defends this method against those who reject it as an innovation which did not exist at the time of Gregory Thaumaturgos. Basil writes:

> But with reference to the charge concerning the singing of the psalms, with which our calumniators greatly frighten the simple, I have the following to say: with the custom as it is presently practiced we stand in agreement and harmony with every church of God. The people betake themselves at night to the house of prayer. With contrition, sorrow and many tears they make confession to God of their sins, get up from their prayers and sing psalms. Now they divide themselves into two groups and sing psalms back and forth; thus they not only grow strong in the contemplation of the words of Scripture but also maintain their attention and keep their hearts from distraction. Then again they leave it to one to begin the singing and the rest fall in. And when they have passed the night in this way in various modes of singing psalms and have also prayed at intervals, when the day breaks they all join together, as from one mouth and one heart, in the psalm of confession to the Lord.[150]

Basil then cites as reference for this type of vigil celebration the Egyptians, Libyans, Thebans, Phoenicians and Syrians — all, in fact, among whom vigils, prayers and the singing of psalms are held in honor. To be sure, Basil does not refute the objection that vigils were celebrated otherwise at the time of Gregory Thaumaturgos, but he recalls other things, such as the litany of penance, which were not done formerly either. It is difficult to determine whether the psalm of confession which Basil tells us was sung in common at the end of the vigil was the *Gloria in excelsis* or Psalm 51. Chrysostom speaks both of the Great Doxology and the Trishagion as vigil songs,[151] while the *Apostolic Constitutions* mention the Great Doxology as a morning song.[152]

We cannot ascertain from Basil's letter whether the people went home after the vigil or remained in the church until the beginning of the morning liturgy. In Jerusalem, according to Egeria, it was left up to those who had attended the Paschal Vigil to remain in church until daybreak or to return home and go to sleep.[153] The space of time between the end of the vigil and the beginning of the morning liturgy was accordingly quite lengthy. Paulinus of Nola writes that the vigil celebration in Nola began late at night, so that the interval between the celebration of the vigil and that of the feast could not have been great. As he reports it, the celebration of the Eucharist just before the vigil preceded the celebration of the vigil as a conclusion to the fasting observed throughout the day. After this everyone went home and had a festive evening meal, followed by a rest. Then, late in the night, they returned to the vigil, drawing out the night with psalms.[154] Sidonius Apollinaris gives a description of the vigil for the feast of Saint Justus of Lyons. He speaks with praise of a large crowd of men and women who gathered together for this nocturnal celebration, and he commends the beautiful singing of the psalms which was done antiphonally by the clerics and monks. He then mentions that the faithful left the church at the end of the vigil,

> but did not go a great distance, so as to be present at the third hour, when the liturgy would be celebrated by the priests.[155]

Thus it seems that, in this instance, there was not time for those present at the vigil to return home.

It is quite clear that this free time could present a danger for many, in that it provided the opportunity for falling back into the customs of the pagan *pervigilia* and feasts of the gods. Most particularly, the people would not desist from music and dancing, which was so elaborate in pagan ceremonies. The history of the vigils and feasts of the martyrs is consequently also the best history of the hard struggle which the Church waged against pagan music.

In the letter of Augustine to Alypius of Tagaste we read that the Church permitted the people to celebrate the feasts of the martyrs "not with the same profanity but with a similar self-indulgence" — similar, that is, to the pagan feasts and *pervigilia*. Music, dancing and feasting were part of this "self-indulgence." If anyone dared to try to take away these customs the people would continually invoke their rights and the antiquity of the customs. As late as the seventh century Bishop Eligius of Noyon (died 659) experienced this. Once, after he had criticized the music and dancing with which the vigil of the Apostle Peter had been celebrated, the people replied menacingly:

> As much as you wish to preach, Roman, you will not succeed in destroying our ancient customs. No man shall forbid us our time-honored amusements which give us such great pleasure.[156]

In fact it had originally even been believed that the martyrs were made happy by music and dancing. For example, in a homily given shortly after 363 on the feast of the martyr Polyeuctus we read:

> But what gift shall we present to the martyr, what would be worthy of him?... If it pleases him we will perform our customary dances in his honor.[157]

Here is a text which clearly shows that the people were within their rights when they said: "Those who did not forbid it before were also Christians!"

At the same time there were strong voices opposing these dances and their musical accompaniment at martyrs' feasts. Just before the commemoration of a martyr Ephraem exhorts his listeners:

> Let us not celebrate as the pagans do, but as Christians. Let us not wreathe the doors, let us not perform dances and enervate our sense of hearing with the music of flute and cithara.[158]

About the year 400 the Egyptian monk Shenute describes one of the feasts of the martyrs that could pass for a feast of the idols:

> People not only chatter, eat, drink and laugh; no, they also fornicate and commit murder. Everywhere drunkenness, debauchery and brawling reign. While in the church the Eucharist is celebrated and psalms are sung, outside there is the noise of cymbals and flutes. Merchants take advantage of the throng to sell their wares — some sell honey, others cattle. People have to be careful that no one will steal their belongings. Many merchants consider it advisable to arrange special overseers who refuse admittance to importunate customers. Even the grossest sensuality is paid homage to in the holy place: old and young anoint their heads and paint their eyes when they go to the martyr's chapel. The tombs and dark corners in the church can attest to the many who have succumbed to the temptation of forbidden things.[159]

These were the relics of paganism against which Shenute fought.

The activities at the feasts and vigils of the martyrs were certainly not as bad everywhere as those which Shenute depicts.[160] Still, opposition to music and dancing at these celebrations existed everywhere. Augustine stressed the great contrast between the behavior of the martyrs themselves and that of many Christians on their feasts when he remarked: "The martyrs achieved the victory *non saltando, sed orando, non potando, sed ieiunando, non rixando, sed tolerando.*[161] It even happened that there was cithara music and dancing in church, as Augustine's second discourse on Psalm 32 (33), mentioned previously, demonstrates.[162] Augustine praises Bishop Aurelius of Carthage, who had forbidden these nocturnal musical performances. Paulinus of Nola, a contemporary of Augustine, particularly decries the singing which went along with the dancing at such vigils. Probably the people were singing songs that they had learned at the pagan *pervigilia.*[163]

In order to remedy this unfortunate situation ecclesiastical law intervened. At first, women were forbidden to attend the vigils, a custom which had often given occasion to excesses. A half century before, Basil of Caesarea had censured the conduct of women at the Paschal Vigil: on that night licentious women

> removed the veils of honor from their heads, contemned God and the angels, displayed themselves shamelessly for every man's eye to see, shaking their hair, dragging their garments and tripping their feet; with lustful eyes they rushed about with unrestrained laughter as if mad, ...dancing in every place before the city where the martyrs had shed their blood and making the holy sites the workshops of their shamelessness. They have sullied the air with their lewd songs and the earth with their unclean feet.[164]

As early as the year 300 the Council of Elvira had forbidden women to hold vigils privately in cemeteries "because they often secretly commit sins under the guise of praying."[165] The Council of Laodicea (c. 360) forbade the holding of banquets in the churches.[166] In the West the Third Council of Carthage in 397,[167] along with many other later councils, maintained these prohibitions. The indecent songs that were sung on the martyrs' feasts in church or in the vestibule or court of the church were the object of concern to the ecclesiastical authorities until the late Middle Ages.[168] The Third Council of Toledo (589) took steps against dancing on the feasts of the martyrs with the following decree:

> The irreligious custom which the common people have of observing the solemnities of the saints — that is, that the people who should be attentive to the divine services try to keep themselves awake with dancing and the

singing of songs of a low sort, thus not only harming themselves but disturbing the services of the monks — is to be entirely eradicated. The elimination of this from all of Spain is committed to the care of the sacred council of priests and judges.[169]

On account of the great dangers monks were also prohibited from attending the vigils and feasts of the martyrs. They could not even go to them simply to pray.[170] On the other hand, however, the pilgrim Egeria mentions the singing of the *monazontes* in Jerusalem during a vigil,[171] and Sidonius Apollinaris also speaks of the participation of monks in the psalmody at a vigil, as has already been noted. A Roman council in 826 legislated against the singing and dancing of women,[172] while in the East Barhebraeus (died 1286) decreed against the relics of the pagan cult of the dead and its commemorations in his *Nomocanon*:

> Women who dance in pagan fashion for their dead and go to the grave with drums, dancing the while, shall be admonished not to do that. But if they do not discontinue they shall be forbidden entrance to the church.[173]

Thus the Church's opposition to pagan music, pagan songs, pagan dances and women's singing was most strongly manifested in her opposition to the pagan *pervigilia* and commemorations of the dead.

NOTES

1. A. Jeremias, *Hölle und Paradies bie den alten Babyloniern* (*Der alte Orient* 1, 3) (Leipzig 1900), p. 9.

2. Lucian, *De lucta* 12 (III 70 Sommerbrodt): οἰμωγαὶ δὲ ἐπὶ τούτοις καὶ κωκυτὸς γυναικῶν καὶ παρὰ πάντων δάκρυα καὶ στέρνα τυπτόμενα καὶ σπαραττομένη κόμη καὶ φοινισσόμεναι παρειαί.

3. Festus, *De verborum significatu: Nenia* (155 Lindsay): Nenia est carmen, quod in funere laudandi gratia cantatur ad tibiam. Cf. Cicero, *De legibus* 2, 24, 62 (IV 429 Müller): Honoratorum virorum laudes in contione memorentur easque etiam cantus ad tibicinem prosequatur, cui nomen neniae, quo vocabulo etiam apud Graecos cantus lugubres nominantur.

4. Cf. the vase picture with the wake scene in Daremberg-Saglio II 1372, no. 3335. The person designated as Παιδαγωγός is holding a lyre in his left hand.

5. P. Haupt, *Akkadisch-Sumerische Keilschrifttexte* (Leipzig 1882), p. 122, no. 19.

6. M. Jastrow, *Die Religion der Assyrer und Babylonier* (Giessen 1912), II 1, 4, 81.

7. Jer. 48:36.

8. There is a small collection of material from Jewish and pagan culture in Z. Hilliger, *Dissertatio de* Αὐλητοῖς *seu Tibicinibus in funere adhibitis* (Wittenberg 1717).

9. Flavius Josephus, *Bellum Judaicum* 3, 9, 5 (2, 173 Dindorf): ὡς ἐπὶ τριακοστὴν μὲν ἡμέραν μὴ διαλειπεῖν τὰς ὀλοφύρσεις ἐν τῇ πόλει, πλείστους δὲ μισθοῦσθαι τοὺς αὐλητάς, οἳ θρήνων ἐξῆρχον αὐτοῖς.

10. Mishna, *Sabbath* 23, 4.

11. Mishna, *Ketub* 4, 4.

12. Cf. F. v. Duhn, "Der Sarkophag aus Hagia Triada," in ARW 7, 271.

13. Inventory no. 643.

14. The frequent presence of the cithara in portrayals of Greek funerals leads S. Eitrem, *Hermes und die Toten* (*Christiania Videnskabs-Selskabs Forhandlinger* 5) (Kristiania 1909), p. 44, to ask if Hermes is pictured with a cithara because it is related to apotropaic music of the dead. There is much to be said for this.

15. There is a reproduction in Th. Klauser, *Die Cathedra im Totenkult der heidnischen und christlichen Antike* (*Liturgiegeschichtliche Quellen und Forschungen* 21) (Münster 1927), table 4. Cf. W. Helbig, *Führer durch die öffentlichen Sammlungen klassischer Altertümer in Rom* I (Leipzig ³ 1912), p. 606.

16. Aristotle, *Politeia* 8, 6, 8 (287 Immisch): φασὶ γὰρ δὴ τὴν Ἀθηνᾶν εὑροῦσαν ἀποβαλεῖν τοὺς αὐλούς· οὐ κακῶς μὲν οὖν ἔχει φάναι καὶ διὰ τὴν ἀσχημοσύνην τοῦ προσώπου τοῦτο ποιῆσαι δυσχεράνασαν τὴν θεόν. The Greeks call this leather band φορβειά. It may be seen on Greek, Roman and Etruscan monuments. Cf. Plate 16 of the present work and A. Schneider, *Zur Geschichte der Flöte im Altertum* (Zurich 1890), p. 32.

17. There is a similar waking scene with a flutist on the limestone relief of a gravestone from Cerveteri, which is presently in the Louvre. There is a reproduction in W. Hausenstein, *Die Bildnerei de Etrusker* (*Atlanten zu Kunst* II) (Munich 1922), table 38.

18. On gravestone 2269 of the Museum of Chiusi there is a scene which refers to these dances; here also the lyrist is present. Cf. Daremberg-Saglio II 1385.

19. It is in Hall 29, no. 9182. Cf. Plate 30 of the present work and R. Paribeni, *Le Terme di Diocleziano e il Museo Nazionale Romano* (Rome 1928), p. 254, no. 762. Cf. also Daremberg-Saglio II 1387, figure 3358, where a sarcophagus is portrayed which seems to depict the moment of death; here too there is the music of the dead.

20. CIL VI 29, 955.

21. Cf., e.g., Petronius, *Saturae* 129, 7 (100 Buecheler): quod si idem frigus genua manusque temptaverit tuas, licet ad tubicines mittas.

22. There is a reproduction of the monument in Klauser, *Die Cathedra*..., table 3 and a detailed description in W. Helbig, *Führer durch die öffentlichen Sammlungen klassischer Altertümer in Rom* II (Leipzig ³ 1913), pp. 30 f. On the three women sitting at the head of the bed cf. Klauser, *Die Cathedra*..., pp. 24 f.

23. On the small cone-shaped coverings over the apertures of the flute cf. Schneider, *Zur Geschichte der Flöte*..., p. 34 and C. Bartholinus, *De Tibiis veterum* (Amsterdam 1639), p. 59. On whether the ancient flute resembled an oboe or a clarinet cf. L. Friedländer, *Darstellungen aus der Sittensgeschichte Roms* II (Leipzig ⁹⁻¹⁰ 1921), p. 165. Cf. also K. Schlesinger, *The Greek Aulos. A Study of its Mechanism and of its Relation to the Modal System of Ancient Greek Music* (London 1939).

24. Lucan, *Bellum civile* VIII 832 (259 Hosius): Nos in templa tuam Romana accepimus Isim Semideosque canes et sistra iubentia luctus.

25. Lucian, *De luctu* 19 (III 72 Sommerbrodt): τί δέ με ὁ κωκυτὸς ὑμῶν ὀνίνησι καὶ ἡ πρὸς τὸν αὐλὸν αὕτη στερνοτυπία καὶ ἡ τῶν γυναικῶν περὶ τὸν θρῆνον ἀμετρία;

26. Plutarch, *De εἰ apud Delphos* 21, 394 (III 26 Bernardakis): Οὐ νάβλα κωκυτοῖσιν, οὐ λύρα φίλα. Καὶ γὰρ ὁ αὐλὸς ὀψὲ καὶ πρῴην ἐτόλμησε φωνήν ἐφ᾽ ἱμερτοῖσιν ἀφιέναι· τὸν δέ πρῶτον χρόνον εἵλκετο πρὸς τὰ πένθη. Cf. the illustrations in Daremberg-Saglio II 1374, figure 3340, 1375, figure 3341 and 1376, figure 3343.

27. Cicero, *De legibus* 2, 23, 59 (IV² 428 Müller): Sumptum minuito, tria si volet reicinia et vincula purpurae, et decem tibicines adhibeto, hoc plus ne facito mulieres genas ne radunto neve lessum funeris ergo habento.

28. Sophocles, *Oedipus Rex* 30 (108 Dindorf): μέλας δ᾽ "Αιδης στεναγμοῖς καὶ γόοις πλουτίζεται.

29. Cicero, *Tusculanae disputationes* 1, 103 (271 Pohlenz): Sed, mihi crede, nemo me vestrum, cum hinc excessero, consequetur.

30. Athenaeus, *Dipnosophistae* 13, 594 (311 Kaibel): τεχνιτῶν τῶν ἐπισημοτάτων χορῷ μεγάλῳ καὶ παντοίοις ὀργάνοις καὶ συμφωνίαις παρέπεμπε τὸ σῶμα.

31. Plutarch, *Aristides* 21 (II 187 Sintenis): τῇ ἕκτῃ ἐπὶ δέκα πέμπουσι πομπήν, ἧς προηγεῖται μέν ἅμ᾽ ἡμέρᾳ σαλπιγκτής ἐγκελευόμενος τὸ πολεμικόν, ἕπονται δ᾽ ἄμαξαι μυρρίνης μεσταὶ καὶ στεφανωμάτων καὶ μέλας ταῦρος καὶ χοὰς οἴνου καὶ γάλακτος ἐν ἀμφορεῦσιν ἐλαίου τε καὶ μύρου χρωσσοὺς νεανίσκοι κομίζοντες ἐλεύθεροι.

32. Persius, *Satura* III, 103 (35 Jahn-Leo): Hinc tuba, candelae, tandemque beatulus alto compositus lecto crassisque lutatus amonis in portam rigidas calces extendit at illum hesterni capite induto subiere Quirites.

33. Seneca, *Apocolocyntosis* 12, 1 (260 Buecheler-Heraeus): tubicinum, cornicinum, omnisque, generis aeneatorum tanta turba, tantus conventus, ut etiam Claudius audire posset. Omnes laeti, hilares...ingenti enim μεγάλῳ χωρικῷ naenia cantabatur anapaestis:

Fundite fletus
Edite planctus...

34. Propertius, *Eleg.* II 13, 19 (294 Rothstein): nec mea tum longa spatietur imagine pompa nec tuba sit fati vana querela mei...desit odoriferis ordo mihi lancibus, adsint plebei parvae funeris exequiae.

35. Servius, *In Vergilii Aeneidos libr.* V 138 (610 Thilo): Sciendum maioris aetatis funera ad tubam solere proferri: Persius hinc tuba, candelae: minoris vero ad tibias, ut Statius de Archemoro [tibia cui] teneros solitum deducere manes.

36. Cf. Plate 31.

37. Cf. CIL IX 4454, 4458–4460, 4465, 4467, 4471 and 4480.

38. C. Huelsen, Bolletino dell' Istituto di corr. archeol.(1890), 72.

39. Lucian, Dialogi mortuorum X 12 (I 1, 137 Sommerbrodt): ἄλλοι δὲ Διόφαντον τὸν ῥήτορα ἐπαινοῦσιν ἐν Σικυῶνι ἐπιταφίους λόγους θιεξιόντα ἐπὶ Κράτωνι τούτῳ. καὶ νὴ Δία γε ἡ Δαμασίου μήτηρ κωκύουσα ἐξάρχει τοῦ θρήνυς ὺν γυναιξὶν ἐπὶ τῷ Δαμασίᾳ.

40. Virgil, Aeneis 11, 184 (338 Janell): Iam pater Aeneas, iam curvo in litore Tarchon constituere pyras. Huc corpora quisque suorum more tulere patrum, subiectisque ignibus atris conditur in tenebras altum caligine caelum. Ter circum accensos cincti fulgentibus armis decurrere rogos, ter maestum funeris ignem lustravere in equis ululatusque ore dedere; spargitur et tellus lacrimis, sparguntur et arma: it caelo clamorque virum clangorque tubarum. Cf. also Lucan, Bellum civile VIII 729 (255 Hosius): Non pretiosa petit cumulato ture sepulchra Pompeius fortuna, tuus non pinguis ad astra ut ferat e membris eos fumus odores, ut Romana suum gestent pia colla parentem, praeferat ut veteres feralis pompa triumphos, ut resonent tristi cantu fora, totus ut ignes proiectis maerens exercitus ambiat armis.

41. Lucian, Charon 22, 519 (I 1, 14 Sommerbrodt): Τί οὖν ἐκείνους στεφανοῦσι τοὺς λίθους καὶ χρίουσι μύρῳ; οἱ δὲ καὶ πυρὰν νήσαντες πρὸ τῶν χωμάτων καὶ βόθρον τινὰ ὀρύξαντες καίουσί τε ταυτὶ τὶ πολυτελῆ δεῖπνα καὶ ἐς τὰ ὀρύγματα οἶνον καὶ μελίκρατον, ὡς γοῦν εἰκάσαι, ἐκχέουσιν; ΕΡΜ. Οὐκ οἶδα, ὦ πορθμεῦ, τι ταῦτα πρὸς τοὺς ἐν "Αιδου· πεπιστεύκασι γοῦν τὰς ψυχὰς ἀναπεμπομένας κάτωθεν δειπνεῖν μὲν ὡς οἶόν τε περιπετομένας τὴν κνῖσην καὶ τὸν καπνόν. πίνειν δὲ ἀπὸ τοῦ βόθρου τὸ μελίκρατον.

42. Lucian, De mercede conductis 28, 687 (I 425 Jakobitz): ἔοικας γὰρ τότε στήλῃ ἑώλου τινὸς νεκροῦ ἄγοντος ἐναγίσματα· καὶ γὰρ ἐκείνου καταχέαντες μύρον καὶ τὸν στέφανον ἐπιθέντες αὐτοὶ πίνουσι καὶ εὐωχοῦνται τὰ παρεσκευασμένα.

43. Cf. A. Erman, Die Ägyptische Religion (Berlin 1909), p. 157. Cf. also F. Cumont. Die orientalischen Religionen im römischen Heidentum (Leipzig-Berlin 1910), p. 278, n. 91, where the "Song of the Harpist," a canonical hymn which was sung in Egypt on the day of burial and which exhorted the deceased "to gladden his heart," is related to the formula εὐψύχει, οὐδεὶς ἀθάνατος.

44. There is a reproduction is F.J. Dölger, ΙΧΘΥΣ IV (Münster 1927), table 233.

45. Cf. Plate 32.

46. Cf. Klauser, Die Cathedra..., p. 38. The Etruscan gravestone from Antella in the Museo Archeologico in Florence mentioned in Klauser is of the same style as our gravestone from Fiesole.

47. There is a reproduction in Dölger, ΙΧΘΥΣ III (Münster 1922), table LV.

48. There is a reproduction in P. Gardner, Museum Oxoniense. Catalogue of the Greek Vases in the Ashmolean Museum (Oxford 1893), plate 20. On Gardner's incorrect explanation of the scene as referring to a music lesson cf. A. Délatte, "La musique au tombeau dans l'antiquité," in Revue archéologique 21 (1913), I 321, n. 1.

49. Cf. Plate 33.

50. Cf. A. Furtwängler, Königliche Museen zu Berlin. Beschreibung der Vasensammlung im Antiquarium I (Berlin 1885), p. 686, no. 2458. There is a reproduction in J. Quasten, "Die Leierspielerin auf heidnischen und christlichen Sarkophagen," in Römische Quartalschrift 37 (1929), table VII.

51. Cf. Plate 34.

52. Lucian, Verae historiae II 5, 108 (II 1, 49 Sommerbrodt): καὶ μὴν καὶ βοὴ σύμ-

μιχτὸς ἠκούετο ἄθρους, οὐ θορυβώδης, ἀλλ' οἷα γένοιτ' ἐν συμποσίῳ τῶν μὲν αὐλούντων, τῶν δὲ ἐπαινούντων, ἐνίων δὲ κροτούντων πρὸς αὐλὸν ἢ κιθάραν. Cf. also the description in Hanno, *Navigatio* 14 (40 Kluge): καὶ φωνὴν αὐλῶν ἠκούεμεν κυμβάλων τε καὶ τυμπάνων πάταγον καὶ κραυγὴν μυρίαν.

53. Stobaios 3, 52, 49 (1089 Hense): τό(τε) δὲ πάσχει πάθος, οἷον οἱ τελεταῖς μεγάλαις κατοργιαζόμενοι. διὸ καὶ τὸ ῥῆμα τῷ ῥήματι καὶ τὸ ἔργον τῷ ἔργῳ τοῦ τελευτᾶν καὶ τελεῖσθαι προσέοικε. πλάναι τὰ πρῶτα καὶ περιδρομαὶ κοπώδεις καὶ διὰ σκότους τινὲς ὕποπτοι πορεῖαι καὶ ἀτέλεστοι, εἶτα πρὸ τοῦ τέλους αὐτοῦ τὰ δεινὰ πάντα, φρίκη καὶ τρόμος καὶ ἱδρὼς καὶ θάμβος. ἐκ δὲ τούτου φῶς τι θαυμάσιον ἀπήντησεν τόποι καθαροὶ καὶ λειμῶνες ἐδέξαντο, φωνὰς καὶ χορείας καὶ σεμνότητας ἀκουσμάτων ἱερῶν καὶ φασμάτων ἁγίων ἔχοντες, ἐν αἷς ὁ παντελὴς ἤδη· καὶ μεμυημένος ἐλεύθερος . . . ὀργιάζει.

54. Cf. Pindar, Fragmentum 129 (318 Schroeder): καὶ τοὶ μὲν ἵπποισί «τε», τοὶ δὲ πεσσοῖς, τοὶ δὲ φορμίγγεσσι τέρπονται.

55. Cf. Plate 35.

56. G. Weiker, *Der Seelenvogel in der alten Literatur und Kunst. Eine mythologisch-archäologische Untersuchung* (Leipzig 1902), p. 11.

57. Cf. the siren with a tambourine in Plate 36. In cabinet 259 in the National Museum in Palermo there is a similar figure — a siren with a lyre on her left arm. It may be noted that sirens were originally death *daemones*. Cf. S. Eitrem, *Opferritus und Voropfer der Griechen und Römer (Videnskapsselskapets Skrifter II. Hist.-Filos. Klasse* 1914, 1 (Kristiania 1915), p. 426.

58. Cf. Délatte, "La musique au tombeau . . . ," 332.

59. Sala mezzogiornio no. 2859.

60. Cf. Plate 37 and W. Helbig, *Führer durch die öffentlichen Sammlungen klassischer Altertümer in Rom* I (Leipzig ³ 1912), p. 430, no. 779.

61. Cf. Plate 38. The tombstone was probably discovered near Xanten. Cf. H. Lehner, *Führer durch das Provinzialmuseum in Bonn* I (Bonn ² 1924), p. 141.

62. Cf. A. Wiedemann, *Zauberei und Magie im alten Ägypten (Der alte Orient 6, 4)* (Leipzig 1904), p. 25.

63. Ovid, *Fasti* 5, 441 (237 Merkel):

Rursus aquam tangit Temesaeaque concrepat aera
et rogat, ut textis exeat umbris suis.

64. Apuleius, *Metamorphoseon* 2, 21, 143 (43 Helm): insistebat lapidem claraque voce praedicabat, si qui mortuum servare vellet de pretio liceretur . . . respondit ille, . . . perpetem noctem eximie vigilandum est exertis et inconivis oculis semper in cadaver intentis nec acies usquam devertenda, immo ne obliquanda quidem . . .

65. A. Jeremias, *Hölle und Paradies bei den alten Babyloniern (Der alte Orient 1, 3)* (Leipzig 1900), p. 20.

66. Statius, *Thebais* 6, 120 (200 Klotz):

Cum signum luctus cornu grave mugit adunco
tibia, cui teneros suetum producere manes
lege Phrygum maesta.

67. Virgil, *Aeneis* 6, 119 (212 Janell):

si potuit manis arcessere coniugis Orpheus
Thraeicia fretus cithara fidibusque canoris.

68. Martianus Capella 9 (347 Dick): Per me [scil. musicam] quippe vestrum homines illexere succursum irasque inferas per naenias sedavere.

69. Herodotus 6, 58 (II 84 Stein): ἀποθανοῦσι δὲ τάδε. ἱππέες περιαγέλλουσι τὸ γεγονὸς κατὰ πᾶσαν τὴν Λακωνικήν· κατὰ δὲ τὴν πόλιν γυναῖκες περιιοῦσαι λέβητα κροτέουσιν.

70. Apollodoros, Schol. Theocrit. 2, 36 (279 Wendel): τὸν δὲ χαλκὸν ἐπῆδον ἐν ταῖς ἐκλείψεσι τῆς σελήνης καὶ ἐν τοῖς κατεχομένοις, ἐπειδὴ ἐνομίζετο καθαρὸς εἶναι καὶ ἀπελαστικὸς τῶν μιασμάτων. διόπερ πρὸς πᾶσαν ἀφοσίωσιν καὶ ἀποκάθαρσιν αὐτῷ ἐχρῶντο, ὥς φησι καὶ Ἀπολλόδωρος ἐν τῷ περὶ θεῶν· τὸ χαλκίον ὡς ἄχει ἀντὶ τοῦ φόφει χροῦε. ἐπεὶ ὁ τοῦ χαλκοῦ ἦχος οἰκεῖος τοῖς κατοιχομένοις. Φησὶν Ἀπολλόδωρος, Ἀθήνῃσι τὸν ἱεροφάντην τῆς Κόρης ἐπικαλουμένης, ἐπικρούειν τὸ λεγόμενον ἠχεῖον· καὶ παρὰ Λάκωσι, βασιλέως ἀποθανόντος, εἰώθασι κρούειν λέβητας.

71. Cf. F. Winter, "Die Typen der figürlichen Terrakotten," in Die antiken Terrakotten, ed. by R. Kekulé v. Stradonitz III (Berlin: 1903), I 13, 5; I 17, 6; I 53, 3; II 139, 13. Cf. P. Delattre, "Figurines trouvées à Carthage dans une Nécropole punique," in Comptes redues de l'Académie des inscriptions et belles lettres (1903), p. 430.

72. Cf. F. Studniczka, "Zu den Sarkophagen von Sidon," in Revue archéologique (1905), II, 46 ff.

73. Pliny, Naturalis historia 36, 13, 92 (V 340 Mayhoff): Supra id quadratum pyramides stant quinque . . ., ita fastigatae, ut in summo orbis aeneus et petasus unus omnibus sit inpositus, ex quo pendeant exapta catenis tintinabula, quae vento agitata longe sonitus referant ut Dodonae olim factum. An earthenware vessel which was found in a grave on the Via Aurelia (Tenuta Bravetta) had a similar aim; on its outer side ϙ-shaped clappers hang which make a noise when the vessel is moved. Cf. K. Lehmann-Hartleben, "Archäologische Funde aus den Jahren 1921 bis 1924 in Italien," in Archäologischer Anzeiger (1926), 105.

74. Diodorus Siculus, Bibliotheca historica 18, 26 (234 Müller): ἐπὶ δὲ τῶν ἄκρων ὑπῆρχε θύσαντος δικτνωτός, ἔχων εὐμεγέθεις κώδωνας, ὥστε ἐκ πολλοῦ διαστήματος προσπίπτειν τόν φόφον τοῖς ἐγγίζουσι. Ibid. 18, 27: ἔκαστος δὲ τούτων [scil. ἡμιόνων] ἐστεφάνωτο κεχρυσωμένῳ στεφάνῳ, καὶ παρ' ἑκατέραν τῶν σιαγόνων εἶχεν ἐξηρτη μένον κώδωνα χρυσοῦν . . .

75. Cf. DACL III 2, 1995.

76. Cf. F.X. Kraus, RE I, 623.

77. Macrobius, In somnum Scipionis II 3 (145 Janus): Mortuos quoque ad sepulturam prosequi oportere cum cantu plurimarum gentium vel regionum instituta sanxerunt, persuasione hac, qua post corpus animae ad originem dulcedinis Musicae, it est ad coelum redire credantur.

78. Philo, De Abraham 260 (57 Cohn): ὡς δ'ἦχον οἱ ἐν τέλει τῶν κατὰ τὴν χώραν συναλγήσοντες, ἰδόντες οὐδὲν τῶν ἐν ἔθει παρ' αὐτοῖς γινομένων ἐπὶ τοῖς πενθοῦσιν, οὐκ ὀλόφυρσιν, οὐ θρῆνον, οὐ κοπετόν, οὐκ ἀνδρῶ οὐ γυναικῶν, ἀλλὰ τῆς συμπάσης οἰκίας εὐσταθῆ καὶ νηφάλιον κατήφειαν. ἐθαύμαζον οὐ μετρίως.

79. On Christianity's influence on pagan funeral customs cf. A.C. Rush, Death and Burial in Christian Antiquity (Studies in Christian Antiquity 1) (Washington 1941).

80. Minucius Felix 12, 6 (CSEL 1, 17 Halm): Non floribus caput nectitis, non corpus odoribus honestatis: reservatis unguenta funeribus, coronas etiam sepulcris denegatis. Cf. also Tertullian, De corona 10 (I 439 Oehler). On the problem of wreathing the dead cf. F.J. Dölger, ΙΧΘΥΣ II (Münster 1922), p. 4, n. 1.

81. Orelli 4793. On the significance of raised hands on tombstones cf. F. Cumont, "Il Sole vindice dei delitti ed il simbolo delle mani alzate," in Atti della Pontificia Accademia Rom. di archeologia, ser. III. Memorie vol. I, parte 1. Miscellanea Giovanni Battista de Rossi (parte 1) (Rome 1923), pp. 65–80.

82. Bolletino di archeologia cristiana IV 1 (1882), 95.

83. Chrysostom, *De SS. Bernice et Prosdoce* (PG 50, 634): Διὰ τοῦτο παρὰ μὲν τὴν ἀρχὴν ἐπὶ τοῖς κοπετοί τινες ἐγίγνοντο καὶ θρῆνοι, νῦν δὲ ψαλμοὶ καὶ ὑμνῳδίαι. Ἔκλαυσαν γοῦν τὸν Ἰακὼβ τεσσαράκοντα ἡμέρας, ἔκλαυσαν καὶ τὸν Μωυσῆν ἑτέρας τοσαύτας οἱ Ἰουδαῖοι καὶ ἐκόψαντο, ἐπειδὴ θάνατος τότε θάνατος ἦν· νυνὶ δὲ οὐχ οὕτως, ἀλλὰ ὑμνῳδίαι καὶ εὐχαὶ καὶ ψαλμοί, δηλούντων ἁπάντων, ὅτι ἡδονὴν ἔχει τὸ πρᾶγμα· οἱ γὰρ ψαλμοὶ εὐθυμίας σύμβολον. Ἐπεὶ οὖν εὐθυμίας ἐσμὲν πεπληρωμένοι, διὰ τοῦτο ψάλλομεν ἐπὶ τοῖς νεκροῖς ψαλμοὺς θαρρεῖν ὑπὲρ τῆς τελευτῆς παρακελευομένους.

84. Augustine, *Confessiones* 9, 12 (CSEL 33, 220 Knöll): Neque enim decere arbitrabamur funus illud questibus lacrimosis gemitibusque celebrare, quia his plerumque solet deplorari quaedam miseria morientium aut quasi omnimoda extinctio. At illa nec misere moriebatur nec omnio moriebatur. Hoc et documentis morum eius et fide non ficta rationibusque certis tenebamus.... Cohibito ergo a fletu illo puero psalterium arripuit Evodius et cantare coepit psalmum. Cui respondebamus omnis domus: Misericordiam et iudicium cantabo tibi, Domine.

85. Gregory of Nyssa, *De vita Macrinae* (PG 46, 992): τῆς παννυχίδος περὶ αὐτὴν ἐν ὑμνῳδίαις, καθάπερ ἐπὶ μαρτύρων πανηγύρεως τελεσθείσης.

86. Jerome, *Epistula* 108 (*Epitaphium sanctae Paulae*) 29, 1 (CSEL 55, 29, 348 Hilberg): Ex hinc non ululatus, et planctus ut inter saeculi homines fieri solet, sed psalmos monachorum linguis diversis examina concrepabant. Translataque episcoporum manibus, cum alii pontifices lampadas cereosque praeferrent, alii choros psallentium ducerent, in media ecclesia speluncae salvatoris est posita. Tota ad funus eius Palaestinarum urbium turba convenit.... Graeco, Latino, Syroque sermone psalmi in ordine personabant, non solum triduo et donec subter ecclesiam et iuxta specum Domini conderetur, sed per omnem hebdomadam cunctis, qui venerant, suum funus, et proprias credentibus lacrymas.

87. J. Leipoldt, *Schenute von Atripe und die Entstehung des nationalägyptischen Christentums* (TU NF 10, 1) (1903), p. 134.

88. R. Raabe, *Petrus der Iberer* (Leipzig 1895), p. 125.

89. Chrysostom, *In Matthaeum homilia* 31, 3 (PG 57, 374): Εἰ γὰρ τότε ἐξέβαλεν ἐκείνους ἔξω, πολλῷ μᾶλλον νῦν. Τότε μὲν γὰρ οὔπω δῆλος ὁ θάνατος ἦν ὕπνος γεγενημένος. νῦν δὲ καὶ αὐτοῦ τοῦ ἡλίου τοῦτο φανερώτερον...Μηδεὶς τοίνυν κοπτέσθω λοιπόν, μηδὲ θρηνείτω, μηδὲ τὸ κατόρθωμα τοῦ Χριστοῦ διαβαλλέτω. Καί γὰρ ἐνίκησε τὸν θάνατον. Τί τοίνυν περιττὰ θρηνεῖς; Ὕπνος τὸ πρᾶγμα γέγονε. Τί ὀδύρῃ καὶ κλαίεις; Τοῦτο γὰρ εἰ καὶ Ἕλληνες ἐποίουν, καταγελᾶν ἔδει· ὅταν δὲ ὁ πιστὸς ἐν τούτοις ἀσχημονῇ, ποία ἀπολογία. τίς ἔσται συγγνώμη τοιαῦτα ἀνοηταίνουσι, καὶ ταῦτα μετὰ χρόνον τοσοῦτον καὶ σαφῆ τῆς ἀναστάσεως ἀπόδειξιν; Σὺ δὲ ὥσπερ αὐξῆσαι τὸ ἔγκλημα σπεύδων, καὶ θρηνῳδοὺς ἡμῖν ἄγεις Ἑλληνίδας γυναῖκας ἐξάπτων τὸ πάθος καὶ τὴν κάμινον διεγείρων, καὶ οὐκ ἀκούεις τοῦ Παύλου λέγοντος· Τίς συμφώνησις Χριστῷ πρὸς Βελίαρ.

90. Chrysostom, *De consolatione mortis* 2, 6 (PG 56, 303): Nos qui iam sub gratia sumus, sub certa spe resurrectionis, quibus omnis tristitia interdicitur, qua fronte mortuos nostros gentilium more plangimus...veluti...bacchantes.

91. W. Riedel, *Die Kirchenrechtsquellen des Patriarchats Alexandrien* (Leipzig 1900), p. 191.

92. Eusebius, *Hist. eccles.* 9, 8, 11 (GCS Eus. II 2, 824 Schwartz): πάντα δ'οὖν οἰμωγῶν ἦν ἀνάπλεα, κατὰ πάντας τε στενωποὺς ἀγορᾶς τε καὶ πλατείας οὐδ' ἦν ἄλλο τι θεωρεῖν ἢ θρήνους μετὰ τῶν συνήθων αὐτοῖς αὐλῶν τε καὶ κτύπων.

93. Basil, *Comment. in Isaiam* 5, 155 (PG 30, 373): Εἶτα πόρρω προϊόντος τοῦ πότου,

αὐλοὶ καὶ κιθάραι καὶ τύμπανα, κατὰ μὲν τὴν ἀλήθειαν ἀποθρηνοῦνται τοὺς ἀπολλυμένους, κατὰ δὲ τὴν ἐπιτήδευσιν τῶν μεθυόντων ὥστε αὐτοῖς πάσας τῆς ψυχῆς τὰς ἡδονὰς τῇ μελῳδίᾳ διεγερθῆναι.

94. Leipoldt, *Schenute von Atripe...*, p. 134.

95. J. Chabot, *Synodicon orientale ou Recueil des Synodes Nestoriens* (Paris 1902), p. 376.

96. O. Braun, *Das Buch der Synhados* (Stuttgart 1900), p. 346.

97. Chabot, *Synodicon orientale...*, p. 486.

98. Canons of the Patriarch Cyriacus 190 in F. Nau, *Les canons et les résolutions canoniques* (Paris 1906), p. 104.

99. H. Petermann, *Reisen Im Orient* (Leipzig 1860), I 121.

100. Tertullian, *De corona* 11 (I 443 Oehler): Mortuus etiam tuba inquietabitur aeneatoris, qui excitari a tuba angeli expectat. The use of the trumpet in the cult of the dead also probably explains a painting in a section of the Catacomb of Saint Lucy in Syracuse; it depicts a man carrying a trumpet in his hand who is about to put it to his mouth. Cf. the report of J.P. Kirsch in *Römische Quartalschrift* 30 (1916–1922), 101.

101. Canon 34 of the Council of Elvira in Hefele-Leclercq I 1, 220: Cereos per diem placuit in coemeterio non incendi, inquitandi enim sanctorum spiritus non sunt. Qui haec non observaverint, arceantur ab ecclesiae communione.

102. Statius, *Thebais* 6, 123 (200 Klotz): exequiale sacrum carmenque minoribus umbris utile.

103. Commodian, *Instructiones* 2, 33, 10 (CSEL 15, 107 Dombart):

> Non provides, quonam merearis ire defunctus?
> Ecce prosequuntur illi, tum iam foste cremaris
> Redactus in Poenam: quid proderit pompa defuncto?
> Incusatus eris qui ob ista collegia quaeris.
> Sub nigrore cupis vivere: te decipis ipsum.

104. There is a reproduction of the gravestone in J.B. de Rossi, *Bolletino di archeologia cristiana* (1864), p. 34.

105. *Constitutiones Apostolorum* VI 30, 10 (381 Funk): καὶ ἐν ταῖς ἐξόδοις τῶν κεκοιμημένων ψάλλοντες προπέμπετε αὐτούς, ἐὰν ὦσιν πιστὰ ἐν κυρίῳ.

106. Gregory Nazianzus, *Oratio* 7, 15 (PG 35, 775): κόνις τιμία, νεκρὸς ἐπαινούμενος ὕμνοις ἐξ ὕμνων παραπεμπόμενος, μαρτύρων βήμασι πομπευόμενος, γονέων χερσὶν ὁσίαις τιμώμενος, μητρὸς λαμπροφορίᾳ τῷ πάθει τὴν εὐσέβειαν ἀντεισαγούσης, δάκρυσι ἡττωμένοις φιλοσοφίᾳ.

107. Chrysostom, *Homilia in Epist. ad Hebraeos* 4, 5 (PG 63, 43): Εἰπὲ γάρ μοι, τί βούλονται αἱ λαμπάδες αἱ φαιδραί; οὐχ ὡς ἀθλητὰς αὐτοὺς προπέμπομεν; τί δὲ οἱ ὕμνοι; οὐχὶ τὸν θεὸν δοξάζομεν χαὶ εὐχαριστοῦμεν ὅτι λοιπὸν ἐστεφάνωσε τὸν ἀπελθόντα, ὅτι τῶν πόνων ἀπήλλαξεν, ὅτι τῆς δειλίας ἐκ βαλὼν ἔχει παρ' ἑαυτῷ; οὐ διὰ τοῦτο ὕμνοι; οὐ διὰ τοῦτο ψαλμῳδίαι; Ταῦτα πάντα χαιρόντων ἐστίν· Εὐθυμεῖ γάρ, φησί, τίς; ψαλλέτω... Ἐννόησον τί ψάλλεις κατὰ τόν καιρὸν ἐκεῖνον· Ἐπίστρεφον, ψυχήμου, εἰς τὴν ἀνάπαυσίν σου, ὅτι Κύριος εὐηργέτησέ σε· καὶ πάλιν, Οὐ φοβηθήσομαι κακά, ὅτι σὺ μετ' ἐμοῦ εἶ· καὶ πάλιν· Σύμου εἶ καταφυγὴ ἀπὸ θλίψεως τῆς περιεχούσης με. Ἐννόησον τί βούλονται οὗτοι οἱ ψαλμοί. Ἀλλ' οὐ προσέχεις, ἀλλὰ μεθύεις ὑπὸ τοῦ πένθους. Κἂν ἐν τοῖς ἑτέρων κηδεύμασι κατανόησον ἀκριβῶς, ἵνα ἔχῃς φάρμακον ἐν τοῖς σοῖς ...εἰ οὖν οὗτος συμβαίη, καί τινες τὰς θρηνούσας ταύτας μισθώσαιντο, πιστεύσατέ μοι λέγοντι, οὐκ ἄλλως γὰρ ἐρῶ, ἀλλ' ὡς ἔχω· ὁ βουλόμενος ὀργιζέσθω· πολὺν αὐτὸν χρόνον τῆς ἐκκλησίας ἀπείρξω ὡς τὸν εἰδωλολάτρην.

108. Jerome, *Epistula* 77 (*Ad Oceanum de morte Fabiolae*) 11 (CSEL 55, 48

Hilberg): Totius urbis populos exequias congregabat. Sonabant psalmi et aurata tecta templorum reboans in sublime alleluia quatiebat.

109. Cf. F. Leitner, *Der gottesdienstliche Volksgesang im jüdischen und christlichen Altertum* (Freiburg 1906), p. 173.

110. Gregory of Nyssa, *De vita Macrinae* (PG 46, 992): ἐπεθορύβει ταῖς οἰμωγαῖς τὴν ψαλμωδίαν.

111. Cf. *supra,* Chapter 4, n. 99.

112. Gregory of Nyssa, *De vita Macrinae* (PG 46, 992).

113. Braun, *Das Buch der Synhados,* p. 341.

114. Justinian, *Novellae* 59, 4 (320 Schoell-Kroll): Sancimus singulo lecto gratis dato unum asceterium dari ascetriarum aut canonicarum, non minus octo mulierum praecedentium . . . psallentium. The participation of κανονικαί at funerals is also mentioned in the inscription of Archbishop Hypatius of Ephesus, which notes that they received pay for their services. Cf. J.N. Bakhuizen van den Brink, *De Oud-christelijke Monumenten van Ephesus* (The Hague 1923), p. 130.

115. Canon 22 in Hefele-Leclercq III 2, 53: Qui ab hac vita recedunt, cum psalmis tantummodo et psallentium vocibus debent ad sepulcra deferri. Nam funebre carmen, quod vulgo defunctis cantari solet, vel in pectoribus se aut proximos aut familias caedere omnino prohibemus.

116. F.J. Dölger, IΧΘΥΣ II (Münster 1922), p. 550. For the dates of the cult of the dead cf. E. Freistedt, *Altchristliche Totengedächtnistage und ihre Beziehung zum Jenseits-Glauben und Totenkultus der Antike (Liturgiegeschichtliche Quellen und Forschungen* 24) (Münster 1928).

117. Dölger, *ibid.,* p. 565.

118. Cf. H. Leclercq in DACL V 2, 2714.

119. *Constitutiones Apostolorum* VI 30, 2 (381 Funk): ἀπαρατηρήτως δὲ συναθροίζεσθε ἐν τοῖς κοιμητηρίοις, τὴν ἀνάγνωσιν τῶν ἱερῶν βιβλίων ποιούμενοι καὶ ψάλλοντες ὑπὲρ τῶν κεκοιμημένων μαρτύρων καὶ πάντων τῶν ἀπ' αἰῶνος ἁγίων καὶ τῶν ἀδελφῶν ὑμῶν τῶν ἐν κυρίῳ κεκοιμημένων.

120. *Ibid.* VIII 42, 1 (552): Ἐπιτελείσθω δὲ τρίτα τῶν κεκοιμημένων ἐν ψαλμοῖς καὶ ἀναγνώσμασιν καὶ προσευχαῖς.

121. W. Riedel, *Die Kirchenrechtsquellen des Patriarchats Alexandrien* (Leipzig 1900), p. 58.

122. Augustine, *Epist.* 158, 2 (CSEL 44, 490 Goldbacher): Exequias praebuimus satis honorabilis et dignas tantae animae; nam per triduum hymnis dominum conlaudavimus super sepulcrum ipsius et redemptionis sacramenta tertio die obtulimus.

123. R. Raabe, *Petrus der Iberer* (Leipzig 1895), p. 130.

124. Dölger, IΧΘΥΣ II, p. 568.

125. Eusebius, *Oratio ad sanctorum coetum* 12 (GCS Eus. I 171 Heikel): ὕμνοι δὴ μετὰ ταῦτα καὶ ψαλτήρια καὶ εὐφημίαι καὶ πρὸς τὸν πάντων ἐπόπτην ἔπαινος. καὶ τοιαύτη τις εὐχαριστίας θυσία τοῖς ἀνδράσιν ἀποτελεῖται, ἁγνὴ μὲν αἵματος ἁγνὴ δὲ πάσης βίας, οὐδὲ μὴν ὀσμὴ λιβάνων ἐπιποθεῖται οὐδὲ πυρκαϊά, καθαρὸν δὲ φῶς ὅσον ἐξαρκέσαι τοῖς εὐχομένοις πρὸς ἔλλαμψιν σωφρονέστατα δὲ πολλῶν καὶ τὰ συμπόσια πρὸς ἔλεον καὶ ἀνάκτησιν τῶν δεομένων ποιούμενα καὶ πρὸς βοήθειαν τῶν ἐκπεσόντων.

126. Tertullian, *Scorpiace* 7 (CSEL 20, 159 Reifferscheid-Wissowa): Sophia in exitibus cantatur hymnis; cantatur et exitus martyrum.

127. Theodoret, *Hist. eccles.* II 24, 8 (GCS 154 Parmentier): πρῶτον διχῇ διελόντες

τοὺς τῶν φαλλόντων χορούς, ἐκ διοδοχῆς ᾄδειν τὴν Δαυιτικὴν ἐδίδαξαν μελωδίαν· καὶ τοῦτο ἐν Ἀντιοχείᾳ πρῶτον ἀρξάμενον πάντοσε διέδραμε καὶ κατέλαβε τῆς οἰκουμένης τὰ τέρματα· οὗτοι τῶν θείων τὰς ἐραστὰς εἰς τοὺς τῶν μαρτύρων σηκοὺς συναγείροντες πάννυχοι διετέλουν σὺν ἐκείνοις τὸν θεὸν ἀνυμνοῦντες.

128. Augustine, *Sermo* 302, 1 (PL 38, 1385): Huic solemnitati sanctae lectiones congruae sonuerunt. Audivimus et cantavimus et evangelicam lectionem intentissime accepimus. *Idem, Sermo* 306, 1 (PL 38, 1400): sicut audivimus et cantando respondimus. *Idem, Sermo* 327, 1 (PL 38, 1450): probamus, quam verum sit, quod cantavimus quia pretiosa in conspectu Domini mors sanctorum eius.

129. Maximus of Turin, *Sermo* 89 (PL 57, 711): cantavimus paulo ante: Laetamini in Domino.

130. Raabe, *Petrus der Iberer*, p. 25.

131. On Ephraem cf. *supra*, Chapter 4, sec. 6. On Marûtâ cf. the 57th chapter of the catalogue of books on the Nestorian Metropolitan 'Abdischo' of Sôbâ in Assemani, *Bibliotheca Orientalis* III (Rome 1720), 73:

> Maruthas Episcopus
> Maypherkatae et medicus peritus
> Composuit librum de martyriis
> et cantus tonosque Martyrum.

132. Juvenal, *Saturae* V 15, 40 (265 Jahn-Leo): Ne laetum hilaremque diem, ne magnae gaudia cenae sentirent positis ad templa et compita mensis pervigilique toro, quem nocte ac luce iacentem septimus interdum sol invenit.... Inde virorum saltatus nigro tibicine, qualiacumque unguenta et flores multaeque in fronte coronae.

133. L. Weniger, *Das Kollegium der sechzehn Frauen und der Dionysosdienst in Elis (Jahresbericht des Gymnasiums su Weimar)* (1883), p. 11.

134. Tacitus, *Annales* 15, 44 (347 Halm-Andresen): Ex quibus supplicatum Volcano et Cereri Proserpinaeque ac propitiata Iuno per matronas, primum in Capitolio, deinde apud proximum mare, unde hausta aqua templum et simulacrum deae perspersum est; et sellisternia ac pervigilia celebravere feminae, quibus mariti erant.

135. Cicero, *De legibus* 2, 9, 21 (IV 2, 413 Müller): Nocturna mulierum sacrificia ne sunto praeter olla, quae pro populo rite fient. Plutarch, *Cicero* 19, 4 (I 1, 375 Lindskog-Ziegler): ἐπειδὴ τὴν ἐκείνου γυναῖκες κατεῖχον ἱεροῖς ἀπορρήτοις ὀργιάζουσι θεόν, ἣν Ῥωμαῖοι μὲν Ἀγαθήν Ἕλληνες δὲ Γυναικείαν ὀνομάζουσι. On the cult of the Bona Dea cf. E. Fehrle, *Die kultische Keuschheit im Altertum* (RVV 6) (Giessen 1910), 126 ff.

136. Cf. *supra*, Chapter 1, n. 36.

137. Cicero, *De legibus* 2, 14, 35 (IV 2, 418 Müller).

138. E. Rohde, *Psyche, Seelenkult und Unsterblichkeitsglaube der Griechen* II (Tübingen ⁵ 1910), pp. 9 ff.

139. Livy 39, 8 (IX 16 Weissenborn).

140. Suetonius, *C. Caesar Caligula* 54 (143 Roth): Nec alia de de causa videtur eo die, quo periit, pervigilium indixisse quam ut initium in scenam prodeundi licentia temporis auspicaretur.

141. Cf. *supra*, Chapter 1, n. 36.

142. Epiphanius, *Panarion haer.* 51, 22, 9 ff. (GCS Ep. II 285–286 Holl): Πρῶτον μὲν ἐν Ἀλεξανδρείᾳ ἐν τῷ Κορίῳ τῷ καλουμένῳ· ναὸς δέ ἐστι μέγιστος, τουτέστιν τὸ τέμενος τῆς Κόρης. Ὅλην γὰρ τὴν νύκτα ἀγρυπνήσαντες ἐν ᾄσμασί τισι καὶ αὐλοῖς τῷ εἰδώλῳ ᾄδοντες, καὶ παννυχίδα διατελέσαντες μετὰ τὴν ἀλεκτρυόνων κλαγγὴν κατέρχονται λαμπαδήφοροι εἰς σηκὸν

τινα ὑπόγαιον, καὶ ἀναφέρουσι ξόανόν τι ξύλινον φορίῳ καθεζόμενον γυμνὸν ἔχον σφραγῖδά τινα σταυροῦ ἐπὶ τοῦ υετώπου, καὶ ταῖς ἑκατέραις χερσὶν ἄλλας δύο τοιαύτας σφραγῖδας καὶ ἐπ' αὐτοῖς τοῖς δυσὶ γονάτοις ἄλλας δύο, ὁμοῦ δὲ τὰς πέντε σφραγῖδας ἀπὸ χρυσοῦ τετυπωμένας. Καὶ περιφέρουσι τοῦτο τὸ ξόανον ἑπτάκις κυκλώσαντες τὸν μεσαίτατον ναὸν μετὰ αὐλῶν καὶ τυμπάνων καὶ ὕμνων, καὶ κωμάσαντες καταφέρουσιν αὐτὸ αὖθις εἰς τὸν ὑπόγαιον τόπον. Ἐρωτώμενοι δὲ ὅτι, Τί ἐστι τοῦτο τὸ μυστήριον; ἀποκρίνονται καὶ λέγουσιν ὅτι, Ταύτῃ τῇ ὥρᾳ σήμερον ἡ Κόρη, τουτέστιν ἡ Παρθένος ἐγέννησε τὸν Αἰῶνα.

143. On the relation of the pagan vigils to the Christian vigils cf. A. Baumstark, *Nocturna Laus. Typen frühchristlichen Vigilienfeier und ihr Fortleben vor allem im römischen und monastischen Ritus*, published from the author's literary remains by O. Heiming (*Liturgiewissenschaftliche Quellen und Forschungen* 32) (Münster ² 1967), pp. 21–26.

144. Tertullian, *Ad uxorem* 2, 4 (I 689 Oehler): Quis enim sinat coniugem suam?... Quis nocturnis convocationibus, se ita oportuerit, a latere suo adimi libenter feret? Quis denique sollemnibus Paschae abnoctantem... sustinebit?

145. Augustine, *Sermo* 219 (PL 38, 1088). The gnostic sect of Basilides was already celebrating a vigil of the feast of Epiphany in the time of Clement of Alexandria. Cf. Clement of Alexandria, *Stromata* 1, 21 (GCS Clem. II 146, 2, 90 Stahlin): οἱ ἀπὸ Βασιλείδου καὶ τοῦ βαπτίσματος αὐτοῦ τὴν ἡμέραν ἑορτάζουσι προδιανυκτερεύοντες ἀναγνώσεσι. Cf. H. Usener, *Das Weihnachtsfest. Religionsgeschichtliche Untersuchung* (Bonn 1889), p. 181.

146. Augustine, *Epist.* 29, 8–9 (CSEL 34, 119, 6 Goldbacher): Iste autem sermo multo habuit contradictores.... Postridie vero, cum illuxisset dies, cui solebant fauces ventresque se parare, nuntiatur mihi nonnullos eorum etiam, qui sermoni aderant, nondum a murmuratione cessasse, tantumque in eis valere vim pessimae consuetudinis, ut eius tantum voce uteretur et dicerent: Quare modo? Non enim, antea qui haec non prohibuerunt, christiani non erant. Quo audito, quas maiores commovendi eos machinas praepararem, omnino nesciebam.... Verum tamen ne illi, qui ante nos tam manifesta imperitae multitudinis crimina vel permiserunt vel prohibere no ausi sunt, aliqua a nobis affici contumelia viderentur exposui eis, qua necessitate ista in ecclesia viderentur exorta. Scilicet post persecutiones tam multas tamque vehementes cum facta pace turbae gentilium in christianum nomen venire cupientes hoc impedirentur. Quod dies festos cum idolis suis solerent in abundantia epularum et ebrietate consumere nec facile ab his perniciosissimis sed tamen vetustissimis voluptatibus se possent abstinere, visum maioribus nostris, ut huic infirmitati parti interim parceretur diesque festos post eos, quos relinquebant, alios in honorem sanctorum martyrum vel non simili sacrilegio quamvis simili luxu celebrarent; iam Christi nomine conligatis et tantae auctoritatis iugo subditis salutaria sobrietatis praecepta auctoritatis iugo subditis salutaria sobrietatis praecepta traderentur.... On Augustine's reorganization of the feasts of the martyrs cf. J. Quasten, "Die Reform des Martyrerkultes durch Augustinus," in *Theologie und Glaube* 25 (1933), 318–331 and *idem*, "Vetus Superstitio et Nova Religio. The Problem of Refrigerium in the Ancient Church of North Africa," in *Harvard Theological Review* 33 (1940), 253–266.

147. The joyful character was particular to the celebrations of the martyrs from their very origins. The Christian community of Smyrna relates already in the middle of the second century that it celebrates the annual commemoration of its Bishop Polycarp with great joy. Cf. *Martyrium Polycarpi* 18, 3 (9 Gebhardt): ἔνθα ὡς δυνατὸν ἡμῖν συναγομένοις ἐν ἀγαλλιάσει καὶ χαρᾷ παρέξει ὁ κύριος ἐπιτελεῖν τὴν τοῦ υαρτυρίου αὐτοῦ ἡμέραν γενέθλιον. It is easy to understand how, with a slackening of religious enthusiasm and zeal, these celebrations could turn into occasions of frivolity and worse.

148. H. Achelis, *Didaskelie* in TU NF 10, 2, 11.

149. Aphraat, *Demonstratio* XII, *De paschate* 13 in *Patrologia syriaca* I 1 (538 Graffin): Ut vero festum singulis annis statuto tempore observetur, haec a nobis requiruntur: ieiunium cum puritate, oratio cum fide, laudatio cum sedulitate et cantus psalmorum quemadmodum opertet. On Aphraat's description of the Easter liturgy cf. J. Duncan, *Baptism in the Demonstrations of Aphraates the Persian Sage* (*Studies in Christian Antiquity* 8) (Washington 1945), pp. 104–107.

150. Basil, *Epist.* 207, 3 (PG 32, 764): Πρὸς δὲ τὸ ἐπὶ ταῖς ψαλμῳδίαις ἔγκλημα, ᾧ μάλιστα τοὺς ἁπλουστέρους φοβοῦσιν οἱ διαβάλλοντες ἡμᾶς, ἐκεῖνο εἰπεῖν ἔχω· ὅτι τὰ νῦν κεκρατηκότα ἔθη πάσαις ταῖς τοῦ θεοῦ Ἐκκλησίαις συνῳδά ἐστι καὶ σύμφωνα. Ἐκ νυκτὸς ὀρθίζει ὁ λαὸς εἰς τὸν οἶκον τῆς προσευχῆς, καὶ ἐν πόν·ῳ κὺὶ θλίψει καὶ συνοχῇ δακρύων ἐξομολογούμενοι τῷ θεῷ, τελευταῖον ἐξαναστάντες τῶν προσευχῶν· εἰς τὴν **ψαλμῳδίαν** καθίστανται. καὶ **νῦν** μὲν διχῇ διανεμηθέντες ἀντιψάλλουσιν ἀλλήλοις, ὁμοῦ μὲν τὴν μελέτην τῶν λογίων ἐντεῦθεν κρατύνοντες …ἔπειτα πάλιν ἐπιτρέψαντες ἑνὶ κατάρχειν τοῦ μέλους, οἱ λοιποὶ ὑπέχουσι· καὶ οὕτως ἐν τῇ ποικιλία τῆς ψαλμῳδίας τὴν νύκτα διενεγκόντες, μεταξὺ **προσευχόμενοι**, ἡμέρας ἤδη ὑπολαμπούσης, πάντες κοινῇ ὡς ἐξ ἑνὸς στόματος καὶ μιᾶς καρδίας, τὸν τῆς ἐξομολογήσεως ψαλμὸν ἀναφέρουσι τῷ Κυρίῳ.

151. Chrysostom, *Homilia in illud, Vidi Dominum* 1, 4 (PG 6, 103): Τὸ πρὸς θεὸν τὴν διάλεξιν ποιεῖσθαι προθεμένους, καὶ αὐτῷ τὴν δοξολογίαν ἀπαπέμποντας, εἶτα ἀφέντας τοῦτον, τὸν πλησίον ἕκαστος ἀπολαβεῖν καὶ τὰ κατ' οἶκον **διατίςεοθαι**.

152. *Constitutiones Apostolorum* VII 47 (455 n. Funk): ροσευχὴ ἑοθινή.

153. Cf. *supra*, Chapter 4, n. 157.

154. Paulinus of Nola, *Carmina* 23, 111 (CSEL 30, 198 Hartel): Nostis eum morem, quo ieiunare solemus ante diem et sero libatis vespere sacris quisque suas remeare domos. Tunc ergo solutis coetibus a templo domini, postquam data fessis corporibus requies sumpta dape, coepimus hymnos exultare Deo et psalmis producere noctem.

155. Sidonius Apollinaris, *Epist.* 5, 17 (PL 58, 547): Conveneramus ad sancti sepulcrum: processio fuerat antelucana, solemnitas anniversaria, populus ingens sexu ex utroque, quem capacissima basilica non caperet, et quamlibet cincta diffusis cryptoporticibus. Cultu peracto vigiliarum, quas alternante monachi clericique psalmicines concelebraverant, quisque in diversa secessimus, non procul tamen, utpote ad tertiam praesto futuri, quum sacerdotibus res divina facienda.

156. C.F. Arnold, *Caesarius von Arelate* (Leipzig 1894), p. 177.

157. B. Aubé, *Homélie inédite, Polyeucte dans l'Histoire* (Paris 1882), p. 79: Τί τοίνυν ἡμεῖς ἀντάξιον δῶρον τῷ μάρτυρι προσοίσομεν;… Χορεύσωμεν αυτῷ, εἰ δοκεῖ, τὰ συνήθη. Cf. also F.C. Conybeare, *The Armenian Apology and Acts of Apollonius and other Monuments of Early Christianity* (London 1896), p. 129.

158. Ephraem, *De poenitentia et iudicio* (Opera graeca-latina 3, 371): μὴ ἐθνικῶς, ἀλλὰ χριστιανῶς· Μή πρόθυρα στεφανώμεξα, μὴ χοροὺς συστησώμεθα. μὴ αὐλαῖς καὶ κιθάραις τὴν ἀκοὴν **ἐχθήλινωμεν**. μὴ ἱμάτια μαλακὰ περιβαλώμεθα…μὴ κώμαις καὶ μέθαις καὶ κοίταις καὶ ἀσελγίαις.

159. J. Leipoldt, *Schenute von Atripe und die Entstehung des nationalägyptischen Christentums* (TU NF 10, 1) (1903), p. 30.

160. Cf. Theodoret's remark on the Syrian ascetic Maris: although in his youth he had frequently sung at the feasts of martyrs he remained unsullied. Such a remark demonstrates the notoriety of these celebrations. Theodoret, *Hist. eccles.* 20 (PG 82, 1429): ἄφθορον διαμεῖναι τὸ σῶμα…καὶ ταῦτα πολλὰς μὲν μαρτύρων πανηγύρεις ἐπιτελέσας, ἡνίκα νέος ἐτύγχανεν, εὐφωνίᾳ δὲ καταθέλξας τοὺς δήμους. Ψάλλων γὰρ ἐπὶ πλεῖστον διετέλεσε

χρόνον, ὥρᾳ τε σώματος λάμπων. Ἀλλ᾽ ὅμως οὔτε τοῦ σώματος τὸ κάλλος, οὔτε τῆς φωνῆς ἡ λαμπρότης, οὐχ ἡ τῶν πολλῶν ἐπιμιξία, τὸ τῆς ψυχῆς ἐλυμήνατο κάλλος.

161. Augustine, *Sermo 326*, 1 *(PL 38, 1449)*.

162. Cf. *supra*, Chapter 4, n. 71.

163. Paulinus of Nola, *Carmina* 27, 556 (CSEL 30, 287 Hartel): Per totam et vigiles extendunt gaudia noctem, laetitia somnos, tenebras funalibus arcent. *Ibid*, 574: ludibria misces. *Ibid*. 576: inter pocula cantas. *Ibid*. 578: ebrius insultas.

164. Basil, *Homilia 14 in ebriosos* (PG 31, 446): ῥίψασαι ἀπὸ τῶν κεφαλῶν τὰ τῆς εὐσχημοσύνης καλύμματα, καταφρονήσασαι τοῦ Θεοῦ, καταφρονήσασαι τῶν ἀγγέλων αὐτοῦ, καταναισχυντήσασαι ἄρρενος ὄψεως, σοβοῦσαι τὰς κόμας, σύρουσαι τοὺς χιτῶνας, καὶ τοῖς ποσὶν ἅμα παίζουσι, ὀφθαλμῷ ἀσελγεῖ, γέλωτι ἐκκεχυμένῳ, πρὸς ὄρχησιν ἐκμανεῖσαι... ἐν τοῖς πρὸ τῆς πόλεως μαρτυρίοις χοροὺς συστησάμεναι, ἐργαστήριον τῆς οἰκείας αὐτῶν ἀσχημοσύνης. τοὺς ἡγιασμένους τόπους πε ποίηται. Ἐμίαναν μὲν τὸν ἀέρα τοῖς ᾄσμασι τοῖς πορνικοῖς, ἐμίαναν δέ τὴν γῆν τοῖς ἀκαθάρτοις ποσίν.

165. Canon 35 in Hefele-Leclercq I 1, 240: Placuit prohiberi, ne foeminae in coemeterio pervigent, eo quod saepe sub obtentu orationis latenter scelera commitunt.

166. Canon 28 in Hefele-Leclercq I 2, 1015: ὅτι οὐ δεῖ ἐν τοῖς κυριακοῖς ἢ ἐν ταῖς ἐκκλησίαις τὰς λεγομένας ἀγάπας ποιεῖν, καὶ ἐν τῷ οἴκῳ τοῦ θεοῦ ἐθίειν καὶ ἀκούβιτα στρωννύειν.

167. Canon 30 in Mansi III 735: Ut nulli episcopi vel clerici in ecclesia conviventur, nisi forte transeuntes hospitiorum necessitate illic reficiant: populi etiam ab huiusmodi conviviis, quantum fieri potest, prohibeantur.

168. Cf. the Synod of Chalons (647), canon 19 in Hefele-Leclercq III 1, 284 and also L. Gougaud, "La danse dans les églises," in *Revue d'histoire ecclésiastique* 15 (1904), 10 ff.

169. Mansi IX 999: Exterminanda omnino est irreligiosa consuetudo quam vulgus per sanctorum solemnitates agere consuevit, ut populi, qui debent officia divina attendere saltationibus et turpibus invigilent canticis, non solum sibi nocentes, sed religiosorum officiis perstrepentes. Hoc enim ut ab omnia Hispania depellatur sacerdotum et iudicum a concilio sancto curae commitatur.

170. F. Nau, *Les canons de Jacques d'Edesse* (Paris 1906), p. 117: "Monks shall not go to the vigils or to the commemorations of the martyrs or to the feasts, not even with the intention of praying at them."

171. *Peregrinatio Aetheriae* 24, 12 (CSEL 39, 74 Geyer): Nox autem recipit se episcopus in domum suam et iam ex illa hora revertuntur omnes manazontes ad Anastasim et psalmi dicuntur et antiphonae usque ad lucum.

172. Canon 35 in *Mon. Germ. hist. Concilia aevi Karolingi* (I 581–582 Werminghoff): Sunt quidam, et maxime mulieres, qui festis ac sacris diebus atque sanctorum nataliciis non pro eorum, quibus debent, delectantur desideriis advenire, sed ballando verba turpia decantando, choros tenendo et ducendo, similitudinem paganorum pergendo advenire procurant; tales enim, si cum minoribus veniunt ad ecclesiam, cum peccatis maioribus revertuntur.

173. Barhebraeus, *Nomocanon* (70-72 Bedjan). Cf. J.A. Wensinck, "Über das Weinen in den monotheistischen Religionen Vorderasiens," in *Festschrift Eduard Sachau z. 70. Geburtstage gewidmet* (Berlin 1915), p. 26.

PLATE 1

Greek vase painting. Sacrificial scene from the cult of Dionysos.
Naples: National Museum. Alinari 11 300b.

PLATE 2

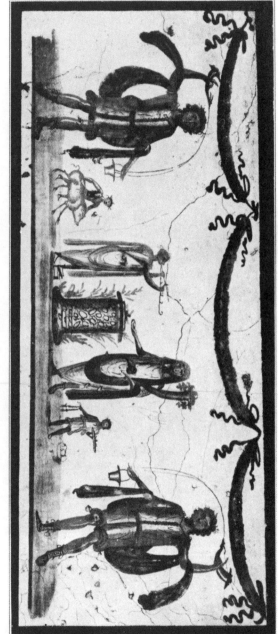

Mural from Pompeii. Domestic sacrifice with a *genius familiaris* and Lares.
Naples: National Museum. Alinari 12 190.

PLATE 3

Altar of the *Lares augusti*. The *vicomagistri* at sacrifice.
Rome: Palazzo dei Conservatori. Moscioni 10 465.

PLATE 4

Sarcophagus showing the sacrifice of a bull.
Florence: Uffizi Gallery. Alinari 1308.

PLATE 5

Bas-relief from the Arch of Constantine. A *suovetaurilium* attended by Marcus Aurelius.
Anderson 2535.

PLATE 6

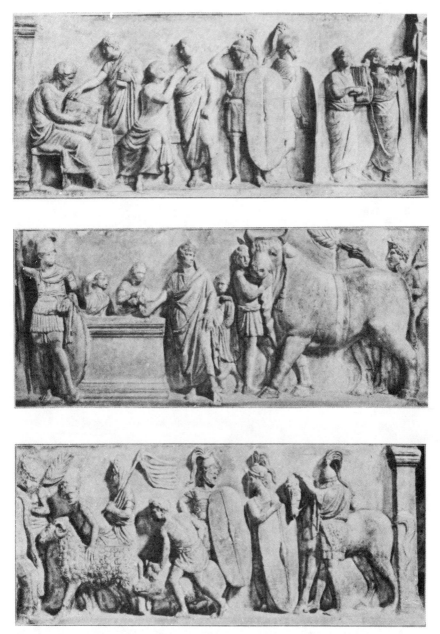

Relief from the altar of the Temple of Neptune in Rome. A military lustration.
Paris: Louvre. Alinari 22 556/7/8.

PLATE 7

Etruscan ash coffer. The sacrifice of Iphigenia.
Rome: Etruscan Museum of the Vatican.

PLATE 8

Grave monument of the *Collegium tibicinum*.
Rome: Palazzo dei Conservatori. Alinari 28 075.

PLATE 9

Base of a small votive temple. Cultic scene with female flutists.
Rome: Museo delle Terme.

PLATE 10

Libation scene from the "Aldobrandini Wedding."
Rome: Vatican Museum. Alinari 7487.

PLATE 11

Altar in the Temple of Vespasian in Pompeii.
Anderson 26 513.

PLATE 12

Relief in clay. Initiation into the Bacchic mysteries.
Hannover: Kestnermuseum.

PLATE 13

Stucco relief from a Roman house. Celebration of the Bacchic mysteries.
Rome: Museo delle Terme. Alinari 6238.

PLATE 14

Mural from the Villa Item in Pompeii. Initiation scene with a cultic dance.
Alinari 39 108.

PLATE 15

Mural from the Villa Item in Pompeii. Lustration scene from the mysteries of Dionysos. Anderson 26 381.

PLATE 16

Detail of a frieze showing an ecstatic procession from the cult of Dionysos.
Naples: National Museum. Alinari 11 164.

PLATE 17

Stucco relief from a Roman house. A Maenad at the lighting of the sacrificial fire.
Rome: Museo delle Terme. Alinari 6286.

PLATE 18

Relief portraying the high priest of Cybele.
Rome: Palazzo dei Conservatori. Moscioni 20 947.

PLATE 19

Bas-relief from the Villa Albani in Rome. Sacrificial scene. Alinari 27 715.

PLATE 20

Stucco relief with a sacrificial scene from the underground basilica near the Porta Maggiore in Rome. Photograph from the German Archeological Institute in Rome.

PLATE 21

1. Detail of a sarcophagus showing a procession from the cult of Cybele.
Rome: S. Lorenzo fuori le mura.

2. Votive table for a safe journey.
Rome: Vatican Museum.

PLATE 22

Relief in clay showing a sacred tree and a sacrifice of fruit.
Rome: Museo delle Terme. Alinari 27 371.

PLATE 23

Mural from Herculaneum. Scene from the cult of Isis.
Naples: National Museum. Alinari 12 035.

PLATE 24

Mural from Herculaneum. Scene from the cult of Isis.
Naples: National Museum. Anderson 23 422.

PLATE 25

Pedestal from the Roman Temple of Isis-Serapis.
Florence: Uffizi Gallery. Alinari 29 347.

PLATE 26

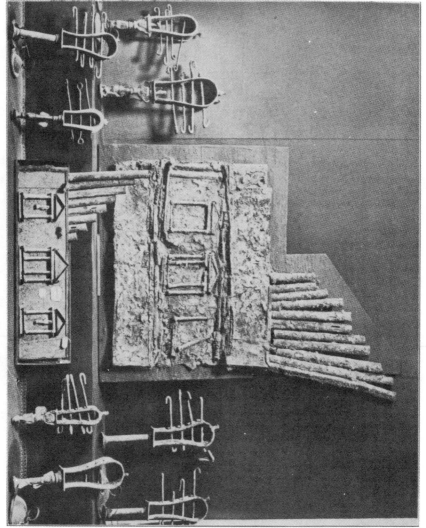

Musical instruments from Pompeii.
Naples: National Museum. Anderson 25 380.

PLATE 27

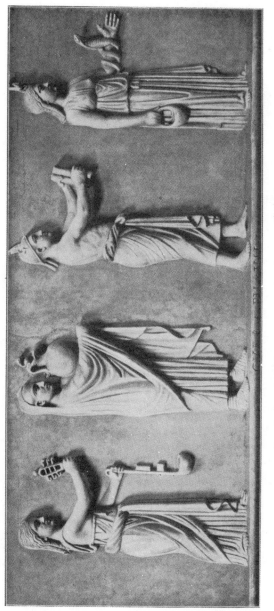

Detail of a relief showing a procession from the cult of Isis.
Rome: Vatican Museum. Alinari 26 981.

PLATE 28

1. Cover of a sarcophagus showing a lute and a scroll in the hands of the deceased.
Rome: Palazzo dei Conservatori. Alinari 6049.

2. Christian sarcophagus with a female lutenist.
Rome: Lateran Museum. Anderson 24 187.

PLATE 29

1. Sarcophagus from Saint-Maximin. Awakening of Tabitha.
Photograph after Wilpert.

2. Terracotta fragment. Singer and organ.
Rome: Museum of the Campo Santo Tedesco.

PLATE 30

Grave relief from the Via Latina.
Rome: Museo delle Terme.

PLATE 31

Relief from Amiternum showing a funeral procession.
Museum at Aquila. Alinari 36 101.

PLATE 32

Etruscan gravestone with a banquet of the dead and dancers.
Fiesole: Museo Etrusco Romano. Alinari 45 780.

PLATE 33

Painting on a Campanian mixing bowl. A deceased person on a gravestone holding a tambourine.
Berlin: Antiquarium. Museum Photograph.

PLATE 34

Oil flask from a Greek cult of the dead. The lyre as a gift for the deceased.
Berlin: Antiquarium. Museum photograph.

PLATE 35

Gravestone of Metrodoros showing music-making sirens.
Berlin: Antiquarium. Museum photograph.

PLATE 36

Lyre-playing siren from a tombstone.
Athens: National Museum. Alinari 24 351.

PLATE 37

Ash urn of L. Lucilius Felix with music-making cupids.
Rome: Capitoline Museum. Alinari 40 920.

PLATE 38

Tombstone of the soldier Marcinus showing a dancing
Maenad.
Bonn: Provincial Museum. Museum photograph.

Index of Personal Names

Index of Anonymous Works

(Names of mythical persons are in the General Index.)

Index of Places, Museums and Landmarks

General Index

The publication of *Music & Worship in Pagan & Christian Antiquity* has been supervised by Daniel Connors, editor. The cover design is by Gerard Valerio, Bookmark Studio, Annapolis, Md. The volume was designed and composed in paladium by Lincoln Graphics, Washington, D.C., and printed and bound by Edwards Brothers, Inc., Ann Arbor, Michigan.